STATES AND DEVELOPMENT IN
THE ASIAN PACIFIC RIM

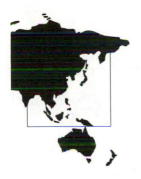

STATES AND DEVELOPMENT IN
THE ASIAN PACIFIC RIM

edited by

Richard P. Appelbaum

and

Jeffrey Henderson

SAGE PUBLICATIONS
International Educational and Professional Publisher
Newbury Park   London   New Delhi

For information address:

SAGE Publications, Inc.
2455 Teller Road
Newbury Park, California 91320

SAGE Publications Ltd.
6 Bonhill Street
London EC2A 4PU
United Kingdom

SAGE Publications India Pvt. Ltd.
M-32 Market
Greater Kailash I
New Delhi 110 048 India

Printed in the United States of America

Library of Congress Cataloging-in-Publication Data

Main entry under title:

States and development in the Asian Pacific rim / edited by Richard P.
    Appelbaum, Jeffrey Henderson.
        p.   cm.
    Includes bibliographical references and index.
    ISBN 0-8039-4034-3 (cl).—ISBN 0-8039-4035-1 (pb)
        1. East Asia—Economic conditions.   2. East Asia—Economic policy.
    3. Industry and state—East Asia.   4. East Asia—Industries.
    I. Appelbaum, Richard P.   II. Henderson, J. W. (Jeffrey William),
    1947-
    HC460.5.S73   1992
    338.95—dc20   92-1150

92 93 94 95 10 9 8 7 6 5 4 3 2

Sage Production Editor: Astrid Virding

Contents

Acknowledgments

This book grew out of the papers presented at a conference held at the University of California, Santa Barbara, on March 22-25, 1990. We would like to thank the University of California Pacific Rim Program, the National Center for Geographic Information and Analysis (NCGIA), the UCSB College of Letters and Sciences, and Environmental Systems Research Institute (ESRI) for their generosity in providing funding for the conference. We would also like to acknowledge the tireless help of Cliff Kono, conference coordinator, as well as the staff of NCGIA in making the detailed arrangements required to host a conference bringing together scholars from four continents. Our thanks also go to the helpful staff at Sage Publications, particularly Marie-Louise Penchoen, Astrid Virding, and Megan McCue. Finally, a special note of appreciation for Michael Goodchild, Director of NCGIA, for realizing the importance of this research to geographers, and providing ongoing support for the several research efforts that have grown out of the original conference.

1

Situating the State in the East Asian Development Process

JEFFREY HENDERSON

RICHARD P. APPELBAUM

The post-World War II economic transformation of East Asia has proven perplexing to development analysts influenced by the African and Latin American experiences. From Paul Baran to Andre Gunder Frank, from Samir Amin to Arghiri Emmanuel, we were led to believe that the possibilities for development in peripheral countries were severely circumscribed by the requirements of the capitalist world economic system.[1] The structures and dynamics of the world economy, controlled as they were from its centers—particularly the United States—locked peripheral societies into an unyielding downward spiral of exploitation and poverty. Under such circumstances it seemed that only one choice was available for Third World societies, and that in Frank's words was between "underdevelopment or revolution" (Frank, 1969a).

Given that revolution was conceived of in socialist terms, there appeared by the mid-1970s to be a number of successful candidates to serve as models of relatively egalitarian development: Cuba, China, Tanzania, and even North Korea appeared to vindicate socialism as the only genuine route to development in the Third World. In all of these countries gross national product (GNP) had expanded, agricultural and industrial productivity had increased, living standards had been improved, and abject poverty seemingly eradicated. When one compared the socialist colossus of China with India, its nearest capitalist equivalent in the Third World, the benefits of socialism seemed incontrovertible. At a minimum, China had fed, housed, rendered literate, and massively improved the health of its population; India, in much the same time frame, had not. On the left, with the exception of Trotskyist critiques of Third World socialism (cf. Harris, 1978, on China), problems of authoritarian rule, of internal repression, of personality cults—of Stalinism—were either not fully understood, or were justified as being no worse than their capitalist counterparts in Brazil, Argentina, or Chile; in Indonesia, the Philippines, or South Korea.

As early as the late 1960s, however, an alternative conception of the possibilities of Third World development under capitalism had begun to emerge. Constructed as it was in contradistinction to the "vulgar" dependency theories of Frank and others, and initially associated with the work of Brazilian sociologist Fernando Cardoso and his collaborators (e.g., Cardoso & Faletto, 1979), this conception began to forge the intellectual tools necessary to grasp the possibility of "dependent development." The argument of the "second wave" *dependistas* was that Third World societies (or at least Latin American ones) were not merely products determined by the structures of unequal exchange within the world economy, but that their present and future possibilities in part were of their own making. Specifically, under certain circumstances, Third World societies were able to achieve sufficient autonomy within the world system to be able to harness the dynamics of global capitalism for their own development purposes. While the economic and political relations of dependence remained a fact of life, and thus set the parameters or external limits to what any Third World society could achieve, some form of genuine development was still a possibility. Central to this possibility was the action of the national state, and in Peter Evans's work (1979), the nature of the triadic alliance that could be forged, at particular historical moments, between the state and indigenous and transnational capital.

The dependent development theorists were reinforced from another front—the American world-systems theorists, centered around Immanuel Wallerstein and the State University of New York's Braudel Center. In Wallerstein's (1979) view, it was possible for certain peripheral societies to break partially from the bonds of dependence and move to an intermediate position within the world economy—termed by Wallerstein the *semiperiphery*—where their economies extracted surplus from the periphery while at the same time yielding surplus to the core. Wallerstein's (1978) analysis emphasized the role of the national state in carving out a space for indigenous economic and political actors to play a role in both the global economy, and in the international state system. At the same time, however, Wallerstein failed to appreciate the restructuring of transnational capital such that some semiperipheral areas might actually become "way-stations" for corporate decision-making and control (Henderson, 1986).

If dependent development and world-systems theorists argued that some degree of development was indeed possible under global capitalism, other theorists sought to demonstrate that capitalism was in fact a precondition to such development. In Britain, Bill Warren and his associates (see Schiffer, 1981; Warren, 1980) extended Marx's analysis of capitalism as a progressive force to the Third World. In Warren's view, by revolutionizing the forces of production, breaking the stranglehold of feudalism, and bringing a working class onto the social and political stage, capitalism created the preconditions for genuine development in the Third World. Mobilizing a wealth of data on economic growth rates, GNP per capita, income distribution and the like, Warren sought to demonstrate that the most economically developed Third World societies were precisely those that were most penetrated by global capitalist relations. Many of Warren's showcase examples were from the East Asian region.

It was, in fact, the case of East Asia that forced a major rethinking of the relationship between global capitalism and Third World economic development. By the mid 1970s, it was clear that a number of East Asian societies were undergoing a process of "late industrialization" (Amsden, 1989). Beginning with Japan in the 1950s, Hong Kong in the 1960s, Taiwan, South Korea, and Singapore in the 1970s and 1980s, and possibly Malaysia today, East Asia seemed to outsiders to have come from nowhere to challenge successfully, and in some cases defeat, the traditional might of U.S. and Western European industrial capitalism. What was more, they seemed to some to have done so by successfully mobilizing the sheer power of the market.

That economies should not only grow, but grow at the spectacular double-digit rates of these East Asian cases, came as no surprise to those with a near-religious belief in the capacities of the "free market". Since the work of Jacob Viner (1953) and the British economists Peter Bauer and Basil Yamey (1957), those imbued with the neoclassical paradigm had been convinced that the blockages to development that existed in the Third World were largely self-imposed. They were alleged to be the result of distortions in markets for labor, capital, natural resources, and technology that arose from the endogenous cultural forms and social practices in many parts of the Third

World (Rostow, 1961), but especially from the meddling (and usually corruption) of the national state. That Japan and subsequently other East Asian countries had deliberately connected themselves to world markets and seemingly applied free market principles through to their logical conclusion, was seen as a vindication of the tenets of neoclassical economics and a defeat for those from Raul Prebisch onward who had argued for autarkic development strategies based upon import-substitution industrialization.[2] That the success of the East Asian economies might well signal the death knell of any socialist route to the modern world was a point to be hammered home by U.S. sociologist Peter Berger in his influential book, *The Capitalist Revolution* (1986).

The concluding part of this chapter, as well as those that follow it, will question the simplistic assumption that the East Asian"miracle" is indeed a vindication of free market capitalism. That notwithstanding, it remains true that for the theoretical traditions reviewed above, the experience of Japan, South Korea, Hong Kong, Taiwan, and Singapore has proven to be something of an enigma. Alice Amsden, for instance, has shown how difficult it is to try to explain Taiwanese development from within a dependency framework (Amsden, 1979), while Andre Gunder Frank (1982) has responded to the problem by simply denying that any genuine development has taken place. Similarly, while some attention has been paid by world-systems analysts to the historical antecedents of development in the region (see in particular Moulder, 1977, on Japan), little of it appears to have been focused on contemporary industrialization (but see So, 1986, on Hong Kong). Additionally, Henderson (1989) has pointed out the deficiencies of a world-system related thesis, that of the "new international division of labor" (Frobel, Heinrichs, & Kreye, 1980), for an analysis of high technology forms of industrialization in the region. Finally, Amsden (1990) has questioned the utility of Alain Lipietz's otherwise stimulating "global fordist" version of regulation theory (Lipietz, 1987) for an analysis of South Korean industrialization.

It seems then that we have not yet reached the point where some general theory of East Asian late industrialization can be advanced; for the moment, all we can do is to provide pointers in that direction. In what follows we offer one pointer by trying to "situate" the state, in a preliminary fashion, in relation to other potential candidates for the determination of East Asian development. The other chapters in this book develop "the case for the state" in detail, with regard to particular facets of state action in Japan, the "four tigers" (South Korea, Taiwan, Hong Kong, and Singapore), and in Malaysia, the society with the greatest recent potential for late industrialization.

Determinants of Development

In this section we assess the relative significance of five factors that have been advanced by a variety of scholars to explain East Asian economic transformation. These factors include the particular historical circumstances out of which their transformation emerged; the role of foreign capital; the importance of free markets; the significance of neo-Confucian cultural forms; and repressive labor systems that ensured supplies of cheap labor. The sixth factor, the role of state policy and influence, is dealt with in a subsequent section.

Historical Legacies

> Is not the present after all in large measure the prisoner of a past that obstinately survives, and the past with its rules, its differences and its similarities, the indispensable key to any serious understanding of the present?

—(Braudel, 1984, p. 20)

Extrapolating from Braudel we can argue that history so infuses the present and sets the parameters for the emergence of the future that any social science that does not place it at the heart of its explanatory system is doomed to deliver woefully inadequate accounts of whatever phenomenon happens to be under scrutiny. Not withstanding the fact that this is precisely one of the central epistemological problems of much which passes for economic science in the contemporary world, history is one of the factors that has been utilized quite heavily in explanations of East Asian economic transformation. History in this sense has been used both in terms of the uniqueness of the national and collective pasts of East Asian societies but particularly in the form of historical conjunctures that have allowed structural space for the emergence of transformative dynamics.

There are five legacies of history that are seen to be of significance. The first concerns the circumstances surrounding the emergence of Japan as an industrializing society in the decades between the Meiji Restoration of 1867-1868 and the First World War. This includes Japan's emergence as an imperial power from the turn of the century and the significance of its incorporation of Taiwan and Korea into its colonial domain. The second concerns the impact of British colonialism in the region. The third relates to the geopolitical conjuncture in the East Asian region from 1945 to the early

1970s. The fourth, partially overlapping with the third, concerns the impact of the expansion of world trade associated with the "long boom" in North America and Western Europe from the late 1940s until the early 1970s. Finally, the reverberations of economic crisis in many of the core economies is regarded as having had important implications for development prospects, particularly amongst the second generation late industrializers (those other than Japan) in the region.

Japanese Industrialization and Colonialism. The "Japanese experience" has been the primary concern of the vast majority of scholars who have studied economic expansion in the region. The reasons for this are obvious given that Japan was the first—and still the only—non-Western economy to make it into the "big league." Its route to the modern world has been significant not only in itself, however, but also because it has constituted the prototype on which other East Asia economies—South Korea and Taiwan in particular— have based their development strategies. In this section we briefly mention some of the key elements that seem to have influenced Japan's own industrialization, before moving on to examine the significance of its imperial expansion for other societies in the region.

Frances Moulder, in her comparative study of Japan and China (1977), argues that contrasting experiences of Western imperialism largely explain the differential economic trajectories of these societies in the nineteenth and early twentieth centuries. Whereas China was absorbed into the expanding capitalist world economy, Japan was not, permitting Japan sufficient flexibility to adopt a relatively autarkic development strategy. As a result, while Japan was able to absorb Western ideas and technology, it was not subject to the economic, social, and political dependencies and exploitation that so often fell to societies touched by Western imperialism. While Moulder goes on to deal with the evolution of the state form, and with its "peculiar" relation with business, it seems clear that she places the weight of explanation on the legacy of the past and particularly the way in which external constraints on imperial expansion provided development opportunities for Japan that were denied other non-Western societies.

Michio Morishima (1982), in his concern to ground Japanese economic success in the articulation of Western technology with the Japanese "ethos," focuses more on the internal evolution of social structures and cultural forms. While his work is a major contribution to the analysis of the relation of a Confucian-based culture to economic expansion, he is at pains to show that Confucian ethics were adapted and transformed over time under the historical conditions that were unique to Japanese culture and society. While he places more emphasis than Moulder on internal historical dynamics, his analysis also emphasizes the conjuncture of Japanese historical isolation from the West with the technological and institutional fruits of contact when it did occur in the late nineteenth and early twentieth centuries. It should be said, in addition, that Morishima also emphasizes the significance of the state-business relation, but for him this arises out of, and in explanatory terms remains secondary to, Japan's unique history and culture.

The significance of imperialism also carries weight in explanations of economic development in Korea and Taiwan. In these cases, however, we are dealing not with Western imperialism, nor with the relative "hands-off" variety of that, which was the Japanese experience. Rather we are dealing with the absorption of both territories into the Japanese empire during the first half of the current century.

The thrust of the Japanese state into Taiwan in 1895 and Korea in 1910 came in the context of Japan's first wave of industrialization. Japan's initial material basis for imperial expansion was its drive to secure sufficient supplies of rice and other agricultural commodities that the rapidly industrializing and urbanizing society could no longer provide domestically. The Japanese were able to enhance agricultural productivity greatly in Korea and Taiwan by removing the absentee landlords and transforming their agricultural systems into smallholder cultivation (S. P. S. Ho, 1978). Additionally, with rising real wages and growing militarization at home in the 1930s, Japanese companies—encouraged by the state—began to invest in manufacturing facilities, particularly in food processing, textiles, wood pulp and paper, fertilizers, aluminum and copper refining, and shipbuilding. The social consequences of these developments were, first, the elimination of the feudal landlord class that has so bedeviled strategies for modernization in other developing societies, and second, the beginnings of the creation of an industrial working class (Amsden, 1979; Cumings, 1987; Gold, 1986). Furthermore, and particularly in the context of Korea, industry emerged in a highly centralized fashion, controlled as it was by six Japanese *zaibatsu* (Amsden, 1989, pp. 31-35). It appears that these firms provided the organizational model for the *chaebol* that have so come to dominate the South Korean economy in more recent years.

There are two other bequests by the Japanese to Taiwan and Korea that seem to have been of significance. First, in order to facilitate imperial control and export (to Japan) of agricultural produce and manufactured commodities, considerable investment went into such infrastructure as roads, railroads, and ports. Secondly, the military nature of Japanese colonial administration ensured the transmission of a military hierarchy with its attendant disciplinary codes and ethos to the colonial societies (Amsden, 1979, 1985; Cumings, 1987), laying the foundations for both a relatively efficient bureaucracy and for the authoritarian state forms that emerged during the Chiang regime in Taiwan and the Rhee and Park regimes in South Korea and that persist, though in a cosmetically democratic form, to the present day.

British Colonialism. The relation of the historical legacies to economic transformation in Hong Kong and Singapore have received less scholarly attention, probably because their historical antecedents are less tangible than those of South Korea and Taiwan. British colonialism in both Hong Kong and Singapore was much more"disinterested" than was its Japanese equivalent. These, after all, were viewed as insignificant backwaters of the British empire, rather than as "jewels in the crown" in the way that South Korea and Taiwan were for the Japanese. Hong Kong and Singapore were entrepôts and naval stations; not the sort of places to be developed for productive purposes.

This is not to say, however, that the legacy of British colonialism is unimportant in explaining development in these two city-states. The British did provide (and in Hong Kong continue to provide) efficient and relatively liberal bureaucratic and legal systems, which remain—particularly in the case of Singapore—probably the least corrupt in the entire region. Furthermore, by being nurtured as key regional nodes for intra-empire trade, both territories benefitted from extensive pre-existing networks of trading houses and specialized services as they began to develop their export-oriented industrialization strategies in the 1950s (Hong Kong) and 1960s (Singapore). It is probably fair to say, however, that in most regards the legacy of Japanese colonialism in Taiwan and South Korea proved to be more significant for subsequent economic development in those two countries than British colonialism did for the two city-states.

In Malaya, the economic requirements of the British Empire boosted tin and established rubber and palm oil production, the latter two remaining central to the Malaysian economy (Jomo, 1990). With the emergence of new industries came the demand for new labor supplies. The preservation of neo-feudal constraints on Malay peasant labor created the need to draw on migrant labor, hence the origins of the Chinese and Indian communities that now make up about 35% and 10% respectively of the Malaysian population. With the economic legacies of colonialism have come racial legacies as well. Superimposed as they have been on class divisions (Jomo, 1986), racial issues have provided a continuing source of potential and actual instability (as in the riots of 1969), and hence of particular legitimation problems not confronted by most of the other states in the region.

"Tradition and previous generations", Marx wrote, "lie like a nightmare on the minds of the living". That this is probably nowhere more true in East Asia than in Malaysia, is a real problem of history that has conditioned that society's development. It may yet be a legacy that derails its future prospects. But it is also a legacy that presents an opportunity of greater global significance than the East Asian newly industrializing countries (NICs). Unlike them, Malaysia is relatively sectorially balanced: it has a vibrant agricultural sector. Also unlike them, it is racially diverse, and it has a democratic state both in form, and generally speaking in content. If Malaysia is successful in its late industrializer strategy, it will, therefore, be a much more apt model for Third World societies than the East Asian NICs could ever be. It would also call into question the notion that there is a necessary connection between late industrialization and authoritarian, non-democratic states.

East Asian Geopolitics. For all but one of the countries dealt with in this book, Malaysia, the geopolitics of the Cold War proved to be an important factor in industrialization. The economies of Japan, Taiwan, and South Korea —and the militaries of the latter two countries—were deliberately built with U.S. aid and technology transfer as bulwarks against communism. Additionally, Japanese industry benefited from the increased demands for steel, military equipment, and uniforms that emerged during the Korean War (1950-1953). Manufacturing in South Korea, Taiwan and particularly in Hong Kong also benefited from the U.S. war in Vietnam (early 1960s to the mid-1970s).

The formation of the Peoples' Republic of China in 1949, and its subsequent involvement in the Korean War, resulted in U.S. and U.N. trade embargoes that all but destroyed Hong Kong's entrepôt function. This, together with an influx of refugees from China, led to massive unemployment (Lin & Ho, 1980, p. 5). Serious social conflict was averted largely because of the growth of a relatively advanced textile and garment industry, based on refugee capital from Shanghai utilizing state-of-the-art technology. Drawing on the pre-existing trading networks referred to above, textile and garment production quickly became the basis for Hong Kong's emergence as East Asia's second industrial power (So, 1986; Wong, 1988; see also Henderson, 1989, pp. 77-80).

Singapore's emergence as a "late industrializer" also arose from regional geopolitics—the confluence of economic, racial and political stresses that had begun with British involvement in the Malayan peninsula during the latter half of the nineteenth century and reached its zenith following the creation of the Federation of Malaysia in 1957. The Chinese, who were numerically dominant in Singapore and economically dominant throughout the Federation, found themselves in conflict with the Malay majority, who held political (but not economic) power. Once Singapore was cut adrift from the Federation in 1965, the rapid development of a high productivity, high wage economy became essential to Singapore's legitimacy and indeed survival (Castells et al., 1990, part 2).

World Trade Expansion. With few exceptions (see, for example, the essays in Deyo, 1987), most analysts of East Asian development have overlooked the fact that the initial industrialization of Japan and the NICs coincided with an unprecedented expansion in world trade, particularly in the markets for manufactured commodities. Without such an historical coincidence, it is highly doubtful that Hong Kong and Singapore could have achieved their double-digit growth rates, or that South Korea and Taiwan could have made the switch from import-substituting to the export-oriented industrialization strategies, in the late 1950s and early 1960s. The sustained "long boom" in the cores of the world economy provided a "window of opportunity" that did not exist before and has not existed since. Without such an expansion in world trade, it is debatable whether there would have been any room for newcomers. The corollary of this, of course, is that the constraints on world trade over the past 10 to 20 years, which have resulted in deepening crisis tendencies within the global economy, may have helped ensure that there will be no more late industrializers (such as Malaysia).

Economic Crisis in the Core. The final set of historical circumstances partially accounting for the economic success of the East Asian NICs can be found in the economic downturns experienced by the industrial nations during the post-1970 period. As Frobel et al. (1980), Bluestone and Harrison (1982), and others have argued, growing trade union bargaining power in the 1950s and 1960s had contributed to a "wage drift" in industrial nations (particularly the United States) that cut into surpluses and damaged profit margins. This profit squeeze was reinforced by the general economic slowdown as well as recessions that further hurt industries in the core economies. In response, many firms—particularly in textiles, garments and electronics— began to locate overseas the more labor-intensive parts of the production process in order to take advantage of the large supplies of cheap, unorganized, and largely female labor that existed on the peripheries of the world economy (Frobel et al., 1980). A number of the East and Southeast Asian countries were among the initial preferred locations for investment in assembly plants. While these developments undoubtedly boosted the flow of foreign manufacturing capital into East Asia (with the exception of Japan), it is important to bear in mind that, with the exceptions of Singapore and Malaysia, foreign investment has not been a dominant feature of capital formation or firm ownership in the manufacturing sectors of the countries under discussion in this volume (see immediately below). Furthermore, direct foreign investment does not in itself ensure genuine economic development, as the dependency theorists, for instance, have clearly demonstrated.

The Role of Foreign Capital

In discussing the relation of foreign investment to economic development in East Asia, it is necessary to distinguish between foreign assistance (primarily by the U.S. government) through the early 1960s, and the foreign direct investment (FDI) and technology transfers on the part of corporations that has occurred since that time.

For South Korea and Taiwan—seen by the United States as East Asian bulwarks in the war against communism—U.S. foreign aid was extremely high prior to the mid-1960s. (Conversely, foreign aid to Hong Kong, Singapore, and Malaysia was negligible during this period.) Between 1953 and 1962, for example, U.S. aid financed 70% of total South Korean imports and 80% of total fixed capital formation; in Taiwan during the same period, U.S. aid financed 85% of the current account deficit and was responsible for 38% of gross domestic capital formation (Haggard & Cheng, 1987, p. 87). This was in addition to $6 billion in military aid to South Korea and $5.6 billion to Taiwan through 1979 (CIA data quoted by Haggard and Cheng, 1987, p. 87). U.S. foreign aid thus played a key role in the initial "take-offs" of South Korea and Taiwan; arguably, only the most corrupt of political economies could fail to develop in the face of such massive amounts of governmental assistance.

Much scholarship, particularly in the dependency tradition, has laid great emphasis on the relation between FDI and Third World industrialization (e.g., Frobel et al., 1980). While there has been much truth to this in Latin America, with the exceptions of Singapore and Malaysia, the significance of FDI to development in Japan, South Korea, Taiwan and Hong Kong has been limited. In terms of exports by value, the share of foreign-invested firms in recent years has been about 18% in South Korea, 15% in Taiwan, and only about 12% in Hong Kong (Henderson, 1989). In the cases of Singapore and

Malaysia, the proportions are about 70% and 45% respectively (Mirza, 1986).

While investment by overseas Chinese has been significant to some of the economies in question (Taiwan, Hong Kong, and Malaysia; see Haggard & Cheng, 1987; Redding, 1990), the acquisition of foreign technologies has been more important. For example, the early development of the Japanese semiconductor industry (in the 1950s) would have been inconceivable without the ability to acquire the technology from U.S. companies under licensing arrangements (Okimoto, Sugano, & Weinstein, 1984). Much the same applies to the development of the semiconductor and consumer electronics industries of South Korea and Taiwan, though in these cases the technology has been acquired largely through "strategic alliances" with U.S. and Japanese companies (Henderson, 1989). Alice Amsden in her work on South Korea (1989) argues that the key to late industrialization has been the ability to learn and adapt technologies and labor processes developed elsewhere. While "industrialization through learning" has indeed been central, the point remains that if it were not for the willingness of foreign corporations to transfer their technology in various ways, the "learning process" would have been more difficult and much slower than was in fact the case.

For many of the East Asian economies, therefore, substantial FDI was not necessary for development; moreover, where it did occur, it was not by itself sufficient. FDI is ultimately significant for economic transformation only when it stimulates local firm production linkages and/or when it results, over time, in shifts to higher value-added forms of production within the subsidiaries of the transnational corporations themselves. While the latter partly explains the successes of Singapore and Malaysia (Henderson, 1989), in other parts of the Third World neither significant linkages nor shifts to higher value-added production have resulted from FDI (cf. Sklair, 1989 on Mexico).

The Question of Free Markets

The free market explanation of East Asian development has probably carried more weight than any other. Indeed, among professional economists, it is difficult to think of any contribution that does not locate "unfettered enterprise" at the core of its explanatory scheme. Interestingly and perhaps surprisingly this is as true for economists indigenous to the region as it is for outside commentators. For instance, one of the region's leading economists, Edward Chen, argues that in the cases of Japan, South Korea, Taiwan, Hong Kong, and Singapore, "state intervention is largely absent. What the state provided is simply a suitable environment for the entrepreneurs to perform their function" (Chen, 1979, p. 41).

According to neoclassical economic reasoning, the East Asian economies (including Japan) have been successful because their governments have sought to maximize efficiencies putatively resulting from market-based resource allocation (Balassa, 1981). These governments, it is argued, have either never intervened in "normal" market allocation functions or if they have, they progressively "liberalized" their economies prior to the initial periods of rapid economic growth associated with export-oriented industrialization. Either way, state-induced market distortions have been kept to a minimum, and as a consequence markets have worked more efficiently than in other developing societies. Additionally, as Wade suggests (1990, pp. 23-24), there has been a secondary theme within the neoclassical literature that has recognized a modicum of state intervention. Here it is argued that at the aggregate level, East Asian governments have successfully balanced domestic market protection with export promotion policies. The overall effect then, has been the neutralization of one set of state-induced market distortions by a second set.

Michael Porter's (1990a, 1990b) influential comparative work on the determinants of economic success among nations, for example, advocates a limited degree of state intervention within a neoclassical framework stressing unfettered market competition as the key. According to Porter, "government's proper role is as a catalyst and challenger; it is to encourage—or even push—companies to raise their aspirations and move to higher levels of competitive performance" (1990a, p. 88). Governments should let wages rise according to the market for labor, permit exchange rates to fluctuate according to market conditions, enforce strict safety and environmental standards in order to assure the highest quality products, sharply limit direct cooperation among industry rivals, eliminate such barriers to competition as state monopolies or fixed prices, enforce strong domestic antitrust policies, and reject all forms of managed trade. Governments should also encourage the creation of a highly skilled, specialized work force, and in general promote goals that lead to "sustained investment in human skills, in innovation, and in physical assets" (Porter, 1990a, p. 88).

Porter partly attributes South Korea's rapid ascent in the world economy to the South Korean government's substantial investments in education and infrastructure, its aggressive export promotion policies (such as providing export insurance and tax credits), and its fostering of a national consensus on the importance of international competitive success. He notes that the South

Korean government has largely limited its intervention in capital markets to channeling heavily subsidized loans to globally competitive industries, and actively pursing technology transfer. While it has (unwisely, in Porter's view) engaged in some protectionism (as well as labor repression, which Porter does not discuss), any adverse effects of such interventions have been offset by intense domestic rivalry and competition.

Despite his professed concern with state policies, Porter tends to deal with the state as a relatively minor player who is best counseled to step out of the way, rather than as central to the dynamic of corporate success and economic transformation. This weakness is particularly noticeable in his chapter on South Korea, where he makes no mention of Alice Amsden's (1989) seminal work on the role of the state in South Korean industrialization. This omission is particularly striking since Amsden and Porter, both colleagues at Harvard Business School, were working on their projects at about the same time.

It is no coincidence that the principal counterweight to neoclassical arguments about the supposed pivotal role of free markets in East Asia has come from those who argue, in effect, that there are varieties of free market economies and that for some of them "free" is very much a relative term. While East Asian economies may indeed have quite small public sectors, and while their domestic economies may be intensely competitive, this does not mean that the role of the state with regard to economic transformation has been minimal. On the contrary, as we will argue in the conclusion of this chapter, late industrialization—and Japan and the East Asian NICs are so far the best examples—demands a decisive role for the state in setting and implementing national goals for economic growth.

In recent years the neoclassical orthodoxy has been successfully challenged in a steady stream of publications. Beginning with Chalmers Johnson's (1982) classic account of role of the Ministry of International Trade and Industry (MITI) in Japan's post-war industrialization, this literature includes Amsden's contributions on South Korea (1990) and Taiwan (1985), Gold's (1986) research on Taiwan, Luedde-Neurath's (1988) work on South Korea, and the chapters by Cumings (1987), Johnson (1987), and Koo (1987) on Northeast East Asia in general in Deyo (1987). Of particular note, however, is Robert Wade's (1990) "governed market theory" of East Asian development. Taking both the "free market" and the more sophisticated "simulated free market" versions of neoclassical theory, he systematically matches them to the empirical realities of economic transformation in the region and finds that they are severely wanting. For Northeast Asia at any rate, it is now simply impossible to argue that free markets have been the primary determinants of economic growth.

Hong Kong and Singapore, however, seem to have followed free market policies to a far greater degree than South Korea, Taiwan, or Japan. Unlike those countries, the two city-states have avoided protectionist policies, sectorially based export promotion, controlled credit, or, in general, controls on business. But as the work of Castells et al. (1990), Schiffer (1991), and Lim (1983) have shown, by means of public housing and other welfare expenditures, they have massively influenced both the price and reproduction of labor power. In the case of Hong Kong, state monopoly of land ownership has been used as a crucial budgetary tool, while in Singapore enforced savings via compulsory employer and employee contributions to the Central Provident Fund have played a similar role.

Collectively this new scholarship on the East Asian economies shows that, if anything, their development has been state-led. Indeed one analyst, speaking of South Korea, has gone as far as to suggest that its success has been "just as much a triumph of state capitalism as . . . the achievements of the first Five Year Plans in the Soviet Union or the People's Republic of China" (Harris, 1987, p. 145). As the chapters in this volume show, to one degree or another these NICs have been led by "developmental states" that sought to secure legitimacy through active pursuit of economic growth policies. Continually to fail to recognize this fact is to persist with the fantasies of pure ideology.[3]

Culture and Development

For 1960s "modernization theory" (Rostow, 1961), traditional cultures were viewed as a barrier to economic development. Extended families, attitudes toward work, hereditary rather than meritocratic systems of advancement, and fatalistic value systems were alleged to be endogenous barriers to transformation and growth in the Third World. Underdevelopment was not the result of exploitative transnational corporations, unfavorable terms of trade, the global state system, or the legacies of colonialism—rather, it was due to the cultural failings of the people themselves. Although modernization theory was subjected to decisive critiques from the dependency theorists and others, it continued to survive in U.S. academic circles (for example, in the pages of *Economic Development and Cultural Change*), as well as within such interstate agencies as the World Bank.

In recent years the relationship of culture to development has taken on new credence through what we might term "neo-modernization" theory (e.g., Berger, 1986; Berger & Hsiao, 1988; Redding, 1990; Wong, 1986). Whereas modernization theory originally saw non-Western cultural forms and social practices as barriers to development in the Third World, the new scholarship argues that in at least one non-Western culture, an East Asian variant is capable of fostering the types of behavior necessary for rapid economic growth. It is suggested that their common Confucian heritage accounts for the developmental success of Japan and the East Asian NICs.

In essence the neomodernization literature suggests that the tenets of Confucianism, which are at the heart of traditional social practices in Chinese societies, Japan, and South Korea, have in recent decades come to constitute the basis of a new economic culture. This neo-Confucian economic culture, at least in the context of capitalist economic systems, has played a role akin to that of Protestantism during the initial rise of capitalism in Western Europe.

The elements of Confucianism that are seen as particularly important to this new economic culture are: filial respect and respect for one's elders and superiors; a high value placed on education; a commitment to meritocratic forms of personal advancement; a capacity for hard work; and an ascetic commitment to deferred gratification. In the neo-Confucian economic culture these elements have been transmuted into deferential attitudes toward managerial authority (resulting in greatly reduced labor relations problems); high rates of personal and corporate savings; a commitment to the firm as a collectivity; and a willingness to forego leisure in favor of long hours of committed work.

Neomodernization theorists do not ignore other determinants of East Asian development. As we have already mentioned, free markets tend to be regarded as a central context for the successful formation and operation of the economic culture, and by implication, therefore, a "light handed" state on the economic tiller is generally seen as an important factor. In the more sophisticated versions of the argument (especially Berger, 1986), the specific historical contingencies discussed above are also seen as important. Even so, however, it is the impact of a Confucian value system that is accorded primacy—an argument that always threatens to give way to racist claims. In the case of Berger's (1986, p. 166) statement that "it is inherently implausible to believe that Singapore would be what it is today if it were populated, not by a majority of ethnic Chinese, but by Brazilians or Bengalis—or, for that matter, by a majority of ethnic Malays," it appears as a peculiar form of inverted racism.

The principal problem with most neomodernization culturalist arguments lies not with their monocausality (Berger is an exception here) nor their tendency to degenerate into racial explanations, but rather in their failure to consider the concrete historical and institutional dynamics of the specific societies themselves. They have problems, for example, in explaining the Japanese "Confucian" stress on loyalty as against the Chinese "Confucian" stress on benevolence (Morishima, 1982); in explaining why there is so much diversity in the business systems of Confucian-based societies—in the nature of the firm, in organizational authority, or in state-business relations (Whitley, 1990, 1991); or, perhaps most significantly, in accounting for the far higher levels of internal political opposition and mobilization currently found in South Korea than any of the other "Confucian" NICs.

The thrust of our argument here is not to reject culture as an important source of "East Asian exceptionalism." Rather, we argue that one cannot understand the significance of culture outside of its relation with other structural elements of specific societies. Far more empirical work is required to identify the importance of culture in particular institutional contexts at particular historical moments.

Repressive Labor Systems

The presence of vast reserves of cheap, unorganized, and disciplined labor in East Asia has been widely used to account for both the region's "economic miracle" and for the corresponding decline in manufacturing and employment in the United States and Western Europe. The argument, developed most forcefully perhaps in Frobel et al.'s (1980) "new international division of labor" thesis, holds that one of the legacies of imperialism was the availability of large supplies of unskilled and underemployed labor on the peripheries of the world economy. The East Asian states, undemocratic, authoritarian, and in some cases (Taiwan and South Korea) militarized, frequently dealt repressively with internal opposition. Antilabor legislation, often banning oppositional trade union activity, meant that sweatshop conditions, long illegal in the core economies, could flourish in the periphery. This, in turn, provided the East Asian NICs, and later Malaysia and Thailand, with a major competitive advantage over the United States and Western Europe, particularly in industries that employed a largely female (and hence presumably culturally more submissive) work force (Heyzer, 1986). As a result, key industries—notably textiles, garments, and electronics—relocated their production operations in the periphery.

While there is clearly merit to the "new international division of labor" thesis, it overstates the importance of cheap labor in accounting for the developmental success of East Asia. First, there are many other parts of the Third World that have large supplies of cheap, unorganized, and frequently repressed labor, that have not experienced genuine development even when they have been the recipients of core-country plants. U.S. garment manufacturers—not to mention manufacturers from Hong Kong and South Korea—now operate factories in Mexico, the Caribbean, and the Indian subcontinent, yet these regions are hardly developing at double-digit rates.

Second, as Deyo (1989) convincingly demonstrates, the empirical record does not support the "docile labor" argument. All of the societies discussed in this volume have experienced major working class mobilizations in the past, and South Korea today remains a major "deviant" case, where internal opposition is widespread despite often violent state repression. In recent years both South Korea and Taiwan have witnessed considerable worker mobilization and the formation of new independent trade unions (Asia Monitor Resource Center, 1988; S. Y. Ho, 1990).

Finally, however important cheap labor may be in the early stages of late industrialization, the East Asian countries prosper today because they have upgraded their manufacturing to produce higher value-added, globally competitive goods. By investing in education, human skills, and technology, these NICs have succeeded in increasing productivity and real wages. Their comparative advantage no longer lies in their ability to deliver cheap, unskilled, and easily replicated labor, but rather in offering highly skilled engineers and technicians (albeit at wage rates far below those of their counterparts in the United States, Europe, or Japan; see Henderson, 1989).

In summary, then, we can say that while the availability of cheap labor was an important factor (among many others) in the early phases of East Asian industrialization, its significance for the more recent phases of industrialization has diminished as labor processes have become increasingly capital-intensive.

Situating the State

Nearly a quarter of a century ago Ralph Dahrendorf drew a distinction between two types of rationality that had begun to infuse industrial society. *Market rationality,* Dahrendorf (1968, p. 219) suggested, was based on the assumption that "a smoothly functioning market is in fact to the greatest advantage of the greatest number"; and it required a "politically passive . . . hands-off attitude in matters of legislation and decision-making." *Plan rationality,* in contrast, "has as its dominant feature precisely the setting of substantive social norms. Planners determine in advance who does what and who gets what" (Dahrendorf, 1968, p. 219). Dahrendorf regarded Western capitalist political economies as the closest empirical approximation to the former, and state socialist societies to the latter.

Dahrendorf's distinctions were developed at a time when liberal European intellectuals still harbored a residue of optimism about soviet-type societies, and when the industrializing societies of Asia, with the partial exception of Japan, were but a blur on the consciousness of most Western scholars. He can thus perhaps be forgiven for not adequately appreciating the inequities— or perhaps irrationalities—that in fact result from the "pure types" of both forms of political economy.

Chalmers Johnson (1982, pp. 18-26), building on Dahrendorf's distinction, has proposed that the concept of plan rationality is more appropriate to an understanding of Japan and other East Asian political economies than it is as a characterization of state socialist societies. He suggests encompassing the latter under a third distinction: *plan ideological*. We suggest completing this logical schema with a fourth distinction that addresses the Reaganite-Thatcherite "new right" economic policies currently in vogue in many parts of the world, including former state socialist societies such as Poland: *market ideological* political economies, according to which public policy is oriented above all toward assuring free market operations. Like plan ideological political economies, market ideological regimes arise from ideological dogma: in the case of the former, the wisdom and benevolence of state managers in a command economy; in the case of the latter, the wisdom and benevolence of an invisible hand in a supposedly unfettered market. In neither case do the requisite conditions in fact exist; in both cases, they are reified by intellectual traditions that remain impervious to disconfirming evidence.

Following the leads of Dahrendorf and Johnson, we refine the definition of market rational political economies to include the regulatory function of the state, which is viewed in such political economies as providing a framework wherein investment, production, and distributional decisions (which remain the preserve of business) can operate in a relatively efficient manner. In a parallel fashion, plan rational political economies are those in which state regulation is supplemented by state direction of the economy as a whole. Here national economic goals are identified, and the state operates with various degrees of influence or pressure to urge companies to act in accordance with these goals. The economy remains largely in private hands, and companies compete with one another under the watchful discipline of the market; yet the state also intervenes to achieve national goals where necessary. Should a sector be lacking what is deemed essential to economic growth, for example, the state will likely induce it, often through price supports, subsidies, and favorable credit arrangements. In Amsden's (1989, pp. 139-155) felicitous phrase, the state will directly intervene to get "relative prices wrong," should this be believed necessary for national economic advancement. The simple and uncritical identification of corporate profits with national economic health—central to market ideological and market rational political economies—is thus broken.

While there are some similarities between plan rational and plan ideological political economies, especially in terms of the state's role in setting national economic goals, their differences are of greater significance. In plan ideological political economies the state owns and controls most if not all economic units. Resource allocations and investment decisions are a state rather than a corporate or market function, supposedly serving an overriding concern with equity in the distribution of wealth and income. Ideological dogma, rather than pragmatic analysis of consequences, dominates policy choices and applications.

These four constructs (market rational, plan rational, market ideological, and plan ideological) should be regarded as ideal types; actually existing political economies combine them in various historically contingent ways. Still, for any particular society, one will typically dominate, facilitating an overall characterization of its prevailing political economy. On the basis of these distinctions, therefore, we can now provisionally diagram the state-economy relations of the societies discussed in the present volume. For the sake of comparison, a number of other industrial and industrializing societies also are included.

Although the contents of Figure 1.1 should be regarded as no more than a first approximation, it does serve to indicate that many of the world's recently most successful political economies can be located in, or close to, the plan rational "quadrant". While it would go far beyond the scope of this chapter to try to justify this positioning for all of the cases so represented, a brief justification of some of the East Asian cases, at least in general terms, is in order.

The argument that the role of the state has been decisive in East Asian economic expansion—what Wade (1990) calls the "governed market" theory—does not rest on direct state ownership of key industries. Although this has been more significant than is often recognized (for example railways and earlier steel and banks in Japan; banks in South Korea; airlines, armaments, ship repairing in Singapore), it is rather the nature of the state-business partnership that has been important. While a corporatist state-business partnership is evident in other societies (such as the European social democracies), what is significant in East Asia, with the exception of Hong Kong, is that the

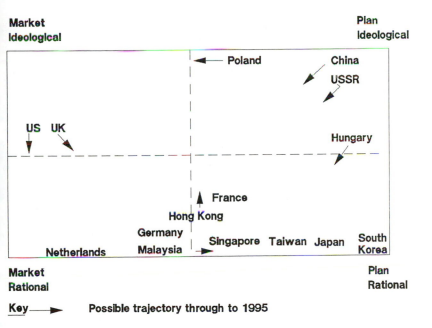

Figure 1.1. National Political Economies in 1991

state has been firmly in the driving seat. At particular historical moments, when the course of growth and development has required it, ministries and planning agencies in Japan and the NICs have engaged in the following forms of intervention:

(1) They have "encouraged" or directed companies into higher value-added, higher wage and more technology-intensive forms of production. They have done this either by systems of constraints, such as controlling credit through the banking system (Japan, South Korea, Taiwan), and/or by rigging prices (Japan, South Korea, Taiwan, Singapore). In the Singaporean case, for instance, manual labor costs since 1978 have more than doubled as a consequence of government-induced increases in employer contributions to the Central Provident Fund (Castells et al., 1990, part 2).

(2) They have legislated to discourage short-term speculative domestic or overseas investment (Japan, South Korea, Taiwan), and thus indirectly have ensured its flow into manufacturing. An extreme example of such state-imposed discipline on investment practices is the South Korean law, dating from the early 1960s, which forbids the export of sums more than one million

U.S. dollars without government permission, on pain of penalties ranging from 10 years imprisonment to death (Amsden, 1990, p. 22).

(3) They have created industrial sectors that did not previously exist either through state companies or through the supply of credit and financial guarantees to private companies. Examples include steel, shipbuilding, transportation, petrochemicals, and semiconductors (Japan, South Korea, Taiwan, Singapore, Malaysia, in some though not all sectors in each case).

(4) They have invested heavily in the creation and refinement of new technologies, usually by setting up government research and development facilities and then transferring the results to private companies without transferring development costs (Japan, South Korea, Taiwan, Singapore).

(5) They have protected domestic markets, either across the board or (more recently) with regard to particular products (Japan, South Korea, Taiwan). For instance, the Taiwanese government still places restrictions on the import of many commodities that are directly competitive with domestic products, but has liberalized trade on those it does not seek to encourage directly, such as certain types of machine tools (Amsden, 1985; Wade, 1990).

(6) They have consistently monitored world markets in search of export opportunities, and in order to identify new types of demand that they may then encourage companies to meet (Japan, South Korea, Taiwan).

(7) They have sometimes used price controls to discourage domestic market exploitation in circumstances of near-monopolistic supply (South Korea), and have created cartels to contain the price of basic foodstuffs (Hong Kong) (Amsden, 1989, 1990; Schiffer, 1991).

(8) They have—in the case of Hong Kong—used state ownership of land as a budgetary mechanism to allow the delivery of a relatively extensive welfare system (by Asian standards), while maintaining low corporate and personal taxation and negligible foreign indebtedness (Castells et al., 1990, part 1; Schiffer, 1991).

(9) They have provided the world's largest public housing systems (in Singapore and Hong Kong), which have served to subsidize wages and legitimate centralized, autocratic—and in Hong Kong, colonial—political regimes (Castells et al., 1990; Schiffer, 1991).

(10) They have subjected companies receiving state-guaranteed credits to rigorous performance standards (including export performance), so as to minimize the possibility that subsidies will result in speculative, nonproductive investments or corruption (South Korea, Japan).

From this brief listing of the ways in which states in East Asia have intervened and directed or substantially influenced the course of economic transformation, it is clear that they have gone far beyond anything that could be encompassed within the neoclassical market ideological or even market rational frameworks. Furthermore, while it is difficult if not impossible, to disaggregate empirically the economic impact of state policy vis-à-vis the other possible determinants of economic growth (cf. Wade, 1990), the weight of circumstantial evidence suggests that state policy has been decisive.

Indeed, we would argue that while the role of the state in Japan and the East Asian NICs must be contextualized both culturally and historically, state policy and influence should now be accepted as the single most important determinant of the East Asian economic miracle. The chapters in this book, although following different theoretical logics, pursue this claim with regard to substantive issues and specific policies.

Notes

1. The principal contributions here are Baran (1957), Frank (1969b), Amin (1974), and Emmanuel (1972). Diana Hunt (1989, pp. 162-197) provides a particularly useful exposition and critique of their work.

2. Bauer and Yamey's (1957) work was an attempt to rebut that of Prebisch and the U.N. Economic Commission on Latin America (ECLA), which itself, at least in Prebisch's hands, had emerged from a critique to the neoclassic paradigm, both in theory and in terms of its policy derivatives and practical consequences (see Hunt, 1989, pp. 293-298).

3. Business economist Neil Kay (1984, pp. 187-188) has expressed the problems of neoclassical economics (including its analytic deficiencies) in more blunt terms: "mainstream economics has continued to be a fertile source of sterile theories . . . the individual intent on pursuing a career as an economist has to be bright enough to understand the abstract ramifications of neoclassical theory and dumb enough to have faith in them."

References

Amin, S. (1974). *Accumulation on a world scale.* New York: Monthly Review Press.

Amsden, A. H. (1979). Taiwan's economic history: A case of "etatisme" and a challenge to dependency theory. *Modern China, 5*(3), 341-379.

Amsden, A. H. (1985). The state and Taiwan's economic development. In P. Evans, D. Rueschemeyer, & T. Skocpol (Eds.), *Bringing the state back in* (pp. 78-106). New York: Cambridge University Press.

Amsden, A. H. (1989). *Asia's next giant: South Korea and late industrialization.* New York: Oxford University Press.

Amsden, A. H. (1990). Third World industrialization: "Global Fordism" or a new model? *New Left Review, 182,* 5-31.

Asia Monitor Resource Center. (1988). *Min-Ju No-Jo: South Korea's new trade unions.* Hong Kong: Asia Monitor Resource Center.

Balassa, B. (1981). *Newly industrializing countries in the world economy*. Elmsford, NY: Pergamon.

Baran, P. (1957). *The political economy of growth*. New York: Monthly Review Press.

Bauer, P. T., & Yamey, B. S. (1957). *The economics of under-developed countries*. London and Cambridge: James Nisbet and Cambridge University Press.

Berger, P. (1986). *The capitalist revolution: Fifty propositions about prosperity, equality and liberty*. New York: Basic Books.

Berger, P., & Hsiao, M. H. H. (Eds.). (1988). *In search of an East Asian development model*. New Brunswick, NJ: Transaction Books.

Bluestone, B., & Harrison, B. (1982). *The deindustrialization of America*. New York: Basic Books.

Braudel, F. (1984). *Civilisation and capitalism 15th-18th century. Volume III: The perspective of the world*. London: Fontana.

Cardoso, F., & Faletto, E. (1979). *Dependency and development in Latin America*. Berkeley: University of California Press.

Castells, M., Goh, L., & Kwok, R. Y. (1990). *The Shek Kip Mei syndrome: Economic development and public housing in Hong Kong and Singapore*. London: Pion.

Chen, E. K. Y. (1979). *Hyper-growth in Asian economies: A comparative study of Hong Kong, Japan, Korea, Singapore and Taiwan*. London: Macmillan.

Cumings, B. (1987). The origins and development of the Northeast Asian political economy: Industrial sectors, product cycles and political consequences. In F. C. Deyo (Ed.), *The political economy of the new Asian industrialism* (pp. 48-83). Ithaca, NY: Cornell University Press.

Dahrendorf, R. (1968). Market and plan: Two types of rationality. In R. Dahrendorf, *Essays in the theory of society* (pp. 215-231). London: Routledge & Kegan Paul.

Deyo, F. C. (Ed.). (1987). *The political economy of the new Asian industrialism*. Ithaca, NY: Cornell University Press.

Deyo, F. C. (1989). *Beneath the miracle: Labor subordination in the new Asian industrialism*. Berkeley: University of California Press.

Emmanuel, A. (1972). *Unequal exchange: A study in the imperialism of free trade*. London: New Left Books.

Evans, P. (1979). *Dependent development: The alliance of multinational, state and local capital in Brazil*. Princeton, NJ: Princeton University Press.

Frank, A. G. (1969a). *Latin America: Underdevelopment or revolution: Essays in the development of underdevelopment and the immediate enemy*. New York: Monthly Review Press.

Frank, A. G. (1969b). *Capitalism and underdevelopment in Latin America: Historical studies of Chile and Brazil*. New York: Monthly Review Press.

Frank, A. G. (1982, June 25). Asia's exclusive models. *Far Eastern Economic Review*, pp. 22-23.

Friedman, M., & Friedman, R. (1981). *Free to choose*. Harmondsworth, UK: Penguin.

Frobel, F., Heinrichs, J., & Kreye, O. (1980). *The new international division of labour*. Cambridge, UK: Cambridge University Press.

Gold, T. (1986). *State and society in the Taiwan miracle*. Armonk, NY: M. E. Sharpe.

Haggard, S., & Cheng, T. J. (1987). State and foreign capital in the East Asian NICs. In F. C. Deyo (Ed.), *The political economy of the new Asian industrialism* (pp. 84-135). Ithaca, NY: Cornell University Press.

Harris, N. (1978). *Mandate of heaven: Marx and Mao in modern China*. London: Quartet Books.

Harris, N. (1987). *The end of the Third World: Newly industrializing countries and the decline of an ideology.* Harmondsworth, UK: Penguin.

Henderson, J. (1986). The new international division of labour and urban development in the contemporary world system. In D. Drakakis-Smith (Ed.), *Urbanisation in the developing world* (pp. 63-81). London: Croom Helm.

Henderson, J. (1989). *The globalisation of high technology production: Society, space and semi-conductors in the restructuring of the modern world.* London: Routledge.

Heyzer, N. (1986). *Working women in Southeast Asia.* Milton Keynes, UK: Open University Press.

Ho, S. P. S. (1978). *Economic development of Taiwan, 1869-1970.* New Haven, CT: Yale University Press.

Ho, S. Y. (1990). *Taiwan—After a long silence.* Hong Kong: Asia Monitor Resource Center.

Hunt, D. (1989). *Economic theories of development: An analysis of competing paradigms.* London: Harvester Wheatsheaf.

Johnson, C. (1982). *MITI and the Japanese miracle.* Stanford, CA: Stanford University Press.

Johnson, C. (1987). Political institutions and economic performance: The government-business relationship in Japan, South Korea and Taiwan. In F. C. Deyo (Ed.), *The political economy of the new Asian industrialism* (pp. 136-164). Ithaca, NY: Cornell University Press.

Jomo, K. S. (1986). *A question of class: Capital, the state and uneven development in Malaya.* Singapore: Oxford University Press.

Jomo, K. S. (1990). *Growth and structural change in the Malaysian economy.* London: Macmillan.

Kay, N. M. (1984). *The emergent firm: Knowledge, ignorance, and surprise in economic organization.* London: Macmillan.

Koo, H. (1987). The interplay of state, social class and world system in East Asian development: The cases of South Korea and Taiwan. In F. C. Deyo (Ed.), *The political economy of the new Asian industrialism* (pp. 165-181). Ithaca, NY: Cornell University Press.

Lim, L. Y. C. (1983). Singapore's success: The myth of the free market economy. *Asian Survey, 23*(6), 752-764.

Lin, T. B., & Ho, Y. P. (1980). *Export-oriented growth and industrial diversification in Hong Kong.* Hong Kong: Chinese University of Hong Kong, Economic Research Centre.

Lipietz, A. (1987). *Mirages and miracles: The crises of global Fordism.* London: Verso.

Luedde-Neurath, R. (1988). State intervention and export-oriented development in South Korea. In G. White (Ed.), *Developmental states in East Asia* (pp. 68-112). London: Macmillan.

Mirza, H. (1986). *Multinationals and the growth of the Singapore economy.* New York: St. Martin's.

Morishima, M. (1982). *Why has Japan "succeeded"?* Cambridge, UK: Cambridge University Press.

Moulder, F. (1977). *Japan, China and the modern world economy.* New York: Cambridge University Press.

Okimoto, D. I., Sugano, T., & Weinstein, F. B. (Eds.). (1984). *Competitive edge: The semiconductor industry in the U.S. and Japan.* Stanford, CA: Stanford University Press.

Porter, M. E. (1990a, March-April). The competitive advantage of nations. *Harvard Business Review,* pp. 73-93.

Porter, M. E. (1990b). *The competitive advantage of nations.* London: Macmillan.

Redding, S. G. (1990). *The spirit of Chinese capitalism.* Berlin: de Gruyter.

Rostow, W. W. (1961). *The stages of economic growth.* Cambridge, UK: Cambridge University Press.

Schiffer, J. (1981). The changing post-war pattern of development: The accumulated wisdom of Samir Amin. *World Development, 9*(6), 515-537.

Schiffer, J. (1991). State policy and economic growth: A note on the Hong Kong model. *International Journal of Urban and Regional Research, 15*(2), 180-196.

Sklair, L. (1985). Shenzhen: A Chinese development zone in global perspective. *Development and Change, 15*, 581-602.

Sklair, L. (1989). *Assembling for development: The maquila industry in Mexico and the United States.* Winchester, UK: Unwin Hyman.

Sklair, L. (1991). Problems of socialist development: The significance of Shenzhen special economic zone for China's open door development strategy. *International Journal of Urban and Regional Research, 15*(2), 197-215.

So, A. Y. (1986). The economic success of Hong Kong: Insights from a world-system perspective. *Sociological Perspectives, 29*(2), 241-258.

Viner, J. (1953). *International trade and economic development.* Oxford, UK: Clarendon Press.

Wade, R. (1990). *Governing the market: Economic theory and the role of government in East Asian industrialization.* Princeton, NJ: Princeton University Press.

Wallerstein, I. (1978). World-system analysis: Theoretical and interpretive issues. In B. B. Kaplan (Ed.), *Social change in the capitalist world economy* (pp. 219-235). Beverly Hills, CA: Sage.

Wallerstein, I. (1979). *The capitalist world economy.* Cambridge, UK: Cambridge University Press.

Warren, B. (1980). *Imperialism: Pioneer of capitalism.* London: Verso.

Whitley, R. D. (1990). East Asian enterprise structures and the comparative analysis of forms of business organisation. *Organisation Studies, 11*(1), 47-74.

Whitley, R. D. (1991). The social construction of business systems in East Asia. *Organisation Studies, 12*(1), 1-28.

Wong, S. L. (1986). Modernization and Chinese culture in Hong Kong. *The China Quarterly, 106*, 306-325.

Wong, S. L. (1988). *Emigrant entrepreneurs: Shanghai industrialists in Hong Kong.* Hong Kong: Oxford University Press.

PART I

THEORETICAL ISSUES

Having assessed the various determinants that have been advanced to explain eco-nomic transformations in East Asia in Chapter 1, we turn, in Part I, to three accounts of the relationship between state policy and economic development in the NICs of the region. These accounts focus on the complex and often contradictory interplay between economies that increasingly produce for a global market, and nationalistic states that seek legitimacy through active pursuit of economic growth.

In Chapter 2, Manuel Castells looks at the "Four Asian Tigers" (Hong Kong, Tai-wan, Singapore, and South Korea) as examples of "developmental states" in which strong and often repressive states single-mindedly pursue development objectives. Contrary to their prevailing images, none of these countries can be regarded as bas-tions of free enterprise capitalism. A detailed examination of the four countries leads Castells to conclude that there are, in fact, marked differences in the developmental paths of each, as well as some common features.

The New International Division of Labor (NIDL) theory, for example, applies primarily to Singapore, where foreign firms overwhelmingly dominate; in Taiwan, on the other hand, foreign firms are a minority. While the South Korean economy is dominated by indigenous chaebols (conglomerates), Hong Kong's phenomenal growth was triggered by smaller local manufacturing firms. Nor did these economies develop through extensive specialization, as the NIDL theory would predict, but rather through flexible response to world economic conditions. In terms of social and labor policy, the welfare state played a more central role in Hong Kong and Singapore than it did in Korea and Taiwan. Despite oppressive labor regimes at various times in

Korea, Singapore, and Taiwan, labor docility has been a recent phenomenon: labor in all four began after World War II as volatile, and has subsequently been tamed. All four NICs ultimately developed through export-oriented industrialization, lacking—or having destroyed—a comprador bourgeoisie whose wealth was based in large landholdings. At the same time, all four fostered a highly educated labor force capable of being reskilled along the lines dictated by rapid industrialization. Inexpensive, efficient, and disciplined labor was therefore a common underlying factor in development. All four countries were able to adapt quickly to changes in the world economy through technical upgrading toward higher value-added production, with the state playing a crucial role in reorienting activities in this direction.

For Castells, the East Asian developmental state relied on economic development to forge a national identity. Economic development is not merely a goal, it is rather a crucial means for elite groups—through state action—to secure political legitimacy. In a country-by-country postwar historical review, Castells concludes that U.S. and British postwar security concerns—while entailing a degree of economic and political vassalage—at the same time provided a developmental space for the four countries. Freed of the need to spend vast sums of resources on defense, the internal elites were able to focus on growth, a path that was acceptable to both U.S. and British interests. In all four countries, increasingly educated workers proved to be a highly productive resource that could be exploited when the objectives of export-oriented industrialization (EOI) dictated repressive labor policies. Contrary to those theorists who explain the exploitation of labor in Asian countries as a direct consequence of an assumed Confucian passivity, Castells documents the repression and violence that often was invoked to keep wages down and workers compliant.

Castells demonstrates that with the partial exception of Hong Kong, the dominant classes were subordinated to the state or destroyed, while the working class was either repressed or incorporated directly into the development process. In this way, the respective states managed to acquire legitimacy by integrating their civil societies behind their development efforts. Yet this very success now seems threatened, as the emergence of powerful, independent capitalists and a growing, consumer-oriented middle class now challenge state power, laying the foundations for a new dialectic of development.

In Chapter 3, Nigel Harris seeks to dispel a number of myths concerning the relationship between state policy and economic development in South Korea, Taiwan, and Singapore. He questions the very notion that independent states exist in a world market. Rather, echoing the other writers in this volume, he argues that there is significant interpenetration of global capital and markets throughout the world. Yet at the same time, Harris argues, states cannot be ignored. There exists today a world political-economic order of competing states and companies, in which the former often contend along geographic and military (rather than economic) lines. While national rivalries and military adventurism at one time went hand-in-hand with economic development—economic growth providing the basis for military strength—this is no longer necessarily true.

With the end of colonialism, the Third World state elites were freed to pursue competitive economic strategies, whose favorable outcomes were partly assured by the rapid growth of global export markets between World War II and the early 1970s. Intense state rivalries thus provided a spur to EOI. Postwar reconstruction in South Korea, Taiwan, and Singapore in particular provided a powerful impulse for growth. The end of Japanese colonialism created a vacuum into which local developmental elites had relatively free play to pursue nationalist objectives through economic development. Capitalizing on an ideological climate that favored strong states, the elites in these countries instituted a variety of economic interventions, including controls over imports, exchange, credits, prices and wages; varying degrees of public ownership and investment; and often direct labor repression. As Castells earlier noted, what united these countries was a single-minded dedication to achieving nationalistic goals through EOI.

Harris—along with Castells—notes that paradoxically the very success of EOI now threatens to undermine the strong states that initially made it possible. Once free to do as they wished, the states in these countries now find themselves challenged by the powerful corporations they helped to spawn and nurture. As Gereffi demonstrates in Chapter 4, domestic and global capital interpenetrate in an export-based global economy, thereby weakening the power of the state. In Harris's apt phrase, the state is transformed "from the incubator of capitalism to one of its many and changing homes."

It would be premature to anticipate the demise of the developmental state, however. In a highly competitive global system, the state must successfully woo highly mobile global capital by assuring appropriate technology, flexible production, marketing opportunities, consumer access, skilled labor, and so forth. Furthermore, there may prove to be some significant barriers to continued economic growth in the NICs. A variety of historical conditions came together in the postwar period to provide the opening for EOI: increased labor productivity, the collapse of geographical barriers in the face of rapidly improving communication and transportation technology, changes in protectionism, the growth of markets in North America and Europe, and— most importantly—the existence of a virtually inexhaustible supply of initially cheap labor that would, through massive educational and training programs, become increasingly skilled. Contrary to Castells, in Harris's view, these conditions—not strong developmental states per se—account for developmental success in the NICs.

In order to better understand the role of the state in economic development, it is necessary to understand the changing nature of capitalism in an export-based global economy. Gary Gereffi provides this analysis in Chapter 4, where he develops the concept of the "commodity chain" as the key production unit in the emerging global manufacturing system. Following Hopkins and Wallerstein, Gereffi defines *commodity chain* as the series of activities involved in commodity production and sales, ranging from raw material extraction to design and production, and ending with final marketing and sales. Gereffi argues that commodity chains are reshaping the geography of capitalism, creating new and distinct regional divisions of labor. By looking at production as a process that occurs over time and space, Gereffi alerts us to the fact that the principal profits need not occur at the manufacturing stage. On the contrary, he argues, profits are increasingly realized through design, marketing and retailing, while manufacturing (now largely done in the NICs) can be done with unskilled labor at low relatively costs (and with little surplus produced).

Within this framework, according to Gereffi, the newly industrializing countries are playing increasingly specialized roles in exporting manufactured goods to the developed nations. By comparing East Asia and Latin America, Gereffi is able to shed light on the degree to which these differing roles contribute to overall industrial development in the NICs of the two regions. Although economic development initially was based on such cheap-labor industries as textiles, clothing, and electronic assembly, increasingly the NICs are turning to higher value-added, high technology manufacturing as a way of remaining competitive and avoiding core country protectionism. Furthermore, while it is widely recognized that export-oriented industrialization (EOI) initially provided the key to developmental success in the NICs, Gereffi argues that in fact a combination of inward- and outwardlooking industrialization has actually occurred. In South Korea and Taiwan, for example, an initial reliance on EOI has been supplemented by a growing emphasis on import substitution, as these countries develop large and prosperous internal markets.

In a case study of the footwear industry, Gereffi argues that in the global division of labor, capitalists in core countries still dictate where much of the manufacturing will occur, in keeping with their own profit considerations. To remain competitive, the NICs must develop distinct "export niches," within which each country specializes in different types of footwear produced through distinct manufacturing systems. In Taiwan, for example, inexpensive men's leather footwear as well as cheap plastic or vinyl footwear is produced through networks of small firms, while in South Korea inexpensive leather footwear as well as athletic shoes are produced by large corporations. Yet as labor costs rise in the NICs, some footwear production is moving back to Mexico and the Caribbean, while the NICs are seeking to protect their market niches by further upgrading and specializing their footwear products.

Gereffi concludes his chapter by identifying the various roles that the NICs can play in the world economy—roles that range from different subcontracting and sourcing arrangements with core country corporations to the production, design, and marketing of their own manufactured goods. In each case, the more autonomy and control a country has, the closer it is moving to core economic activities. Gereffi calls for a new development theory for the 1990s, one that will take into account both local specialization and regional development in an increasingly integrated global economy.

2

Four Asian Tigers With a Dragon Head

A COMPARATIVE ANALYSIS OF THE STATE, ECONOMY, AND SOCIETY IN THE ASIAN PACIFIC RIM

MANUEL CASTELLS

The saga of economic development of the newly industrialized countries (NICs) in the Asian Pacific (South Korea, Taiwan, Hong Kong, and Singapore) in the last 25 years is now a well-known story.[1] But the understanding of the social processes that led to the dramatic improvement of overall economic conditions in these countries, albeit at the price of high social costs and political repression, remains obscured by the passion of ideological debate, although recent research contributions are setting a new, more promising course to find an adequate explanation for one of the most extraordinary experiences in the history of economic growth and structural change (see especially Deyo, 1987a). Indeed, the performance of these economies challenges the conventional wisdom of both dogmatic dependency analysis and neoclassical free market approaches in the field of development theory. Against the prevailing left-wing view, according to which sustained

AUTHOR'S NOTE: I wish to acknowledge the intellectual help provided by a number of colleagues and graduate students who educated me in whatever understanding I acquired of very complex, and for me very alien, social and historical realities. Among the literally dozens of scholars and social actors who agreed to share their time and knowledge with me, I want to name: Hsing You-tien, Hsia Chu-Joe, Kim Joo-Chul, Reginald Y. W. Kwok, Chua Beng-Huat, Lee Goh, Chin Pei-Hsiung, Jeff Henderson, Jonathan Schiffer, Miron Mushkat, and Victor Sit. Naturally, the analyses, statements, and opinions expressed in this text are my exclusive responsibility, and they should not be held accountable, directly or indirectly, for any such statements since I did not consult with them when writing this text.

economic development could not take place for dependent societies under the conditions of an integrated capitalist system, the four Asian "tigers" maintained the highest rate of GNP growth in the world over 25 years, and won substantial shares of the world market economy, entirely transforming in the process their economic structure and their social fabric. Furthermore, while exploitation and oppression were integral components of the development process (as was the case in the industrialization of Europe during the nineteenth century), economic growth was coupled with substantial improvement of basic living conditions for most of the population (as shown by health, education, and housing indicators), and with a less unequal income distribution in the society at large (although the trend toward improvement in income equality during the 1960s stabilized in the 1970s and deteriorated during the 1980s, it still shows a more equal distribution, according to the Gini Index, than the one existing in the early stages of the development process) (Barrett & Chin, 1987). To be sure, this process took place under extremely repressive political and ideological conditions, but such are also the conditions of most developing societies that remain, at the same time, unable to overcome the structural obstacles to economic development imposed upon them by their colonial or semicolonial heritage (Collier, 1979).

On the other hand, the economic success of the four Asian "tigers," while raising hope and a desire for emulation in a number of other industrializing countries, has fueled the ideological discourse of free market economists and politicians who try to find in the legendary reconstruction of the process of economic development in the Asian Pacific the lost paradise of "laissez faire" capitalism. And yet, any serious, unbiased observer of the Asian Pacific scene knows that systemic and comprehensive state intervention in the economy, as well as the state's strategic guidance of the performance of national and multinational companies located on the shores of its territory, has been a fundamental factor in creating the conditions for economic growth, as well as in ensuring the transition of the industrializing economies to each one of the different stages they were reaching in their evolving articulation to the world economy (Gereffi, 1989). Using the now classical concept proposed by Chalmers Johnson (1982) in his analysis of Japan's economic transformation, the "developmental state" lies at the core of the experience of the newly industrialized economies. There is widespread recognition of such fact for South Korea, Taiwan, and Singapore. On the basis of another stream of less well-known studies, including my own research, I will argue that such is also the case for Hong Kong.

But arguing that the state has been the driving force in the process of economic development of these countries raises more questions than it answers for development theory and for development policies. Because, given the widespread and generally inefficient state intervention in most of the Third World, we must reconstruct the complex web of relationships between the society, the state, and the economy in order to understand the historical structural sources of the specific mode of state intervention and the causes for the (always relative) success of such intervention in terms of the development outcome.

In the following sections I try to accomplish this task from within the framework of the historical-structural approach to development. The order of presentation begins with the most statist and ends with the least statist of the four economies in question.

Singapore: Multinational Corporations,
the National State, and the
Changing International Division of Labor[2]

In econometric terms, the analysis by Tsao Yuan (1988, pp. 17-65) on the sources of growth in Singapore for the 1965-1984 period shows the influx of capital as the main contributing factor, with labor input also being a positive factor, while total factor productivity had a negligible contribution, in a structure quite different from that demonstrated by Solow (1957) and the aggregate production function school for the advanced industrial economies.

Concerning labor, in 1966 Singapore had 9% unemployment with a 42.3% labor force participation rate. In 1983, the unemployment rate had gone down to 3%, with labor force participation of 63.8%, coming mainly from the massive incorporation of women into the labor force. A crucial factor was the substantial improvement in the education of the labor force, with mandatory English in the school system, and the expansion of vocational training.

But the critical factor was the massive flow of capital from two main sources: (a) Direct foreign investment that oscillated between 10% and 20% of gross domestic product (GDP) during the 1970s, and (b) an exceptional rate of growth of gross national savings that reached 42% of gross domestic product (GDP) in the mid-1980s, the highest savings rate in the world. For the overall period 1966-1985, gross national savings represented more than 74% of total gross domestic capital formation. Much of it was generated by the public sector (46%), mainly through the Central Provident Fund, a government controlled Social Security scheme designed to impose savings on the economy. However, only some of these savings were invested by the

government, much of it in social and physical infrastructure, some in public
corporations (more than 500 public companies), and in investments abroad
to decrease the vulnerability of government revenues vis-à-vis the cycles of
the Singapore economy. About one quarter of total government revenue was
kept in a government development fund to stabilize the economy and allow
for strategic government expenditures, actually providing the government
with a substantial instrument to ensure monetary stability and to control
inflation.

This left the responsibility of the dynamism of the economy to foreign direct
investment. The Singapore government decided from the moment of its independence, in 1965, that its impoverished, tiny territory could only prosper by
offering itself as an export platform to multinational corporations. In this sense,
the origins of Singapore's growth fit well with the thesis of the new international
division of labor as an expression of the process of productive decentralization
from core to periphery in search of cheap, efficient labor, and political stability
(Deyo, 1981). Still, it was the role of the Singapore government to provide the
necessary incentives to attract foreign capital, and to reach out through the creation of an Economic Development Board that did strategic planning on the
future directions of the international economy, and successfully sold Singapore
to prospective investors through a network of offices across the world. Among
the critical factors attracting a continuous flow of investment, initially in manufacturing, were: a favorable business environment including low labor costs,
social peace (after the repression of independent trade unions in the early 1960s),
an educated labor force, and lack of government environmental and industrial
regulation; excellent industrial and communications infrastructure; an advantageous inflation differential; stable fiscal policy; and political stability (P. S. J.
Chen, 1983).

In addition, the Singapore government was essential in making economic
diversification possible and in upgrading the level of operations performed
in Singapore, enhancing the value of the activities over time. Singapore
shifted gradually from traditional services to manufacturing and to advanced
services; from low-skill assembly manufacturing to advanced production
processes, including R&D and wafer fabrication in electronics; and from an
economy dominated by maritime trade and petroleum refining to a highly
diversified economic structure, including machinery industries, electronics,
transport equipment, producer services, and international finance. The government was also responsible for such upgrading by creating the necessary
educational and technological infrastructure (including some of the best telecommunications and air transportation infrastructure in the world); by organ-

izing the advanced services economy; and by upgrading labor through a series
of bold measures, including a substantial increase in labor costs in 1979 to
squeeze out companies looking for unskilled cheap labor, once the Singapore
economy had overcome the survival stage of the 1960s. Efficient government
management and political stability ensured through ruthless domination and social integration mechanisms gave the multinationals enough reasons to believe
Singapore was the safest haven in a generally troubled world. Public housing of
increasingly decent quality for 87% of the population, and heavily subsidized
public health, public education, and mass transit, together with rapid economic
growth, improved living conditions for the whole population and helped to calm
the social, ethnic, and political unrest that had characterized Singapore in the
1950s and early 1960s. A sophisticated security apparatus took care of the few,
generally middle class, political dissenters.

  While the restructuring process of the early 1980s, to upgrade the technological and educational basis of the economy, plunged Singapore into its
only recession (1985-1986), new measures aimed at liberalizing the economy and at articulating it more closely with the movements of the most dynamic sectors (in finance, advanced services, high technology
manufacturing, and R&D) again propelled Singapore into the high growth
path beginning in 1987 (rates of growth greater than 9% per annum). Coming
from a devastated economy in the mid-1960s, forcibly cutoff from its natural
Malaysian hinterland in 1965, and abandoned as entrepôt and military bases
by the retreating British Empire in 1968, Singapore has established itself as
a showcase of the new development process, building a national identity on
the basis of multinational investment attracted and protected by a developmental city-state.

South Korea: The State Production
of Korean Oligopolistic Capitalism, or,
When Foreign Debt Becomes
an Instrument for Development[3]

  In the case of South Korea, although American intervention was fundamental in creating the basis for a modern economy in the 1948-1960
period (basically through land reform and by a massive influx of foreign aid
that allowed the reconstruction and survival of the country after one of the
bloodiest wars of modern history), the process of economic development is

associated with the inception of the Park Chung Hee Regime, established by
the military coup of May 1961, and institutionalized as the Third Republic
by the rigged election of October 1963.

On the basis of military, financial, and political support from the United
States—a support determined by the strategic interests of the Cold War
against Communism in Asia, with the 38th Parallel in Korea playing the role
of the Berlin Wall in Europe—the South Korean Military, and its political
expression, the Democratic Republican Party, undertook the construction of
a powerful South Korean economy as the foundation for its nationalist project. In the initial stages of the development process, the state assumed an
entrepreneurial role via public corporations and government investments.
Thus, in the 1963-1979 period, purchases by government and public enterprises represented an annual average of almost 38% of gross domestic capital
formation. The Park Regime, however, heavily influenced by the Japanese
model, aimed at creating a solid industrial structure based on large Korean
companies organized in the form of conglomerates. To do so it established
strong protectionist measures to preserve the domestic market, but given the
narrowness of such a market for accumulation purposes, it privileged the
expansion of export-oriented Korean manufacturing companies. By using
the control of the banking system and of export and import licenses it deliberately pushed existing Korean companies to merge and constitute large conglomerates (the *chaebol*), similar to the Japanese *zaibatsu* but without
financial independence. By 1977, 2.2% of Korean enterprises employed
more than 500 workers each and together accounted for 44% of the labor
force.

Through a series of 5-year economic plans established and implemented
by the Economic Planning Board, the government also guided Korean companies toward the sectors considered strategic for the national economy, either in terms of creating self-sufficiency or in order to foster competitiveness
in the international economy. Thus South Korea systematically walked the
sectoral path of economic growth, investing sequentially in textiles, petrochemicals, shipbuilding, steel, electrical machinery, consumer electronics,
and (in the 1980s) automobiles, personal computers, and microelectronics
(with some spectacular successes in this field, including endogenous design
capacity of 256K chips) (Lee, 1988). Often some of the strategic decisions
were grossly misguided, leading to economic setbacks (Johnson, 1987). But
the government was there to absorb the loses, reconvert the factories, and
secure new loans (Lim & Yang, 1987).

As in the case of Singapore, but on a much larger scale, the critical role of
government was to attract capital and to mobilize and control labor to make

possible the formation and growth of the *chaebol* during the 1960s and 1970s. A critical share of capital was of foreign origin, but with a crucial difference from the Singapore experience. The nationalism of the Korean government rejected an excessive presence of foreign multinational corporations, fearful of their influence on the society and on the political fate of the Korean nation. Thus capital influx into South Korea mainly took the form of loans, guaranteed by the government under the sponsorship of the United States. Public loans (mainly from international institutions, such as the World Bank) were provided to the government to build the productive infrastructure. Private loans were channeled by the government to Korean companies, according to their compliance with the government's strategic plans. Foreign capital thus accounted for 30% of all gross domestic capital formation between 1962 and 1979, and thus the ratio of foreign debt to GNP rose to more than 26% in 1978, making South Korea one of the most endebted economies in the world by the early 1980s. Debt service as a proportion of exports was not excessive, however, and in fact declined from 19.4% in 1970 to 10.5% at the end of that decade. Indeed, the ratio of exports and imports to the GNP had jumped from 22.7% in 1963 to 72.7% in 1979. This well-known characteristic of the South Korean economy strongly indicates that endebtedness per se is not an obstacle to development: It is the proper use of the loans received that determines the outcome. Given U.S. military assistance to South Korea, the huge defense budget of the South Korean government did not need to have recourse to foreign lending for its financing, as was the case in several Latin American countries (particularly in Argentina), since the United States was paying the bill for this bulwark of anticommunism.

Only during the 1970s, when the foundations of the South Korean economy were established under the tight control of the *chaebol*, supported and guided by the state, did the government actively solicit direct foreign investment. But even then, strong restrictions were imposed on foreign companies: foreign equity holding was limited to a maximum of 50%, forcing them into joint ventures with Korean firms except in the Export Processing Zones isolated from the Korean market. Also, the government was very selective in allowing foreign investment, looking particularly for companies that could facilitate some technology transfer. Thus although Japanese companies invested in textiles, electrical machinery, and electronics, and American companies established a presence mainly in petroleum and chemicals, overall foreign direct investment remained quite limited, accounting in 1978 for only 19% of South Korean exports and for 16% of total manufacturing output.

While supporting and shaping the emergence of large Korean corporations aiming at the world market (and they indeed became major multinational players in the world economy during the 1980s), the South Korean developmental state organized the submissive incorporation of labor into the new industrial economy. Clearly, establishing the principle of producing first, redistributing later, Korean labor was, as in the other East Asian countries, a critical factor in Korean economic growth, being highly educated and generally hard working. However, the mode of incorporation of labor into the industrial structure was much more brutal and repressive in South Korea than in the other societies (Deyo, 1987b). Their concentration in large factories organized by means of quasi-military management favored the emergence of militant trade unionism, but autonomous workers' unions were forbidden, activism was severely repressed, and working conditions both at the factory and in terms of housing were kept at the minimum possible standards. Such repressive attitudes led to steady resistance among Korean workers, and has led to the formation of the most militant labor movement in East Asia, as the frequent and often violent strikes of the 1980s have shown. Keeping wages growing at a rate substantially lower than productivity and profits was a cornerstone of the government's economic policy.

Living conditions in general did improve, however, for the population at large as well as for industrial workers, because of the impressive performance of the economy under the impulse of export-led industrialization. But the benefits of growth were unevenly shared. For instance, during the critical period of the 1970s, between 1972 and 1979, government revenues increased at an stunning annual rate of 94.7%, the top 46 *chaebol* collected an annual increase in value-added of 22.8%, and real wages, while growing substantially by international standards, still trailed that performance, growing at an annual rate of 9.8%. Thus, while South Korea has a relatively equitable income distribution (better than the United States), mainly because of the phasing out of the landed class in the 1940s and 1950s, income distribution worsened during the 1970s, although living conditions improved for everybody (for instance, the share of the population below the poverty line went down from 41% in 1965 to 15% in 1975).

Finally, emphasis on science and technology and the upgrading of the quality of products and processes in Korean industry have been the obsession of all Korean governments since the mid-1960s, creating and staffing a series of specialized R&D institutes and linking them to industry under the guidance of the Ministry of Science and Technology. South Korea is probably the industrializing country that has most rapidly climbed the technology ladder in the new international division of labor (Ernst & O'Connor, 1990). For instance, between 1970 and 1986 Korea's engineering exports grew at an annual average rate of 39%, far exceeding the performance of Japan at 20% per year.

Thus behind the performance of "Asia's next economic giant," one that increased its share of the world's gross domestic production by growing by 345% between 1965 and 1986 (Federation of Korean Industries, 1987), lies the nationalist project of a developmental state that deliberately orchestrated the creation of major Korean multinational companies able to become influential players in the world economy on the basis of foreign lending, American military support, and ruthless exploitation of Korean labor.

Taiwan: The Rise of Flexible Capitalism
Under the Guidance of an Inflexible State[4]

Even by the high standards of the Pacific Rim development experience, Taiwan is probably *the* success story, in terms of the combination of a sustained high rate of economic growth (annual average of 8.7% for 1953-1982, and of 6.9% for 1965-1986), increase in world share of GDP (multiplied by a factor of 3.63 in 1965-1986), increase in the share of world exports (that reached 2.08% in 1986, above all other NICs including South Korea), increase in the share of the world's manufacturing output (multiplied by a factor of 6.79 in 1965-1986 as compared to South Korea's growth factor of 3.59), and this within the context of relatively equal income distribution (Gini coefficients of .558 in 1953 to .303 in 1980, much better than the United States or the average of the EC, although the situation has deteriorated during the 1980s [Kuo, 1983]), substantial improvement of health, education, and living standards (Gold, 1986), and social stability (enforced by harsh police repression) for the period from 1950 to 1977.

At the core of Taiwanese economic growth lies the notion of flexible production, put into practice in Taiwan (Greenhalgh, 1988) before American academics discovered it on their Italian vacations. The flexibility concerns both the industrial structure itself, and the adaptability of the overall structure to the changing conditions of the world economy, under the guidance of an all-powerful state, supported and advised in the initial stages by U.S. Aid. In fact, throughout the historical process of development the logic of the model of economic growth changed quite dramatically, from import-substitution emphasis in the 1950s, to export-oriented industrialization in the 1960s (the take-off period), to what Thomas Gold (1986) calls "export-oriented import substitution" (that is, the deepening of the industrial base to feed exports of manufactured goods) during the 1970s and 1980s. In the 1980s, as Taiwan became an economic power in its own right, Taiwanese companies took on the world market, internationalizing their production and investments both in Asia (particularly in China) and in the OECD countries (particularly in the United States).

At each one of these four stages in the process we observe a different industrial structure that evolves and superposes on itself without major crises. But in all instances two features are critical for the understanding of the process; the Kuomintang (KMT) state is at the center of the structure and the structure itself is highly diversified, decentralized, and made up of networking relationships between firms, between firms and the state, and between firms and the world market through trading companies (mainly Japanese) and worldwide commercial intermediaries.

During the 1950s, the KMT state, with massive economic aid and military protection from the United States, undertook the reform of the economy after taking total control of the society through ruthless and bloody repression in the 1947-1950 period. An American-inspired land reform destroyed the land-owning class and created a large population of small farmers that, with state support, dramatically increased agricultural productivity. Agriculture was the original device for surplus accumulation, both in the form of transfer of capital and in terms of providing cheap food for the urban-industrial labor force. The government forced the farmers into unequal exchange with the industrial economy by controlling credit and fertilizers and organizing a barter system that exchanged agricultural inputs for rice. With the control of the banks (they were, and still are in the majority of cases, government owned) and control of import licenses, the government geared the Taiwanese economy toward import substitution industrialization, forming the beginning of a capitalist structure in a totally protected market. The government, with American aid, provided the necessary production and communications infrastructure and placed major emphasis on educating the labor force. To implement this strategy a series of government institutions, including four-year economic plans, were established.

Because of the exhaustion of the domestic market as potential demand to stimulate growth at the end of the 1950s, the state followed the advice (indeed, the instructions) of the U.S. agencies and embarked on an ambitious restructuring of the economy based on an outward orientation. In 1960, the 19-Point Program of Economic and Financial Reform liberalized controls on trade, stimulated exports, and designed a strategy to attract foreign investment. Taiwan was the first country to invent the notion of Export Processing Zones, and implemented one in Kaoshiung at the southwestern tip of the island. In 1964, General Instruments pioneered electronics assembly offshoring in Taiwan. Japanese *medium-sized* companies quickly moved to benefit from low wages, educated labor, and government support. Yet the nucleus of Taiwanese industrial structure was made up of a large number of local enterprises, set up with family savings and cooperative savings networks and supported by government bank credits, many of which were (and still are) located in the rural fringes of metropolitan areas, where family members work on the land and in the industrial shop at the same time. For instance, about half of the world's umbrellas come from a network of small companies, many of which are located in the semirural area near Tanyung, as I saw for myself during field work in the region. Thus the Taiwanese state attracted multinational investment as a way to generate capital and to obtain access to world markets. But foreign corporations were linked through subcontracting arrangements to a wide network of small firms that provided the substantial base of industrial production. In fact, with the exception of electronics, direct foreign investment does not represent a major component of the Taiwanese economy. For instance, in 1981 direct capital stock of foreign companies in Taiwan represented only 2% of the GNP, employment in foreign companies amounted to 4.8% of total employment, their output only 13.9% of total output, and their exports only 25.6% of total exports (Purcell, 1987, p. 81). A more important phenomenon in facilitating critical access to world markets was the intermediary role played by Japanese trading companies and by representatives of American large commercial chains looking for direct supplies from Taiwanese industrialists.

Thus the outward orientation of the economy did not imply control of the economy by the multinationals (as in Singapore), nor the formation of large Taiwanese conglomerates as the dominant force (although a number of major industrial groups did develop under the auspices of the state). Rather, it was enacted by a flexible combination of a decentralized network of Taiwanese firms acting as subcontractors for foreign manufacturers located in Taiwan (large American multinationals, medium-sized Japanese firms), and as suppliers of international commercial networks, either through Japanese trading companies or through representatives of large (mainly American) department stores. This is how "Made in Taiwan" merchandise ended up entering the whole realm of our everyday life: K-Mart acted as a KMT agent . . .

However, in spite of the importance of Taiwanese medium and small firms in the process of winning competitiveness through flexibility, I must insist on the fact that the state was the central actor in guiding and coordinating the whole process of industrialization, by setting up the needed infrastructure, attracting foreign capital, deciding the priorities for strategic investment, and imposing its conditions when necessary (for instance, the first attempt to initiate a Taiwanese automobile industry failed when the government refused to accept the conditions required by Toyota).

A critical factor in the growing productivity of the Taiwanese economy, as in the case of the other "tigers," was the high yield of labor through the combination of low wages, decent education, hard work, and social peace. Social control of labor in Taiwan was achieved first by establishing the precedent of unrestrained repression to any challenge to the state authority. But in addition to repression, a number of factors contributed decisively to diffuse conflict and to integrate workers into the industrial fabric. The state did provide a safety net in the form of subsidized health and education, but not housing, although housing cooperatives (helped by government banks) were a factor in delaying the housing crisis until it exploded in the 1980s in one of the most dramatic issues in today's Taiwanese society (Chin, 1988). But the most important factor contributing to social peace was the industrial structure itself, made up of thousands of small companies, many of which were based on family members and primary social networks, sometimes linked to part-time agricultural activity. In the multinational corporations, the bulk of the unskilled labor force, as in other Asian societies, were young women, who were subjected to the double patriarchalism of family and factory, thus effectively reducing them into subservience, since they actually came to see factory life as a space of relative freedom compared with life at home. While the situation is changing, with the formation of a conscious female working class, the gender structure of the work force was an important factor ensuring social peace during the critical moment of the industrial take-off.

In the 1970s and 1980s, to fight the threat of protectionism in the core markets and to counter the danger of political isolation after the entry of the People's Republic of China into the international community, the KMT state engaged in a process of upgrading and modernization of industry, particularly in high technology, including the creation of one of the most successful high technology parks in Asia, in Hsinchu, articulating the major government research institute in electronics, two leading technical universities, foreign firms, and Taiwanese companies, some of them spin-offs from the research institute. Taiwan has made rapid progress in electronics, particularly in personal computers and peripherals, and a number of Taiwanese firms have become major suppliers to electronics giants such as DEC or IBM

(Ernst & O'Connor, 1990). Other industrial sectors (in particular garments and textiles) have been pushed by the government to raise the quality of their goods in order to circumvent protectionism by going into higher value-added merchandise while not increasing the quotas calculated in volume terms.

In the 1980s Taiwan became such a mature, thriving economy that the Taiwanese industrial bourgeoisie developed a more assertive mood, increasingly breaking away from the state and trying to establish its own presence in the world, through its links with international capital. The most spectacular change refers to massive investment in China in open defiance of official KMT policy, very often using centuries-old village networks, which remain in place. Because of rising wages and increasing workers' organization in Taiwan, together with the tightening of quotas vis-à-vis Taiwanese-origin merchandise, the largest Taiwanese companies are offshoring production in China and other East and Southeast Asian countries (for instance, it is estimated that 40% of Taiwanese shoe manufacturing actually takes place in China [Hsing, 1990]) in a striking demonstration of the endogenous character of Taiwanese capitalism, finally reaching maturity at the very moment the KMT's ideology becomes irreversibly obsolete and the KMT state is losing its grip on the complex, industrial society it helped to create.

The Hong Kong Model
Versus the Hong Kong Reality:
Small Business in a World Economy
and the Colonial Version of the Welfare State[5]

Hong Kong remains the historical reference for the free-market, free-trader, free-wheeler advocates of unrestrained capitalism whose ideology wrecked the American economy in the 1980s.[6] While the prominent role of the state in the hypergrowth economies of Japan, South Korea, Taiwan, and Singapore is too obvious to be denied, Hong Kong, with its early take-off during the 1950s and its apparently laissez faire brand of capitalism, reinforced by the Hong Kong government's stated policy of "positive non-intervention," incarnates the dreams of classical state-free capitalism and makes them into a model destined to survive the 1997 deadline for a society built "in a borrowed place, on borrowed time."

And yet, a careful analysis of the process of economic development of Hong Kong since the mid-1950s reveals a decisive role by the state in creating the conditions for economic growth, though in a more subtle, more indirect but not less important way than the intervention described in the case of the three other countries analyzed here (Leung et al., 1980; Schiffer, 1983; Youngson, 1982).

Let us first review certain facts. In the free-market paradise of Hong Kong, all land (with the exception of communal village land in the New Territories) is Crown Land, which the government has leased—not sold—over the years, in a land market entirely manipulated by government control to increase its revenue and subsidize its public housing projects as well as government-developed industrial estates and flatted factories.[7] Furthermore, during the critical years of economic take-off (1949-1980) while GDP grew by a factor of 13 (impressive in itself), real government expenditure grew by 26 times, and government expenditure in welfare (including housing, education, health, and social welfare) grew by an astounding amount of 72 times. Thus government expenditure as a proportion of GDP reached 20.3% in 1980. The government share of total capital formation grew during the 1960s and 1970s from 13.6% in 1966 to an all time high of 23.4% in 1983 before declining to about 16% during the mid-1980s (Ho, 1979; Youngson, 1982; also see statistical sources in Castells, Kwok, & Goh, 1990).

But more significant than the size of government expenditures or than the real extent of regulation (quite important, for instance, in the banking industry after a series of scandals threatened to wreck the financial markets during the early 1980s [Ghose, 1987]), is the strategic role played by government in making possible the specific mode of development that made Hong Kong into a nest of competitiveness in the thriving world economy of the 1960s. Thus we must briefly sketch the components of such a development process, to understand the crucial importance of indirect government intervention on the conditions of production and collective consumption that are at the source of the competitiveness of Hong Kong's business.

The classic econometric study by Edward K. Y. Chen (1979) on the sources of economic growth in Hong Kong for the period 1955-1974 shows that capital and labor inputs played a much greater role in Hong Kong than in the growth of advanced industrial economies. Also, he identifies export and international trade as the leading factors in explaining Hong Kong's growth. This interpretation is confirmed and expanded in the careful statistical analysis by Tsong-Biau Lin, Victor Mok, and Yin-Ping Ho (1980) on the close relationship between exports of manufacturing goods and economic growth, hardly a surprising finding but an observation full of meaning, particularly when the rise of Hong Kong as a financial and trade center in the 1980s tends to blur the original sources of the Territory's prosperity.

Their study also shows that exports have concentrated over time in the same few industries—textiles, garments, footwear, plastics, consumer electronics—in a different pattern than that observed in the other three countries. However, the expansion of exports is mainly due to what the authors call "changes due to differential commodity composition," that is, changes of product line and in the value of the products within the same industry. In this sense, what has been fundamental is the flexibility of Hong Kong manufacturers to adapt quickly and effectively to the demand of the world market within the same industries.

We still need to explain the competitiveness of these industries besides their ability to adapt to demand. Another econometric study by E. K. Y. Chen (1980) provides the clue: The critical explanatory variable in Hong Kong's growth equation is the differential between Hong Kong's relative prices and the level of income in the United States, the main market for Hong Kong's exports. The level of prices for manufactured goods in Hong Kong being mainly determined by wage levels in labor-intensive industries, it was the capacity of Hong Kong firms to keep wage increases well below the increase in U.S. income while still assuring an efficient, skilled, and motivated labor force that provided the ground-base for the expansion of manufactured exports, and thus for economic growth. Thus flexibility of manufacturing and competitive prices on the basis of low production costs are the main factors that explain Hong Kong's export success, which underlies Hong Kong's growth. But these "explanatory variables" are themselves the result of a specific industrial structure and of a given institutional environment that made possible the flexibility and competitiveness of the economy.

On the one hand, the flexibility is the result of an industrial structure characterized by small business; more than 90% of manufacturing firms in Hong Kong in 1981 employed less than 50 workers, and large enterprises (more than 100 workers) accounted for only 22.5% of manufacturing's contribution to GDP. Since 90% of manufactured goods are exported, we may assume that small businesses are similarly important in this area, although there are no data to show it directly. We do know that foreign manufacturers account for a small proportion of Hong Kong's manufacturing exports (10.9% in 1974, 13.6% in 1984). In fact the average size of manufacturing establishments in Hong Kong decreased over time: from an average of 52.5 workers per establishment in 1951 to 20 in 1981. The mystery is how these small firms were able to link up with the world market. Unlike in Taiwan, foreign trading companies were not important in Hong Kong. There were indeed the traditionally established British trading "hongs" (such as the legendary Jardine

Matheson or Swire groups), but their role in manufacturing exports was actually small. About 75% of exports, according to the study by Victor Sit (1982), were handled by local export/import firms. The great majority of these small firms were small businesses themselves: There were more than 14,000 such firms in Hong Kong in 1977. It was only in the 1980s that large department stores from the United States, Japan, and Western Europe established their own channels in Hong Kong to place orders with the local firms. Thus the basic industrial structure of Hong Kong consisted of networks of small firms, networking and subcontracting among themselves on an ad hoc basis, following the orders channeled by small firms specializing in export/import. Such a flexible structure, originating from the initial nucleus of Shanghainese textile entrepreneurs that immigrated after the Chinese revolution with little more than their know-how, became in fact the most adequate instrument for adapting to rapidly changing demand in a world market expanding at an increasing rate.

But how were these small businesses able to obtain information about the world market, to upgrade their production, to improve their machinery, to increase their productivity? The Hong Kong government played a significant though not decisive role in the matter. First, it organized the distribution of export quotas allowed under the MultiFibre Agreement among different companies in the textile industry, actually shaping the production networks under the guidance of the government's Industry Department. Second, it established (in the 1960s) a series of information and training centers, such as the Hong Kong Productivity Center, engaged in training programs and consulting and technology services, and the Hong Kong Trade Development Council, with offices around the world to promote exports and to disseminate information among Hong Kong's firms. Other services, such as the Hong Kong Credit Insurance Corporation, served to cover some of the risks incurred by exporters. In the late 1970s, when the need for restructuring and upgrading Hong Kong's economy became necessary to answer the challenge of protectionism in core markets, the government appointed a committee on Industrial Diversification that elaborated a strategic plan for Hong Kong's new stage of industrialization, a plan that was implemented by and large during the 1980s.

The fundamental contribution, however, of Hong Kong's government to the flexibility and competitiveness of small businesses was its widespread intervention in the realm of collective consumption, particularly through a huge public housing program that houses about 45% of the population in subsidized apartments whose initial appalling quality has considerably improved over time with the building of new towns and large housing estates. In addition, a comprehensive system of public education, public health, subsidized mass transit, social services, and subsidized foodstuffs, was put into place over the years, amounting to a major subsidy of indirect wages for the labor force. Schiffer (1983) calculated the impact of nonmarket forces on household blue-collar expenditures for 1973-1974: On average it amounted to a 50.2% subsidy for each household. In another study concerning only the public housing subsidy, Fu-Lai Yu and Si-Ming Li (1985) estimated a transfer-in-kind to the average public housing tenant equivalent to 70% of the household's income. Thus public housing and the special brand of welfare state that emerged in Hong Kong subsidized workers and allowed them to work long hours without putting too much pressure on their employers, most of them with little margin to afford salary increases. By shifting onto the government's shoulders the responsibility for the workers' well being, small businesses could concentrate on competitive pricing, shrinking and expanding their labor force according to the variations of demand.

Hong Kong's Colonial welfare state did perform two other important functions directly related to the competitiveness of the economy:

(a) It made possible industrial peace for a long period, a matter of some consequence given the historical tradition of social struggle (often overlooked) among the Hong Kong working class, an underlying current that surfaced with rampaging violence in the urban riots of 1956, 1966, and 1967 (Chan et al., 1986; Chesneaux, 1982; Endacott & Birch, 1978; Hong Kong Government, 1967).

(b) It created a safety net for low-risk entrepreneurialism that characterized the scene of small business in Hong Kong. In fact, small businesses in Hong Kong, as everywhere else, had a very high mortality rate (Sit, 1982), particularly in the presence of the black box of a distant world market. But most businesses were started by workers who bet their small savings and relied on family support and on the safety net of public housing and subsidized collective consumption to take their chance, withdrawing to their relatively secure position when their entrepreneurial attempt went wrong.

Thus social stability and subsidized collective consumption were critical for the moderation of direct wages, for stable industrial relations, and for the creation of a burgeoning nest of small and medium-sized entrepreneurs who were indeed the driving force of Hong Kong's development, but under social and institutional conditions quite different from those depicted by Milton Friedman in his novels about the economy.

Commonalities and Dissimilarities
in the Process of Economic Development
of Asia's Newly Industrialized Economies:
Are They Four Tigers or
One Dragon With Four Tiger Tails?

I have tried to reconstruct, as precisely as possible, the underlying specific logic of the process of economic development in the four countries under consideration. In my opinion, this is the necessary starting point for all attempts aimed at building a new theory of development. But to make progress on the path of theorizing we must now shift gears and reflect comparatively on the processes just described. The commonalities and dissimilarities in such processes should lead us to clues to understand the *social* sources of development in the new world economy.

Let us start with the *uncommon factors,* those that clearly differ in each case, and that therefore cannot be considered critical elements in the development process.

The most important dissimilarity is the industrial structure of each country. In particular, we should reject the "new international division of labor" thesis, according to which the new industrialization in the periphery is mainly the result of productive decentralization by multinational corporations from the core. They are fundamental for Singapore, but they played a secondary role in Taiwanese industrialization, and they are clearly minor players in South Korea and Hong Kong (although in Hong Kong international *financial* corporations became important during the 1980s). As we know, the industrial structure of Singapore is characterized by the direct connection between multinational corporations and the state; the South Korean economy is centered around the Korean *chaebol* nurtured and guided by the state; Taiwan blends into a flexible structure of large national firms, small and medium-sized businesses, and a significant but minority presence of foreign firms, either large (American) or medium (Japanese); and Hong Kong's economic growth, until the 1980s, was engineered by local manufacturing firms, most of them small and medium, supported by a benevolent colonial state that provided productive infrastructure and subsidized collective consumption. Thus there is no relationship between a given industrial structure and economic growth. They were all stunning success stories, but they reached similar rates of growth through seemingly different paths.

Nor is the sectoral specialization of the economies a common feature. It was not the concentration of industrial effort on textiles or on electronics that explains the competitiveness of these economies, since South Korea—and Taiwan to a lesser extent—gradually diversified their activities into a variety of sectors. Singapore started from the beginning on petroleum and electronics (mainly semiconductors), and Hong Kong basically deepened and upgraded its original specialization in textiles, garments, plastics, footwear, and consumer electronics. The one common feature is the adaptability and flexibility needed to deal with world market demands, but this was performed either by a simultaneous presence in various sectors, or by a succession of priority sectors (as in South Korea), or by upgrading the traditional sectors (as in Hong Kong). Economic competitiveness does not seem to result from "picking the winners" but from learning how to win.

The existence of a welfare state of sorts, through subsidized collective consumption, was a decisive element in the development of the city-states—Singapore and Hong Kong—but was clearly not so in South Korea (where the state did not take care of workers' needs and only the *chaebol* introduced some elements of social paternalism, such as company housing), nor in Taiwan where the state deliberately intended to improve the living conditions of the population and to lower income inequality, but it let the market provide the basic goods for the population, while it concentrated on providing education and ensuring that the economy would generate jobs and income.

Last but not least, the myth of social peace as a major component of the development process in East Asia does not stand up to research observations when data are gathered from historical records and direct interviewing of the social actors. Singapore became stable after massive repression and outlawing of the main trade union movement in the early 1960s. Taiwan was pacified after the 1947 massacre of an estimated 10,000 people resisting the imposition of the KMT state, and although it has been a politically conflictual society since at least the 1977 Chung Li riot, conflicts have not fundamentally endangered its economic dynamism. Hong Kong had for a long time a relatively high degree of unionized workers (Lethbridge, 1980) with the largest union federation controlled by Chinese communists; its "social peace" was repeatedly shattered by the riots of 1956, 1966, and 1967 (Miners, 1986; Lau, 1982), the last one being followed by several months of protests, including bombings. Since the late 1970s, powerful mobilizations at the community level have created the foundations of what is today an extremely active "democracy movement" that raises great concern both in Hong Kong and in Beijing. South Korea went from the 1960 student uprising that toppled Syngman Rhee to an endless succession of student demonstrations, workers struggles (most of them subdued and ignored), and citizen-workers insurrections, most notably the 1980 Kwangju uprising that was repressed at the price of more than 1,000 victims. Although South Korea's growth has recently been challenged by political instability, the occasional violent conflicts (actually triggering the process that ended the military dictatorship) as well as daily workers' resistance during the entire process of economic development, did not undermine the economic performance of the country (S. K. Kim, 1987; Park, 1990).

Thus while it is true that the search for social stability, and the partial achievement of such a goal, was a fundamental element in the development policy of the four countries, it was not a given of the society. Quite the opposite: All four countries started from potentially volatile social and political situations that had to be tamed, repressed, and later on controlled and prevented in order for the economy to work. Social stability was not a prerequisite but an always uncertain result of the process of economic growth in the Asian Pacific.

But we also find some *commonalities* in our observation. Without them, we could not even think about a recurrent pattern that would shed light on our understanding of the new historical processes of development.

The first common factor concerns the existence of an emergency situation in the society, as a result of major tensions and conflicts at the international level. It is obvious in the cases of South Korea and Taiwan. It should also be recalled that Hong Kong dramatically changed as a consequence of the Chinese revolution, losing most of its traditional role as entrepôt for China trade, thus being forced into manufacturing exports as a way to survive without being a burden on the Crown's budget. Indeed it was its role vis-à-vis China, together with its economic success that prevented Hong Kong from joining the decolonization process, since neither the United Kingdom nor China could accept its independence. That was also the case for Singapore, first prevented by British troops from being annexed by Indonesia, then expelled from the Federation of Malaysia and abandoned to its fate by Britain in 1965-1968, then saved politically and economically because of its support for the American effort in the Vietnam War. The critical element here, as compared for instance to the situation in Latin America, is that the United States perceived most of Asia as being clearly in danger of a general communist takeover (and in fact, there were enough elements to support such a perception). Therefore strategic considerations overshadowed all other calculations for U.S. policy in the region, which in fact gave much more freedom to maneuver to the local states in the running of their economies, although on the condition of remaining "vassal states" in terms of foreign policy and of repressing domestic communism (a condition to which they gladly agreed). If there is a fundamental common thread to the policies of the four countries (including Hong Kong) it is that, at the origin of their process of development we find *policies dictated by the politics of survival.* Another consequence of this context dominated by the Asian Cold War was the importance of American and British support for these governments and for their economies. As we know, American aid was the major element in the economies of South Korea and Taiwan during the 1950s. Although Hong Kong contributed to Britain more than the United Kingdom did to Hong Kong, some crucial functions like defense remained on British shoulders. Singapore did not receive much direct aid, and its economy could start only in the mid-1960s because of the profitable oil and ship repairing commerce with American forces in Vietnam.

A second major common factor is that *all four development processes were based on an outward orientation of the economy, and more specifically on their success in exporting manufactured goods.* Although for both South Korea and Taiwan import-substitution policies were extremely important at the onset of the process, particularly to set up an industrial base, they only prospered when they engaged in export-oriented manufacturing. In this sense, the explosion of world trade in the 1960s and the growing interdependence of the world economy form an indispensable background for understanding the success of the Asian tigers—which brings up the question of the historical replicability of such an exceptionally favorable situation.

A third common factor is the *absence of a rural landowning class,* nonexistent in Hong Kong and Singapore, and practically destroyed (or reconverted into an industrial bureaucracy) by the American-inspired land reforms of South Korea and Taiwan in the 1950s. It would appear that the existence of a powerful landowning class is indeed a major obstacle to the development of dynamic capitalism in the Third World, because when they convert themselves into "businesses" (as in Indonesia, for instance) they tend to confuse money making with capital accumulation, actually undermining the modernization efforts of the country and the improvement of its relative position in nontraditional exports (Yoshihara, 1988).

A fourth common, and critical, factor in the development of the four countries is the *availability of educated labor, able to reskill itself during the process of industrial upgrading, with high productivity at a level of wages very low for international standards. A fundamental factor for all the countries has been the ability to keep labor under control, in terms of work discipline and labor demands.* This goal has been achieved, by and large, through different means, but the success of labor policies cannot be equated with the existence of social peace, as already stated. Disciplined, efficient, cheap labor is a fundamental factor in the process of development of the

Asian NICs. But their discipline or effectiveness does not come from the supposedly submissive nature of Asian labor (plainly a racist statement) nor, in a more sophisticated vein, from Confucianism. Confucianism does explain the high value placed on education and therefore the high quality of labor once the state provides the minimum conditions for access to education. But Confucianism does not explain submissiveness, since in the Confucian philosophy authority must be legitimate and exercised in legitimate ways. Indeed, the long story of popular uprisings and social revolts in China, as well as the long tradition of a revolutionary working-class movement in Shanghai and Guangdong Province stands against the ill-informed statements of managerial ideology. In all cases labor discipline was imposed first by repression, as indicated in the specific analyses of each country. But in all cases there were also powerful elements of social integration that explain why an historically rebellious population ultimately accommodated to the exploitative conditions for most of the people for most of the period under study. Paramount among the integrative factors is the actual betterment of living conditions for workers. What was a low wage for an American or Japanese worker was a fortune for the new industrial labor force of extremely poor Asian countries. Furthermore, data show an improvement in income inequality during the first stage of the process and a dramatic improvement in real wage earnings overall. Besides, in the case of Hong Kong and Singapore a peculiar version of the welfare state, materially organized around public housing projects and new towns, did provide the privileged a channel both for the improvement of living conditions and for the establishment of social and political control by the state. In the case of Taiwan, the integration of rural and urban life and the vitality of primary social networks provided, at the same time, the social net to resist the shock of rapid industrialization and the mechanism of peer-group social control to discourage the highly risky enterprise of challenging the system. Thus through a combination of state repression, state integration, economic improvement, and social network protection and control, an increasingly educated labor force (many of whom were women) found it in their best interests to fulfill the expectations of a system that was as dynamic as it was ruthless. Only when the survival stage was passed did spontaneous social resistance start to take the shape of a labor movement dreaming of political alternatives, particularly in South Korea.

A fifth common factor in the Asian experience of rapid industrialization is the *ability of these economies to adapt to the changing conditions of the world economy, climbing the ladder of development through technological upgrading, market expansion, and economic diversification.* What is particularly remarkable (as in the case of Japan, which provided the role model for all the experiences with the possible exception of Hong Kong) is their understanding of the critical role played by R&D and high technology sectors in the new international economy (Ernst & O'Connor, 1990; Purcell, 1989). This emphasis on science and technology that mainly characterizes South Korea and Taiwan but is also present in the city-states, was decided and implemented by the state, but it was welcomed and adopted by industrial firms. Thus the four countries have in fact made their transition into the advanced productive structures of the informational economy, and while many activities remain rather primitive (as also happens in New York) it would be a fundamental mistake to consider their competitiveness to be based still on low-paid, low-skilled labor. It is the ability to shift from one level of development to another and from one form of incorporation into the world economy to a more competitive one, generating higher value, that was the clue for a cumulative process of development that led to endogenous economic growth, in contrast with the short-lived phases of economic growth followed by stagnation and crisis that was the experience of most of Latin America in the 1970s and 1980s (Fajnzylber, 1983).

Behind most of the critical factors found to be common to the four experiences appears what seems to be the most important of all commonalities: *the role of the state in the development process of each country.* The production of high-quality labor and its subsequent control, the strategic guidance through the hazardous seas of the world economy, the ability to lead the economy in periods of transition, the process of diversification, the creation of a science-and-technology base and its diffusion in the industrial system— these are all critical policies whose success determined the historical possibility of the overall process of development. And policies are, of course, the outcome of politics, enacted by the state. Thus in the various configurations of the industrial structure we have examined, the only invariant is the centrality or importance of the state. While the process of development gradually freed the economy and society from the tight control of the state, the historical origin and the main explanatory structural element in the generation of cumulative growth was the action of the state, as a number of empirical analyses presented here have shown. Thus to understand the secret of the new sources of economic development we must unveil the logic of the state. Behind the economic performance of the Asian tigers breathes the dragon of the developmental state.

The Historical Specificity
of the Developmental State in
the East Asian Newly Industrialized Countries

On the Concept of Developmental State

If the hypotheses presented in this text are plausible, understanding the development experience of the Asian NICs requires, first of all, a sociological and political analysis of the historical experience of the developmental state in these countries. Without such an analysis, the economists' efforts at replicating "the model" are doomed and likely to lead to ideologically driven economic policy, the worst possible recipe for developing societies.

In good methodology, the historical-structural approach I present in this analysis would at this point require a careful reconstruction of the socio-political process leading to the specific mode of state intervention in the economy of each of the four countries under consideration. However, I doubt the already too patient reader would tolerate such an exercise. Thus, I will try to summarize the main lines of the argument, while illustrating it, for each point of the presentation, with specific references to the social structure and political history of each country.

First, I need to define the precise meaning of *development state*. While I do not disagree with the main explicit or implicit notions of the developmental state in the social sciences literature (those of Chalmers Johnson, Peter Evans, or Frederic Deyo, for instance), I believe it would be clarifying to be unequivocal about my own use of the concept, as it emerges from the analysis of the East Asian experience (although, I think it can be extrapolated to other contexts).

A state is developmental when it establishes as its principle of legitimacy its ability to promote and sustain development, understanding by development the combination of steady high rates of economic growth and structural change in the productive system, both domestically and in its relationship to the international economy. This definition is misleading, however, unless we specify the meaning of *legitimacy* in a given historical context. Most political science theorists remain prisoner of an ethnocentric conception of legitimacy, related to the democratic state. Under such a conception, the state is legitimate when it establishes hegemony or consensus vis-à-vis the civil society. Yet, this particular form of legitimacy presupposes the acceptance by the state itself of its submission to the principle of representation of society as it is. But we know that states that have tried over history to break away from the existing order, did not recognize civil society-as-it-was as the source of their legitimacy. And yet, they were not pure apparatuses of naked power, as was the case with defensive military dictatorships in many historical instances. The clearest examples are revolutionary states, particularly those emerging from communist revolutions or national liberation movements. They never pretended to be legitimate in terms of the acquiescence of their subjects, but in terms of the historical project they embodied, as avant-gardes of the classes and nations that were not yet fully aware of their destiny and interests. The obvious and significant political and ideological differences between the communist and revolutionary states and the right-wing dictatorships of East Asia have, in my opinion, led to the overlooking of some fundamental similarities that go beyond formal resemblances to the heart of the logic of the state: the legitimacy principle holding together the apparatus, and structuring and organizing the codes and the principles for accessing power and for exercising it. In other words, the legitimacy principle may be exercised on behalf of the society (the democratic state) or on behalf of the societal project. When the state substitutes itself for society in the definition of societal goals, when such a societal project involves a fundamental transformation of the social order (regardless of our value judgment on the matter), I refer to it as the *revolutionary state*. When the societal project respects the broader parameters of social order (although not necessarily the specific social structure) but aims at a fundamental transformation of the economic order (regardless of the interests or desires of the civil society) I propose the hypothesis that we are in the presence of what we call the *developmental state*. The historical expression of such a societal project generally takes the form (and such was the case in most of the East Asian experience) of the building or rebuilding of national identity, affirming the national presence of a given society or a given culture in the world, although not necessarily coinciding with the territorial limits under the control of the developmental state (e.g., the Kuomintang state speaking on behalf of the "Republic of China," behind the safe refuge provided by the U.S. Seventh Fleet).

Thus ultimately for the developmental state, economic development is not a goal but a means.[8] To become competitive in the world economy, for all the Asian NICs, was first, their way of surviving, both as a state and as a society. Second, it also became their only way to assert their national interests in the world, that is, to break away from a dependency situation, even at the price of becoming unconditional military frontliners for the United States. In a deliberate parallel with Marx's theory of social classes, I propose

the idea that the developmental state effects the transition of a political
subject "in itself" to a political apparatus "for itself" by affirming the only
legitimacy principle that did not seem to be threatening for the international
powers overseeing its destiny: economic development. The basic logic of
such a transition is nonetheless a fundamentally political logic, directly ex-
pressing a nationalist project, even if, in the same moment, the leaders of the
new nation did personally benefit from their power, by ransacking the society and the economy as all nondemocratic states do.

The Rise of the Developmental State:
From the Politics of Survival
to the Process of Nation-Building

The general hypothesis I propose is that the East Asian developmental
state, outside Japan, was born out of the need for survival, and then it grew
on the basis of a nationalist project of self-affirmation of cultural/political
identity in the world system.
Survival came first.
Singapore was a nonentity at the onset of its independence in 1965. An
abandoned military outpost of the crumbled British Empire, a bankrupt
entrepôt economy cut off from its ties with Indonesia, an integral part of
Malaysia expelled from the Federation of Malaysia, and a multiethnic society subjected to the pressure of its Malay environment and torn by the internal violent ethnic and religious strife between the Chinese majority and the
Muslim Malay and Hindu Tamil minorities. It could have easily become
another Sri Lanka. The first concern of the People's Action Party (PAP) that
led the anticolonial struggle against British domination was to hold Singapore together and to make it viable, while fighting off what was perceived as
the menace of the guerrillas of the Malaysian Communist Party, led by Chinese and supported by the People's Republic of China (PRC).
South Korea had just survived an all-out assault from communist North
Korea, and had barely escaped being caught in the middle of a nuclear war
between MacArthur's imperial dreams and the quasi-victorious Chinese
People's Liberation Army. In 1953 the country was in a shambles, the nation divided, and Syngman Rhee's First Republic was but a superstructure
for America to build a strong defensive line (based on a new, modern Korean military) on the Northern Asian frontier in the relentless war against
communism.
Taiwan was not Taiwan. It was an impoverished and terrorized island that
had become the last bastion of the vanquished Kuomintang armies, kept in

reserve by America as a potential threat and as a political standpoint against the rising power of the PRC. In fact, only the communist invasion of South Korea decided America on drawing the line in the Taiwan Straits, a decision that probably saved the KMT and allowed it to start living the ideological fantasy of reconstructing the Republic of China from Taiwan Province, a fantasy not shared by Chinese capitalists who migrated elsewhere.

Hong Kong was rapidly becoming an anachronism, after the Chinese Revolution and the embargo on China imposed by the United Nations on the occasion of the Korean War. With its entrepôt commerce with China downgraded to smuggling, it was on its way to being the last colony of a fading empire. Fundamental doubts about China's willingness to let it live outside Chinese control, as well as political fears that either the Labour Party or British public opinion would include the Territory in the next round of decolonization, kept Hong Kong wondering about its fate while wave after wave of Chinese immigrants/refugees were making the colony into their own trap, out of their escape either from revolution or misery.

The first reflex of the state apparatuses that later became developmental (the PAP state in Singapore, the Park Regime in South Korea, the KMT in Taiwan, and the colonial state in Hong Kong) was to ensure the physical, social, and institutional viability of the societies they came to be in charge of. In the process, they constructed and consolidated their own identity as political apparatuses.

However, according to the hypothesis I am proposing, *they shaped their states around the developmental principle of legitimacy on the basis of specific political projects that had, in each case, specific political subjects, all of which were created in rupture with the societies they were about to control.*

In Singapore (Chua, 1985) the PAP did lead the anticolonialist struggle, but it did so in the 1950s in close alliance with the left-wing movement (including the left-wing unions), and even with the communists, until the events of the early 1960s convinced the undisputed national leader, Lee Kwan Yew, that he had to repress the left (which he did ruthlessly) and to establish an autonomous political project aimed at transforming Singapore, out of necessity, from a colonial outpost into a modern nation. The PAP was in fact organized along Leninist lines, with tight mechanisms of social control and social mobilization, centralized forms of party power, and direct guidance of the economy through a well-paid, well-trained state technocracy. The social policies of the PAP, including public housing and community services, aimed at blending into one national culture the complex multiethnic structure of Singapore, while the emphasis on Confucianism and on Mandarin literacy among the Chinese deliberately sought to break up the subcultures organized around dialects and Chinese networks of various regional origins. Economic development was the means to achieve the goals of both making Singapore a viable nation and of affirming its presence in the world.

An even clearer case underlies the constitution of the developmental state in Taiwan (Gold, 1986). Once the KMT had to accept the reality of having lost China, it tried to convert Taiwan both into a platform for the mythical reconquest of the Mainland, and a showcase of what the reformed KMT could do for China and for the Chinese, after recognizing the disastrous economic management and the damage that their unrestrained corruption had done to their political control over China. A quasi-Leninist party, explicitly organized on the principles of democratic centralism, the KMT attempted to reform itself, made its adherence to Sun Yat-Sen's "three principles of the people" official ideology, and derived from it the emphasis on land reform, relative income equality, and providing for education of the population. The critical matter, however, was to assure the economic prosperity of the island, both to mobilize the population around the regime and to offer to the Chinese in the world at large an alternative project to Communist China. Indeed, the Chinese Open Door Policy of the 1980s was partly an answer to the impact of Taiwan's economic miracle, not only among the informed Chinese population, but among the Chinese leadership itself.

The origins of the Park Regime in South Korea can also be traced back to the emergence of a new political subject, breaking away both from the colonial order and from the corrupt, inefficient Rhee regime that had seen the remnants of the pro-Japanese bourgeoisie prosper through the state redistribution of American aid, while the country continued to suffer under the devastation of the war (Cole & Lyman, 1971; Lim, 1982). Although the 1961 coup actually toppled the short-lived civilian government of John Chang, its ideology and its practice were only partially linked to a law-and-order reflex. Its leaders were young nationalist military officers (Scalapino, n.d.) of a low rank, with the exception of Major General Park, who was in fact trained in Japan and who had served in the Japanese Army in Manchuria. The South Korean Military was an entirely new institution, whose organization and growth was obviously linked to the war. It grew from 100,000 in 1950 to 600,000 in 1961, making it one of the most numerous, well trained, and more professional armies in the world. Given the priority military interest of the United States in Korea, most of the effort of modernization and support was focused on the military. Thus the army's professional training and organizational capacity seems to have been quite above the rest of Korean society in the 1960s, with the exception of the small group of students and the intelligentsia. Thus in the presence of the disintegration of the state, economy, and society, the military officers who seized power in 1961-1963 seem to have been closer to the "Nasserite" brand of nationalist military regimes than to the mainstream Latin American tradition of pro-oligarchic military coups (Stepan, 1971). Lacking a social basis and feeling uncertain of the support of the United States toward the national projection of Korea beyond its limited military function, the Park Regime actually conceived, in explicit terms, the developmental strategy as an instrument of rebuilding the Korean nation and of winning shares of political autonomy.

But what about Hong Kong? How did the half-hearted, more subtle brand of Hong Kong's semidevelopmental state come into being? How could a colonial government identify itself with the destiny of the colony? If the traditional hongs and the new entrepreneurs cared only about their business, if the old British families dreamed about their retirement in Surrey, and the new Chinese industrialists about their green cards in Los Angeles, how could a political subject emerge in Hong Kong to make it into a thriving city-state projecting itself into the world economy?

Institutional power in Hong Kong during the entire development process was concentrated in the hands of the Colonial Governor, appointed by Westminster. Once appointed, however, the Governor was almost entirely autonomous in deciding domestic Hong Kong policies (Miners, 1986). More specifically, since 1957 the Hong Kong budget did not require formal approval from London. Thus the Colony was run by an autonomous state centered in the Governor and in a series of appointed Committees, headed by Secretaries also appointed by the Governor. This Executive Branch of government relied on the support of a number of legislative and advisory bodies made up of official and unofficial members, most of them also appointed by the government until the political reforms of the 1980s. These institutions are served by a numerous, well-trained, and extremely efficient government public service, numbering 166,000 civil servants in the 1980s. However, behind this formal structure of power, the political science study by Miron Mushkat (1982) and the historical-anthropological monograph by Henry Lethbridge (1970), as well as a number of other studies (Kwan & Chan, 1986) including my own field work, reveal an astounding, indeed fascinating power structure. The core of the Hong Kong power structure seems to be in the hands of what Miron Mushkat calls the "administrative class," a small, select group of civil servants who, until the 1970s, were recruited overwhelmingly in Britain by the Colonial Civil Service, generally out of the best British universities, and in general from Oxford and Cambridge. Between 1842 and 1941 there were only 85 "cadets" (as they were called until 1960) of the Hong Kong Colonial Civil Service. Even after the huge expansion of personnel in the 1970s, including massive recruitment of Chinese, there were only 398 "general grades administrative officers" in 1983 (Scott & Burns, 1984). It was this administrative class, with strong social and ideological cohesion and shared professional interests and cultural values, that seems to have controlled power within the Hong Kong state for most of the history of the Colony. They exercised this power while keeping in mind the interests of the business elite, but only to the extent that business would assure the economic prosperity of Hong Kong on which the power, income, prestige, and ultimately the ideological self-legitimation of the administrative class depended. Their interest in relationship to the future of Hong Kong was two-fold: to maintain the Colony in the midst of the turmoil of decolonization and the threatening anticolonial stands of the British Labour Party; and to show the world that the Colonial Service, on behalf of what was left of the tradition of the British Empire, was more able than any other political institution (including the new independent national states) to ensure the prosperity of the new Asian world, including to a large extent the well-being of its people, in a paternalistic attitude that could be considered typical of what history knows as "enlightened despotism." Although my ethnographic material on the matter is too unsystematic to be conclusive, it did convince me that the dedication and effectiveness of the elite colonial civil service of Hong Kong was tantamount to the last hurrah of the British Empire, building Hong Kong's prosperity as an ideological monument to their historical memory, along with the side-benefit of taking care of their retirement years.

Thus under different forms specific to each society, the developmental state in the Asian newly industrialized countries seems to have been the instrument of a nation (or city) building (or rebuilding) process enacted by political subjects largely autonomous vis-à-vis their societies. However, it was only because such political subjects were able to both mobilize and control their civil societies that they were able to implement their development strategy.

The State and Civil Society in the Restructuring of the Asian Pacific Region: How the Developmental State Succeeded in the Development Process

To identify the historical subjects of the development process in the Asian Pacific does not solve the fundamental issue of why they were able to succeed, if by success we understand the achievement of their particular vision of economic development. Thus I will conclude this chapter by formulating some additional hypotheses about the factors that made possible such success. Fundamentally, they have to do with three series of questions: the relationship between developmental states and other states in the international system; the internal logic of developmental states; and the relationship between development states and their civil societies.

First, it is important to remember that the success of the East Asian developmental states cannot be explained without referring to the geopolitical context of their birth: the Asian Cold War and the unconditional, politically and militarily motivated support by the United States to these regimes. While we must reject the leftist oversimplification of seeing these states as "puppets of American imperialism" (in fact, they did show their strong autonomy as nation-building political subjects), it is equally important to recognize the historical specificity of their development process, including the crucial help they received in every aspect in the initial stages of their take-off process, both from the United States and, to a lesser extent, from Britain. I will propose the concept of "vassal states" for this particular political form. By *vassal state,* using the analogy of the feudal system, I understand a *state that is largely autonomous in the conduct of its policies, once it has abided by the specific contribution it has to make to its "sovereign state."* Thus these were not just "dependent states" in the precise sense in which dependent societies and dependent states are defined by the structural-historical theory of dependency. These are states with very limited autonomy in their contribution to the overall geopolitical system to which they belonged, in exchange for which they received protection along with a significant degree of autonomy in the conduct of their domestic affairs. I propose the notion that South Korea and Taiwan were—at least until the early 1970s in Taiwan and the early 1980s in South Korea—vassal states of America, while Hong Kong was all along a vassal state (rather than a classic colony) of the United Kingdom, and Singapore was a semivassal state of the United Kingdom during the 1960s and then of the United States until the early 1980s, including some curious linkages such as the training of its military by the Israelis. This "vassal" condition created a security umbrella, relieved much of the burden of the huge defense budget, and played a role in the critical initial stages in facilitating access to world markets (for Hong Kong to the Commonwealth markets; for Taiwan and South Korea to the U.S. market; for South Korea after its 1965 treaty with Japan to the Japanese market).

The second element explaining the success of the development strategy is *the construction of an efficient, technocratic state apparatus.* This has little to do with the traditional dichotomy between corrupt bureaucracies and clean bureaucracies. Corruption was widespread in South Korea, significant in Taiwan, much more limited (but present) in Hong Kong and Singapore. And yet the South Korean state or the KMT state were able to operate with a high level of efficiency, served by well-trained civil servants, and organized on flexible lines that changed according to the needs of each stage of development. In functional terms corruption is only an obstacle to efficiency when it prevents the apparatus from fulfilling its assigned performance. In the South Korean case, for instance, corruption was part of the pay-off for government officers and for the government party for running the country along policy lines that created huge benefits for the newly created Korean industrialists. Overall, these states were more technocratic than bureaucratic, since their apparatuses were set up to implement a strategic, historical project, and not only (but also) to reap the benefits of dictatorship.

Yet *the fundamental element in the ability of developmental states to fulfill their project was their political capacity to impose and internalize their logic on the civil societies.*

I have already objected to the Western racist myth of the submissive nature of Asian labor. While this relative submissiveness could apply (in Asia and elsewhere) to teenage women subjected to societal patriarchalism at the beginning of their life as workers (but not 10 years later), it certainly does not apply to the historical experience or to the cultural characteristics of Chinese or Korean workers. Thus the autonomy of the developmental states and their ability to implement their project with few concessions to the demands of civil society must be explained in empirical, historical terms, without referring to the metaphysics of Confucianism.

The first explanation is a simple one: *repression.* The Kuomintang executed between 10,000 and 20,000 people in establishing its hold on the island of Taiwan in 1947-1950, particularly in the Kaoshiung massacre of May 9, 1947, and went on for the next decades to establish a ruthless political control apparatus that arrested, tortured, and killed political dissenters from right or left, all being lumped under the communist label. The PAP in Singapore liquidated all serious political opposition in the 1961-1965 period, banning the main trade union and arresting the leaders of the opposition Barisan Socialists, which motivated the expulsion of the PAP from membership of the Socialist International. It later used the British Colonial Internal Security Act, allowing the government to detain with no charge for an indefinite period anyone suspected of "subversion." Hong Kong used British troops to quell the riots of 1956, 1966, and 1967, and kept a very large and efficient police force of more than 20,000 people, who did not hesitate to deport to China any dissident who became dangerous to the public order. And South

Korea, under the aegis of one of the most effective repressive apparatuses in the world, the Korean CIA, arrested, tortured, imprisoned, and killed dissidents, occasionally by the thousands, while forbidding all independent union activity and most independent political activity until the demise of the authoritarian regime in the 1980s.

Most Third World countries, however, practice the same repressive policies without much success in either containing protest or, even less, mobilizing their societies in their development path. Thus other factors must account for the organizational capacity demonstrated by the developmental states vis-à-vis their societies.

An important element is that *the dominant classes were either destroyed, disorganized, or made totally subordinate to the state, with the partial exception of Hong Kong.* Land reforms in Korea and Taiwan, and the absence of a noncolonial bourgeoisie in Singapore, actually destroyed the traditional oligarchy in these societies. What was left of the commercial-industrial bourgeoisie was made an appendix of the development strategy decided by the state. With no domestic base from which to accumulate, the role of the state as gatekeeper to the world economy made any local capitalist entirely dependent on bureaucratic licenses and government-sponsored credits. In Singapore, the multinationals quickly understood that the Lion City could be a tropical paradise for them only on the condition of not "messing up" with the government, and certainly of not giving orders in the way they used to do in Latin America or, closer to home, in Marcos's Philippines. In Hong Kong, as usual, a more complex pattern developed. The bourgeoisie, both traditional (the British Hongs) and newcomers (the Shanghainese industrialists), were co-opted via a number of government committees. The Chinese bourgeoisie was left to run its own business on the condition of reporting to the government and abiding by its instructions (Castells et al., 1990; see also King & Lee, 1981; Lethbridge, 1987; Scott, 1987). The Jockey Club socially "glued" the political and business elites together, but under the clear leadership of the arrogant, allpowerful "cadets." And a significant number of high-ranking government officials retired to become representatives of Hong Kong business associations, thus establishing an informal but effective channel of communication between government and business in a harmonious division of labor that was generally led by the government's enlightened technocracy.

As for the working class, the four states devised strategies of integration to complement repression and if possible to substitute for it in the long run. All four states counted on economic growth and the improvement of living standards, including access to education and health, to keep the workers content. In fact, the strategy was effective for most of the period. In spite of their exploitative working and living conditions, the rise of living standards in the four countries was the fastest in all of the world, including Japan. And, as we know, people judge according to the standard of their own experience, not in comparison to life in a Los Angeles suburb.

In addition, Taiwan practiced for some time a deliberate policy aimed at income redistribution, with substantially positive results. And both Singapore and Hong Kong created an Asian version of the British welfare state, centered around public housing and social services organized in new towns, that actually played a fundamental role in social integration and, in the case of Singapore, interethnic pacification. South Korea practiced a much harsher policy toward the working class and as a result it is now confronting one of the most militant labor movements in Asia. However, the extraordinary improvement of living conditions in general and the emergence of an affluent middle class allowed South Korea to maintain relatively stable industrial relations until the 1980s, paving the way for the creation of competitive advantage in the international markets.

Thus the developmental states were fully aware of the need to integrate their civil societies to the extent that such integration remained compatible with the economic conditions necessary to be competitive in the world economy. They were not just repressive dictatorships. Their project consisted of a two-edged plowshare that they did not hesitate to transform into a sword when required.

However, *the process of development they succeeded in implementing not only transformed the economy but completely changed the society.* A new, more assertive capitalist class, ready to take on the world, emerged in the 1980s, increasingly confident that they no longer needed a state of technocrats, racketeers, and political police. A new, consumer-oriented, educated, liberal middle class decided that life was all too good to be sacrificed for the historical project of an artificially invented nation. And a new, more conscious, better organized working class appeared ready to follow the same historical path that has been walked by any other working class in the history of industrialization: class struggle.

The success of the developmental states in East Asia ultimately leads to the demise of their apparatuses and to the fading of their messianic dreams. The societies they helped to engender through sweat and tears are indeed industrialized, modern societies. But their actual historical projects are being shaped by their citizens, now in the open ground of history making.

Notes

1. Detailed statistical and documentary references are not given for every figure or fact cited in this text, to avoid making it even more cumbersome. All citations must be considered "sources of sources" that could lead the reader to the appropriate empirical contrast of the hypotheses I suggest here. For a summary view of some statistical data on Asian NICs see: Dalhman, 1989, pp. 51-94; for an excellent analytical overview of the themes under discussion see White, 1988.

2. The analysis of Singapore relies on my own research in Singapore in 1987 and 1989, presented in Castells, 1988. A useful economic analysis of Singapore is in Krause, Koh Ai Tee, and Lee (Tsao) Yuan, 1987.

3. Useful sources for the analysis of the process of economic development in South Korea are Lim, 1982, a revised version of his excellent 1982 Harvard doctoral dissertation; and K.-D. Kim, 1987, particularly pp. 169-460. I also relied on a brief period of my own field work and interviewing in the fall of 1988.

4. The basic social analysis of Taiwanese development is in Gold, 1986. Another interesting source regarding our own interpretation of the process is Winckler and Greenhalgh, 1988. I also grounded this analysis in some field work and interviewing conducted in Taipei, Tanyung, and Kaoshiung in January 1989.

5. My analysis of Hong Kong is based on research I conducted at the University of Hong Kong in 1983 and 1987. For a presentation of my research findings and analyses see Castells, Goh, and Kwok, 1990.

6. Milton Friedman has been the main ideologue propagating the myth of the "Hong Kong Model," but his information relies on research conducted in Hong Kong by his disciple, Alvin Rabushka (see Rabushka, 1979).

7. In Hong Kong, people live, work, and produce goods "in the sky." Factories are organized vertically, in buildings reminiscent of blocks of apartments or "flats" (using the prevailing British English of the colony).

8. Japan's experience as a developmental state driven by a nationalist project fits, in my opinion, in the analysis presented here. See an important and often overlooked book on the political origins of the Japanese economic strategy by London School of Economics professor A. J. Allen (1979).

References

Allen, A. J. (1979). *The Japanese economy.* London: Macmillan.

Barrett, Richard, & Chin, Soomi. (1987). Export-oriented industrializing states in the capitalist world-system: Similarities and differences. In Frederic Deyo (Ed.), *The political economy of the new industrialism.* Ithaca, NY: Cornell University Press.

Castells, Manuel. (1988). *The developmental city state in an open world economy: The Singapore experience.* Berkeley: University of California, Berkeley Roundtable on the International Economy.

Castells, Manuel, Goh, Lee Kwok, & Reginald Y. W. (1990). *The Shek Kip Mei syndrome: Economic development and public housing in Hong Kong and Singapore.* London: Pion.

Chen, Edward K. Y. (1979). *Hypergrowth in Asian economies: A comparative analysis of Hong Kong, Japan, Korea, Singapore, and Taiwan.* London: Macmillan.

Chen, Edward K. Y. (1980). The economic setting. In David Lethbridge (Ed.), *The business environment of Hong Kong.* Hong Kong: Oxford University Press.

Chan, M. K., et al. (Eds.). (1986). *Dimensions of the Chinese and Hong Kong labor movement.* Hong Kong: Hong Kong Christian Industrial Committee.

Chin, Pei-Hsiung. (1988). *Housing policy and economic development in Taiwan.* Berkeley: University of California, Institute of Urban and Regional Development.

Chen, Peter S. J. (Ed.). (1983). *Singapore: Development policies and trends.* Singapore: Oxford University Press.

Chesneaux, Jean. (1982). *The Chinese labor movement: 1919-1927.* Stanford, CA: Stanford University Press.

Chua, Beng-Huat. (1985). Pragmatism and the People's Action Party in Singapore. *Southeast Asian Journal of Social Sciences, 13*(2).

Cole, David C., & Lyman, Princeton N. (1971). *Korean development: The interplay of politics and economics.* Cambridge, MA: Harvard University Press.

Collier, David (Ed.). (1979). *The new authoritarianism in Latin America.* Princeton, NJ: Princeton University Press.

Dalhman, Carl J. (1989). Structural trade and change in the East Asia newly industrial economies and emerging industrial economies. In Randall P. Purcell (Ed.), *The newly industrializing countries in the world economy* (pp. 51-94). Boulder, CO: Lynne Rienner.

Deyo, Frederic C. (Ed.) (1987a). *The political economy of the new industrialism.* Ithaca, NY: Cornell University Press.

Deyo, Frederic C. (1987b). State and labor: Modes of political exclusion in East Asian development. In Frederic C. Deyo (Ed.), *The political economy of the new Asian industrialism.* Ithaca, NY: Cornell University Press.

Deyo, Frederic C. (1981). *Dependent development and industrial order: An Asian case study.* New York: Praeger.

Endacott, G. B., & Birch, A. (1978). *Hong Kong eclipse.* Hong Kong: Oxford University Press.

Ernst, Dieter, & O'Connor, David C. (1990). *Technological capabilities, new technologies and newcomer industrialization: An agenda for the 1990's.* Paris: OECD Development Centre.

Fajnzylber, Fernando. (1983). *La industrializacion Truncada de America Latina.* Mexico: Nueva Imagen.

Federation of Korean Industries. (1987). *Korea's economic policies (1945-1985).* Seoul: Federation of Korean Industries.

Gereffi, Gary. (1989). Rethinking development theory: Insights from East Asia and Latin America. *Sociological Forum, 4*(4).

Ghose, T. K. (1987). *The banking system of Hong Kong.* Singapore: Butterworths.

Gold, Thomas B. (1986). *State and society in the Taiwan miracle.* Armonk, NY: M. E. Sharpe.

Greenhalgh, Susan. (1988). Families and networks in Taiwan's economic development. In Edwin A. Winckler & Susan Greenhalgh (Eds.), *Contending approaches to the political economy of Taiwan.* Armonk, NY: M. E. Sharpe.

Ho, H. C. Y. (1979). *The fiscal system of Hong Kong.* London: Croom Helm.

Hong Kong Government. (1967). *Kowloon disturbances, 1966: Report of Commission of Inquiry.* Hong Kong: Hong Kong Government.

Hsing, You-Tein. (1990). [Untitled.] Doctoral dissertation in progress. Berkeley: University of California, Department of City and Regional Planning.

Johnson, Chalmers. (1982). *MITI and the Japanese miracle*. Stanford, CA: Stanford University Press.

Johnson, Chalmers. (1987). Political institutions and economic performance: The government-business relationship in Japan, South Korea and Taiwan. In Frederic C. Deyo (Ed.), *The political economy of the new Asian industrialism*. Ithaca, NY: Cornell University Press.

Kim, Kyong-Dong. (Ed.). (1987). *Dependency issues in Korean development*. Seoul: Seoul National University Press.

Kim, Seung-Kuk. (1987). Class formation and labor process in Korea. In Kyong-Dong Kim (Ed.), *Dependency issues in Korean development*. Seoul: Seoul National University Press.

King, Ambrose Y. C., & Lee, Rance P. (Eds.). (1981). *Social life and development in Hong Kong*. Hong Kong: The Chinese University Press.

Krause, Lawrence B., Koh Ai Tee, & Lee (Tsao) Yuan. (1987). *The Singapore economy reconsidered*. Singapore: Institute of Southeast Asian Studies.

Kuo, Shirley W. Y. (1983). *The Taiwan economy in transition*. Boulder, CO: Westview.

Kwan, Alex Y. H., & Chan, David K. K. (Eds.). (1986). *Hong Kong society*. Hong Kong: Writers and Publishers Cooperative.

Lau, Siu-Kai. (1982). *Society and politics in Hong Kong*. Hong Kong: The Chinese University Press.

Lee, Chong Ouk. (1988). *Science and technology policy of Korea and cooperation with the United States*. Seoul: Korea Advanced Institute of Science and Technology, Center for Science and Technology Policy.

Lethbridge, Henry. (1970). Hong Kong cadets, 1862-1941. *Journal of the Hong Kong Branch of the Royal Asiatic Society*, 10, pp. 35-56.

Leung, Chi-Keung, Cushman, J. W., & Wang, Gungwu. (Ed.). (1980). *Hong Kong: Dilemmas of growth*. Hong Kong: University of Hong Kong, Centre for Asian Studies.

Lim, Hyun-Chin. (1982). *Dependent development in Korea: 1963-79*. Seoul: Seoul National University Press.

Lim, Hyun-Chin, & Yang, Jonghoe. (1987). The state, local capitalists, and multinationals: The changing nature of a triple alliance in Korea. In Kyong-Dong Kim (Ed.), *Dependency issues in Korean development* (pp. 347-359). Seoul: Seoul National University Press.

Lin, Tsong-Biau, Mok, Victor, & Ho, Yin-Ping. (1980). *Manufactured exports and employment in Hong Kong*. Hong Kong: The Chinese University Press.

Miners, N. J. (1986). *The government and politics of Hong Kong*. Hong Kong: Oxford University Press.

Mushkat, Miron. (1982). *The making of the Hong Kong administrative class*. Hong Kong: University of Hong Kong, Centre for Asian Studies.

Park, Young-Bum. (1990). *Public sector labor market and privatization in Korea* (Discussion Paper/25/1990). Geneva: International Institute for Labour Studies.

Purcell, Randall P. (Ed.). (1989). *The newly industrializing countries in the world economy*. Boulder and London: Lynne Rienner.

Rabushka, Alvin. (1979). *Hong Kong: A study in economic freedom*. Chicago: University of Chicago Press.

Scalapino, Robert A. (n.d.). Which route for Korea? *Asian Survey*, 2(7), 1-13.

Schiffer, Jonathan. (1983). *Anatomy of a laissez-faire government: The Hong Kong growth model reconsidered*. Hong Kong: University of Hong Kong, Centre for Urban Studies.

Scott, Ian. (1987). *Policymaking in a turbulent environment: The case of Hong Kong.* Unpublished report. Hong Kong: University of Hong Kong, Department of Political Science.

Scott, Ian, & Burns, John P. (Eds.). (1984). *The Hong Kong civil service.* Hong Kong: Oxford University Press.

Sit, Victor F. S. (1982). Dynamism in small industries: The case of Hong Kong. *Asian Survey, 22,* pp. 399-409.

Solow, Robert. (1957). Technical change and the aggregate production functions. *Review of Economics and Statistics, 39,* pp. 312-320.

Stepan, Alfred. (1971). *The military in politics.* Princeton, NJ: Princeton University Press.

Tsao, Yuan. (1986). Sources of growth accounting for the Singapore economy. In Lim Chong-Yah & Peter J. Lloyd (Eds.), *Singapore: Resources and growth.* Singapore: Oxford University Press.

White, Gordon. (Ed.). (1988). *Developmental states in East Asia.* New York: St. Martin's.

Winckler, Edwin A., & Greenhalgh, Susan. (Eds.). (1988). *Contending approaches to the political economy of Taiwan.* Amonk, NY: M. E. Sharpe.

Yoshihara, Kunio. (1988). *The rise of ersatz capitalism in southeast Asia.* Oxford, UK: Oxford University Press.

Youngson, A. J. (1982). *Hong Kong: Economic growth and policy.* Hong Kong: Oxford University Press.

Yu, Fu-Lai, & Li, Si-Ming. (1985). The welfare cost of Hong Kong's public housing program. *Urban Studies, 22,* pp. 133-140.

3

States, Economic Development, and the Asian Pacific Rim

NIGEL HARRIS

This chapter considers two questions. First, what has been the role of the State in the process of economic development, and does this conform to what happened in South Korea, Taiwan, and Singapore (Hong Kong is omitted, since this raises special issues outside the range of this chapter[1])? Second, how far was the development of the three economies a unique phenomenon?

States and Economic Development

The analysis of the relationship between economic activity and States is bedeviled by a number of fictions, the most extreme of which is the distinction between the domestic and the external. Once the polarity is assumed, then relating them becomes a problem; countries are "inserted" in the world, or the world "penetrates" the country, as if any countries had, in a serious sense, not been part of the world for much of recorded history.

Other assumptions can be no less debilitating. Take, for example, two. First, some observers politicize the world market, making it into an arena for the struggle of embattled national fiefdoms, each with a clearly demarcated territory, a peculiar people and a discrete segment of capital; then each of the terms, *society, economy,* and *culture,* have comfortingly simple territorial perimeters, and *national* is the only feasible adjective to go with each concept. This is the tunnel vision from the vantage point (or better, slit trench) of each government. So far as the unity of government and capital is concerned, such a geopolitical vision was considerably more plausible between 1870 and the 1950s than either before or afterward, but even in its heyday, the perspective in effect denied a significant role to the most important source of change, world markets. All was decided in the chancelleries of the Great Powers.

On the other hand, some versions of Marxism reduce the political—of which the State is the preeminent institution—to an epiphenomenon, a cork—as it were—floating on the tides of economic activity (nowadays, a rare version) or of the domestic collision of classes. As a result of such a case, some leading Marxists at the time of the First World War assumed the integration of the European economy had rendered nationalism redundant, or, at most, restricted to the marginal issue of culture or language; they thus wildly underestimated the viability of nationalism in Europe and its material embodiment, the State. Without the idea of contradiction, such a view might suggest that world government would inevitably be the result of the integration of a world economy: politics was no more than a reflex of economics (Harris, 1990). A different error was to reduce the State to no more than the mouthpiece of a private capitalist class; indeed, public actions were seen as the means of identifying what the immediate interests of capital were, a proposition enshrining a methodology beyond empirical disproof (and one that excluded the possibility of the State making mistakes). Those, however, who shared the general approach but felt uncomfortable with the resulting tautology, were obliged then to embrace an addendum: on the "relative autonomy" of the State, or—in a cruder variant—"Bonapartism" (that is, the State is able temporarily to escape the control of the dominant classes by, in certain specific historical circumstances, playing one off against another). It should be noted in passing that whereas the first account subordinates all domestic conflict to the "external" struggle (it corresponds therefore to the viewpoint of the competitive State itself); in the second, there is often no external context at all; classes (or "fractions") struggle within national boundaries, and public action is primarily the reaction of capital to domestic issues.

The problems arise from a misspecification of the issues, a misspecification heightened by the changing nature of the world order. There are at least two systems operating in the world that are conceptually distinct although in practice continually interwoven and interacting: a system of competing companies (whether owned privately, by governments, or other agencies) that make and distribute a priced output of goods and services and, in sum, constitute a world economy; and a system of competing States, that administer clearly defined territories and populations and make up a world political order. There are—as is well known—quite different characteristics, functions, areas of primary operation, and powers associated with each set of agencies. States are defined by territory, by geography, companies in principle are not (although some may be); States have a monopoly within their territory of the use of physical power while companies rarely have more than security guards. The main source of finance of State power is expropriation, taxes. Companies engage directly in the process of production and distribution of goods, and so forth.

There are analogies. Firms can be bankrupted and liquidated; States can be destroyed. Companies can experience boardroom coups or takeovers, just as heads of States can be removed by coup and countries can be conquered. But they are only analogies and serve to underline the differences rather than the similarities, and particularly, the contrast between an institution characterized by the use of physical force and based upon the appropriation of value generated outside the public sector, and the financial power of an agency directly engaged in the generation of value.

The most important feature of States is that they compete with each other, and they do so, like companies, to secure their survival. Unlike companies, a crucial means to compete is precisely in the area of physical power. The primary task of States is to defend their national independence, and military competition is a key element in this. Of course, the more developed the world becomes, the greater the perceived dangers of rivalries to all States, so there are various attempts to cartelize the world order, establish stabilizing alliances, rules, fora for discussion, and so forth. The Concert of Europe was an early version of the attempt to establish a regulated order, and depended upon the Great Powers acting as self-appointed policemen to put down rebellions that threatened the State-system. However, the lack of an overarching power, a world government, mobilizing sufficient physical force to control all participants, undermines any simulation of national legal systems: if the issue at stake is sufficiently important, the strongest States can always defy international law. A Great Power, a participant with a particular interest, cannot be accepted for long as the embodiment of universal interests. Furthermore, today the cost of global policing is beyond even the richest powers and appears to be steadily increasing; the United States could only with difficulty sustain one Vietnam War—10 would have been impossible.

In the past, this continuing theme of military rivalry can be seen clearly. Indeed, competition in war-making capacity is itself an important element in the creation of the modern State, a point summarized in Charles Tilly's aphorism, "War made the State, and the State made war" (Tilly, 1975, p. 42). If war making or war preparation is in the foreground of the history of European governments, finding the means to pay for it is the obsession of much of the background. Late medieval rulers spent much of their time in desperate schemes and subterfuges to raise adequate funds to fight. It is this which so often led to administrative reforms, increasing centralization, the overriding of local liberties and extraordinary burdens of taxation—that in turn provided the source for the many rebellions that mark the path to the creation of the modern European State. It is also the source of the growing interest of monarchs—or their high officers—in economic questions and the growth of domestic capitalism. Capitalism owes much to the patronage of rulers searching for the revenues that would ensure the capacity to fight— rather than that patronage indicating the control of the State by capital. Of course, in a more general sense, the State's fundamental role in a world divided into competing States is to provide leadership for the whole ruling order (which includes the duty of *defining* what the national interest is, rather than simply reflecting interests defined elsewhere), and a private capitalist class may be part of that order; but this cannot simply be reduced to the interests of companies.

National economic development—as opposed to companies just making a profit—is invariably a by-product of the competition of States, not a spontaneous outgrowth of the operation of markets. Of course, the process may be more or less conscious. In the first case of industrialization historically, that of Britain, the role of the State and of warfare was crucial, but, one presumes, unconscious. During the 127 years between 1688 and 1815 when the key industrial transition was made, England (later Britain) was engaged in major wars for roughly 70 years. In the closing phases of this period during the Napoleonic Wars, there were 350,000 men under arms (1801), and half a million in 1811 (that is, equal to nearly 10% of the labor force), with many other hundreds of thousands engaged in keeping them supplied with arms, clothing, foodstuffs, and transport. For some 50 years (1780-1830), government consumption was larger than the value of exports, so that it appears that British economic development was, in the first phase, government, rather than export, led. By 1801, gross public expenditure may have been equal to over a quarter of total national expenditure (Deane, 1975, p. 91). Thus government and its military activities, the cost of systemic rivalries, raised and sustained output, transformed its structure (with disproportionate growth in the metallurgical and coal industries), and flattened the fluctuations that would have arisen from a market-led pattern of growth. The curtailment of imports from Europe added an element of import substitution stimulation that helped force an increase in the utilization of the factors of production. The process seems to have been based upon a familiar redistribution of income between classes: "the bulk of the increased indirect taxation necessitated by war seems to have been borne by consumers rather than producers, and the new direct taxes touched the mercantile and manufacturing classes relatively lightly" (Deane, 1975, p.97).

At the other end of the nineteenth century, Japan provided a striking parallel. Between 1874 and 1945, Japan was engaged in 10 major wars, two of them World Wars. From 1886, military spending was on average equal to 10% of the gross national product, and 12% in the three decades up to 1945. Initially, the country had very little modern military capacity, but by the 1920s Japan had become the third largest naval, and fifth largest military, power. Military demands were the source of both the giant subcontracting *zaibatsu* and the prodigious growth of the key industries: heavy and chemical, electrical equipment, and vehicles. Morishima (1982, pp. 96-97) concludes:

> This economic growth was certainly not achieved through using the mechanism of the free operation of the economy; it was the result of the government or the military, with their loyal following of capitalists, manipulating and influencing the economy in order to realize national aims . . . the price mechanism scarcely played an important role, and the questions of importance were how to raise capital to meet the government's demand and the nature of the demand generated from the enterprises at the receiving end of a government demand.

There are a sufficient number of other well documented examples of international rivalries impelling States to reorganize their domestic economies in the interests of military preparedness (Harris, 1986, p. 155 ff.) for it to seem a common theme. Of course, the conditions in which such rivalries take place are different, not only in terms of military technology (and the balance between imports and home produced equipment), the scale of required firepower, but also the organization of the domestic economy and labor force in order both to finance arms and to use them effectively. More refined measures of relative standing are derived, with much emphasis on comparative levels of labor productivity, education, and training, rather than simply firepower.

By the late nineteenth century, the emergence of a mass society in Western Europe and North America added a different dimension, for now the State was required to pursue its purposes in full public gaze and with some measure of popular participation—some accommodation to popular interests became the condition of effective policy; in turn, popular participation eased the two ancient restrictions on war-making capacity, the unwillingness of people either to pay taxes or to fight. Now, the concerns of the competitive

State increasingly went beyond the domain of the ruler or government to encompass the whole society. There was emerging a program of social transformation—from, for example, industrialization, mass education, and participation—required of an effective competitor.

The State system of the world and the rivalries of its leading powers set the terms of competition. Given the extraordinary inequality of States, the majority cannot match the most advanced levels of competition, but the largest make some attempt to do so, regardless of the per capita income of their countries (those developing countries that are said to possess nuclear weapons or the capacity to make them illustrate this). The majority of States, however, could not realistically defend themselves against the most powerful governments. They are not usually required to do so, only to defend their national independence against such things as local rivals or freebooters. The price of failure is the loss of independence or its radical qualification.

Governments in economically backward countries are thus today obliged by a competitive system to pursue economic development. Yet this itself imposes upon their societies new and extraordinary disciplines. Industrialization promotes an unprecedented degree of social and administrative centralization as well as new and quite frequently horrifying work disciplines, major social upheavals, moral revolutions, and so forth. For many of those in countries that recently attained national independence, it might seem the new disciplines are more onerous than those of being a colony: national liberation turned out to be only a means to force the liberated to compete. Indeed, it might appear that it was the State that was liberated, not the inhabitants.

The capacity to compete is powerfully influenced by the economic context. The output of each country is unique, so its relationship to world markets is highly specific, and therefore its capacity to earn the export revenues required to purchase vital imports, including defense equipment. The years after the Second World War were a sharp contrast to the interwar period in this respect. The possibilities of a growth of exports were much greater up to 1973 than either before the war or after 1973. The newly independent governments of this period were the unwitting beneficiaries of this generalized growth, able to claim that it was political independence itself that brought economic success rather than an unprecedented growth in world demand.

How does this relate to the development of South Korea, Taiwan, and Singapore? In essence, the military competition that drove the early developers to transform their domestic economies was, if anything, even more extreme for these three, particularly the first two (for Singapore, *Konfrontasi* was, however, of much importance, particularly after the break with Malaya and the evacuation of the British). The competition was much more severe than anything comparable in Latin America or Africa. In the case of Korea, it included extraordinary destruction from the cataclysm of a world war fought exclusively across its territory. In addition to this primary drive for survival, the State in both Korea and Taiwan was for a time peculiarly free of the social restrictions imposed by entrenched dominant classes. The entire ruling order of 1940 (except for part of the landed class) was Japanese and left when the Japanese empire collapsed. Given the third factor, the extraordinary growth in the world economy after 1950, if governments were able, by luck or design, to adopt nonobstructive policies, the prospects for high growth were most favorable. As we know, governments in South Korea, Taiwan, and Singapore went considerably further than this in promoting growth.

Rivalries promoted economic development in developing countries after the war. They had generated a no less sustained drive to *étatisme* in the industrialized countries in the 1930s. Two world wars and the Great Depression created a climate of opinion in which it was taken for granted that government power should supersede markets. The language of the war economy was bequeathed both to those who introduced protectionism after the interwar slump and to those who strove to develop backward countries after the Second World War. From the imperatives of Stalin's Soviet Union (where development, or "constructing socialism," coincided with preparation for war) to the milder corporatism of Britain in the 1930s, culminating in the period of Labour Government after 1945, there was a common theme of the control or supersession of market forces. Theorization about this supposedly new form of economy came much later; indeed, the Owl of Minerva (Galbraith, 1967; Shonfield, 1965) appeared in the mid-1960s when the counterrevolution was already beginning.

Thus the intellectual inheritance of the developing countries in the postwar period placed overwhelming emphasis on the role of the State. It is hardly surprising therefore that extreme forms of economic nationalism became almost universal among developing countries—import controls, overvalued exchange rates, large-scale public ownership and investment initiatives, directed investment with managed interest rates, prices and wages, and so forth. The program was embraced regardless of the political persuasion or external alliance of different governments—Chiang Kai-shek's Kuo Min Tang program of 1938 or Ngo Dinh Diem's aspirations in South Vietnam are hardly distinguishable from Nehru's brand of "socialism." The program was impelled by the exigencies of external competition rather than domestic social priorities. South Korea, Taiwan, and to a lesser extent Singapore, were not particularly different in this respect. Their singularity lay not in their domestic arrangements or control of the national economic frontiers, but in their single-minded concentration on overseas markets for manufactured exports—at a time when, as will be suggested in the next section, a quite unanticipated and radical change in the structure of world demand was occurring.

However, success in the endeavor of building competitive capacity through economic development had a contradictory result. For where a domestic private sector was allowed to survive as a means to accelerate growth, the greater the success a government had in propelling development, the more it created a strong private capitalist class, ultimately capable of challenging the priorities of State policy where these collided with its interests. The public emergence of this conflict can be seen in the late 1970s in South Korea when the heavy industrial plans of General Park (more closely related to building a self-sufficient military power than the type of civil economy market imperatives might promote) were increasingly questioned, particularly when they seemed to be starving high exporting light industry of investment and driving the economy to crisis. Similar issues emerged around the same time in Taiwan (Harris, 1987). In Singapore, overwhelmingly dominated by foreign capital, the fantasies of Mr. Lee were of much less significance for a multinational capitalist class.

The change in the social weight of the business class at home is not the only implication. As the world economy becomes increasingly integrated, the mark of maturity of a national capitalist class is that world competition drives it to operate internationally, to merge increasingly with global capital. This is only feasible with the liberation of capital from all that mass of restrictions which national governments seek to impose in order to capture a larger share of any surplus (and to protect what was initially seen as their capital from foreign competition). National liberation freed the State; restructuring and liberalization now freed capital. A second range of issues between business and government in South Korea concerns such things as the type of controlled currency regime, rights to borrow abroad, or rights to import freely. We might hazard a guess that similar forces are at work in the managerial stratum of Eastern Europe and the former Soviet Union, a proto-capitalist class that might reasonably expect to inherit the newly privatized corporations; this might partly account for the speed of the transition.

Thus, paradoxically, national economic development that was impelled by the rivalries within the State system now produces a new component in the market system that in part contradicts the independence of the State. Governments become preoccupied with retaining a group of powerful companies within their borders and seeking to beg or bribe international companies to invest there in order to secure privileged access to the surpluses generated by world, rather than national, capital. The State moves from being the "executive committee of the (national) bourgeoisie" (if such a phrase was ever adequate) to a local authority for a world bourgeoisie, from the incubator of capitalism to one of its many and changing homes.

The role of the State, however, remains important for the economy, for world capital will locate in the country concerned only if the government can guarantee certain conditions of production of goods, the reproduction of labor of a certain quality and price, and of effective management. Competition by States in the economic field now shifts from geographically specific advantages (such as raw material endowments) to much less tangible elements. As DeAnne Julius recently put it,

> What is most important to competitive success is no longer a country's land or mineral endowment or even, in many cases, its labour costs. Rather it is a whole range of nongeographical factors: access to technology, flexible management techniques, marketing strategy, closeness to consumers, speed of response to changes in the marketplace etc. All these are firm-specific not territorially based. (Julius, 1990, p. 82)

How Unique Was the Economic Growth Process of the Gang of Four?

The type of public sectors and governments developed in the industrialized countries between 1930 and—say—1960, and that were constructed in the developing countries in the postwar period, were responses to systemic rivalries in a world where up to that time capital accumulation was founded upon a national basis (even if the national core was part of a wider empire). It was taken for granted that all capital was nationally identifiable and had a loyalty much as inhabitants were supposed to have. However, at different times in different sectors—for example, finance, capital movements, commodity trade—these assumptions began to change, particularly from the 1950s. Accumulation began to assume a primarily global form. Thus the conditions for effective macroeconomic policy were transformed. All the machinery constructed to protect a national economy became, if not redundant, positively obstructive in the task of increasing the power of any particular government in a world economy. It is this radical shift that has meant that almost all economies seem perpetually engaged in "restructuring," seeking to adjust national policy and structure to the new world economy, and transforming the public role to one of "facilitation" rather than implementation. From the continuing decontrol and privatization of the industrialized countries to the structural adjustment of much of the developing world to the momentous changes in Eastern Europe and the Soviet Union, all can be seen as continuing efforts to unwind the structures of the earlier period in order to reestablish the new conditions for sustained growth.

One of the first signs of the emergence of the new world economy in trading terms was the quite extraordinary growth of the Four Little Tigers of East and Southeast Asia. The most important case was Hong Kong simply because of the unusual openness of its economy which reacted to changes in world demand without public mediation through commodity or currency control. The growth of the four was faster and sustained over a longer period of time (despite fluctuations in the world economy) than other developing countries. But it was nonetheless part of a general change in the system, reflected to a greater or lesser degree in almost all developing countries. Indeed, the precipitation of quite rapid growth in the 1960s seems much cruder and simpler in purely economic terms than is often suggested. Where the structure of current output and pricing (including the exchange rate) were favorable, then it became possible to enter the learning process that, with luck and persistence, produced the goods to fit a particular niche in the world market for manufactured goods. In practice, initially few countries were socially and politically equipped to start, and it is here that the major obstacles to growth lie (and that the superiority of the Four Little Tigers was most clearly apparent). Furthermore, starting the process did not guarantee it could be continued: there were failures (Morawetz, 1982), particularly as world economic conditions became more unstable in the 1970s.

A key indication of a country's successful adjustment to the new structure of world demand was its capacity to export manufactured goods into the heartlands of the industrial world, in Europe and North America. No one in the development field in the 1950s had envisaged such an audacious possibility, and much ingenuity was devoted to explaining why it was impossible. Yet the change is clearly apparent. In an earlier analysis of the 27 developing countries exporting goods worth more than $1 billion in 1980 (Harris, 1986)—countries covering some 54% of the world's population—it could be seen that virtually all experienced a rate of growth of exports from 1960 well ahead of the increase in world trade. Some had rates of expansion that, for periods, were as dramatic as those in the Four Little Tigers. Furthermore, in all 27 countries, the increase in the export of manufactured goods was much faster than the growth of exports as a whole. Israel increased the share of manufactured goods in its exports between 1960 and 1980 from 62% to 82%; Yugoslavia from 38% to 73%; Portugal from 54% to 72%. Finally, in all cases, the skill intensity of manufactured exports increased (if we take as a surrogate of this, exports of machinery and transport equipment, which on average increased from 2% to 10% of the total, and for the nine leading countries, from 4% to 23%).

If we extend the period to include the 1980s when many developing countries experienced much greater obstacles to growth, the picture is the same, showing that the tendency is long term. Of the 77 countries with comparative data in the *World Development Report* (World Bank, 1990) (now including the countries of Eastern Europe), 12 had negative rates of growth but 22 had 4% or more annually (1980-1988), and this included some of the largest countries—China with 10.3%; Pakistan, 6.5%; Thailand, 6.0%; and India, 5.2%. In terms of exports, 22 had negative growth but 34 an annual growth of 4% or more; many cases here had extraordinary rates of growth in the 1980s—seven of them, more than 11% annually (Paraguay, 15.7%; Turkey, 15.3%; South Korea, 14.7%; Taiwan, 13.9%; China, 11.9%; Portugal, 11.6%; Thailand, 11.3%). Sixty-one of the 81 countries for which there are data increased the share of manufactured goods in their exports, and by now 50% or more of the exports of 21 countries are manufactured goods, although few rival the 91%-93% share of Taiwan, South Korea, or Hong Kong—the nearest are Portugal (81%), South Africa (80%), Haiti (74%), China (73%), India (73%), all well ahead of Singapore (at 55%) (World Bank, 1990).

What were the factors at stake in this remarkable expansion of manufactured exports by developing countries? There are some obvious features— the spread of education and infrastructure following decolonization and in conditions of relatively high growth. Health status has improved consistently in developing countries. The effects of these changes have been enhanced because they have been concentrated in particular localities (generally in and around the large cities). They make possible a narrowing of the gap in labor productivity in comparable plants in developed and developing countries. That was helped by specific industrial promotion programs and rising levels of domestic savings.

There were other factors that reduced the significance of geographical distance for selected commodities. Thus, the costs of transport and communications fell because of innovations in both equipment and fuel efficiency. As the costs of movement fell, the geographical perimeter of potential production sites extended.

Third are the changes in protectionism in the main markets, the developed countries. This has made for new patterns of territorial specialization and new comparative advantages making it impossible for firms in developed countries to compete in markets for labor-intensive manufactures.

Many of these factors, however, would have facilitated the redistribution of some manufacturing capacity but not caused it. For that we must assume not only general growth in the world system, but also a radical change in the world economy, in the geographical distribution of comparative advantages. A key element in this was the rapid exhaustion of labor supply in Europe in the 1950s, sending buyers beyond Europe in search of new sources of supply. Hong Kong, unlike the other three Little Tigers, was completely open to changes in external markets, and responded to this quite new demand, precipitating a process of remarkable self-transformation. The change is historically specific, since Hong Kong had always been an open economy but had not industrialized before. The other three of the Four then copied the process of export-led growth, but through deliberate State intervention (where the Japanese model became relevant, although Japanese growth at a comparable stage was not export-led).

The 1950s were crucial for this transition. It was then that rapid European growth transformed the demand for labor. The agricultural labor force was swiftly drawn into nonagricultural work. An increasing number of women were drawn out of the household into paid employment. Finally, immigrant workers became an increasingly important component of the labor force.

Thus as migrant workers moved one way, buyers of goods moved in the other in search of new supplies. Once begun, countries were able quite swiftly to upgrade the technical quality of their output, to develop.

By the 1970s, the process had become so advanced, it could scarcely be reversed. The industrial output of the more developed—let alone, the consumption level—depended upon imported manufactured goods. It is for this reason that the return of slump to the system in the 1970s did not produce a level of protectionism that, in the Great Depression of the interwar years, destroyed the world trading system.

The change in the structure of world demand does not explain why some countries rather than others were able to exploit the process so far as to transform their domestic economies. But that question has to presuppose the much larger factor of a fundamental change in the world economic order, beginning the creation of an integrated world manufacturing economy and a global capital. The role of the State in that context is radically changed.

Conclusions

With the benefit of hindsight, we can now see the period since 1930 as the heyday of State economic power. There was no clear date for the ending of this period—and it does not coincide with a reversal in the share of national incomes taken by the public sector. There were stages in the industrialized countries—in terms of finance, the convertibility of currencies, the emergence of offshore money markets, the floating of exchange rates, the different "Big Bangs" in different countries. Each step was pragmatic; that is, a response to specific short-term conjunctures rather than the implementation of a premeditated strategy. The same is true in developing countries, where pragmatic experiments in the promotion of manufactured exports as well as elements of liberalization have continued for long periods (and on occasions been reversed).

In the end, however, a new world economic order had been created. The old project of national economic development, creating a fully diversified independent national economy supplying the domestic market, had become both utopian and, for some, economically disastrous. Both the structures of public power and the corporatist social alliances that supposedly vindicated that power became redundant. World markets required increased specialization and so increased differentiation. The government still captained the boat, but with no power over wind and wave. It was less and less the leader, patron and manager of a discrete segment of world capital relating to an autonomous domestic market and controlled currency area. It was more the administrator of part of a world economy, a junction point for transactions that began and ended far beyond its authority. The key to public power lay not in access to domestic resources or capital, but in providing the right environment for external forces.

It was this new context that forced liberalization on most of the countries of the world. Three of the Four Little Tigers, South Korea, Taiwan, and Singapore, had conformed to the old prescription for national economic development and created a powerful directing State and a large public sector in a closely protected market (this last feature did not occur in Singapore). The State structures were defensive, to protect the country in a fiercely competitive State system. What was unusual in the postwar context was not this but that, by a series of accidents, they came to focus upon external markets for manufactured goods, thus directly connecting their economies to the most dynamic forces of growth in the world economy. It could not have been done without a fundamental change in world demand, a change which controverted most of the social science wisdom on the subject.

The ramifications of this change will be working themselves out long into the future—for the changes are not merely in the role of the State and its relationship to economic questions, nor in the geography of production. In a closed economy, the pricing of capital and labor, their relative scarcity, and the effect of this upon technology, optimal scales of production and the organization of work, are very different from what holds in a world economy. There is no scarcity of labor in the open economy, no necessity for labor saving innovations. Capital intensity, scales of concentration (of capital as well as in production units) and work patterns—between formal and informal—may all change radically as liberalization proceeds. Many cherished assumptions are being eroded, and many surprises are in store.

Note

1. Hong Kong's government administered no economically significant controls on external trade or currency movements, and this distinguishes it from almost all other governments. It was interventionist in certain respects (in land release and development, housing, etc.), but again, this was relatively small compared to another open economy, Singapore. Hong Kong reacts to world demand with very little public mediation, so it must be treated as a quite different case to the other three. This is discussed by me elsewhere (Harris, 1986).

References

Deane, Phyliss. (1975). War and industrialization. In J. M. Winter (Ed.), *War and economic development: Essays in memory of David Joslin.* London: Cambridge University Press.

Galbraith, J. K. (1967). *The new industrial state.* London: Hamish Hamilton.

Harris, Nigel. (1986). *The end of the Third World: Newly industrializing countries and the decline of an ideology.* London: Tauris.

Harris, Nigel. (1987). *Newly emergent bourgeoisies?* Working Paper, Hong Kong: University of Hong Kong, Centre for Urban Studies and Urban Planning. [To be republished in Harris, N. (in press). *Cities, class and trade: Economic and social change in the Third World.* London: Tauris.]

Harris, Nigel. (1990). *National liberation.* London: Tauris/Penguin.

Julius, DeAnne. (1990). *Global companies and public policy: The growing challenge of foreign direct investment.* London: Royal Institute of International Affairs/Pinter.

Morawetz, David. (1982). *Why the emperor's new clothes were not made in Colombia* (World Bank Staff Working Paper, 368). Washington, DC: World Bank.

Morishima, Michio. (1982). *Why has Japan "succeeded"? Western technology and the Japanese ethos.* Cambridge, UK: Cambridge University Press.

Shonfield, Andrew. (1965). *Modern capitalism: The changing balance of public and private power.* London: Royal Institute of International Affairs/Oxford University Press.

Tilly, Charles. (1975). Reflections on the history of European state-making. In Charles Tilly (Ed.), *The formation of nation states in western Europe.* Princeton, NJ: Princeton University Press.

World Bank. (1990). *The world development report 1990.* Washington, DC: World Bank.

4

New Realities of Industrial Development in East Asia and Latin America
GLOBAL, REGIONAL, AND NATIONAL TRENDS

GARY GEREFFI

Industrial capitalism on a world scale has undergone significant shifts during the past two decades. Industrialization today is the result of an integrated system of global production and trade, buttressed by new forms of investment and financing, promoted by specific government policies, and entailing distinctive patterns of spatial and social organization. The objective of this chapter will be to sketch some of these new trends at the global, regional, and national levels.

I will outline four central arguments. First, we are witnessing the emergence of a global manufacturing system that has different institutional foundations than in the past. Although government policies in core and peripheral nations have combined with new technologies to fuel this process, export networks are a significant new focal point in development studies.

Second, the concept of commodity chains offers an important analytical framework for understanding both productive and spatial interdependencies. Commodity chains permit us to engage in a rigorous analysis of industries that highlights the importance of productive networks and the social embeddedness of economic activities. The footwear industry will be used to exemplify this approach.

Third, distinct regional divisions of labor are reshaping the geographical anatomy of industrial capitalism. Though ultimately subordinate to the overall international division of labor, these regional configurations contain their own cores and peripheries with particular sets of unequal transactions, dependencies. and development possibilities. Illustrations of these trends will be drawn from the electronics and automobile sectors in East Asia and Latin America.

Fourth and finally, the newly industrialized countries (NICs) within these regional divisions of labor are playing specialized roles within the world economy. As we move from the dynamics of global production down to the specifics of region, community, and place (and back again) to explain the nature of these roles, it is necessary to introduce a complex set of intermediate variables that link the macro and micro levels of analysis. These include industrial organization, new process and product technologies, industrial and commercial subcontracting relationships, and social ties such as gender, ethnicity, kinship, and class.

A Global Manufacturing System

There have been striking changes in the structure and dynamics of the world economy during the past several decades. The growth in manufacturing since the 1950s has been fueled by an explosion of new products, new technologies, the removal of barriers to international trade, and the physical integration of world markets through improved transportation and communication networks. International trade has allowed nations to specialize in industry as distinct from other economic sectors, in different manufacturing branches, and increasingly even in different stages of production within a single industry. This situation has led to the emergence of a global manufacturing system in which production capacity is dispersed to an unprecedented number of developing as well as industrialized countries (see Harris, 1987; Gereffi, 1989a).

Trade and industrialization have reinforced each other. Between 1980 and 1986, the number of Third World countries (classified by the World Bank as low- and middle-income, excluding the high-income oil-exporting countries) that exported goods worth $1 billion or more increased from 27 to 49 (Harris, 1987, p. 93; World Bank, 1988, pp. 242-243). This expansion of Third World export capacity, particularly for manufactured goods, embraces such a diverse array of countries that it appears to be part of a general restructuring in the world economy.

The newly industrializing countries (NICs) from East Asia and Latin America are pivotal actors in the global manufacturing system. East Asian nations have clearly established themselves as the Third World's premier exporters. Hong Kong topped the list in 1988 with $63.2 billion in exports, followed closely by South Korea and Taiwan with export totals of just over $60 billion each. The People's Republic of China had $47.5 billion in exports and Singapore $39.2 billion. Brazil was the leading Latin American exporter at $33.7 billion, followed by Mexico with an export total of $20.7 billion. Several other Asian nations emerged as "near-NICs" by 1988 on the basis of their export performance: Malaysia, $20.8 billion in exports; Indonesia, $19.7 billion; and Thailand, $15.8 billion (see Table 4.1).

The rapidity of change in the Third World's export capacity is indicated by comparing these 1988 figures with those only three years earlier in 1985. East Asia's three "super-exporters"—Hong Kong, South Korea, and Taiwan—each doubled their official export totals between 1985 and 1988. The other Asian near-NICs also experienced major export gains during this period, with the exception of Indonesia whose exports rose only slightly (6%). Thailand's export total more than doubled (an increase of 123%), Singapore's and China's exports jumped by nearly 75% each, while Malaysia's rose by 36%. Brazil's exports increased by about one-third from 1985 to 1988, while Mexico experienced a slight export decline, explained in large part by the significant drop in the value of Mexico's oil sales abroad.

One explanation for this recent dramatic growth in exports, especially among the East Asian NICs, is the marked appreciation of their currencies vis-à-vis the U.S. dollar since the mid-1980s, which augmented the official value of their export totals in these years. The upward shift in the export capacity of these nations is far more than a statistical artifact, however, when one takes into account that nearly all the countries listed in Table 4.1, including Brazil and Mexico whose currencies were significantly devalued versus the dollar after 1985, had substantial export increments, especially of manufactured products. (Even though Mexico's overall exports declined slightly because of falling oil sales, its exports of manufactures nearly doubled from $5.9 billion to $11.4 billion between 1985 and 1988.)

This shift toward a prominent and growing role for manufactured exports in the NICs is readily apparent in Table 4.1. Manufactured products constituted more than 90% of total exports in Hong Kong, South Korea and Taiwan in both 1985 and 1988. While manufactures did not dominate the export profiles of any of the other NICs to this same extent, the seven remaining nations in Table 4.1 all showed remarkable gains in their manufactured exports between 1985 and 1988. Mexico, for example, doubled the manufacturing share in its export total from 27% in 1985 to 55% in 1988. Similarly, China's "manufactured exports expanded from 54% to 73% of its total

Table 4.1 Exports by the East Asian and Latin American NICs, 1985 and 1988

Country	Exports (US$ billions)		Exports/GDP (percentage)		Percentage Share of Exports[a]							
					Primary Commodities		Textiles and Clothing		Machinery and Transport Equipment		Other Manufactures	
	1985	1988	1985	1988	1985	1988	1985	1988	1985	1988	1985	1988
East Asian NICs												
Hong Kong	30.2	63.2	92[d]	108[b]	8	8	32	29	24	25	36	37
South Korea	30.3	60.7	35	35	9	7	23	22	36	39	32	32
Taiwan	30.7	60.4	52	57[b]	9[c]	8	18[c]	15	29[c]	34	44[c]	43
Singapore	22.8	39.2	131	164	41	26	4	5	32	47	22	23
Latin American NICs												
Brazil	25.6	33.7	14[d]	10	59[d]	52	3[d]	3	14[d]	18	24[d]	27
Mexico	21.9	20.7	12	12	73[d]	45	1[d]	2[b]	16[d]	33	11[d]	20
Other Asian Near-NICs												
People's Republic of China	27.3	47.5	10	13	46[d]	27	24[d]	24[b]	6[d]	4	24[d]	45
Malaysia	15.3	20.8	49	60	73[d]	55	3[d]	4	19[d]	26	5[d]	15
Indonesia	18.6	19.7	21	24	89[d]	71	2[d]	8	1[d]	1	8[d]	20
Thailand	7.1	15.8	19	27	65[d]	48	13[d]	17	7[d]	11	15[d]	24

SOURCE: World Bank (1987), pp. 220-223, 206-207; World Bank (1988), p. 244; World Bank (1990), pp. 182-183, 204-205, 208-209. The 1985 and 1987 export and gross domestic product figures for Taiwan are given in Council for Economic Planning and Development (1988), pp. 23, 208.
NOTES: a. Percentages may not add up to 100 due to rounding error.
b. 1987.
c. 1986.
d. 1984.

exports between 1985 and 1988, Thailand from 35% to 52%, Malaysia from 27% to 45%, and Indonesia from 11% to 29%.

Equally impressive are the figures which show the diversity of these manufactured exports. Hong Kong, South Korea, and Taiwan have retained a relatively strong base in two of the traditional industries that have been economic mainstays since the start of their export-led industrialization nearly three decades ago, textiles and clothing. What is surprising is the fact that machinery and transport equipment now is the leading export sector for three of the four East Asian NICs (the exception being Hong Kong), as well as for Mexico, Brazil, and Malaysia. The machinery and transport equipment sector comprises a set of capital- and technology-intensive industries that mark a definitive shift in emphasis from the labor-intensive exports of the past, despite the fact that some traditional products like clothing or footwear are still significant export items. Nontraditional textile/apparel exports now represent between three fifths and three fourths of all exports in the four East Asian NICs and around one half of total exports in the Latin American NICs. (The nontraditional label is an approximation based on the exclusion of textiles and clothing from the manufacturing total. There are some products within the "Other Manufactures" category, such as footwear, that ordinarily would be added to the traditional exports list.)

Finally, it should be pointed out that the NICs vary considerably in the degree of their external orientation. The East Asian nations are export-led economies in which exports in 1987-1988 accounted for 57% and 35% of gross domestic product (GDP) in Taiwan and South Korea, respectively, and for 108% and 164% of GDP in the entrepôt city-states of Hong Kong and Singapore (see Table 4.1). This compares with export/GDP ratios of only 10% to 12% in the much larger Latin American NICs, 13% in China, and about 25% in Indonesia and Thailand. Malaysia's export orientation was especially high at 60% of GDP. Thus, the East Asian NICs are far more dependent on external trade than their Latin American or other Asian counterparts (including Japan, which had an export/GDP ratio of only 9.3% in 1988).

In summary, the international division of labor has evolved beyond the old pattern by which developing nations exported primary commodities to the industrialized countries in exchange for manufactured goods. Today, developing countries like the East Asian NICs are among the world's most successful exporters of manufactures. Furthermore, the NICs have diversified from traditional labor-intensive exports, such as textiles, or those based on natural resources—such as plywood, leather, paper, and basic petrochemicals—to more complex capital- and skill-intensive exports like machinery, transport equipment, and computers.

While the diversification of the NICs exports toward nontraditional manufactured products is now a clear trend, less well recognized is the tendency
of the NICs to develop higher levels of specialization in their export profiles.
The global manufacturing system that has emerged in the last several decades and the related expansion in export activity by the NICs has led to
increasingly complex product networks and an unprecedented degree of geographical specialization. The NICs within a given region, such as East Asia
or Latin America, are becoming increasingly differentiated from one another
as each nation is establishing specialized export niches within the world
economy (see Gereffi, 1989a for illustrations of this trend). Export networks
and export niches thus are becoming key units of analysis in the contemporary global manufacturing system.

National Development Strategies

National development strategies nonetheless have played an important
role in shaping these new productive relationships in the world economy.
Conventional economic wisdom has it that the NICs have followed one of
two alternative development strategies: an inward-oriented path of import-
substituting industrialization (ISI) pursued by relatively large, resource-rich
economies in which industrial production is geared mainly to the needs of a
sizable domestic market; and an outward-oriented approach (export-oriented
industrialization, or EOI) adopted primarily by smaller, resource-poor nations that depend on global markets to stimulate the rapid growth of their
manufactured exports. Whereas the Latin American NICs have been most
closely associated with ISI. The East Asian NICs are considered as paradig-
matic exemplars of the virtues of EOI.

This simplified view of the development trajectories of the Latin American and East Asian NICs, while useful up to a point, can be profoundly misleading, especially in terms of its policy implication that other Third World
nations ought to attempt to emulate the successful economic experience of
the East Asian NICs (for a fuller consideration of these issues, see Gereffi,
1989a and 1989b; Gereffi & Wyman, 1990). With regard to the relevance of
national development strategies to the global manufacturing system described above, I want to highlight several major points.

First, it is a mistake to think of inward-oriented and outward-oriented development strategies as mutually exclusive alternatives. Each of the NICs in
Latin America and East Asia has pursued a combination of both initial and

advanced phases of ISI and different types of EOI in order to avoid the in-herent limitations of an exclusive reliance on domestic or external markets. This mixed approach also facilitates the industrial diversification and up-grading that are required for these nations to remain competitive in the world economy (see Gereffi, 1989b; 1991). Rather than being mutually exclusive alternatives, the ISI and EOI development paths in fact have been comple-mentary and interactive.

Second, the sharp divergence between inward-oriented and outward-ori-ented development strategies in the Latin American and East Asian NICs, respectively, in the 1960s, masks a significant convergence in their eco-nomic trajectories during the subsequent two decades. The countries in both regions established or expanded second-stage ISI industries to meet a variety of domestic development objectives and ultimately to enhance the flexibility of their export structures (this point is amply documented in Gereffi and Wyman, 1990). In the 1970s, South Korea and Taiwan launched major "Heavy and Chemical Industrialization" programs with a focus on steel, ma-chinery, automobiles, shipbuilding, and petrochemicals. Singapore used its links with transnational corporations (TNCs) to push into capital-intensive sectors like oil refining, petrochemicals, telecommunications equipment, of-fice and industrial machinery, and electronics in the 1970s. These shifts to-ward heavier industries in the East Asian NICs paralleled similar kinds of investments in the Latin American NICs a decade or two earlier. They also laid the groundwork for a far more diversified range of manufactured exports by the East Asian NICs in the 1980s.

The Latin American NICs moved toward a strategy of export diversifica-tion in the 1980s as well. In Mexico, sharp currency devaluations led to a spectacular increase of labor-intensive manufactured exports from the *maquiladora* ("bonded-processing") industries located along the U.S. bor-der. In Brazil, the composition of industrial exports evolved toward more skill-intensive metalworking and machinery products initially developed for their domestic markets during the second stage of ISI, such as consumer durables, transport equipment, and capital goods. The automobile industry, for example, has emerged as one of the most dynamic export sectors for Mexico and Brazil in the 1980s. This industrial deepening along ISI lines in the Latin American and East Asian NICs contributed to a more diversified pattern of export growth in each region, illustrating the often unexpected synergy between inward-oriented and outward-oriented development strategies.

Third, EOI in the East Asian and Latin American NICs has been over-whelmingly centered on the U.S. market since the onset of their export-promotion efforts in the 1960s. Nonetheless, the degree of export reliance on the United States varied considerably among the NICs in the late 1980s. Mexico's dependence on the American market was the greatest in 1987, at 65%, followed by Taiwan at 44%; South Korea, 39%; Hong Kong and Brazil, around 28%; and Singapore, 25% (United Nations, 1989; Council for Economic Planning and Development, 1988, p. 222).

However, the willingness and ability of the United States to continue to fuel the NICs' export growth in the future is very doubtful. The United States had a world-record trade deficit of nearly $180 billion in 1987. With the exception of Germany, most of the other West European nations are running trade deficits as well. The political pressures for protectionism in the developed countries are well documented and likely to grow. How the NICs respond to this challenge rests to a large degree on their ability to diversify their export markets, both geographically and through product specialization.

Fourth, significant industrial upgrading has occurred in many of the EOI industries in the NICs, often in response to specific government policies. While the first significant wave of exports from the East Asian NICs in the late 1950s and the 1980s came from traditional, labor-intensive industries like textiles, apparel, and footwear that relied on low wages and an unskilled work force, there has been a very pronounced shift in the 1980s toward an upgraded, skill-intensive version of EOI. These new export industries include higher value-added items that employ sophisticated technology and require a more extensively developed, tightly integrated local industrial base. Products range from computers and semiconductors to numerically controlled machine tools, televisions, videocassette recorders, and sporting goods. This export dynamism in East Asia does not derive solely from introducing new products, but also from continuously upgrading traditional ones.

The Latin American NICs also have developed a sophisticated array of exports on the basis of their earlier import-substituting industries. American automobile companies are setting up world-class engine plants in Mexico, for example, partly to cope with Japanese competition (Shaiken & Herzenberg, 1987). Brazil too has developed state-of-the-art, technologically advanced, and increasingly export-oriented industries from an ISI base in fields like automobiles, computers, armaments. and assorted capital goods. Fifth, EOI industries in the NICs are spatially segregated from the older ISI industries, they have different kinds of labor forces, they attract alternative forms of capital investment, and they are promoted by distinctive government policies in the NICs and the core countries. In many of the NICs, governments want to move away from unskilled labor enclaves both because of rising labor costs and in order to create higher levels of domestic value-added. Core-country protectionism (tariffs, quotas, and voluntary export restraints) has had the perhaps unanticipated effect of encouraging industrial upgrading in the main exporting NICs. This often leads to import displacement as higher value-added NIC exports replace those lower on the value-added chain, rather than to effective import substitution favoring domestic producers in the core.

Sixth, the growing prominence of EOI industries in the NICs has created a qualitative shift in the international division of labor. Whereas the ISI industries established a pattern of national segmentation in which parallel national industries were set up to supply highly protected domestic markets, the turn to EOI has promoted a logic of transnational integration based on geographical specialization and global sourcing. Thus, national development strategies have helped to foster the emergence of a global manufacturing system.

Commodity Chains and
the Footwear Industry

In the global manufacturing system of today, production of a single good commonly spans several countries, with each nation performing tasks in which it has a cost advantage. This is true for traditional manufactures, such as footwear and garments, as well as for modern products, like automobiles and computers. In order to analyze some of the implications of this worldwide division of labor for specific sets of countries like the East Asian and Latin American NICs, it is very helpful to utilize the concept of commodity chains.[1]

Commodity Chains

A *commodity chain,* as defined by Hopkins and Wallerstein (1986, p. 159), refers to "a network of labor and production processes whose end result is a finished commodity." One must follow two steps in building such a chain. First, to delineate the anatomy of the chain, one typically starts with the final production operation for a manufactured good and moves sequentially backward until one reaches the raw material inputs. The second step in constructing a commodity chain involves identifying four properties for each operation or node in the chain: (1) the commodity flows to and from the node, and those operations that occur immediately prior to and after it; (2) the relations of production (i.e., forms of the labor force) within the node;

(3) the dominant organization of production, including technology and the scale of the production unit; and (4) the geographic loci of the operation in question (Hopkins & Wallerstein, 1986, pp. 160-163).

The NICs are pivotal production sites in the commodity chains that cut across national boundaries and that help define core-periphery relations in the world system. However, the complexity of commodity chains for the kinds of export-oriented manufacturing industries that the NICs are predominant in today requires that the model proposed by Hopkins and Wallerstein be extended in several ways.

First, the dynamic growth of the NICs has revolved around their success in expanding their production and exports of a wide range of consumer products destined mainly for core-country markets. This means that it is extremely important to include forward as well as backward linkages from the production stage in the commodity chain. In the footwear industry, a full commodity chain encompasses the entire spectrum of activities in the world economy: the agro-extractive sector (cattle for leather, and crude oil as the basis for plastic and synthetic rubber inputs), the industrial sector (footwear manufacturing), and the service sector (the activities associated with the export, marketing, and retailing of shoes).

Second, the extension of commodity chains beyond production to include the flow of products to the final consumer market has important implications for where economic surplus is concentrated in a global industry. In the case of footwear, the comparative advantage of the NICs lies primarily in footwear production because of the relatively low labor costs in these non-core countries. A corollary of this fact, however, is that the main source of economic surplus within the footwear commodity chain generally is not at the production stage, but rather at the last stage of the chain where service activities predominate (i.e., the marketing and retailing of shoes). Product differentiation by means of heavily advertised brand names (e.g., Nike, Reebok, Florsheim) and the use of diverse retail outlets allows core-country firms, rather than those in the semiperiphery, to capture the lion's share of economic rents in this industry.

Third, an export-oriented industry like footwear provides a convenient baseline for measuring the relative success of countries as they compete with one another for shares of the world market. I will concentrate on footwear exports to the United States, which is the world's largest market for manufactured consumer exports from the NICs (Keesing, 1982). By mapping the changing shares of the major footwear exporters to the U.S. market during the past two decades, one gets a remarkably clear picture of competition not only among the East Asian and Latin American NICs, but also between these NICs and core-country exporters like Italy and Japan.

Figure 4.1 outlines a commodity chain for the global footwear industry. It is composed of four major segments: (1) raw material supply; (2) production; (3) exporting; and (4) marketing and retailing. In addition, the major footwear export niches in the U.S. market are included in order to illustrate the specialized nature of the competition that occurs among the major footwear exporters.

Patterns of Competition
Among the Footwear-Exporting NICs

The footwear industry is a very instructive case for exploring the mobility of the NICs in the contemporary world economy. Footwear has been the top export item from South Korea, Taiwan, and Brazil to the United States throughout most of the 1980s, and it is of growing importance to China. Although each of these countries has a very diversified profile of manufactured exports (see Table 4.1), it is notable that footwear continues to be a major export commodity, despite the fact that the export momentum of the NICs is shifting toward more sophisticated products such as automobiles, computers, color television sets, and videocassette recorders.

The United States is the largest footwear market in the world. During the past two decades, imports have steadily displaced local production within the American market. In 1968, imports accounted for 21.5% of all nonrubber footwear consumed in the United States; in 1979, one out of every two pairs of shoes purchased in the United States was imported; and by 1989, four out of every five pairs of shoes bought in the United States were made abroad (Footwear Industries of America [FIA], 1990).

The pattern of footwear exports to the American market shows several clear shifts. These can be seen in Table 4.2, which identifies the major sources of nonrubber footwear imports to the United States from 1968 to 1989. (Nonrubber footwear accounts for about 80% of all U.S. footwear imports.) In the late 1960s, the main footwear exporters to the American market were Italy, Spain, and Japan, This trio of nations accounted for three quarters of all U.S. footwear imports by value in 1968 (Gereffi & Korzeniewicz, 1990, table 1). Italy was the dominant exporter that year, with a market share of 41% by value and 34% by volume.

By the mid-1970s, however, the East Asian NICs were beginning to displace their European rivals, while Japanese imports had virtually disappeared from the American market. Taiwan led the way, followed by South

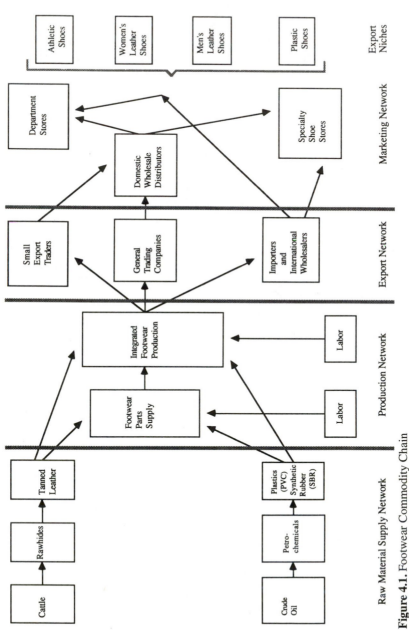

Figure 4.1. Footwear Commodity Chain
SOURCE: Gereffi and Korzeniewicz (1990).

Table 4.2 Major Sources of U.S. Nonrubber Footwear Imports, 1968-1989 (Millions of Pairs and Percentage Share of World Total)

	1968 Pairs	1968 %	1976 Pairs	1976 %	1981 Pairs	1981 %	1983 Pairs	1983 %	1985 Pairs	1985 %	1987 Pairs	1987 %	1989 Pairs	1989 %
Italy	59.0	33.7	47.2	12.7	50.1	13.3	56.3	9.7	74.7	8.8	47.7	5.1	41.7	4.8
Spain	14.2	8.1	38.7	10.5	18.9	5.0	26.7	4.6	55.5	6.6	28.2	2.9	22.6	2.6
Taiwan	15.3	8.7	155.7	42.1	118.5	31.6	243.4	41.8	372.5	44.2	427.0	45.5	262.1	30.5
South Korea	0.7	0.4	43.9	11.9	44.0	11.7	118.8	20.4	137.2	16.3	191.8	20.5	172.8	20.1
Brazil	a	0	26.7	7.2	43.0	11.5	64.4	11.1	113.2	13.4	108.2	11.6	112.8	13.1
China	a	0	0.8	0.2	7.1	1.9	7.2	1.2	20.8	2.5	47.3	5.1	143.5	16.7
All Other	86.1	49.1	57.0	15.4	94.0	25.0	65.1	11.2	68.8	8.2	87.5	9.3	104.9	12.2
World Total	175.3	100.0	370.0	100.0	375.6	100.0	581.9	100.0	842.7	100.0	937.7	100.0	860.4	100.0

SOURCE: U.S. Department of Commerce, Bureau of the Census, cited in Footwear Industries of America (1990).
NOTE: a. Less than 50,000 pairs.

Korea. In 1976, Taiwan exported 156 million pairs of nonrubber footwear to the United States, which represented 42% of total U.S. imports, more than triple the volume of Italy or South Korea, its closest competitors. The market position of the two East Asian NICs reached its zenith in 1987, when Taiwan and South Korea were supplying two thirds of U.S. nonrubber footwear imports (Table 4.2). Since the import share of the American footwear market has been more than 80% since 1985, this means that one out of every two pairs of shoes sold in the United States in 1987 was made in either Taiwan or South Korea.

In the early 1980s, Brazil emerged as a major shoe exporter to the United States, with China also entering the field in both rubber and nonrubber shoes by the end of the decade. In 1989, four nations—Taiwan, South Korea, China, and Brazil—accounted for more than 80% of all nonrubber footwear imports in the U.S. market (see Table 4.2).

This dramatic increase in the role of the East Asian and Latin American NICs in the American footwear market during the 1970s and 1980s is evidence of dynamic new sources of international competitiveness in this global industry. Mobility within the world-system is tied to a country's ability to upgrade its mix of core-peripheral economic activities. In order to advance in the world economy, countries typically strive to play a major role in those segments of commodity chains with the highest ratio of core to peripheral activities—that is, where the economic surplus is greatest.

The location of economic surplus in the footwear commodity chain is conditioned by four factors: labor, core and peripheral capital, the state, and economic organizations. First, footwear production is a relatively labor-intensive activity. Labor costs thus tend to drive the competitive strategies of footwear exporters, and are a major factor in explaining geographical shifts in the industry. Relatively inexpensive labor in the NICs is the key reason these nations acquired a significant cost advantage vis-à-vis core rivals like the United States and Italy. Since labor costs in the NICs (especially in East Asia) have been rising quite rapidly, however, these semiperipheral nations have had to select export niches which allow them to economize on labor and attain higher levels of value-added in the industry. This offers some measure of protection from cheap-labor footwear exporters like those in China, Mexico, and Thailand.

The connection between the cost of labor and its impact on the average value per pair of nonrubber shoes sold in the U.S. market can be seen in Table 4.3. For the three European nations (France, Italy, and Spain) and the United States, the relationship is quite direct: the higher the total hourly compensation (wages plus benefits) in the footwear industry in 1988, the higher

Table 4.3 Average Value per Pair of U.S. Imported Nonrubber Shoes and Overseas Wages in the Footwear Industry, 1988

Country	*Average Value Per Pair of Nonrubber Shoes Imported into the United States (in U.S. dollars)*	*Total Hourly Compensation in the Footwear Industry (in U.S. dollars)*
United States	16.75[a]	7.80[b]
France	31.19	11.08
Italy	18.55	9.77
Spain	15.48	5.52[c]
South Korea	10.83	1.71[b]
Brazil	8.42	0.65[d]
Taiwan	6.52	2.27[e]
Hong Kong	5.89	2.71
China	2.90	NA

SOURCE: Footwear Industries of America (1989, p. 4; 1990).
NOTES: a. Average factory price, cited in U.S. Department of Commerce (1990, pp. 36-46).
b. Nonrubber footwear.
c. Includes clothing and leather; 1987 data.
d. 1985 data.
e. Leather and leather products.
NA = Not available.

is the average value per pair of imported shoes. (This generalization also holds for the average factory price of domestically made shoes by U.S. manufacturers.) The linkage is less clear-cut for the NICs, however: Hong Kong and Taiwan have the highest levels of hourly compensation in the footwear industry ($2.71 and $2.27, respectively), followed by South Korea ($1.71) and Brazil ($0.65). Nonetheless, the average value per pair of imported shoes is greatest in South Korea ($10.83) and Brazil ($8.42), followed by Taiwan ($6.52), Hong Kong ($5.89), and China ($2.90). The most likely explanation for these discrepancies in the price/wage comparisons lies in the different export niches that each country occupies in the U.S. market, which will be discussed below, since these niches reflect diverse levels of value-added in the industry.

Second, the footwear industry requires a reconceptualization of the roles of core and peripheral capital in contemporary consumer-goods export industries in the world economy. The footwear industry is highly competitive at the international level, with little direct involvement by multinational corporations in the production and exporting of footwear. Local private capital, usually made up of small and medium-sized firms, is the principal actor in the footwear industry in the NICs.

Core capital does play a significant role, however, in the distribution and marketing stage of the footwear commodity chain. Unlike capital- and technology-intensive industries where multinational corporations frequently set up facilities for overseas production, core capital shapes the growth and evolution of the footwear industry in a more indirect way, mainly as a subcontractor and buyer of footwear made to the specifications of shoe companies and retail outlets in the United States.

The available information suggests that the most profitable segment of the footwear commodity chain is the distribution and marketing of shoes, rather than footwear production. The distributors' margins in the core countries are very large. In the United States, these margins averaged 50% in the mid-1970s, but were closer to 80% for imported goods. In Japan, "the price [of footwear] approximately doubles between the departure of the goods from the factory and their purchase by the consumer. The successive increases appear to be as follows: factory 55%, wholesaler 70%, and retailer 100%" (Organization for Economic Co-operation and Development, 1976, p. 39). A similar situation seems to prevail in Europe, where distribution costs amount to at least 100% of the manufacturers' price. The economic surplus that accrues to footwear distributors and retailers in core countries undoubtedly is much higher when production is done overseas rather than domestically.

Third, the state so far has maintained a relatively low profile in the footwear industry in both the semiperiphery and the core, contrary to the expectation in world-systems theory that semiperipheral states will play a leading role in upgrading the mix of core-peripheral economic activities. Within the semiperiphery, the state has no involvement in footwear production at all (in contrast to the prominence of state enterprises in heavy or strategic industries such as steel, oil, petrochemicals, and mining). The main impact of the state on manufactured exports from the NICs is in the area of exchange rate policies, export promotion schemes, and protection for domestic producers.

State policies in a core country like the United States are primarily important in terms of selectively restrictive trade measures such as tariffs, quotas, and other nontariff barriers that could impede footwear imports. In the footwear industry, for example, the United States established Orderly Marketing

Agreements (OMAs) with Taiwan and South Korea for a four-year period beginning in June 1977 (U.S. Department of Commerce, 1990, pp. 36-37). After the OMAs expired in 1981, imports from these two countries, which had declined during the OMA period, began to accelerate rapidly and by 1987 they had nearly quadrupled from their level of six years earlier (see Table 4.2).

Until recently, state policies in both the semiperiphery and the core have fostered a rapid expansion of footwear exports from the NICs. There is a growing perception, however, that the more or less open trading environment that has been supported by core states in the postwar world economy will become more closed. In particular, the favorable access to the U.S. consumer market on the part of East Asian manufacturers may be reduced as the geopolitical map of Asia is redrawn. An even more drastic scenario that has been mentioned is the possible emergence of regional trading blocs (Garten, 1989). This would fundamentally alter the role of the NICs in the world economy, and transform the structure of export-oriented industries like footwear.

Finally, the footwear industry demonstrates convincingly the importance of looking at economic organizations and other institutions within the NICs to explain their individual patterns of export success. Footwear firms in South Korea and Taiwan, for example, are quite different from one another in their organizational aspects, which reflects their distinct national industrial structures and social contexts. These contrasts help explain why these two nations have targeted diverse footwear export niches in the U.S. market, and why their future strategies in the industry are likely to vary.

In terms of size, the Taiwanese footwear industry is composed mainly of small firms, while the South Korean industry is dominated by very large companies. In Taiwan, the number of establishments with 500 workers or more comprised about 20% of value-added in the footwear sector in 1976; in South Korea, establishments of this size provided 90% of all footwear value-added (Levy, 1988). The relatively concentrated industrial structure in South Korea was enormously helpful in the mass-production of athletic footwear that followed the rapid boom in the demand for jogging shoes, and the entry of Nike into South Korea in 1976 and Reebok in the early 1980s. The Korean footwear sector has remained quite dependent on this one product (athletic footwear), however, which has shown cyclical patterns of growth. The smaller size of Taiwanese footwear producers, on the other hand, seems to have resulted in greater organizational flexibility that permits them to be responsive to design and fashion changes in core-country markets, and thus to respond more rapidly to shifting consumer preferences.

Export Niches in the U.S. Market

Export niches are segments or shares of world and national markets captured by firms of a single nationality within an industrial sector. The concept of export niches is a crucial analytical tool in understanding the trajectories of semiperipheral mobility. Export niches help explain how South Korea, Taiwan, Brazil, and China captured large shares of the American footwear market by specializing in products that were well suited to their raw material supply networks and domestic industrial capabilities.

The major export niches in the U.S. footwear market in 1989 are depicted in Table 4.4. (The term *export niche* is used because it helps to describe the distribution of exports by major footwear-producing nations, although from the vantage point of the United States these could also be called "import niches.") Men's leather footwear imports are quite widely distributed between Taiwan (19%), Brazil (16%), South Korea (14%), China (14%), and Italy (8%). A more pronounced division of labor emerges, however, when one looks at the average value of the men's leather footwear exported to the United States by each of these countries. The bulk of Italy's exports of men's leather shoes are in the most expensive "over $25" price category: Taiwan's and South Korea's men's leather footwear exports cluster in the $8 to $20 range; Brazil overlaps with the two East Asian NICs, but also has a large number of shoes whose average import value is $5 to $8; and China's exports are concentrated at the least expensive end of the price continuum, "not over $1.25" (FIA, 1989).

There are far higher levels of concentration by exporting countries in the other footwear niches identified in Table 4.4. Taiwan and China were the largest suppliers of vinyl or plastic footwear imports, with 49% and 31%, respectively, for men's shoes (not shown in the table); 68% and 24% for women's shoes; and 56% and 30% for juvenile footwear. South Korea accounted for nearly two thirds of the athletic leather footwear imported into the United States in 1989 and for almost one third of the juvenile leather shoes. The primary niche for Brazil was women's leather footwear (42% of total U.S. imports), while China was the largest exporter of rubber and fabric shoes (mainly sneakers) to the United States (50% of the total), followed by South Korea (18%) and Taiwan (11%).

In terms of the raw material supply networks highlighted in the global footwear commodity chain (see Figure 4.1), Italy, Spain, South Korea, and Brazil have all specialized in *leather* footwear, although the European producers have occupied the high-priced fashion shoe niches (especially Italy), South Korea an intermediate niche, and Brazil the lowest price ranges.

Table 4.4 Export Niches in the U.S. Footwear Market, 1989 (Thousands of Pairs and Percentage Share of Total World Imports)

Footwear Niches Country	Men's Leather		Women's Leather		Women's Vinyl/Plastic		Juvenile Leather		Juvenile Vinyl/Plastic		Athletic Leather		Rubber/Fabric	
	Pairs	%	Pairs	%	Pairs	%	Pairs	%	Pairs	%	Pairs	%	Pairs	%
Italy	5,014	7.7	25,630	11.5	1,685	1.1	5,770	12.9	298	0.4	1,061	0.7	NA	NA
Spain	3,620	5.6	14,115	6.4	335	0.2	2,670	6.0	286	0.4	104	0.1	NA	NA
Taiwan	12,196	18.8	24,529	11.1	103,998	67.5	5,746	12.8	38,471	56.4	27,417	17.2	20,619	10.9
South Korea	9,050	13.9	19,393	8.7	2,589	1.7	12,980	29.0	4,339	6.4	102,502	64.5	33,840	17.8
Brazil	10,419	16.1	92,388	41.6	609	0.4	7,148	16.0	628	0.9	1,117	0.7	NA	NA
China	8,859	13.6	22,170	10.0	37,656	24.5	4,408	9.9	20,766	30.4	8,736	5.5	95,252	50.1
All Other	15,764	24.3	23,864	10.7	7,152	4.6	5,991	13.4	3,463	5.1	17,919	11.3	40,345	21.2[a]
World Total	64,922	100.0	222,089	100.0	154,024	100.0	44,713	100.0	68,251	100.0	158,856	100.0	190,056	100.0
Export Niche Share[b]	[7.5]		[25.8]		[17.9]		[5.2]		[7.9]		[18.5]		c	

SOURCE: U.S. Department of Commerce, Bureau of the Census, cited in Footwear Industries of America (1989).

NOTES: a. Mexico has 12.4% and Hong Kong 4.1% of U.S. rubber/fabric footwear imports.

b. The bracketed percentages represent the share of each niche in total U.S. nonrubber footwear imports of 860.4 million pairs in 1989. These six niches account for 82.8% of total U.S. nonrubber footwear imports.

c. This niche covers what is not included in the nonrubber footwear market.

NA = Not available.

Taiwan and China have been the primary suppliers of *plastic* and *vinyl* shoes, while China also has been the main producer of *rubber* and *fabric* footwear. Thus footwear-manufacturing nations are trying to consolidate and upgrade their international market positions within as well as between different categories of footwear that have diverse raw material starting points. In order to be competitive in these product clusters, a country has to have an assured and high quality source of raw material supply. This is particularly problematic for shoe producers relying on leather inputs (see Korzeniewicz, 1990).

The empirical evidence presented above helps piece together several interesting "stories" about global footwear production in the 1970s and 1980s. The East Asian and Latin American NICs succeeded in capturing important segments of the U.S. market, but they did so in different ways (Gereffi & Korzeniewicz, 1990). *South Korean producers* captured an extraordinarily dynamic market for athletic footwear at the time when the fitness boom hit a peak in the United States. South Korean shoemakers showed an amazing ability to dominate a niche that in a few years grew to comprise about 20% of the overall U.S. footwear import market. *Taiwanese producers* captured a rapidly growing market that was already in place, that of plastic and vinyl shoes, and competed most directly with American producers. Taiwanese firms seem to have been more effective than other shoemakers in diversifying their exports into various footwear sectors. *Brazilian producers* showed a capacity to capture a very large niche in their exports of women's leather footwear, in effect cutting Italy's share of this product market by more than one half during the 1970s and 1980s. This is an impressive record, even if part of this outcome reflects Brazilian producers filling niches that the Italian footwear firms abandoned by moving to higher-value shoes. Finally, *Chinese producers* have been the most recent major entrant into the U.S. footwear market. They have targeted the least expensive end of the footwear spectrum, with an emphasis on rubber shoes and women's and children's types of vinyl footwear.

The fierce competition that has thrown continuous waves of new entrants into the American footwear market shows no signs of abating, despite the fact that the American consumer is not buying as many shoes as before. The per capita consumption of footwear in the United States, which peaked in 1986 at 4.9 pairs, has fallen to about 4.4 pairs in 1990 (Fischer, 1990, p. 26). Although this decline in consumption has been matched by a decline in imports which fell from their record high of 941 million pairs in 1986 to 860 million pairs in 1989, import penetration during these years has remained stable at just over 80%.

The established East Asian and Latin American footwear exporters are in the process of upgrading their product offerings, just as the European shoe-makers did over a decade ago, in order to stay ahead of the competition from lower cost footwear-producing nations. Much of the low-cost production of women's and children's vinyl shoes has shifted from Taiwan to China, for example, as Taiwan has consciously upgraded its product mix to leather-type footwear. This is because manufacturers generally have been able to achieve higher profit margins on leather footwear compared with shoes made from other materials. As a result, the average value per pair of imported nonrubber shoes from South Korea, which emphasized leather athletic footwear since the late 1970s, was 66% higher than that of Taiwan in 1989 ($10.83 and $6.52, respectively) (see Table 4.3). However, South Korea also has been affected by competition from lower-cost countries. Thailand and Indonesia have quadrupled and doubled, respectively, their footwear exports to the United States from 1988 to 1989 as branded athletic footwear importers began to shift their sources of supply from South Korea to lower-cost facto-ries in these countries (U.S. Department of Commerce, 1990).

Finally, while the Pacific Rim is certainly unparalleled among U.S. foot-wear sources, there is another quietly growing source in what might be called the "Atlantic Rim." While Brazil manufactures almost 85% of the U.S. foot-wear imports from Latin America, its exports have stagnated at around 110 million pairs since 1984. Mexico, the Dominican Republic, and Colombia have begun to grab larger shares of the U.S. market during the past five years, although they have started from much smaller bases (Fischer, 1990). A good deal of this production is shoes and slippers made from precut footwear parts exported from the United States for final assembly abroad. The finished products are then re-exported to the United States under Section 807 of the U.S. Tariff Schedule, in which duties are then assessed only on the value-added content.

Whether the East Asian and Latin American NICs will get closer to the core countries, or whether any of them will actually enter the core, ultimately depends on their capacity for technological and institutional innovation, and their ability to adjust to the changing opportunities and constraints in the international political economy. What succeeded in the past is no guarantee for the future. The openness of the U.S. market has been a key factor in the rapid economic growth of all the export-oriented NICs, especially those in East Asia. Continued easy access to the American market is very much in doubt, given the staggering trade deficits that confront the world's leading core nation. For the NICs to ascend in the world economy, they will have to find new ways to move to the most profitable end of commodity chains. This requires a fundamental shift from manufacturing in the semiperiphery to marketing in the core, a daunting task indeed.

Differentiating the Roles
of the NICs in the World Economy

The foregoing analysis of the Latin American and East Asian NICs allows us to identify a differentiated set of roles that semiperipheral nations play in the world economy. From the perspective of world-systems theory, these roles reflect the mix of core-peripheral economic activities in the NICs, as well as the significance of core and peripheral capital in carrying out these development efforts. The roles are not mutually exclusive, and their importance for a given country or set of countries may undergo fairly dramatic shifts over time. These roles in the world economy are largely determined by domestic conditions, such as the pattern of economic, social, and political organization within the NICs, and thus are not simply a response to the "needs" of core capital.

This framework focuses on export production in the NICs, since this is the best indicator of a country's international competitive advantage. The NICs can be characterized in terms of at least five basic types of international economic roles: (1) the commodity-export role; (2) the commercial-subcontracting role; (3) the export-platform role; (4) the component-supplier role; and (5) the independent-exporter role.

The *commodity-export role* is of prime importance for the Latin American NICs, where natural resources account for two thirds or more of total exports, and also for Singapore, which processes and re-exports a large volume of petroleum-related products. Peripheral capital controls many of these natural-resource industries at the production stage in Latin America, with the petroleum and mining industries usually being run by state-owned enterprises. The agricultural and livestock industries often are owned by local capital, although foreign-owned food-processing companies still predominate in many of Latin America's most profitable lines of commercial agriculture. In Singapore, TNCs are the proprietors of most of the petroleum-related industries. These commodity exports are sent to a wide range of nations, with the main share going to core countries. The export and distribution networks are usually controlled by core capital.

The next three types of roles in the world economy refer to various kinds of international subcontracting arrangements (see Holmes, 1986). The first major distinction is between "commercial subcontracting" in which the finished goods output of the subcontracting firms is sold to either a wholesaler or a retailer, and "industrial subcontracting" in which parts production is carried out for use by other manufacturing firms. Furthermore, there are two major types of industrial subcontracting: "export platforms" with an emphasis on foreign-owned, labor-intensive assembly operations; and "component-parts supply" in capital- and technology-intensive industries in the periphery.

The *commercial-subcontracting role* refers to the production of finished consumer goods by locally owned firms, where the output is distributed and marketed by large chain retailers and their agents (Holmes, 1986, p. 85). This is one of the major niches filled by the East Asian NICs in the contemporary world economy. In 1980, three of the East Asian NICs (Hong Kong, Taiwan, and South Korea) accounted for 72% of all finished consumer goods exported by the Third World to OECD countries, other Asian countries supplied another 19%, while just 7% came from Latin America and the Caribbean. The United States was the leading market for these products, with 46% of the total (Keesing, 1983, pp. 338-339). In East Asia, peripheral capital controls the production stage of the finished-consumer-goods commodity chains (see Gereffi, 1990; Haggard & Cheng, 1987), while core capital tends to control the more profitable export, distribution, and retail marketing stages. While the international subcontracting of finished consumer goods is growing in Latin America, it tends to be subordinated to the export-platform and component-supplier forms of production.

The *export-platform role* corresponds to those nations that have foreign-owned, labor-intensive assembly of manufactured goods in export-processing zones. These zones offer special incentives to foreign capital, and tend to attract firms in a common set of industries: garments, footwear, and electronics. Virtually all of the East Asian and Latin American NICs have engaged in this form of labor-intensive production, although its significance tends to wane as wage rates rise and countries become more developed. In Taiwan and South Korea, export-processing zones have been on the decline during the past 10 to 15 years, largely because labor costs have been rapidly increasing. These nations have been trying to upgrade their mix of export activities by moving toward more skill- and technology-intensive products. The export-platform role in Asia is now being occupied by low-wage countries like China, the Philippines, Thailand, Indonesia, and Malaysia.

In Latin America, on the other hand, export-platform industries are on the upswing because the wage levels in most countries of the region are considerably below those of the East Asian NICs, and recent currency devaluations in the Latin American NICs make the price of their exports more competitive internationally. The export platforms in Latin America also have the advantage of geographical proximity to the most important core-country markets in comparison with Asian export platforms. Mexico's *maquiladora* industry, which was set up in 1965 as an integral part of Mexico's Northern Border Industrialization Program, is probably the largest and most dynamic of these export areas. The *maquiladora* industry doubled its foreign-exchange earnings from 1982 ($850 million) to 1987 ($1.6 billion). In the latter year, *maquila* exports were Mexico's second largest source of foreign exchange, surpassed only by crude oil exports (see Carrillo-Huerta & Urquidi, 1989). There are similar zones in Brazil, Colombia, Central America, and the Caribbean. Core capital controls the production, export, and marketing stages of the commodity chains for these consumer goods. The main contribution of peripheral nations is cheap labor.

The *component-supplier role* refers to the production of component parts in capital- and technology-intensive industries in the periphery, for export and usually final assembly in the core country. This type of international industrial subcontracting has at least two important subcategories: (1) "capacity" (or concurrent) subcontracting, in which the parent firm and the subcontractor engage in the fabrication of similar products in order to handle overflow or cyclical demand; and (2) "specialization" (or complementary) subcontracting, in which the parts produced by the subcontractor are not made in-house by the parent firm. Whereas "capacity subcontracting" involves a horizontal disintegration of production, "specialization subcontracting" is a vertical disintegration of production (see Holmes, 1986, p. 86).

Component supply has been a key niche for the Latin American NICs' manufactured exports during the past two decades. Brazil and Mexico have been important production sites for vertically integrated exports by TNCs to core-country markets, especially the United States, since the late 1960s. This is most notable in certain industries like motor vehicles, computers, and pharmaceuticals (see Newfarmer, 1985). American, European, and Japanese automotive TNCs, for example, have advanced manufacturing facilities in Mexico and Brazil for the production of engines, auto parts, and even completed vehicles for the U.S., and European markets.

This pattern is a striking contrast to the earlier version of Japanese automobile production, pioneered by Toyota, in which manufacturing efficiency seemed to require highly integrated production networks with factories clustered within a few miles of one another in a vast urban-industrial complex such as Toyota City (Hill, 1987). As countries like Mexico have developed their own networks of reliable parts suppliers in the automobile industry, facilitated in part by the investments of foreign auto manufacturers, and as protectionist barriers have made it more difficult for major exporting nations to penetrate core-country markets from centralized production sites, highly dispersed yet still coordinated production and export networks linking geographically distant nations have emerged for a wide variety of consumer goods (see Uchitelle, 1990, for a detailed discussion of these new trends in Mexico).

In Latin America, the manufacturing stage of the commodity chain in component-supplier production typically is owned and run by core capital, sometimes in conjunction with a local partner. The export, distribution, and marketing of the manufactured items are handled by the foreign firm. A major advantage of this production arrangement is that it is the one most likely to result in a significant transfer of technology from the core nations.

In East Asia there are two variants of the component-supplier role. The first is similar to the Latin American arrangement in which *foreign subsidiaries* manufacture parts or subunits in East Asia for products like television sets, radios, sporting goods, and consumer appliances that are assembled and marketed in the country of destination (most often, the United States). The firms that engage in this form of subcontracting can be considered to be "captive" companies that supply the bulk of their production (usually in excess of 75%) to their parent corporation.

The second variant of the component-supplier role in East Asia involves production of components by *local firms* for sale to diversified buyers on the world market. These "merchant" producers, in contrast to the captive companies mentioned above, sell virtually all of their output on the open market (see Henderson, 1989, p. 169, fn. 1). The importance of merchant producers is illustrated in the semiconductor industry. South Korean companies have focused almost exclusively on the mass production of powerful memory chips, the single largest segment of the semiconductor industry, which are sold as inputs to a wide range of domestic and international manufacturers of electronic equipment. Taiwan, on the other hand, has targeted the highest value-added segment of the semiconductor market: tailor-made "designer chips" that perform special tasks in toys, video games, and other machines. Taiwan now has 40 chip-design houses that specialize in finding export niches, and then develop products for them ("Sizzling Hot Chips," 1988). While the South Korean companies are engaging in a form of "capacity subcontracting," the Taiwanese producers of specialty semiconductor chips represent a third form of industrial subcontracting known as "supplier sub-contracting." Here the subcontractor is "an independent supplier with full control over the development, design and fabrication of its product, but is willing to enter into a subcontracting arrangement to supply a dedicated or proprietary part to the parent [or purchasing] firm" (Holmes, 1986, p. 86). Taiwan, with its technological prowess, is acquiring the flexibility to move into the high value-added field of product innovation. However, without their own internationally recognized company brand names, a substantial advertising budget, and appropriate marketing and retail networks, Taiwan's ingenious producers will find it difficult to break free of the commercial-sub-contracting role. South Korea probably has more potential to enter core-country markets successfully because its large, vertically integrated industrial conglomerates (*chaebols*) have the capital and technology to set up overseas production facilities and marketing networks. Thus South Korea's leading auto manufacturer, Hyundai Motor Company, has become one of the top importers into both Canada and the United States since the mid-1980s (see Gereffi, 1990).

The fifth role in this typology is the *independent-exporter role*. This refers to finished-goods export industries in which there is no subcontracting relationship between the manufacturer and the distributor or retailer of the product. These goods can range from construction materials (like cement, lumber, and standard chemicals) to a wide variety of food, clothing, and electronics items (such as beer, watches, jewelry, radios, etc.).

This typology of the different roles that the Latin American and East Asian NICs play in the world economy shows that the standard development literature has presented an oversimplified picture of the semiperiphery. The East Asian NICs have been most successful in the areas of commercial subcontracting and component supply, with secondary and declining importance given to the export-platform role emphasized in the "new international division of labor" literature. The Latin American NICs, on the other hand, have a different kind of relationship to the world economy. They are prominent in the commodity-export, export-platform, and component-supplier forms of production, but they lag far behind the East Asian NICs in the commercial-subcontracting type of manufactured exports.

Although each of these roles has certain advantages and disadvantages in terms of mobility in the world system, the prospects for the NICs can only be understood by looking at the interacting sets of roles in which these nations are enmeshed. If development theory is to be relevant for the 1990s, it will have to become flexible enough to incorporate both increased specialization at the commodity and geographical levels, along with new patterns of regional and global integration.

Note

1. This section is adapted, in part, from Gereffi and Korzeniewicz, 1990.

References

Carrillo-Huerta, Mario, & Urquidi, Victor L. (1989). *Trade deriving from the international division of production: Maquila and postmaquila in Mexico.* Unpublished manuscript, El Colegio de México, Mexico City.

Council for Economic Planning and Development (CEPD). (1988). *Taiwan statistical data book, 1988.* Taipei, Taiwan.

Fischer, John. (1990, August). Per capita consumption affects imports and domestic production. *American Shoemaking,* pp. 26-27.

Footwear Industries of America. (1989). Quarterly report, 4th quarter 1989. *Statistical Reporter.* Washington, DC: Footwear Industries of America.

Footwear Industries of America. (1990, February 27). *Nonrubber footwear industry in the United States: Fact sheet.* Washington, DC: Footwear Industries of America.

Garten, Jeffrey E. (1989). Trading blocs and the evolving world economy. *Current History,* 88(534), 15-56.

Gereffi, Gary. (1989a). Development strategies and the global factor. *Annals of the American Academy of Political and Social Science, 505,* pp. 92-104.

Gereffi, Gary. (1989b). Rethinking development theory: Insights from East Asia and Latin America. *Sociological Forum, 4*(4), pp. 505-533.

Gereffi, Gary. (1990). Big business and the state. In G. Gereffi & D. Wyman (Eds.), *Manufacturing miracles: Paths of industrialization in Latin America and East Asia.* Princeton, NJ: Princeton University Press.

Gereffi, Gary. (1991). International economics and domestic policies. In Neil J. Smelser & Alberto Martinelli (Eds.), *Economy and society: State of the art* (pp. 231-258). Newbury Park, CA: Sage.

Gereffi, Gary, & Korzeniewicz, Miguel. (1990). Commodity chains and footwear exports in the semiperiphery. In William Martin (Ed.), *Semiperipheral states in the world-economy* (pp. 45-68). Westport, CT: Greenwood Press.

Gereffi, Gary, & Wyman, Donald. (Eds.). (1990). *Manufacturing miracles: Paths of industrialization in Latin America and East Asia.* Princeton, NJ: Princeton University Press.

Haggard, Stephan, & Cheng, Tun-jen. (1987). State and foreign capital in the East Asian NICs. In Frederic C. Deyo (Ed.), *The political economy of the new Asian industrialism* (pp. 84-135). Ithaca, NY: Cornell University Press.

Harris, Nigel. (1987). *The end of the Third World.* New York: Penguin.

Henderson, Jeffrey. (1989). *The globalisation of high technology production: Society, space and semiconductors in the restructuring of the modern world.* London: Routledge.

Hill, Richard Child. (1987). Global factory and company town: The changing division of labor in the international automobile industry. In Jeffrey Henderson & Manuel Castells (Eds.), *Global restructuring and territorial development* (pp.18-37). Newbury Park, CA: Sage.

Holmes, John. (1986). The organization and locational structure of production subcontracting. In Allen J. Scott & Michael Storper (Eds.), *Production, work, and territory: The geographical anatomy of industrial capitalism* (pp. 80-106). Boston: Allen & Unwin.

Hopkins, Terence K., & Wallerstein, Immanuel. (1986). Commodity chains in the world-economy prior to 1800. *Review, 10*(1), 157-170.

Keesing, Donald. (1982). *Exporting manufactured consumer goods from developing to developed economies: Marketing by local firms and effects of developing country policies.* Mimeo. Washington, DC: World Bank.

Keesing, Donald. (1983). Linking up to distant markets: South to north exports of manufactured consumer goods. *American Economic Review, 73,* 338-342.

Korzeniewicz, Miguel. (1990). *The social foundations of international competitiveness: Footwear exports in Argentina and Brazil.* Unpublished doctoral dissertation, Duke University.

Levy, Brian. (1988). *Transaction costs, the size of firms, and industrial policy: Lessons from a comparative study of the footwear industry in Korea and Taiwan.* Research Memorandum Series. Williamstown, MA: Williams College.

Newfarmer, Richard. (Ed.). (1985). *Profits, progress and poverty: Case studies of international industries in Latin America.* Notre Dame, IN: University of Notre Dame Press.

Organization for Economic Co-operation and Development (OECD). (1976). *The footwear industry: Structure and governmental policies.* Paris: OECD.

Shaiken, Harley, with Stephen Herzenberg. (1987). *Automation and global production: Automobile engine production in Mexico, the United States, and Canada.* Monograph Series, 26. La Jolla: University of California, San Diego, Center for U.S.-Mexican Studies.

Sizzling hot chips: Asia is the source of the semiconductor industry's spectacular growth. (1988, August 18). *Far Eastern Economic Review,* pp. 80-86.

Uchitelle, Louis. (1990, September 25). Mexico's plan for industrial might. *The New York Times,* pp. C1-C2.

United Nations. (1989). *1987 International trade statistics yearbook, Vol. 1.* New York: United Nations.

United States Department of Commerce. (1990). Leather and leather products. *1990 U.S. Industrial Outlook.* Washington, DC: Bureau of the Census.

World Bank. (1987). *World development report 1987.* New York: Oxford University Press.

World Bank. (1988). *World development report 1988.* New York: Oxford University Press.

World Bank. (1990). *World development report 1990.* New York: Oxford University Press.

PART II

ECONOMIC POLICY

In Part II we examine further the interplay of state policy and economic development through four case studies—two of Korea, one of Malaysia, and one of Japan.

In Chapter 5, Hagen Koo and Eun Mee Kim focus on the relationship between state policy and capital accumulation in South Korea. The strong Korean state, Koo and Kim argue, has been largely autonomous from civil society, and therefore has been able to exert significant control over both domestic and foreign capital in the interests of spurring economic development. In examining the ways in which the Korean state helped to secure accumulation for the large *chaebols* (conglomerates), Koo and Kim look at differing policies during four phases of postwar Korean history: U.S. assisted import substitution during the 1950s; EOI based on cheap labor during the 1960s; "industrial deepening" in exports combined with import substitution in the 1970s; and the liberalization and globalization of the Korean economy during the past decade.

During the 1950s, the war-devastated Korean economy was highly dependent on U.S. military and economic assistance. Although the Rhee dictatorship was more concerned with U.S.-funded military buildup than with economic development, the preconditions for development were nonetheless established. Land reform virtually eliminated the landlord class, paving the way for a fairly open class structure. Japanese properties, and state owned enterprises and banks, were privatized and turned over to the Korean ruling elite, giving birth to today's Korean capitalist class. By the time a worker-student uprising toppled the Rhee regime in 1960, the economy was already beset by inflation, unemployment, and a decline in U.S. economic aid.

113

After a brief democratic interlude, Park Chung Hee's 1961 military coup launched a state-controlled "development decade" that he would oversee for twice that long. Elaborating on Castells and Harris, Koo and Kim's historical analysis shows that a primary objective of economic growth was to secure the legitimacy of Park's military regime (as well as fund it, in the face of declining U.S. military aid). This established a long-lasting alliance between capital and the military, an alliance that has left its stamp on the Korean economy. Koo and Kim argue that "guided capitalism" became the Park regime's "sacred mission." Given the historic weakness of civil society in Korea, the regime possessed the necessary autonomy to pursue its growth objectives. Through a series of five-year development plans, encouraged by foreign advisors from the International Monetary Fund (IMF) and the U.S. Agency for International Development, exports emerged as a key component of Korea's growth objectives. Export and currency policies were liberalized, and relations with Japan were normalized, partially opening the door to Japanese investment. Domestic private investment was steered toward the export sector by means of tight credit controls and artificially maintained below-market interest rates. Economic performance—as well as political connections (see Chon's detailed analysis in the next chapter)—dictated who received subsidized capital. Despite abuses (for example, land and credit speculation), these policies resulted in substantial private investment in both export and import substitution industries.

By the end of the 1960s, the limits of this approach had been reached. Firms found themselves increasingly in debt, resulting in an increasing number of bankruptcies; unemployment rose; and IMF-imposed austerity measures contributed to mounting student and worker unrest. Park responded to the impending crisis by issuing a series of emergency statutes that severely curtailed the right of labor to organize, strike, and even bargain. By 1972, he had declared himself lifetime president with unchecked powers. By a series of decrees he forgave a great deal of the accumulated private debt. The *chaebols* were protected from their creditors, providing a new foundation for growth at the expense of both finance capital and the thousands of middle class families involved in money lending. With the Heavy and Chemical and Industrialization Plan in 1973, Park also began to deemphasize the increasingly uncertain cheap labor approach to exports that Korea had pursued. Economic growth, achieved by investment in heavy industry, would secure domestic peace. The *chaebols* grew in strength, and substantial international investment flowed into Korea by the end of the decade. Exporting became the monopoly of a handful of government-licensed conglomerate giants who were able to finance their export activities through cheap government loans. By the end of the 1970s, rising debt, declining exports, and inflation threatened this economic success. An austerity response triggered labor unrest. As strikes spread across the country, Park was assassinated by the head of the Korean CIA in 1979. A broad alliance of workers, farmers, small business people, and the middle class—the *Min Jung* (People's) movement—mobilized support against the *chaebols* during the early 1980s. A 1979 military coup by Major General Chun Doo Hwan led to demonstrations and bloody repression. Lacking in legitimacy, the Chun government, as had its predecessor, sought legitimacy through economic expansion.

Economic growth was stabilized, limited welfare programs were introduced, and workers' wages were frozen. Although government economic policies were directed at promoting the growth of small and medium size firms, the *chaebols* have continued to grow in size and strength, fueled by growing exports and favorable international trade conditions. This economic success of the *chaebols* during the past decade has strengthened their position vis-à-vis the Korean state, while creating "new class forces"—the middle and working classes. As the strength of the *Min Jung* has increased along with the power of the *chaebols,* the relative autonomy of the developmental state has declined. Whether this will undermine development in the future remains to be seen.

In Chapter 6, Soohyun Chon extends the analysis of the relationship between politics and development in Korea, focusing specifically on the geographical origins of the developmental elite. She first shows that economic development in Korea has been uneven among the various regions of the country. Per capita income, for example, is highest in the southeastern provinces. There has been a significant redistribution in recent years in manufacturing employment from the Cholla provinces to rapidly growing provinces such as Kyonggi and Kyongsang. Historically, the Cholla provinces formed the seat of Korea's prosperous agricultural economy. But, with the shift to heavy industrial production described in the previous chapter, the economic fortunes of that region have declined relative to other areas of the country. Furthermore, while the Cholla provinces were at one time the rice bowl of Korea, urbanization has favored dry crops (fruit and vegetables) over rice production, resulting in geographical shifts that have been reinforced by investment in transportation and other infrastructure.

Industrial growth has occurred primarily in the northwest and southeast portions of the country. Textiles and precision machinery, two engines of Korea's rapid economic development, were found initially in Kyongsang and in the Seoul-Kyonggi provinces, although they have subsequently dispersed from these two provinces to adjacent areas. Chon explains the geographical concentration of specific industries as resulting from the logic of EOI pursued by the Park government. While government incentives encouraged exports, other policies promoted the import of intermediate products that could be used as inputs into the export-oriented industries. This simultaneous promotion of exports and imports required that industries locate themselves near ports as well as near sources of cheap labor. South Korea—like Hong Kong, Singapore, Taiwan, and Japan—is a relatively small country in which few areas are distant from the shoreline, an obvious advantage in a world where economic growth is dictated by the growth of external markets. According to Chon, "the geography of ports largely determines the location of industries" along the southeast and eastern coasts, with Pusan—the closest Korean port to Japan—emerging as the chief port. This geographical specialization was encouraged by railroads and express highways that linked Pusan with Seoul.

But economic and geographic factors are not the only explanations for the uneven geographical distribution of development in Korea. The internal politics of development amplified these patterns. Two out of the three presidents since Park have had geographic origins in the Kyongsang provinces. To legitimate his 1961 coup, Park sought to build a broad power base along classical Korean lines—"school, clan, and geographical affiliation." Park's close geographical ties with the north Kyongsang provinces reinforced the political power of a region that had historically been over-represented in prominent positions in government and industry. Chon shows that top-ranking officials as well as industrialists are disproportionately drawn from Seoul, with the Kyongsang provinces second. State development policies focused on particular favored industries rooted in the Kyongsang provinces—a pattern that was reinforced by intermarriage among the political, military, and economic elites.

Yet this pattern of geographical concentration may be undermined by the very success of Korean economic development. Because of skyrocketing real estate prices, the government now plans to disperse infrastructure and economic activities, with many of the new high technology industries to be located along the west coast. Such dispersal should also help to legitimate the Korean government, in the face of popular dissatisfaction over the geographical maldistribution of the fruits of economic development. Just as economic development now threatens the historical autonomy of a state that sought to legitimate itself through development (see Koo and Kim, Chapter 5), so it challenges the legitimacy of excessively spatially concentrated industrial development.

In Chapter 7, Paul Lubeck addresses the question of the "replicability" of the "East Asian model," focusing on the experience of Malaysia. Unlike the "four tigers," Malaysia has an ethnically heterogeneous social structure with a strong Muslim component, and is seeking export-driven industrialization a generation later—during a time of sluggish growth in the world economy when the competition for exports is fierce. To some degree, Malaysia fits the economic model of the developmental state: it has achieved impressive average annual growth rates of 7%-9%, relatively high per capita income, and has devoted a significant proportion of its economy to such export-oriented manufacturing as electronic components. At the same time, exports have been fueled by cheap labor, although in recent years labor shortages have encouraged illegal (although tolerated) immigration by as many as a million workers from Indonesia and other neighboring countries.

Malaysia's New Economic Policy (NEP)—instituted in 1971—was designed to incorporate the indigenous (Bumiputera) peoples—primarily Malays—into economic growth, promoting interethnic harmony through equalizing economic control among the Chinese, Malay, and other ethnic groups. Yet despite its seemingly impressive performance, Lubeck argues, the Malaysian economy masks structural weaknesses and deep ethnic divisions that distinguish it from the other East Asian NICs. Despite substantial government expenditure, globally competitive national industries have failed to develop; exporters are supplied by multinationals from Japan and other East Asian countries rather than indigenous firms. The key difficulty can be traced to ethnic separation between political and economic power: despite two decades of NEP, the Chinese continue to dominate business, while the Malays control the state, often acting as a comprador bourgeoisie in relationship to foreign capital while jealously seeking to control indigenous Chinese business growth.

Lubeck traces the historical roots of ethnic identities and cleavages to the ethnic division of labor imposed by British colonialism, which utilized "scientific" racial theories to allocate the "industrious" Chinese to business and trade activities, the "docile" Indians to rubber plantation labor, and the "indolent" but "courteous" Malays to farming (rice production). This stratification system reinforced pre-existing economic roles, contributing to a stereotyping that remains strong today.

Furthermore, unlike Japanese colonial policy in Korea and Taiwan—which destroyed the large landowning class, thereby paving the way for industrialization—the British supported the Malay feudal aristocracy, bringing it directly into colonial administration. As a result, Lubeck concludes, the bourgeoisie today remains weak relative to the rentier Malay administrative class, which—comfortably housed within the state bureaucracy—lacks both the temperament and history to function as a developmental state. It is this historical legacy that accounts for the "weak state technocratic impulse" whereby the Muslim aristocracy continues to wield enormous power, "blocking avenues of capitalist development for commoner Malays."

Why, after 20 years of NEP, have neither the Chinese nor the Malays overcome this historical legacy? Lubeck rejects cultural explanations that locate the explanation in the absence of a Confucian value system among the Muslim Malays, or a weakened Confucianism among the Chinese, many of whom also derive income as rentiers rather than industrialists. Rather, he argues, it is state industrial policy itself—which makes possible the amassing of fortunes without developing an indigenous industrial base—that is responsible. Lubeck argues that Islam is elsewhere associated with the rise of merchant capitalism, and that Muslim texts could well be reinterpreted to provide the basis for a highly equitable form of economic development, if political institutions favored such a reinterpretation. For the present, however, lacking "the confidence of the Chinese industrialists or a confident Malay class of industrialists," the country must continue to depend on foreign investment for its growth.

What does the future hold? Rapid demographic shifts favoring the Malay population, combined with growing income inequality, may exacerbate economic strains and undermine the NEP. While ethnic polarization is one possible outcome, a rethinking of the present arrangements is another. Some advisors are already calling for deep economic restructuring, promoting indigenous firms to support the export-oriented economy. There are strong pressures to encourage industrial development independent of ethnicity; whether these will prove sufficient to overcome the resistance of political elites remains to be seen. Until the Malaysian state fully commits itself to a broadly based development effort, however, it cannot be termed "developmental" along the lines of the other East Asian NICs.

In Chapter 8, Haruhiro Fukui offers some reflections on the role of the Japanese state that provide important insights into the nature of state-driven capitalism in the "four tigers." Fukui argues that Japanese capitalism is an "unorthodox and deviant" form, one that has muted class differences and emphasized national purpose and unity, a pattern that is repeated to varying degrees in the East Asian NICs.

Japanese capitalism has its roots in the strongly nationalistic and paternalistic Meiji Restoration of the mid-nineteenth century. The renegade samurai who led the revolt against the Tokugawa shogunate were determined to protect Japanese independence from Western colonialism. This they hoped to achieve through rapid industrialization and military power. The state sought to promote a high degree of domestic harmony and consensus, both through promotion of the emperor cult and the suppression of all opposition, particularly class-based politics: Marxist ideologies were banned, and socialist parties, leftist unions, and labor movements in general were ruthlessly suppressed. At the same time, industrial harmony was promoted through corporatist legislation that provided minimal protections for workers. These are all avenues that have been well-traveled in the East Asian NICs.

Furthermore, Fukui argues, systematic indoctrination of youth into the Shintoist emperor cult and Confucianist beliefs in state loyalty helped to promote national harmony and unity. Shinto became the state religion, and was self-consciously used to promote allegiance to the state; public pronouncements extolled the Confucian virtues of unity, family loyalty, and moral conduct. Mass public education inculcated these values, as children were taught to be "loyal, cooperative, and industrious, as well as literate and able workers in the service of the state." Nationalist values were guaranteed by strict state controls over curriculum and materials at the primary and secondary school levels, designed to assure appropriate "moral education." Youth groups and other organizations were formed with a similar intent.

In the industrial sector, unions were either incorporated into industry or destroyed. Thanks to literate, hard-driving, and nationalistic workers, manufacturing accounted for nearly one third of GDP by World War II, and annual growth rates exceeding 5% had already been achieved. Following the war growth continued and accelerated, despite (and perhaps because of) sweeping postwar reforms dictated by the armistice. These reforms banned ultranationalism and the emperor cult, democratized the educational system, assured freedom of assembly and speech, and guaranteed the right to organize and unionize. But these postwar changes did not seriously challenge the more moderate forms of nationalism, nor the Japanese psychological hostility to divisive ideologies. In fact, unionization, emancipation of women, and the opening up of the educational system all served to mute class-based ideologies. Undoubtedly, this is partly attributable to the emergence of a vast middle class (more than 90% of Japanese so identify), and partly through an educational system that stubbornly remains conservative, having successfully contained efforts by its often leftist teachers to introduce class-based materials into the classroom.

Perhaps nowhere is the defeat of class-based ideology more apparent than in the corporatist quality circle (QC) that is widely viewed as the hallmark of Japanese industry. Like many Japanese products, the QC is an American import that has thrived in Japanese factories, now reaching as much as 40% of the work force. They account in part for the high levels of productivity and quality in Japanese factories, as well as a leveling of all employees to common standards and commitments. This "groupism" actively promotes loyalty to the firm (and strongly discourages disloyalty as well)— loyalty reinforced by lifetime employment guarantees and seniority-based promotion and wage systems.

Despite its apparent success, Japanese capitalism—like that in the East Asian NICs—is presently undergoing significant changes. First, like capitalism elsewhere, it is becoming internationalized, as high labor costs, protectionism, and the appreciation of the yen have driven Japanese capital abroad. Of these three factors, protectionism is probably the decisive factor: growth in Japanese foreign investment has been especially rapid in North America and Europe, where hourly wage gains have been even more rapid than those in Japan. Capital flight has not led to unemployment, however; on the contrary, a severe labor scarcity exists in Japan, a problem addressed in part by a growing reliance on cheap immigrant labor. Whether Japanese firms on foreign soil can continue to retain their highly corporatist orientation is doubtful.

Second, lifetime employment and pay systems are experiencing difficulties. Always restricted to a minority of employees, the system depended on a much larger pool of part-time or temporary labor, typically women whose wages are slightly more than half those of their male counterparts. Japanese production also consists of elaborate networks of much smaller subcontractors who do not enjoy the same corporatist protections as are provided in the large industries. Even within the latter, however, lifetime security guarantees and seniority-based pay schemes have declined significantly recent years.

Third, despite continuing increases in real wages, the current real estate boom has threatened to undermine the consuming power of Japanese workers. Rampant real estate speculation has ballooned prices to a point where few workers can afford to buy apartments. High consumer prices—among the highest in the industrial world—also threaten to undermine workers' gains. Upsets in the July 1989 elections, where the long-dominant LDP suffered significant reversals, portend difficulties in the near future.

Fukui concludes that despite Japan's phenomenal success in creating one of the most rapidly growing and economically egalitarian industrial economies in the world, there are nonetheless problems below the surface that will likely change the nature of "Japanese-style capitalism" during the last decade of this century. We can add to this conclusion the observation that similar difficulties are likely to surface in the "four tigers" that are pursuing the Japanese model. As we have seen in Chapters 2, 3, 5, and 6, strong development states secured rapid growth through a variety of economic interventions, social policies, and labor controls, yet the extraordinary success of these policies now threatens to undermine the authority of state power. In Part III of this book, we turn directly to these issues, examining the social and labor policies that undergirded the East Asian development model.

5

The Developmental State and Capital Accumulation in South Korea

HAGEN KOO

EUN MEE KIM

By now there is no serious disagreement among scholars about an important role played by the state in the economic development of developing countries. The state is more than "brought back in." In fact, the statist perspective appears to be quickly establishing itself as a major paradigm in the development literature, spawning a large body of empirical work that seeks to explain economic development in the Third World, especially in East Asia, in terms of state intervention in the economy. At the center of these analyses is the developmental state—the state that intervenes in the economy in a positive way, in a "market-promoting" or "market-sustaining" way rather than in a "market-distorting" way.

A developmental state is most commonly defined by two characteristics: (1) its autonomy from societal forces—its economic bureaucracy can devise long-term economic policies without interference from private interests, and (2) its strength or capacity to implement economic policies effectively—the state can exercise a large measure of control over the behaviors of domestic and foreign capital (Haggard, 1990; Johnson, 1982, 1987; Wade, 1990). But as the concept becomes widely used in the development literature, the exact meaning of *developmental state* becomes increasingly vague and elusive. Not only do these concepts of state autonomy and strength involve variable empirical referents, but also the specific connections between these attributes of the state and development outcomes are unclear (Haggard & Moon,

1990; Moon, 1989). Furthermore, these concepts are often used in a somewhat tautological fashion, equating economic success to state strength post factum, or even measuring state strength by its presumed outcome.

It seems increasingly clear that in order for the statist perspective to move ahead, it must resist a temptation for reification and seek to develop theoretical specification based on grounded empirical analyses of the complex interactions among the state, market, and societal forces. The most critical void in the current literature on development is the lack of knowledge about the specific ways in which *political processes* circumscribe the nature and the behavior patterns of a developmental state.

The major aim of this chapter is to provide an analysis of the specific ways in which the South Korean developmental state has shaped the capital accumulation process in interactions with economic and political actors in the changing international and domestic economic environments. Several excellent studies of the South Korean political economy are available (Amsden, 1989; Cheng, 1991; Cole & Lyman, 1971; Haggard, 1990; Haggard & Moon, 1990; Jones & Sakong, 1980; S. K. Kim, 1987; Koo, 1987; Woo, 1990). The objective of this study is more specific, that is, to analyze the process of capital accumulation by focusing on the interactions between the state and capital. The analytic focus is on the process of capital accumulation rather than the general character of the South Korean political economy or the institutional character of the Korean developmental state. In this analysis, the developmental state is taken not simply as a *structure* but as a *process,* and not simply as an economic process but also as a political process. An important objective of the analysis is to examine *how* and for what specific *purposes* state managers use state organizations in the process of economic development. Thus we pay close attention to political processes as much as economic processes of development. By focusing our attention on the process of capital accumulation rather than economic growth, we can get closer to these dynamic processes of economic development.

Since its birth in 1948, South Korea has pursued four stages of economic development: (1) import-substitution industrialization (ISI) based on U.S. economic aid in the 1950s; (2) export-oriented industrialization (EOI) based on labor-intensive, light manufacturing in the 1960s; (3) industrial deepening along with export-oriented industrialization with selective use of ISI in the 1970s; and (4) liberalization and internationalization of the economy in the 1980s. Each stage is characterized by a particular kind of development strategy, state-economy relations, and development alliances. Thus our analysis follows through these four stages, attempting to isolate interesting patterns in the political economy of South Korean capital accumulation, with special attention to the dynamics of the state and the chaebol.[1]

The 1950s

After coming out of political and economic chaos in the postindependence period and the highly devastating Korean War (1950-1953), the South Korean economy more or less survived on the basis of U.S. economic and military aid in the 1950s. Between 1953 and 1961, the United States gave more than $4 billion in economic and military aid (Mason et al., 1980, p. 182). It was these foreign aids that determined not only the development strategy of the Rhee regime, but also the entire economic and social structures of Korea during the 1950s. Although this period is characterized by import-substitution industrialization, this was actually not a strategic choice of the state but was largely a response to the economic exigencies of the period. Preoccupied with domestic politics to maintain his ever decaying power, Rhee gave no systematic attention to economic development. Had there existed any strategic choice by Rhee, it was aid maximization, to squeeze as much economic and military aid possible from the United States by skillfully manipulating U.S. security interest in the peninsula (Cole & Lyman, 1971; Woo, 1990). The unrealistically overvalued exchange rates and other financial policies adopted during this period clearly reflected Rhee's primary interest in aid maximization.

While the economy drifted along with ISI, a few important economic changes took place during the Rhee period that were to have a serious impact on later development. The first was land reform, carried out in 1948-1950, which drastically changed the Korean class structure. There are many conflicting evaluations of this land reform. Many Korean scholars define it as a failure, because the reform measures passed by the landlord-dominated national assembly were far too moderate and because the implementation had been delayed so long that landlords had enough time to hide and sell their land. Nonetheless, the land reform achieved something only few nations in the world have done: the virtual elimination of the landlord class, and the creation of a relatively egalitarian class structure.

The second important change was the distribution of Japanese-owned properties (land, property, and production facilities) and privatization of state-owned enterprises and later state-owned banks. All these properties were distributed, at extremely low prices, to the individuals who had close political connections with the ruling elites. Practically, this was the origin of the modern-day Korean capitalist class. Having acquired these properties, many "political capitalists" further used their political connections to accumulate in well-protected import-substitution industries with privileged access to cheap U.S. dollars and aid materials (K. D. Kim, 1976). On his part, Rhee fostered these ties in order to squeeze maximum political funds, allowing widespread rent-seeking activities among leading businesspersons.

The downfall of the Rhee regime came in April 1960 with the uprising of the students, joined by workers and urban middle-class citizens, against the rigged presidential election. But even before this student revolution, the regime had been reaching its economic limits, caused by the exhaustion of ISI, the spiralling rates of inflation and unemployment, and most important, a drastic curtailment of U.S. economic aid.

After the fall of Rhee, the first democratic government was formed under the leadership of Chang Myon. Chang inherited the ill-managed economy with enormous economic problems, and he faced inordinate expectations for an immediate delivery of economic welfare and political democracy. Yet, comprised as it was of old opposition politicians with conservative class interests and no clear political or economic vision, the new regime was indecisive and slow in developing any coherent program to attack economic and social problems. The continuing economic difficulties combined with political instability invited a military coup on May 16, 1961. Korea's new economic era began with the emergence of the military regime.

The 1960s

Park Chung Hee, who led the coup and became a supreme ruler for the next two decades, distinguished himself from his two predecessors in terms of his strong commitment to economic development. He justified the coup in terms of the urgent need to "rescue the nation from the brink of starvation" as well as to defend it from the communist threats. A nation of wealth and power was not merely a political slogan but also his "dream," his firm conviction. No sooner had he captured the state power than he took bold steps to push the development plans.

A son of a poor farmer, with a strong anti-urban ideology, Park instantly relieved farmers of their private debts, guaranteed higher prices to farmers through subsidies, and created banks to allocate more funds to agricultural and small-to-medium businesses. More significantly, the junta arrested leading businesspersons on charges of "illicit wealth accumulation" during previous regimes, with full intention to punish them. Yet, very soon Park turned around completely, pardoning those arrested in exchange for economic cooperation. He asked them to participate in his ambitious industrialization projects as leading entrepreneurs, and subsequently allocated to them the bulk of foreign and domestic capital along with many other trade and tax privileges. This is the second time these large merchant capitalists (already called *chaebol* in the 1950s) escaped this accusation of "illicit wealth accumulation"; they had been convicted on the same charge during the Chang regime. This time, however, they not only escaped the crisis, but also found golden opportunities to prosper.

It was this narrow development alliance between the military regime and select large capitalists that eventually shaped the capital accumulation process during the period of export-oriented industrialization. Why did the Park regime forge this narrow developmental alliance rather than a broader "distributional alliance," as was the case in Taiwan, for example, that pursued a similar strategy of export-oriented industrialization? There are several reasons, but the most important was the urgent need of the military junta to establish its political legitimacy and consolidate its power. Park sought to achieve these goals by delivering impressive economic growth, and he believed that the quickest and the most reliable way to do this was by collaborating with the already proven group of large capitalists. This collaboration was also a convenient means to solve an immediate need of the military junta to raise a large sum of political funds to institutionalize its rule—the Democratic Republican Party and the Korean Central Intelligence Agency. Thus this "sword-won alliance" was the product of political exigencies and the existing class structure. The presence of a group of large capitalists with sizeable capital and organizational resources and entrepreneurial skills, a product of the previous period of accumulation, limited the choices of the new state elites—and thereby affected the capital accumulation process in the new stage. Once formed, this alliance had a lasting effect on the evolution of the Korean economy.

One of the most remarkable achievements of the Park leadership in the first years of its coming to power was the swift reorganization of the state structure into the so-called developmental state. He overhauled the bureaucracy, purging hundreds of corrupt and incompetent bureaucrats; he created the Economic Planning Board (EPB), a central economic decision-making agency with a large degree of autonomy from private interests and other agencies; and he restructured the financial system by nationalizing banks and bringing the central bank (The Bank of Korea) under the authority of the Ministry of Finance. Economic development was taken as the most important goal, a sacred mission, of the state, by which the power holders hoped to be judged by the people as to their right to rule. The regime's guiding economic philosophy was not really a free market economy, but a "guided capitalism."

Park's strong economic orientation, as he acknowledged himself, was shaped by his biographical background. But a more important reason is a structural one. As mentioned above, the 1950s was the period of enormous economic hardship and growing political instability arising from high unemployment and runaway inflation; it was also accompanied by widespread political discontent. As Cole and Lyman (1971) suggest, no one who came to power in the 1960s could ignore the huge popular demand for economic well-being. Park correctly perceived it and attempted to base his political legitimacy on economic performance.

State rulers' motivations and ideologies, however, explain only part of the emergence of a developmental state. A developmental state is a state that has a considerable amount of autonomy to adopt policies without interference from class interests and a capacity to implement these policies effectively. Fortunately, the Park regime inherited a state structure that had stood historically above the civil society, with an enormous amount of coercive capacity based on large police and military forces. The civil society, on the other hand, was weak and relatively undifferentiated, with no powerful class. In short, the historical conditions of state-society relations in Korea were amenable to the transformation of the Korean state into a developmental state. Given these structural preconditions, a critical variable that was required to transform a non-developmental state into a developmental one was the ideology, interest, and motivation of those who captured state power.

While restructuring the state structure, Park was anxious to move ahead with development plans. He ordered the technocrats to develop the first Five-Year Economic Development Plan, which they did by adapting an earlier plan adopted by the Chang Myon regime. The stated goal of the plan was to create a "self-reliant economy by terminating the previous aid-dependent and consumption-oriented structure." The plan selected 22 priority projects in such industries as electricity, fertilizer, oil-refining, synthetic fiber, and cement. Clearly, the policy priority was on import-substitution industries, not export industries. The government did stress the importance of promoting exports, not as a new development strategy but mainly to increase necessary foreign savings in order to improve the balance of payment situations. The transition to export-oriented industrialization occurred gradually in the following years mainly as a result of the strong advice by foreign advisers from the IMF and the U.S. AID mission, as well as the surprisingly positive market response to export promotion policies. The EOI strategy emerged as Korea's dominant development strategy around 1964, not as a conscious choice of the developmental state, but as a consequence of the unanticipated interactions of the world economy and domestic capital (Lim, 1985).

Between 1963 and 1965, the Park government carried out a set of major economic policy reforms, which included: (1) fiscal reform to promote government savings in 1963; (2) exchange rate and trade policy reforms to promote exports in 1964; and (3) an interest rate reform to promote domestic savings in 1965. These liberal policy reforms significantly reduced distortions in the market and stimulated export activities. Indeed, "getting the prices right" played a crucial role in this early transition to outward-oriented development strategy. In order to solve the capital shortage problem in Korea, the government adopted the Foreign Capital Inducement Law in 1966, while pushing through the enormously unpopular Normalization Treaty with Japan in 1965. This latter measure brought in a huge sum of reparation money ($500 million) from the Japanese government and opened the door to a large flow of Japanese private capital (Cole & Lyman, 1971; Mason et al., 1980).

The Park leadership took a cautious attitude toward foreign capital. It showed a preference toward public and commercial loans to foreign direct investment (Haggard & Cheng, 1987). Foreign loan capital provided the necessary foreign exchange without the involvement of management and control by the multinational corporations (MNCs). Foreign dominance in any form was lamented by the intellectual community as well as the public, due to the recent experience of Japanese colonialism and historical incidents of foreign invasion. Allowing MNCs to enter and operate in the Korean economy was interpreted as a first step toward economic and political domination by others. MNCs did not show interest in investing in Korea in the early 1960s. Korea was barely out of the ruins of the devastating Korean War, its GNP per capita was below $200, and it had very few natural resources.

In Korea, state strength has been enhanced by the inflow of foreign capital in the form of public as well as commercial loans.[2] The government distributed public loans to sectors it deemed important for its economic development plans. A large majority of foreign loans (approximately 90%) required government guarantees for payment and put the government in charge of distribution. But a more powerful mechanism of state control over the private sector was its control over domestic banks, which the military junta wrested from private ownership in the first months of coming to power. To a great extent, as Woo (1990) argues, the autonomy and capacity of the Korean developmental state resides in its control over the financial system.

The key feature of the Korean pattern of capital accumulation has been not really macro-economic policies ensuring the "right prices" but the specific manner by which the government has used its control over the allocation of domestic and foreign capital to mould the behaviors of private capital. Credit allocation has been clearly the most important tool of government control of business. Throughout the period of the Park government, domestic interest rates have been maintained artificially far below the real market prices; in fact, when adjusted to the inflation rates, they were negative in several years (see Table 5.1).[3] Foreign loans were even better. In the period between 1965 and 1970, the effective interest rates of dollar-denominated loans (nominal interest rate adjusted by changes in the foreign exchange rate) were between 5.6% and 7.1%, as compared with 25% to 30% for domestic bank loans (S. K. Kim, 1987, p. 123). Thus, obtaining bank loans itself constituted a major source of profits.

But access to these subsidized loans has been very selectively distributed. Bank credit allocation has been closely tied to the allocation of another key mechanism of capital accumulation, the investment licenses. Those who obtained major investment licenses received cheap loans through government-controlled banks; and those who were in a position to obtain a large loan were in an excellent position to obtain a new, profitable license. At the nexus of the two, there lies the most critical ingredient of Korean capital accumulation, that is, access to state power. Unlike the previous Rhee regime, the Park regime stressed economic performance as a major criterion of the allocation of both loans and investment opportunities (Amsden, 1989; Jones & Sakong, 1980). But there was no question that it was political connection, not just a firm's capability, that determined who could participate in profitable projects doled out by the government.

The vast majority of the projects specified in the First Five Year Economic Development Plan were monopolized by a group of the current *chaebols* that had been accused of illicit wealth accumulation. The decisions on the allocation of major investment licenses were personally made by Park himself (Institute of Korean Political Study, 1987; H. Lee, 1968). Park's main emphasis was consistently on the economies of scale and rapid economic growth that would result from it. His developmental orientation was clearly inclined toward the unbalanced, concentrated pattern of growth over which

Table 5.1 Interest Rates of Domestic Banks and the Curb Market, and Inflation
Rates, 1961—1985 (%)

Year	Bank Lending Rates (A)[a]	Inflation (B)[b]	Real Interest Rate (A-B)	Curb Market Lending Rate
1961	17.5	14.0	3.5	N/A
1962	16.6	18.4	−1.8	N/A
1963	15.7	29.3	−13.6	52.6
1964	16.0	30.0	−14.0	61.8
1965	26.0	6.2	19.8	58.9
1966	26.0	14.5	11.5	58.7
1967	26.0	15.6	10.4	56.5
1968	25.2	16.1	9.1	56.0
1969	24.0	14.8	9.2	51.4
1970	24.0	15.6	8.4	50.2
1971	22.0	13.9	8.1	46.4
1972	15.5	16.1	−0.6	39.0
1973	15.5	13.4	2.1	33.2
1974	15.5	29.5	−14.0	40.6
1975	15.5	25.7	−10.2	47.9
1976	18.0	20.7	−2.7	40.5
1977	16.0	15.7	0.3	38.1
1978	19.0	21.9	−2.2	41.7
1979	19.0	21.2	−2.2	42.4
1980	20.0	25.6	−5.6	45.0
1981	17.0	15.9	1.1	35.3
1982	10.0	7.1	2.9	30.6
1983	10.0	3.0	7.0	25.8
1984	10.0	4.1	5.9	24.7
1985	10.0	3.6	6.1	N/A

SOURCES: Kim, S. K. (1987, p. 176); Bank of Korea (1972, p. 1221).
NOTES: a. At year end, one year maturity.
b. Change of GNP deflator.

the government exercised close supervision and guidance. The *chaebols* fitted in perfectly in this developmental orientation.

A major success of Park's developmental state in the 1960s was the transformation of merchant capital into industrial capital, thereby changing the accumulation process from a "zero-sum game" into a "positive-sum game" (Jones & Sakong, 1980). But this does not mean that profit making through rent-seeking activities was eliminated. To the contrary, a great deal of rent-seeking behavior existed in the 1960s and afterward, too. The most important source of such accumulation was real estate investment. Land investment was extremely profitable, not only because land prices increased much faster than inflation rates but also because real estate could be used as a collateral for bank loans. Large capital owners had access to secret information on new real estate development, and could reap handsome profits out of real estate investments.[4] Although no accurate information is available on the extent of land speculation among large business owners, it was serious enough to make the Park government enact regulations about the limit of land ownership by *chaebol* groups in the 1970s.

Another important source of rent-seeking is money lending in the underground money market. In the 1960s and through the first part of the 1970s, there existed a huge curb market in Korea. It was reported that in 1964, the estimated outstanding assets and liabilities in the informal financial market was almost double the commercial bank loans outstanding (S. K. Kim, 1987). Between 1964 and the end of 1969, the size of informal loans increased by 450% (Cole & Park, 1983, p. 126). The people who participated in the curb market as money lenders included professional money lenders and propertied middle-class people as well as business owners and top managers of the same industrial firms that were borrowing money from the curb market. Cole and Park reported, "[As of August 3, 1972] about 25 percent of the total informal debts (of all the business enterprises) were 'disguised informal loans', in that they were made by the owners, major stockholders, or executives of the borrowing firms" (Cole & Park, 1983, p. 127).

In sum, the large capitalists utilized a double-edged strategy of accumulation in the 1960s: one is productive investment in export and import-substitution industries, and the other is participation in speculative land investment and money lending in the curb market. For both types of investment, businesspersons depended heavily upon external finances. Given that interest rates of domestic and foreign loans were substantially lower than the unregulated market prices, those who obtained official loans had several easy avenues of making money. Productive investment was only one of them at this time.

Partly due to the investment structure, and partly due to the changes in world market conditions, the South Korean economy entered its first major crisis of export-oriented industrialization near the end of the 1960s. Of the two, changes in the world market conditions were more serious. At the end of the 1960s, the first principal payment was due on many commercial loans. At the same time, a continuous devaluation of the Korean currency raised Korean firms' costs of foreign debt servicing (the official rate of exchange increased from Korean won 272 to U.S. $1 in 1967, to 392 to 1 in 1972)

(Economic Planning Board, 1990). The debt service ratio as percentage of exports increased from 9.5% in 1968 to 13.7% in 1969, and to 19.4% in 1970 (World Bank, various years). Thus many firms had to turn to the curb market for their immediate cash flow needs. A large number of firms, small and large, which had overexpanded in the middle of the 1960s, went into bankruptcy. Business failures were especially serious among many foreign invested firms. It was reported that 45% of Japanese invested firms declared bankruptcy (D. Lee, 1984). Thus the government had to take over several dozens of "ill-managed companies" between 1969 and 1971, assuming the responsibilities to pay back their foreign debts.

What aggravated these financial and market troubles was increasing labor volatility toward the end of the 1960s. Also, as the labor market tightened with a substantial reduction of unemployment and underemployment in the latter half of the 1960s, wages increased fast, at an 8.8% annual rate of real wage increase between 1965 and 1969. The International Monetary Fund (IMF) forced the Park government to carry out stabilization measures, which aggravated the financial condition of firms that had already heavy debt burdens. In the political arena, Park's attempt to extend his tenure beyond the constitutional limit of two terms triggered strong opposition from students and the opposition party. Thus, after several years of smooth export-led growth, the Korean economy faced a major crisis.

The 1970s

Park took two drastic measures to address the growing economic and political crisis: He imposed severe restrictions on organized labor, while attacking financial capital. Both measures demonstrate both the strength and the "relative autonomy" of the Korean capitalist state very well. The state was willing and able to act against both labor and segments of capital, in the long-run interest of capitalists as a whole.

In 1969, Park proclaimed the Provisional Exceptional Law concerning labor unions and the settlement of labor disputes in foreign-invested firms. It imposed severe restrictions on labor organization, prohibiting strikes in foreign-invested firms. It was followed in 1971 by the proclamation of the state of emergency and the Law Concerning Special Measures for Safeguarding National Security, which suspended indefinitely the workers' right to collective bargaining and action. The culmination of all these authoritarian legislative actions was the installation of the Korean version of the bureaucratic-authoritarian regime, the *Yushin* regime, in October 1972. With this internal coup, Park closed all the political space and bestowed upon himself a lifetime presidency with unchecked executive power.

On the economic frontier, in order to rescue industrialists from serious debt problems, Park took a measure that would be difficult to conceive of in democratic capitalist societies. On August 2, 1972, Park announced the Presidential Emergency Decree for Economic Stability and Growth to become effective the next day (popularly called the "8-3 measure"). The decree included (1) the nullification of all the loan agreements between business firms and private money lenders as of August 3, 1972, replacing them with the requirement that borrowers would be given a three-year grace period, after which they would have to repay their informal loans over a five-year period at a substantially lowered interest rate; and (2) the replacement of a large amount of short-term loans (worth more than $500 million) by long-term loans at a lower interest rate payable over a five-year period after a three-year grace period. In addition, the government established a new industrial rationalization fund with some $125 million and lowered the overall bank interest rates (Bank of Korea, 1973).

Although this Emergency Decree was meant for capitalists in general, the results show that the largest *chaebols* were the main beneficiaries, while the small and medium-sized businesses were not helped substantially.[5] As a result, the emergency decree sought to rescue industrial capital from the private money lenders, even while threatening the sanctity of the private property system. The measure brought relief to business owners, providing new ground for dynamic growth in the 1970s. On the other hand, this bold attack on money capital hurt not only financial capitalists but also thousands of middle-class families who were involved in private money lending activities.[6]

These measures were preparatory steps toward a more ambitious project of Park's developmental state. In his New Year's address in January 1973, Park announced the Heavy and Chemical Industrialization Plan. The Plan was received with much reservation and criticism from both domestic and foreign capital. Nevertheless, the Park regime mobilized all the institutional and material resources at its disposal to push forward. The government selected six strategic industries: steel, electronics, petrochemicals, shipbuilding, machinery, and nonferrous metals. More than ever before, the Park government was willing to concentrate its resources in order to promote these target industries.

There were several reasons why the Park regime made this hasty move into heavy and chemical industrialization in the early 1970s. Both international economic conditions and internal political and economic factors influenced this decision. The international financial system became very unstable with the collapse of the Bretton Woods system in 1971. Economic nationalism began to rise, accompanied by increasing protectionism. As a result, continuous dependence on labor-intensive export industries seemed less promising, especially as domestic wages had been rising fast in this period. Another important factor was that Japan was moving into high-tech industries, and was willing to relinquish some of the labor-intensive sectors of heavy industries.

More important than these economic factors was the political environment of the period. In the early 1970s, significant changes took place in Far Eastern geopolitics. Nixon's visit to China and the ending of the "old" Cold War brought uncertainty to the Korean peninsula. The Nixon Doctrine stressed greater effort for self-defense among U.S. allies, and the Nixon administration made a partial withdrawal of U.S. military forces from South Korea in 1971. A former general, Park felt a great threat in all these changes and determined to strengthen Korea's military power domestically. His decision to promote steel and chemical industries was very much influenced by defense considerations.

But probably the most important factor was the changing domestic political situation. By the early 1970s, South Korea became a far more differentiated and politically active society than it had been in the early 1960s. Labor conflicts began to rise, student and political opposition movements intensified, the agricultural sector showed signs of disaffection, and the opposition party grew into a more formidable force under the leadership of a shrewd charismatic politician, Kim Dae Jung. Park was nonetheless intent on staying in power beyond the constitutional limit of two four-year terms. He changed the constitution and ran for the 1971 presidential election, in which he narrowly escaped defeat at the hands of Kim Dae Jung despite all the propaganda and alleged vote-buying by the regime. The installation of the *Yushin* system in October, 1972 was Park's response to these domestic political changes.

In short, the march to heavy and chemical industrialization was clearly a politically motivated plan to diffuse popular discontent and to mobilize people's energy for a new economic goal. This was justified in the name of building a prosperous nation that would be able to join the club of advanced industrial countries. Economically, this development strategy might have been a premature move but it proved to be a wise choice politically. In his January 1973 presidential press conference, Park made a promise to deliver a "$10 billion export, $1,000 GNP per capita, and my-car age" by the end of the decade. Once again, Park sought to buy political legitimacy with an economic delivery. And once again, recent Korean economic history suggests that political exigencies played a more important role in determining a development strategy than market factors.

The oil crisis in 1973, however, delayed the implementation of the heavy industrialization plan. Korea's oil import bill rose dramatically, and the growth rate of exports slowed down due to a low demand in the depressed world market. Foreign investment was very sluggish, and so was domestic investment in heavy industries. Many of the large-scale plants suffered from excess capacities and a poor financial situation, while many other projects that had not yet been undertaken were either canceled or postponed. As the world economy gradually overcame the first oil shock, and as the Middle East construction boom provided anew big investment opportunities, the South Korean economy began to bounce back after 1975. Exports increased noticeably, and the overseas construction business brought in a large amount of repatriated savings.

With this economic turnaround, the government and conglomerates resumed active investments in heavy and chemical industries. The *chaebols* were a critical element in implementing the government industrialization plan throughout the 1970s. The collusive relationships between the bureaucratic authoritarian state and big business deepened in this period. The *chaebols* were to deliver impressive economic performances and the state was to provide all the necessary conditions for capital accumulation.[7] During the 1970s, the *chaebols* were able to expand and entrench themselves as a formidable power bloc in the Korean political economy. Initially somewhat cautious and skeptical toward investment in heavy industries, the *chaebols* rushed in to obtain the state's investment licenses in these prime sectors of capital accumulation. Fierce competition for territorial expansion ensued amongst them.

International capital began to flow in large volume in the second half of the 1970s. As we can see in Table 5.2, the vast majority of international capital was composed of public and commercial loans; direct foreign investment constituted a very small portion. The MNC investments were restricted to a few limited areas.

In 1975, the state created a new organization, the General Trading Company (GTC), that had a tremendous impact on the Korean industrial structure. Modeled after the Japanese *Sogo-Shosha*, the government licensed a small number of large-scale GTCs to operate as the nation's export windows. By linking the trade-specialized organizations to small-sized manufacturing firms, both of them could specialize in their respective activities and at the same time improve their competitive positions in the world market. Thirteen *chaebols* were given GTC licenses (later three lost their licenses). These

Table 5.2 Inflow of Foreign Capital, 1959-1989[a](in $1,000)

Year	Total Foreign Capital	Loan			Direct Foreign Investment
		Total	Public	Commercial	
1959-1961	4,386	4,386	4,386	0	0
	(100.0)[b]	(100.0)	(100.0)	(0.0)	(0.0)
1962-1965	138,276	118,775	52,836	65,939	19,501
	(100.0)	(85.9)	(38.2)	(47.7)	(14.1)
1966-1970	1,757,232	1,692,772	549,396	1,143,376	64,460
	(100.0)	(96.3)	(31.3)	(65.1)	(3.7)
1971-1975	4,998,780	4,510,598	2,027,250	2,483,348	488,182
	(100.0)	(90.2)	(40.6)	(49.7)	(9.8)
1976-1980	12,280,637	11,748,708	4,774,606	6,974,102	531,929
	(100.0)	(95.7)	(38.9)	(56.8)	(4.3)
1981-1985	11,371,912	10,635,083	7,499,026	3,136,057	736,829
	(100.0)	(93.5)	(65.9)	(27.6)	(6.5)
1986-1989	11,192,059	8,383,000	3,357,000	5,026,000	2,809,059
	(100.0)	(74.9)	(30.0)	(44.9)	(25.1)

SOURCE: Economic Planning Board, *Major statistics of Korean economy* [various years].
NOTES: a. The figures may not add up to 100.0% due to rounding
b. The figures in parentheses are percentages.

licenses were accompanied by an attractive package of trade, finance, and tax advantages, including a license to import raw materials, low-rate export financing, import financing for raw materials, and preferential treatment from the GTCs' overseas offices. An exporter who had valid evidence of an export order could borrow from the banks up to 90% of the dollar amount of the export at an interest rate far below the regular bank lending rate.[8] Thus the establishment of the GTC structure played an instrumental role for top-ranking *chaebol* firms to grow into an unchallengeable position in the economy.

The acquisition of ill-managed companies was another important source of the *chaebols'* accumulation. A major reorganization of these ill-managed companies did not take place until the early 1980s. But during the 1972-1979 period, 17 of them were sold to other private firms. Of these, 13 were purchased, at bargain prices and with additional financial and tax privileges, by the *chaebols* in the top-10 list. This acquisition allowed some *chaebols,* such as Daewoo, to make a strategic entry into key industries such as automobiles and shipbuilding, while Hyundai acquired Inchon Steel Co.

The developmental state of South Korea was at its peak in the second half of the 1970s. Industrial targeting was widely practiced, and the government was in tight control of the allocation of capital. In order to support strategic heavy and chemical industries, the government created the National Investment Fund in 1974. In the second half of the 1970s, somewhere between 53% and 63% of the total domestic loans were distributed as "policy loans" at a preferential rate. Approximately 70% of the policy loans went to the heavy and chemical industry sector. The majority of these loans were given to *chaebols,* since they were the ones who were assigned these strategic projects.

Thus the industrial deepening in the 1970s provided existing *chaebols* with golden opportunities to expand and strengthen their businesses. The 1970s was the period of empire building for the top 10 *chaebols.* Their accumulation strategy was mainly to diversify into many industries in order to strengthen their market positions in relation to the state. Growing big meant obtaining a stronger position to participate in the state's priority projects, and obtaining policy loans and other bank credits. Their dominance in the Korean economy grew tremendously in the 1970s (see Table 5.3).

In Korea, the *chaebols'* common strategy of territorial expansion was widely called the "octopus style" of accumulation, a strategy of stretching one's reach all around and swallowing up existing small-to-medium enterprises. The *chaebols'* horizontal and vertical integrations increased tremendously during the latter part of the 1970s. Between 1972 and 1979, the average number of firms owned by these 10 largest *chaebols* grew from 7.5 per *chaebol* in 1972 to 25.4 in 1979. And the number of different industries in which they operated increased from an average of 7.7 industries (by 2-digit industrial classification) in 1972 to 17.6 in 1979. In the same period, the 10 largest *chaebols* achieved a 47.7% compound average annual growth rate in terms of assets, while the annual average growth rate of the GNP (in real terms) was 10.2% (E. M. Kim, 1991). The figures in Table 5.4 show the tremendous growth of the top 10 *chaebols* in the 1970s.

The main source of this rapid growth of the *chaebols* was more or less the same as in the 1960s—the preferential allocation of subsidized loans. In general, *chaebol* firms relied more heavily on debts for investment. In the 1972-1979 period, 78.8% of the asset growth among the top 10 *chaebols* was financed by debt, compared to 59.7% for the average Korean firm.

Table 5.3 Dominance of the Top 50 Chaebols

Year	The Share of Top 10 Chaebols Sales in GNP
1974	15.1%
1977	26.0%
1980	48.1%
1984	67.4%
1987	68.8%

	The Share of Top 50 Chaebols		
Year	Shipment Shares	Employment Shares	Value Added in GNP
1977	35.0%	16.9%	13.4%*
1982	37.5%	16.0%	
1987	30.9%	14.5%	15.6%

SOURCES: Jones and Sakong (1980), p. 266; S. K. Kim (1987), p. 2; Lee and Lee (1990), p. 26; Management Efficiency Research Institute (1988), p. 29.
NOTE: * The figure is for the 46 largest chaebols' value added in GDP in 1975.

Table 5.4 The Growth of the Ten Largest Chaebols, 1971-1983

Rank[a]	Chaebol	Total Assets[b]		Average Annual Rate of Asset Growth (%)[c]		
		1971	1983	1971-1980	1981-1983	1971-1983
1.	Hyundai	158,261	4,469,342	38.0	19.2	32.1
2.	Samsung	415,978	3,371,603	18.4	35.4	19.1
3.	Daewoo	34,679	3,340,367	53.7	11.6	46.3
4.	Lucky-Gold Star	437,060	2,714,511	17.2	16.4	16.4
5.	Ssangyong	310,424	1,711,715	16.8	13.3	15.3
6.	Sun Kyong	40,049	1,477,873	36.7	0.6	35.1
7.	Han Jin	83,734	1,340,120	32.9	7.5	26.0
8.	Korea Explosives	256,424	1,173,064	11.7	37.0	13.5
9.	Dae Lim	64,522	943,307	31.8	5.7	25.1
10.	Kukje	153,489	896,205	19.3	8.8	15.8

SOURCE: Kim, E. M. (1973-1982); Maeil Kyungje Shinmun (1984; 1986).
NOTES: a. Ranking based on total assets in 1983.
b. Total assets in 1980 constant Korean thousand Won.
c. Average annual growth rate was calculated using 1980 constant prices.

Table 5.5 Debt and Debt Service, 1970-1987

Year	Total Long-Term Debt Disbursed and Outstanding[a]		Debt Service[b] as Percentage of	
	in $ million	% of GNP	GNP	Exports
1970	1,797	23.3	3.0	19.4
1980	16,274	28.8	4.9	12.2
1981	19,964	32.1	5.8	13.1
1982	20.061	28.3	5.2	13.1
1983	21,472	—	—	12.3
1984	29,990	37.0	6.6	15.8
1985	35,756	43.0	8.6	21.5
1986	34,304	36.1	10.8	24.4
1987	30,644	25.8	13.0	27.5

SOURCE: The World Bank, *World Development Report* (various years).
NOTES: a. Figures for 1970-1982 are based on public debt outstanding and disbursed.
b. Figures for 1984-1987 are based on total long-term debt service.

At the end of the 1970s, the South Korean economy faced several structural problems that originated from both external and internal sources. Externally, a recession in the world economy following the second oil shock in 1979 was a serious blow to the South Korean economy, which was by now very dependent on the world market. Korea's oil import bill doubled, while its exports slowed down due to decreasing demands and to the creeping protectionism in the advanced industrial economies. The current account deficit of Korea increased from US $1.1 billion in 1978 to $5.3 billion in 1980. By the early 1980s Korea's foreign debt had reached a dangerous level, and many foreign banks began to seriously question Korea's creditworthiness. The total long-term debt disbursed and outstanding increased from $2.0 billion in 1970 to $35.8 billion in 1985. Moreover, its share as percentage of GNP rose to 43.0% in 1985, almost double that of 23.3% in 1970 (see Table 5.5). Korea found it increasingly difficult to obtain long-term loans, thus relying more on short-term, high-interest loans.

Internally, the massive investment in heavy machinery and chemical industries resulted in severe overcapacity and a poor financial situation for many large firms. Chronic problems of high debt combined with export decline, especially in shipping and construction industries, pushed many firms toward insolvency. Throughout the 1970s, the inflation rate was generally high, but it was particularly high toward the end of the decade. The consumer price index rose by 28.7% in 1980 as compared to 14.5% in 1978. The business sector strongly complained that they were losing competitiveness in the export market due to a high rate of wage increase in the latter part of the 1970s.

The IMF pressured the Park government to undertake a stabilization program. In April 1979, the government adopted the Comprehensive Stabilization Plan, which was aimed at price stabilization and liberalization of the economy. The stabilization plan included a wage freeze, and the liberalization plan included cutting down on low-interest export loans to businesses and farm subsidies.

These economic problems and responses contributed to a rising level of labor unrest and protests by the urban poor. In 1979, a labor strike at a wig factory, the Y. H. Company, triggered a major political crisis when the striking women workers moved to the opposition party headquarters to continue their protest when they were forcefully evicted from their factory by the police. The opposition party's support of the workers and the violent police repression deepened the political crisis as angry protests and labor strikes spread across major industrial cities in the south. Faced with this crisis, the ruling group split internally, which eventually led to an abrupt ending of one chapter of Korean history. Park Chung Hee, the architect of the two decades of growth, was assassinated by the head of the Korean CIA on October 26, 1979.

During a short period of political liberalization following Park's death, a wave of labor unrest erupted across the country. Most labor conflicts were concerned with wage issues and layoffs, but a major focus of workers' struggles was to create independent labor unions and to destroy management-controlled (*oyong*) unions. Workers' resentment against the co-opted union leadership ran very deep, and their linkages with activist students and progressive church groups became closer and stronger in the latter part of the 1970s.

The 1980s

The turn of the 1980s saw the formation of a loosely formed "distributional alliance" under the banner of the *minjung* movement. *Minjung* (the people or the masses) is a broad alliance against the dominant governing coalition, the *chaebols,* and foreign capital. The rise of the *minjung* movement was a reaction to both the *Yushin* regime and the *chaebol-*dominated capital accumulation process. A strong sense of distributive injustice spread across diverse sectors of the population: factory workers, farmers, small-business persons, and white-collar workers. Although they did not belong to the same class, they were bound together by their common moral anger against the collusive relationships between the authoritarian state and the *chaebols.* The *minjung* movement grew as a reaction to the *Yushin* regime, and by the early 1980s it had become a potent political and social movement.

This short period of political liberalization and popular democratic aspirations was dashed, however, by a military coup in December 1979, led by Major General Chun Doo Hwan, then head of the Defense Security Command. The military junta declared martial law and arrested hundreds of dissident leaders. In May 1980, thousands of students and citizens of Kwangju revolted against the imposition of martial law and the arrest of Kim Dae Jung, the opposition leader who came from this region. But the military junta massacred some 200 people in its bloody repression of the rebellion. In February 1981, Chun elected himself to the presidency.

Coming to power without popular support, and with enormous economic troubles inherited from the previous regime, the Chun regime had to undertake bold economic restructuring. The pressure came from both international and domestic capital. International capital demanded that the Korean government open up its market for both foreign imports and foreign capital investment. The IMF and World Bank also kept up pressure on the new government to carry out a substantial stabilization program by freezing wages, reducing money supplies, and cutting government expenditures. The domestic sectors made conflicting demands. The business sector demanded that the government come to their rescue and save their ailing businesses, while the popular sectors demanded measures to control the growth of the *chaebols* and to increase distributive justice.

The military junta created a Standing Committee for Emergency National Security Measures on May 31, 1980, which implemented a few radical reforms. The general policy direction was to respond to both international and domestic pressures, especially to the former. The keystone of the new economic policies was *liberalization*: reduced government intervention in the economy, promotion of market mechanisms through enhanced competition, wider opening of the domestic market to foreign goods, and encouragement of direct foreign investment. Two rounds of liberalization measures were taken, in 1981 and 1982, which opened many new industries to foreign investors. In July 1984, important liberalization measures took place via the

Foreign Capital Inducement Law to attract more foreign direct investment. Instead of allowing only a few industries to be open for foreign direct investment (positive system), a negative system was adopted. This change increased the share of the manufacturing industries open to foreign direct investment to 92.5%. An automatic approval system was adopted as well to facilitate foreign investment (Economic Planning Board, 1986, pp. 31-33).

In the financial sector, the state privatized the ownership of city banks, although it did not relinquish its control over their personnel and key decision matters. The size of policy loans was reduced, and preferential interest rates applied to strategic industries were abolished. Similarly, large tax privileges that were previously given to target industries were reduced substantially as the system of designating target industries changed.[9] The government's priority was given to stable and balanced growth rather than to accelerated growth with which Park's economic planners had been so preoccupied. Chun modified Park's stabilization plan and implemented his new Comprehensive Plan for Stabilization and Structural Reorganization. The plan called for devaluation of the foreign exchange rate, reduction of domestic interest rates, and tightening of the money supply and government expenditure, as well as a curb on wage and dividend payments.

At the same time, responding to the demands of the "distributional coalition," to use Olson's terms (Olson, 1982), the regime promised that it would bring social welfare and distributive justice and would "purify" the corrupt political and business worlds. The usual five-year economic plan would now embrace social welfare goals, thus the 1982-1986 plan was labelled the Fifth Five-Year Economic and Social Development Plan.

While publicly stressing social welfare and broader distribution, however, the Chun regime took a harsher measure against labor than any previous regime. Hundreds of labor activists were arrested or fired, unions were restructured into enterprise-level unions, and collective action by new restrictive labor laws. Furthermore, workers' wages were frozen in the name of economic stabilization.

With regard to capital, the Chun regime was able to make a few changes. The most serious problem Chun faced was that of duplicate investment and excess capacity in the heavy and chemical industries. In August 20, 1980, the military junta issued the Investment Reorganization of the Heavy and Chemical Industries to reorganize the power plant equipment and automobile industries. Under the 8-20 measures, Daewoo was to integrate and monopolize the power plant equipment production sector by taking over Hyundai Heavy's and Hyundai International's investment, and Hyundai was to integrate the passenger automobile sector by merging with Daewoo Motors.

Kia Motors was to specialize in the production of special-purpose non-passenger cars. A similar measure followed in October to reorganize heavy electrical machinery, engine production, copper refining, and other industries. These measures were not fully implemented, in part because of the protests from the foreign joint-venture partners.[10]

In a similar move, the junta announced the "Measure to Rationalize Corporate Structure" on September 27, 1980. The Measure selected 26 *chaebols* and forced them to reorganize their group structure around specialized primary businesses. In order to accomplish this, the government urged them to relinquish their sideline businesses, sell non-business-related real estate, offer their stocks in the stock market, and improve their financial structures. The committee selected 135 firms (from the total of 631 firms owned by the 26 *chaebols*) as the "main line business firms," and ordered them to give up 166 firms by 1984. The government investigated all the real estate owned by the *chaebols* and their owner families, and told them to dispose of the majority of the land ownership.

The result was, however, far below the initial target. The *chaebols* gave up some of their firms but bought almost the same number of new firms. The 10 largest *chaebols* sold 18 member companies and merged 21 companies with their other member companies, but then purchased or created 38 new companies. The average number of firms owned by the top 10 *chaebols* remained practically the same between 1979 and 1985—24.3 and 24.2, respectively (Management Efficiency Research Institute, 1986). The *chaebols* were forced to sell their land in 1981 and 1982, but they purchased it back again as soon as the government and public campaign over the issue ended. They were also reluctant to go public; as of June 1984, only 24% of the firms owned by the 10 largest *chaebols* had gone public.

The government adopted the Fair Trade Act in April, 1981. The Fair Trade Committee was established in the EPB to monitor collusion and unfair behavior of firms, and an Assistant Deputy Prime Minister was appointed the director of the committee. The state selected the largest *chaebols* and put under close supervision their financial status and expansion through merger and acquisition. The government also monitored subcontracting practices between large and smaller firms in order to reduce abuses by the former. However, the fate of this Fair Trade Act was similar to previous measures to control the *chaebols;* the bark was much stronger than the bite.

At the same time, the Chun government adopted a few policies to promote small- and medium-sized firms. Banks were ordered to direct 40% to 50% of their total loans to small- and medium-sized firms. The government designated 110 product groups as off-limits to large firms, while allowing small and medium companies some collective monopolies in some designated areas. The government also concentrated its effort on selecting 5,000 "promising small and medium companies" for extra financial support and technical guidance. In spite of all these public gestures, the share of loans made to the small and medium enterprises actually declined from 45.2% in 1981 to 32.4% in 1985 (*Maeil Kyungie Shinmun,* September 5, 1985).

Thus despite much public fanfare, state actions taken against the *chaebol* firms in the early 1980s had no apparent effect in containing *chaebol* growth. The *chaebols* continued to achieve impressive growth in the 1980s. Between 1979 and 1985, the sales of the top 10 *chaebols* (top 10 in 1985) grew at an annual rate of 34.5%, and their assets grew 21.8% annually. As previously noted, however, the average number of member companies of the 10 largest *chaebols* remained constant. Their degree of diversification in terms of the 2-digit standard industrial classification showed a moderate increase from 16.7 in 1979 to 18.9 in 1985. These changes suggest that *chaebols* have entered a maturing stage in their evolution.

Since the mid-1980s, the *chaebols* have experienced rapid growth due to some favorable changes in the international economy. The popularly named "Three Low Period" has since 1986 allowed the *chaebols* to capitalize on lowered interest rates of major foreign banks, lowered exchange rate of the U.S. dollar against the Japanese yen, and the lower price of crude oil. The export business boomed for the *chaebols,* since the U.S. market found Japanese products to be increasingly unaffordable, and sought cheaper goods from Korea. This export boom allowed the *chaebols* to expand rapidly in the 1980s. It was very fortunate for Korean industry that the international economy turned upward at the same time the state was turning away from direct subsidies and other preferential treatment. Despite the changing policy environment, the success of the *chaebols* in exports significantly increased their leverage in dealing with the state and helped them become increasingly more self-reliant. The accumulation strategy of the *chaebols* also had to shift from relying on state guidance and support to the market mechanism. The *chaebols* became more active in striking deals with MNCs on their own without the supervision and mediation of the state, and have begun to establish subsidiaries abroad.

Conclusion

Several tentative conclusions can be drawn from this analysis of the political economy of capital accumulation in South Korea during the past three decades.

First, the strength of the state derived partly from the institutional inheritance from the past (such as a centralized bureaucracy, large police forces, and executive dominance) and partly from *statecraft,* that is, the ways in which state rulers use state instruments to enhance their power over civil society. Having inherited the same state institutions, Syngman Rhee and Park Chung Hee presided over states of quite different strength and autonomy. State strength also derives from both internal and external sources. The Rhee and Park regimes both used Korea's strategic geopolitical position skillfully to enhance its bargaining power with core nations considerably, while at the same time enhancing their own power inside the country.

Second, it is the character of a *regime* rather than a state structure that determines whether or not the state is developmental. There were no great differences in terms of state structure among the Rhee, Park, and Chun periods, but the specific manner in which the state intervened in the economy varied significantly among these three regimes. The most important element that determines the character of a regime, and consequently the ways in which state instruments are used, seems to be the manner and the social context in which state rulers came to power. Park came to power through a military coup in a social context that made heavy demands for economic welfare and in a historical period when economic development had a powerful ideological appeal. Park Chung Hee sought to establish his regime's political legitimacy on the basis of economic performance. The emergence of the Korean developmental state is intimately related to his quest for political legitimacy.

Third, the state's choice of a *developmental strategy* and major economic policies is not only determined by domestic and world market factors but also by *political* considerations. The Korean state's decision to make a hasty move into heavy and chemical industrialization in the early 1970s is a good example. It was not economic rationality but political rationality—a response to domestic politics and security threats—that propelled the Park regime to make such a move.

Fourth, the class character of the *development alliance* between the state and segments of capital shapes the dominant form of capital accumulation. Park Chung Hee forged a narrow development alliance with conglomerate capital (*chaebol*) in order to pursue rapid economic growth. This state-*chaebol* alliance facilitated a remarkably rapid rate of economic growth, but produced enormous capital concentration and a skewed distribution of wealth, engendering a wide sense of distributive injustice.

Fifth, the very success of development policies based on a narrow development coalition worked to undermine the unity of this coalition, by bringing into being *new class forces*. The expansion of the working class and the middle classes in Korea, the outcome of rapid export-led industrialization, led to the formation of the loosely organized "distributional coalition" under the banner of *minjung* (the people or the masses). The rise of the *minjung* movement in the 1980s strained the relationships between the Chun regime and the *chaebols*, as the state could no longer protect and favor this privileged segment of capital. But by the 1980s, the relative autonomy of the state vis-à-vis conglomerate capital declined considerably, and so did the ability to control the behavior of the *chaebols*. Consequently, the scope and effectiveness of the Korean developmental state diminished considerably.

Finally, a broader implication of the last two points is that the behavior pattern of a developmental state must be understood within the context of *class structure*. Until recently, the Korean state pursued an unbalanced, highly concentrated pattern of capital accumulation based on a narrow development alliance with the *chaebols*, largely because of the absence or weakness of "distributional alliances." The weakness of organized labor and other popular sectors allowed the capitalist state to adopt blatantly pro-capital and antilabor, or pro-growth and antidistributional policies. The effectiveness of the Korean state's development policies derived largely from the *consistency* of its policy implementation in favor of large capital. This consistency in the mode of state intervention in the economy has ensured "business confidence" and has promoted a favorable investment climate for both domestic and international capital. As the balance of class power changed, however, the state could not maintain a consistent approach, caught among pressures from big business, small business, labor, and farmers, resulting in a considerable weakening of the state's ability to manage the economy.

Notes

1. The *chaebol* is a large business conglomerate owned and managed by family members or relatives. Its main characteristics include large market share and wide range of businesses. Detailed analyses of *chaebol* organizations are available in E. M. Kim (1991); Steers et al. (1989); and Yoo & Lee (1987).

2. The first study that showed the positive impact of foreign capital on a less developed country was done by Jeff Frieden (1981). Frieden showed that loan capital, unlike foreign direct investment can strengthen and support state power in less developed countries. A similar argument is made by E. M. Kim (1989) and by Stallings (1991). Their studies showed that public loans strengthened state autonomy and capacity while foreign direct investment and some commercial loans undermined state autonomy.

3. In 10 of the 18 years of Park's regime (1961-1979), the rate of inflation was higher than the interest rate of domestic banks. In the years 1963, 1964, 1974, and 1975, the rate of inflation was greater than the interest rate of the banks with a difference of more than 10% (S. K. Kim, 1987, p. 176).

4. For example, Samsung Life Insurance Company of the Samsung *chaebol* bought land in Seochodong in Seoul between 1987 and the fall of 1989. The land was initially designated as a site for a public bus terminal. The plan to build the terminal was suddenly abandoned, however, and the lot was rezoned in December 1989 for commercial use. Therefore, the property value jumped and Samsung made a handsome profit. There are three possible explanations. One is that Samsung received information of the rezoning prior to the announcement, and another is that Samsung purchased the land and effectively lobbied the City for rezoning. Whichever the case may be, circumstantial evidence points to the influence and power of Samsung. The third and least plausible explanation is that Samsung was extremely lucky. Another incident was reported at the National Assembly meeting on April 16 and 17, 1990 by Lee Hae Chan of the Pyungmin-dang. According to this report, Hyundai, Samsung, and Keukdong Oil purchased land (200 thousand *pyung*) in the Choongnam Province. The problem was that the property was purchased at a cheap price before the land was approved for a land fill. The price of the land skyrocketed from $1.8-2.2 to $118-221 per *pyung* with the announcement. Therefore, the three *chaebols* made an enormous profit. Once again, no conclusive evidence was presented to prove that these *chaebols* had access to inside information. However, incidents such as this only fuel the suspicion that the *chaebols* do indeed have privileged access to critical information, and that they have real influence on the government. See Ham (1990) for more information.

5. The large *chaebols* were the largest borrowers of the curb market loans, thus becoming the main beneficiaries of the emergency relief measure. Furthermore, the results of the allocation of bank loans and the industrial rationalization fund showed that the *chaebols* were disproportionately favored. The fund and loans were targeted mainly for capital- and technology-intensive industries, which had large debts. The *chaebols* were predominant in such industries, and therefore became the largest recipient of the low-interest bank loans and funds. As a result, the *chaebols* came out once again as the winners.

6. Since banks' savings interest rates were unreasonably low, many middle-class families lent their money to business borrowers at that time. In 1971, the year preceding the emergency decree, the curb market lending rate was 46.4%, while that of the banks was only 22%. It is estimated that over $866 million worth of curb market loans were affected by this emergency measure, which was equivalent to 34% of the then outstanding domestic credit of the banking sector. See Bank of Korea (1972); Cole and Park (1983); and S. Lee (1985).

7. For example, the 10 largest *chaebols'* growth rate of total assets was more than 27% between 1971 and 1980. This rate is more than 2.5 times the rate of growth of the entire Korean economy (Economic Planning Board, 1990).

8. Between 1975 and 1979, the bank lending rates for each year were 15.5%, 18.0%, 16.0%, 19.0%, and 19.0%. On the other hand, the corresponding interest rates for export financing were 7.0%, 8.0%, 8.0%, 9.0%, and 9.0%. This shows that the interest rate for export loans was about half that of the domestic banks. See Economic Planning Board, *Major Statistics of Korean Economy* (various years).

9. During the drive for heavy and chemical industrialization in the 1970s, six target industries were chosen for heavy government support and protection under the government's careful planning. By the early 1980s with liberalization measures taking place, "targeting" took on a new meaning. Instead of being a long-term commitment of the government to allow for certain industries to grow under the auspices of the government, it became a short-term protection plan

for infant and declining industries. The changes, therefore, meant that becoming a target industry was no longer a guarantee for huge wind-fall profits, due to government subsidies, low-interest loans and tax cuts, and monopoly or oligopoly of the market. The selection of industries also changed from those that were deemed strategic and important by the government planners, to those requiring assistance due to market conditions. (Based on interviews with government officials in the Ministry of Commerce and Industry and the Economic Planning Board by Eun Mee Kim during the summer of 1988.)

10. For example, General Motors, which had been the joint-venture partner of Daewoo Motors, strongly opposed the 8-20 measure, forcing the government to back off from the initial plan.

References

Amsden, Alice H. (1989). *Asia's next giant: South Korea and late industrialization.* New York: Oxford University Press.

Bank of Korea. (1972). *Economic statistics yearbook.* Seoul: Bank of Korea.

Bank of Korea. (1973). *Full report on the president's decree of August 3, 1972.* Seoul: Bank of Korea.

Cheng, Tun-jen. (1991). Political regimes and development strategies: South Korea and Taiwan. In Gary Gereffi & Donald Wyman (Eds.), *Manufacturing miracles: Paths of industrialization in Latin America and East Asia.* Princeton, NJ: Princeton University Press.

Cole, David, & Lyman, Princeton. (1971). *Korean development: The interplay of politics and economics.* Cambridge, MA: Harvard University Press.

Cole, David C., & Park, Yung Chul. (1983). *Financial development in Korea, 1945-1978.* Cambridge, MA: Harvard University Press.

Economic Planning Board. (1986). *Analysis of economic policies of the 1980s.* Seoul: Economic Planning Board.

Economic Planning Board. (1990). *Major statistics of Korean economy.* Seoul: Economic Planning Board.

Frieden, Jeff. (1981). Third World indebted industrialization: International finance and state capitalism in Mexico, Brazil, Algeria, and South Korea. *International Organization, 35,* pp. 407-431.

Haggard, Stephen. (1990). *Pathways from the periphery: The politics of growth in the newly industrializing countries.* Ithaca, NY: Cornell University Press.

Haggard, Stephen, & Cheng, Tun-jen. (1987). State and foreign capital in East Asian NICs. In Frederic Deyo (Ed.), *The political economy of the new Asian industrialism.* Ithaca, NY: Cornell University Press.

Haggard, Stephen, & Moon, Chung-in. (1990). Institutions and economic policy: Theory and a Korean case study. *World Politics, 12,* pp. 210-237.

Ham, Young Jin. (1990, June). Speculative real estate investments by the chaebols [in Korean]. *Wolgan Chosun,* pp. 180-203.

Institute of Korean Political Study. (1987). *Park Chung Hee Sidae Kyungie Bihwa* [Economics behind stories during Park Chung Hee era]. Seoul: Tongkwang.

Johnson, Chalmers. (1982). *MITI and the Japanese miracle.* Stanford, CA: Stanford University Press.

Johnson, Chalmers, (1987). Political institutions and economic performance: The government-business relationship in Japan, South Korea, and Taiwan. In Frederic Deyo (Ed.), *The political economy of the new Asian industrialism* (pp. 136-164). Ithaca, NY: Cornell University Press.

Jones, Leroy, & Sakong, Il. (1980). *Government, business, and entrepreneurship in economic development: The Korean case.* Cambridge, MA: Harvard University Press.

Kim, Eun Mee. (1973-1982). Industrial organization and growth of the Korean *chaebol.* In *Korean company handbook.* Seoul: Korea Productivity Center.

Kim, Eun Mee. (1989). Foreign capital in Korea's economic development, 1960-1985. *Studies in Comparative International Development, 24,* pp. 24-45.

Kim, Eun Mee. (1991). The industrial organization and growth of the Korean chaebol: Integrating development and organizational theories. In Gary Hamilton (Ed.), *Business networks and economic development in East and Southeast Asia.* Hong Kong: Hong Kong University Press.

Kim, Kyong Dong. (1976, May). Political factors in the formation of the entrepreneurial elite in South Korea. *Asian Survey, XVI*(5), 465-477.

Kim, Seok Ki. (1987). *Business concentration and government policy: A study of the phenomenon of business groups in Korea, 1945-1985.* Unpublished D.B.A. dissertation, Harvard University.

Koo, Hagen. (1987). The interplay of state, social class, and world system in East Asian development: The cases of South Korea and Taiwan. In Frederic Deyo (Ed.), *The political economy of the new Asian industrialism* (pp.165-180). Ithaca, NY: Cornell University Press.

Lee, Dae Keun. (1984). The evolution of the loan-dependent economy [in Korean]. In Dae Keun Lee & Un Young Chung (Eds.), *Hankook Chabon Juuiron* [On Korean capitalism] (pp. 163-190). Seoul: Kkachi.

Lee, Hahn-been. (1968). *Korea: Time, change, and public administration.* Honolulu: University of Hawaii Press.

Lee, Kyu Uck, & Lee, Jae Hyung. (1990). *Gieob gyeolhab qwa gyeongjeryeog jibjung (Business groups and economic concentration). Seoul: Korea Development Institute.*

Lee, Sung Hyung. (1985). State, class and capital accumulation—Focusing on the 8.3 measure [in Korean]. In Jang Jip Choi (Ed.), *Hankook Chabon Chuuiwa Kookka* [Korean capitalism and the state] (pp. 229-286). Seoul: Hanul.

Lim, Hyun-Chin. (1985). *Dependent development in Korea 1963-1979.* Seoul: Seoul National University Press.

Maeil Kyungje Shinmun. (1984). *Maekyung: Annual corporation reports.* Seoul: Maeil Kyungje Shinmun.

Maeil Kyungje Shinmun. (1985). *Maekyung: Annual corporation reports.* Seoul: Maeil Kyongje Shinmun.

Maeil Kyungje Shinmun. (1986). *Maekyung: Annual corporation reports.* Seoul: Maeil Kyungje Shinmun.

Management Efficiency Research Institute. (1986). *Analysis of financial statements—Fifty major business groups in Korea.* Seoul: MERI.

Mason, Edward, et al. (1980). *The economic and social modernization of the Republic of Korea.* Cambridge, MA: Harvard University, Council on East Asian Studies.

Moon, Chung-in. (1989). Beyond statism: Rethinking the political economy of growth in South Korea [Special issue on East Asian development model, edited by Steve Chan & Cal Clark]. *International Studies Notes.*

Olson, Mancur. (1982). *The rise and decline of nations: Economic growth, stagflation, and social rigidities.* New Haven, CT: Yale University Press.

Stallings, Barbara. (1991). The role of foreign capital in economic development: A comparison of Latin America and East Asia. In Gary Gereffi & Donald Wyman (Eds.), *Manufacturing miracles: Paths of industrialization in Latin America and East Asia.* Princeton, NJ: Princeton University Press.

Steers, Richard, et al. (1987). *The chaebol.* New York: Harper & Row.

Wade, Robert. (1990). *Governing the market: Economic theory and the role of government in East Asian industrialization.* Princeton, NJ: Princeton University Press.

Woo, Jung-En. (1990). *Race to the swift: State and finance in Korean industrialization.* New York: Columbia University Press.

World Bank. *World development report.* (various years).

Yoo, Sangjin, & Lee, Sang M. (1987, Summer). Management style and practice of Korean chaebols. *California Management Review,* pp. 95-110.

6

Political Economy of Regional Development in Korea

SOOHYUN CHON

Since 1961, the Korean government has carefully planned and closely monitored the economic growth of the country. Through an intricate profit allocation system devised to promote export industries, the government was able to achieve impressive growth. As a result of Korea's successful economic growth in the past three decades, the living standard of the country's population has increased significantly. But the policy also had the effect of concentrating the benefits in the hands of a few large corporations and people from certain regions. While most of the industrial and urban activities are now concentrated in the Seoul and Pusan metropolitan areas, the central part of Korea—including the Chungchong provinces as well as the Cholla provinces in the southwest—lag behind in their economic development (Figure 6.1). This chapter is an attempt to explain how rapid economic growth and state intervention have affected spatial economic development. The author has sought to find explanations using:

(1) the economic structural transformations that favored regions with industrial bases;
(2) the relative agricultural income growth among different regions in Korea; and
(3) the political and elite power structure that consists of a majority of leaders from the southeast.

AUTHOR'S NOTE: The author would like to express sincere gratitude to Dr. Jin Yong Oh of the Sejong Institute and Professor Shin Haeng Lee of Yonsei University for their support, advice, and comments during the writing of this chapter. I would also like to thank Anneke Vonk for the maps.

Figure 6.1. Provinces of Korea

Table 6.1 Income Level by Regional Groupings (1983)

	Population (in Millions)	Per Capita Income (Percentage of National Average)
Central Provinces	5.9	80.1%
Southwestern Provinces	4.4	80.0%
Southeastern Provinces	10.4	112.0%

SOURCE: Ministry of Construction (1987).

The uneven distribution of economic growth is best illustrated by the skewed income distribution among these regions. A report by the Ministry of Construction provides income statistics that are not readily available from other sources (Ministry of Construction, 1987).[1] According to the report the "central provinces," including North and South Chungchong provinces as well as part of North Cholla province, had 5.9 million people comprising approximately 14.6% of the total population in 1983 (Table 6.1). The economies of the "central provinces" are under represented as their share of output amounted to only 12.3% of the total national output. Per capita income of the central region is about 80.1% of national per capita income as well.

The "southwestern provinces" include the entire South Cholla province and part of North Cholla province. This area contains 4.4 million people, about 10.7% of the total population of the country in 1983. The share of regional output of this area was 9.1% of the total national output of the country in 1983. The per capita income of this region also amounted to 80% of national per capita income in 1983. On the other hand, the "southeastern provinces," which include Pusan, Taegu, 13 cities, and 31 *kuns* (counties) in the southeast, had 26.7% of the total population of the country in 1983. Per capita income of this area was 112% of national per capita income in 1983.

The uneven distribution of economic development is not an anomaly that exists only in Korea, because factors of production are rarely distributed evenly. The regional disparity in Korea, especially between that of the Cholla provinces in the west and the Kyongsang provinces in the east, however, is an extreme case where political institutions and the economic structure has had a significant impact on redirecting resources and investment away from the Cholla provinces to the Kyongsang provinces. This has resulted in the Cholla's underdevelopment and the sense that Cholla's people have received a low share of the benefits from Korea's economic develop-

Table 6.2 Concentration Index of Industrial Output by Regions (1982)

	AP	AS
Cheju	0.08	0.04
Kangwon	0.19	0.06
Kyonggi	1.59	1.35
North Cholla	0.42	0.26
South Cholla	0.55	0.65
North Chungchong	0.57	0.26
South Chungchong	0.63	0.43
North Kyongsang	1.15	0.43
South Kyongsang	2.03	1.83
Inchon	2.52	40.63
Pusan	1.15	24.12
Seoul	0.74	23.73
Taegu	0.99	8.86

SOURCE: Korea Research Institute for Human Settlement (1985).

NOTE: $AP = \dfrac{\text{Regional Industrial Value Added / Total National Value Added}}{\text{Regional Population / Total National Population}}$

$AS = \dfrac{\text{Regional Industrial Output / Total National Industrial Output}}{\text{Area of Each Region / Area of South Korea}}$

ment. As illustrated in Table 6.2, for example, the share of the Chollas' man-ufacturing value-added falls far behind that of the Kyongsang provinces. This has led to deep resentment that divides these regions among different political parties.

The Cholla and Kyongsang provinces started out as the two most populous areas in the country comprising approximately 25% and 28% of the total population respectively in 1949. Today, the Kyongsang provinces have nearly 30% of Korea's population and the Cholla provinces approximately 12%. Such a drastic decrease in the proportion in the Cholla provinces is attributable to the lack of employment opportunities in manufacturing and hence of migration out of the area. For example, the share of manufacturing employment in the Chollas as a percentage of total Korean manufacturing employment has decreased from 13.1% in 1958 to 5.4% in 1983. The share of the Chollas' value-added has also decreased from 10.4% to 8.0% during the same period. Since the Korean economy has grown substantially during this period, the absolute total employment in manufacturing in Cholla has increased approximately three to four times in both North and South Cholla. However, this does not compare favorably with the more than 10-fold increase in employment in other economically vibrant provinces such as the Kyonggi and Kyongsang provinces. The Kyongsang provinces' share of manufacturing employment has increased from 28.6% to 41.0% between 1958 and 1983, and the share of value-added has increased from 35.2% to 40.2% during the same period. Table 6.2 presents a concentration index of industrial output by regions in 1982, as a measure of the degree of industrialization for each province. Here again, the prominence of Kyonggi and the Kyongsang provinces as industrial centers is apparent.

The Chollas experienced negative population growth between 1970 and 1985. North Cholla's population decreased from 2.4 million in 1970 to 2.2 million in 1985, while the population of South Cholla decreased from 4.0 million to 2.8 million during the same period. Out-migrants from the Chollas are found in large numbers in urban centers, living below the poverty level. In Seoul, people from North and South Cholla provinces comprise 28.3% of the total urban poor (M. H. Kim, 1988, p. 493). Since the Cholla's total population is approximately 12% of the total population of Korea, North and South Cholla provinces represent a disproportionately large share of urban poverty. Although it would be expected that recent immigrants would comprise a larger proportion of the underprivileged than the existing population as a whole, no statistics are available that permit this hypothesis to be tested. It would be of interest to compare recent urban immigrants from the Chollas versus other rural areas to find their share of the poor and to determine how quickly they assimilate into the middle class. Since there is a cultural bias against people from the Cholla provinces, one could expect that their assimilation into the middle class would be impeded (M. H. Kim, 1987).[2] The feeling of alienation both in their places of origin and of destination causes Cholla people to align themselves with a political party representing their own regional interests, the Peace and Democratic Party headed by Kim Dae Joong.

Table 6.3   Annual Growth Rate of Gross National Product

Year	Growth Rate (Percentage)	Year	Growth Rate (Percentage)
1955	5.4	1973	16.7
1958	5.2	1976	15.5
1961	4.8	1979	7.0
1962	3.1	1982	7.2
1964	8.6	1985	7.0
1967	7.8	1988	12.2
1970	7.9	—	—

SOURCE: Mason et al. (1980), p. 98; Korea Development Institute (1989), p. 27.

Structural Reasons for Underdevelopment in Cholla

Economic development, which encouraged fast industrialization with aggressive export promotion policies, had a significant impact on the structure of the Korean economy. As is always the case, economic development meant an increase in the importance of the industrial sector and a decrease in the relative importance of agriculture. Traditionally, the Cholla provinces were the most prosperous agricultural areas in Korea. The Far Eastern agricultural system, especially that of Korea and Japan, is characterized by a division of wet rice paddies and upland dry fields. Because rice is the major crop and has the highest productivity per unit land, the topography and availability of water largely determined the prosperity of an agricultural area. The Cholla provinces are endowed with fertile plains suitable for rice cultivation. They used to be the most wealthy agricultural areas in Korea and were known as the "Rice Bowl." It is not a coincidence that some of Korea's first modern entrepreneurial families, such as the Samyangsa Group, had its origins in fortunes built on Cholla agricultural wealth.[3]

Starting from 1961 when the military government of President Park Chung Hee came into power, Korea's economy started to grow at an accelerated rate due to the successful execution of the Five Year Economic Plans (Table 6.3). With fast economic growth, there emerged two trends that worked against the relative regional prosperity of the Cholla provinces compared to other areas. Rapid economic growth was accompanied by an increase in urban populations and their income. This was conducive to the production of high value dry-field crops such as fruits and vegetables. Consequently, North Chungchong, North Kyongsang, and Cheju Island, which used to be relatively poor agricultural sectors due to a high percentage of dry fields to total cultivable land, began to show fast growth in agricultural production. Between 1960 and 1974, North Chungchong province, North Kyongsang province, and Cheju Island experienced an average annual output growth rate of 6.2%, 4.7%, and 10.4% respectively (Ban, Moon, & Perkins, 1982, pp. 116-127). In contrast, areas such as South and North Cholla, as well as South Kyongsang, which are and have been major rice production areas, experienced decreases in their share of total agricultural output of the country. In North Cholla province, which has the highest percentage of paddy land, agricultural output grew by only an average of 1.7% per annum between 1960 and 1974. This compares unfavorably with the average annual agricultural output growth rate of 4.0% for the whole country during the same period.

As illustrated in Table 6.4, total agricultural output in monetary terms reveals that the differentials between the rate of growth in the rice growing regions and the predominantly dry-field regions are not as drastic as in the case of total output in tonnage. This is because rice's per unit land yield in monetary terms is as high as most commercial vegetables and fruits. It does show, however, that the agricultural output measured in monetary terms increased faster in regions with a higher percentage of dry fields. Again, areas with a high percentage of dry fields to total agricultural area, such as Cheju, North Kyongsang, and North Chungchong, show more than a 2.5 times increase in their farm output in monetary terms, while North Cholla and South Chungchong show the lowest increase.

Between the initiation of economic development by the military government in the early 1960s and early 1980s, most of the transportation network, especially highway construction, strengthened the existing Seoul-Pusan artery rather than building roads in poorly connected areas such as the Chollas. This pattern of infrastructure development put the Chollas at an even further disadvantage in commercial crop cultivation for major markets in urban centers (Ban et al., 1982, pp. 147-158; Keidel, 1979). Only recently in the 1980s, have four-lane highways connecting the capital city of South Cholla—Kwangju—to Seoul, Pusan, and Taegu been constructed.

Second, because the Cholla provinces were the most prominent agricultural regions at the outset of Korea's economic development, their relative

Table 6.4 Farm Output (Current Prices), 1960-1974 (Unit: Million 1970 Won)

	1960	1965	1970	1974	Percentage Increase (1960-1974)
Cheju	6,801	12,760	11,014	18,033	265
Kangwon	19,785	27,213	32,543	44,491	225
Kyonggi	52,313	62,621	92,849	118,487	226
North Cholla	47,810	73,440	82,585	103,246	216
South Cholla	65,220	104,274	116,570	149,688	230
North Chungchong	26,969	43,626	53,497	71,259	264
South Chungchong	52,703	75,880	89,725	113,870	216
North Kyongsang	67,305	120,398	130,806	169,835	252
South Kyongsang	54,374	107,637	106,353	124,481	229
Pusan	0	2,476	1,923	1,979	—
Seoul[a]	4,361	5,915	5,080	4,286	98

SOURCE: Keidel (1979), p. 211, Table B-17.
NOTE: a. Decrease in agricultural production around Seoul is an obvious case of speculation by landholders arount a fast growing urban center.

position against other provinces slipped when the share of industry and services in the Korean economy started to rise. Grouping investment sectors indicates that the industrial sector has received an increasingly larger share of total capital formation. While capital formation in the industrial sector increased from 42.8% in 1953-1955 to 57.5% in 1970-1972, the agricultural sector's capital formation decreased slightly from 9.6% to 9.0% during the same period (Kuznets, 1977, pp. 68-69). The gap continued to increase throughout the 1970s and 1980s. This might be due to the fact that estimating agricultural fixed capital formation can have a downward bias since the value of nonmonetized land improvements play a crucial role in agricultural output increases, but are relatively hard to measure. A large part of the investment channeled into improving agricultural capital—such as paddy or dry-field construction and maintenance—come from the labors of small-scale farmers. As a result, the investment is often left out of national account estimates. Nevertheless, agriculture's small investment share largely reflects the top priority given industrial development in the initial stages of the Five Year Economic Development Plans. With the decrease in relative importance of the agricultural sector in the economy, the Cholla provinces, which were predominantly agricultural regions, were adversely affected in their relative importance compared to other parts of the country.

Determinants of Industrial Locations

One glance at the distribution of different industries in Korea reveals that there is a heavy concentration in the northwest and southeast of the country. As the maps in Figure 6.2 and Figure 6.3 illustrate, most of the textile and precision machinery industries are located in the Kyongsang provinces and in the Seoul-Kyonggi area. Textiles are representative of light manufacturing, which played a major role at the initial stage of Korea's economic development. Even in 1983-1984, textiles comprised 21.6% of the country's total exports. Initially, textile industries were heavily concentrated in the Seoul and Pusan metropolitan areas comprising 40.0% of total textile employment in 1970. In 1984, the share of textile employment in these two metropolitan areas decreased to 27.0% as textile plants began to disperse to adjacent areas of Seoul and Pusan, such as Kyonggi and North Kyongsang provinces. In turn, the share of employment in textile industries in the Kyongsang provinces increased by 29.7% between 1970 and 1985, while Kyonggi province showed an increase of 42.0% during the same period. North Cholla province also experienced a 69.0% increase in its share of textile industry employment during the same period. This is partly because North Cholla started out with a small base comprising only 2.6% of total textile employment in 1970. By 1984, North Cholla's share was 4.4%. The share of the rest of the country, North Chungchong, South Chungchong, South Cholla, and Kangwon provinces decreased from 13.4% to 10.4% between 1970 and 1985. In the machinery, metals, and electronics industries that the government started to promote aggressively from 1973, concentration around Seoul and Pusan is even more pronounced. The Seoul and Pusan areas occupied 76.7% of the total employment in these industries in 1970. Precision industries also experienced dispersion of their locations to nearby provinces of Seoul and Pusan between 1970 and 1980. By 1984, Kyonggi province, excluding Seoul, occupied 38.6% of the total employment in precision machinery while North and South Kyongsang provinces, excluding Pusan, came to occupy 32.2%. Establishment of the Kumi and Changwon industrial complexes in North Kyongsang and South Kyongsang provinces respectively, accounts for the dispersion of these industries to the nearby provinces. In 1984, the Seoul-Kyonggi area and the Pusan-Kyongsang area had a total of more than 96.1% of the employment in precision machinery. On the other hand, the share of precision machinery manufacturing employment in North Chungchong, South Chungchong, North Cholla, South Cholla, and Kangwon provinces had remained the same—changing slightly from a meager 3.8% in 1970 to 3.6% in 1984. Similar patterns can be discerned in fabricated metal industries, electric machinery industries, and general machinery industries as illustrated in Table 6.5. Chemical industries are an exception, in that South Cholla's share is significant. This is because the second largest oil refinery and petrochemical complex in Korea is located in Yosu in the South Cholla province.

As much as the structural change of the Korean economy influenced differential regional growth levels, the existing geographical patterns of infrastructure and industry, along with the economic development policies of the Korean government, contributed to the concentration of industries in certain parts of Korea. At the initial stages of economic development, the military government of President Park Chung Hee decided that the route to fast economic growth would be fueled by an aggressive export-promotion policy. For Korea to secure foreign currency, which is needed to import such vital items as petroleum and food and to resolve chronic balance of payment deficit problems, it was necessary to promote export-oriented economic growth. Korea's limited market size is another factor that necessitated exports so that certain industries could achieve economies of scale.

Since the growth of exports depended on the enthusiastic cooperation of business with the government, the government devised various profit incentives to promote exports. Many benefits and incentives were given to export-oriented industries resulting in phenomenal economic growth. Such aggressive export-promotion policies and profit allocation schemes—more detailed examples of these profit allocation schemes to export industries are illustrated in the following section—given to export industries created a number of distortions in the structure of the Korean economy. Of the many impacts that these export-promotion policies had on the Korean economy, one of them was the profound imprint left on the country's industrial structure.

To achieve export goals, the Korean government became overly concerned about total export volume and hence geared its policies to reward

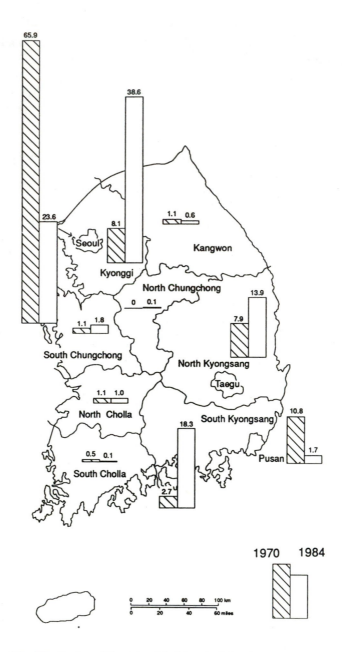

Figure 6.2. Distribution of Precision Machine Tool Employment in Korea (%)
SOURCE: Korea Educational Development Institute (1988, p. 353).

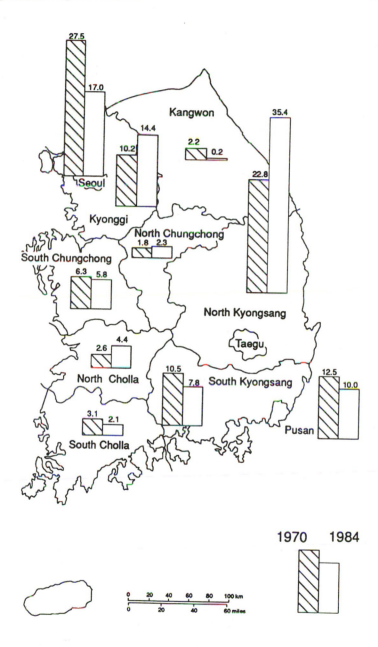

Figure 6.3. Distribution of Textile Employment in Korea (%)
SOURCE: Korea Educational Development Institute (1988,p. 348).

Table 6.5 Regional Distribution of Industrial Employment in Korea
(Unit: Percentage of Total National Employment)

| | Textiles | | Precision Machinery | |
	1970	1984	1970	1984
Kangwon	2.21	0.28	1.11	0.67
Kyonggi	10.20	14.45	8.12	38.61
North Cholla	2.66	4.45	1.12	1.07
South Cholla	3.19	2.17	0.57	0.14
North Chungchong	1.88	2.35	0.00	0.17
South Chungchong	6.34	5.83	1.16	1.88
North Kyongsang	22.88	35.49	7.91	13.95
South Kyongsang	10.54	7.80	2.72	18.31
Pusan	12.51	10.02	10.84	1.75
Seoul	27.55	17.05	65.90	23.67

| | Fabricated Metals | | Electric Machinery | |
	1970	1984	1970	1984
Kangwon	0.50	0.22	0.02	0.43
Kyonggi	10.05	28.71	17.40	36.32
North Cholla	3.46	1.00	0.25	0.64
South Cholla	2.99	0.90	6.65	0.43
North Chungchong	0.78	0.71	0.05	2.20
South Chungchong	3.06	2.15	0.67	1.23
North Kyongsang	15.12	8.49	2.06	5.29
South Kyongsang	2.23	17.27	1.31	15.27
Pusan	17.75	14.61	17.17	3.62
Seoul	43.77	25.87	54.37	29.29

| | General Machinery | |
	1970	1984
Kangwon	3.03	0.50
Kyonggi	9.00	25.47
North Cholla	1.69	0.37
South Cholla	4.93	1.66
North Chungchong	1.75	5.55
South Chungchong	7.43	2.32
North Kyongsang	13.53	11.05
South Kyongsang	13.24	22.13
Pusan	15.20	10.29
Seoul	29.69	20.65

SOURCE: Lee et al. (1988), pp. 348, 353.

businesses that had the highest volume of exports, instead of those with the highest value added. Therefore, exporters did not have much incentive to invest in the manufacturing of parts and intermediate products that required long-term investment in capital and technical resources. Instead, they reaped the benefits given to large exporters by importing parts and assembling products for export. This caused industry to rely heavily on imported inputs. As a result, Korea became import dependent as well as export dependent. While Korea's exports increased from $US 55 million in 1962 to $US 35 billion in 1986, imports increased from $US 442 million to $US 32 billion during the same period.[4]

This heavy dependency on both imports and exports necessitated that exporting industries locate near ports to have the advantage of low transportation costs. Often, the economic success of export-oriented market economies of the NICs' is credited to having highly skilled, low-wage labor that allowed them to build industries based on supplying labor-intensive products to world markets at competitive prices. Few scholars note their geographical advantage as relatively small countries with easy access to waterborne transportation. Hong Kong and Singapore are basically port cities. In Taiwan and Korea, and even in Japan, the most remote inland location is less than 100 miles from the coast. This geographical advantage has played an important role in allowing these newly industrialized countries to have an edge in transportation costs over other countries. This is especially true when one compares the NICs and Japan to geographically large countries such as the United States and Australia.

For Korea to compete with other NICs in the world market for labor-intensive low value products, it was essential to locate export industries near ports and along the major transportation arteries connected to ports. Because of the importance of access to waterborne transportation, the geography of ports largely determined the location of industries in Korea. In general, the east coast of Korea has favorable physical geography for deep seaports so that large ships can dock. Not only does the east coast have great water depth offshore, but also the tidal differences are a minimal 50 cm compared to tides of 1,000 cm on the west coast. For this reason, the major exporting ports are highly concentrated on the east and southeast coasts of Korea. On the west coast, Seoul's Inchon port is the only major cargo and container exporting port. On the southeast and east coasts, Mukho, Pohang, Ulsan, Masan, and Kwangyang are the exporting ports that handle the majority of cargo traffic. Pusan, located in the southeast corner of Korea and equipped with container as well as cargo handling facilities, is the prime port city of Korea, serving the entire nation.

Until very recently, the existing transportation network also played an important role because easy access to ports from inland was vital for exporting industries as well. This also explains the heavy concentration of industries along the Seoul-Pusan axis. Major railroad trunk lines built during the Japanese occupation to access resources in Manchuria connected Pusan to Shineuju via Seoul. The four-lane express highway constructed during the 1960s that served as the major transportation artery also linked Pusan to Seoul, inducing further development of the areas along the route.

There are other economic and geographical reasons as to why industries are concentrated in the Seoul and Pusan areas. Seoul has always enjoyed the advantage of being the prime city, since it has been the country's capital since the Lee Dynasty (1392-1910). With nearly 25% of the country's total population and 58% of total bank loans directed to industries concentrated in the city, it is only natural that business is attracted to Seoul. Access to skilled labor, infrastructure, and markets are only a few of the amenities Seoul can offer.

There are also inherent locational advantages to Pusan compared to the southwestern part of Korea. During the Japanese occupation, Pusan had the advantage of being the major Korean port close to Japan. Thus, before Japan initiated massive heavy and chemical industrial development in North Korea as part of its industrialization efforts in Manchuria, Pusan served as the major light manufacturing center of Korea. To maintain these light manufacturing activities, the colonial government established the basic infrastructure in this area. Also, during the Korean War, as the only part of South Korea that was not largely destroyed by the war and occupied by the communists, South Kyongsang province drew the majority of refugees. Consequently, there was a massive transfer of wealth from the rest of the country to South Kyongsang province, especially to Pusan. From the combination of these two reasons, the Kyongsang provinces emerged from the war with 24.4% of the total manufacturing employment in the country. Following the war, the Kyongsang provinces received a large share of infrastructure investment through soft loans from international agencies such as the United Nations Korea Reconstruction Agency (UNKRA). The Kyongsang provinces' share of total Korean reconstruction aid amounted to 17.3% of the total, second only to Seoul which received 19.8% (M. H. Kim, 1987, pp. 32-33).

Having an export-oriented market economy heavily dependent upon imports of raw materials and intermediate products dictates that industrial locations be concentrated near the ports or along major transportation arteries. Because existing infrastructure and industry were concentrated in Seoul and Pusan at the initial stages of development, and because ports were easier to build on the east and southeast coasts of Korea, it was economical to locate new industries in these areas. Considering that much of the risk for new projects in developing countries comes from undertaking big infrastructure investments, it was an economically rational decision to take such locational factors into account. Thus, fast economic growth, with a heavy emphasis on nurturing industry and exports, found development along the Seoul-Pusan axis to be cost effective. This also allowed export industries to have the competitive advantages of cheap transportation costs and the agglomeration of activities. Such a policy might have been economically rational, but it brought about the uneven distribution of industrial development in Korea and political discontent in the regions that received a low share of the benefits from industrialization. Resolution of regional tension in the Chollas is becoming more urgent now that the new political alignment of Kim Young Sam and Kim Jong Pil with Roh Tae Woo may further alienate this area from the rest of the country.[5]

Geographical Affiliation of Political Power

If the existing economic structure and the existing infrastructure caused the concentration of industries in the Seoul-Kyonggi and Pusan-Kyongsang areas, the political power structure of the Korean government had the impact of exaggerating the locational advantages of these areas. Two of the three presidents since Park have geographical affiliations with the Kyongsang provinces. This has left a profound impact on the elite structure of the country and subsequent allocation of benefits to different parts of the country.

When President Park Chung Hee came to power in 1961 through a military coup, he needed to establish justification of his regime, since a coup is not a legitimate means of assuming a ruler's position. The interim government that Park toppled to grab power was established by the 1960 student revolt against the dictatorship of Syngman Rhee. Even though the interim government was extremely inefficient in dealing with the legacies and corruptions of the Rhee regime, it was symbolic in that it was the product of a successful democratic struggle against a decade-old dictatorship. Park's coup was a jolting event in which the democratization process of Korea regressed. In order to legitimize his rule, which signified regression to dictatorship and military rule, he had to build a broad power base with a large number of supporters.

With military rule, power is monopolized by the officers who participated in the coup and shared the risk. The officers who planned the coup with President Park were alumni of Taegu Sabum (Teacher's Vocational Training School of Taegu) and the Military Academy. Even though they held the most important positions in the government and government-owned corporations, the number of graduates from these schools was not large enough to draw upon as a power base. In a society where school, clan, and geographical affiliations are of crucial importance for social advancement, Park needed to establish his power base by connecting himself with other groups that could broaden his ties and help him establish his legitimacy. Park solved this problem by relying on his regional affiliation with the city of Taegu and the Kyongsang provinces.

The Taegu area of North Kyongsang traditionally had a strong core elite group dating back to the early part of the Lee Dynasty. As descendants and disciples of Yoo Sung Yong and Lee Toi Gey, who were prominent Confucian scholars and leaders of the *Namin* faction during the Lee Dynasty, these scholars held a tight informal network. Confucian schools (*Sawon*) located in Andong, Sangju, and Sunsan were the centers of their gatherings. Even though these groups of Confucian scholars had not held high ranking positions in the government since the latter part of the Lee Dynasty, they managed to maintain a close relationship through the modern period. During the Japanese occupation, their ties were strong enough that they could organize a relatively effective resistance against the colonial regime. Because the Taegu area used to be the center of education for both North and South Kyongsang provinces, these elites educated their children at Kyongbook High School in Taegu. The linkages drawn from these social and school connections were quite extensive and it was this geographical affiliation that Park could tap because he was born in Sunsan. By doing so he managed to establish ties with the elites of the most populous province of Korea, which now comprises approximately 30% of the total population.

The affiliation of a political leader with one region has many implications in the development of a country. Unusually large numbers of people from the Kyongsang provinces entered positions of influence throughout government and industry. They have consistently dominated high-level positions in the cabinet, politically appointed national assembly seats, and supreme court appointments. Statistics compiled by Kim Man Heum (M. H. Kim, 1987, pp. 22-23) shows that 32.0% of the high-level officials[6] from the Second Republic through the Fifth Republic have their family origins in the Kyongsang provinces.[7] A total of 14.6% and 13.0% of the high-level officials during this period were from the Chungchong provinces and Seoul respectively, while the Chollas produced 13.0% of the high-level officials. Examination of the chronological data indicates that the number of high-level officers from the Kyongsang provinces started to rise significantly during the Second Republic when the military government came into power, and reached its peak at 43.6% during the Fifth Republic. The Cholla provinces' share of high-level officers, on the other hand, steadily declined from 16.3% in the Second Republic to 9.6% in the Fifth Republic.

M. H. Kim standardized these figures by the population size of each province to determine whether any given province was producing a disproportionately large number of high-ranking officials. Regional affiliation in Korea is not determined by place of residence, but by the place of one's family origin. The population in each province does not necessarily reflect the number of people born in that province. The most reliable data on population by family origin was first compiled by the Japanese Colonial Government in 1943. Since then the population has been quite mobile within the country. Few statistics have been collected in classifying populations at the destination of migration by place of origin since then; therefore, the 1943 data is the best available source for determining the number of people by place of origin. The data have problems, however; for example, assumptions had to be made that the mortality and fertility rates of each province were uniform over half a century. Also it had to be assumed that there was no interregional migration of population within the country. Given these assumptions, certain demographic models can project population growth in a closed system given birth- and death rates by age and sex categories. Since the assumptions used by these models—such as mortality and fertility rates being uniform throughout the entire country in both urban and rural areas—are too unrealistic, thus the projections are rough estimates.

Using the base population data from 1943, the percentage of high-level officers from each province was divided by the percentage base population of each province.[8] The ratios reveal that Seoul still has the highest share ratio of 3.7 of top ranking officers from the Second Republic through the Fifth Republic. The Kyongsang provinces rank second to Seoul with a ratio of 1.5. Chungchong, Cholla, and Kangwon provinces have ratios of 1.4, 0.7, and 0.7, respectively. From this data, M. H. Kim concludes it is clear that a disproportionately large share of high ranking officers come from the Kyongsang and Seoul areas.

In some ways, the overrepresentation of the Seoul and Kyongsang provinces is not an anomaly in that these areas are economically more prosperous than other provinces. During the Fifth Republic, however, the Kyongsang provinces were overrepresented by 2.2 times their base population—a marked increase from their overrepresentation ratio of 1.5 in the Third and Fourth Republics.

Not only is there a quantitative difference in the number of high ranking officials from the Kyongsang and Cholla provinces, but there are also qualitative differences in the type of positions to which they are assigned. Since the Kwangju incident in 1980, no one from the Chollas has been appointed to security-related positions such as Minister of Justice, public procurator-general, or attorney general (Chun, 1988, p. 264). There was also a concerted effort to appoint at least one person from the Kyongsang provinces in either the public procurator-general's position or in the Minister of Justice position since the Fifth Republic (Chun, 1988, p. 266).

The overrepresentation of the Kyongsang provinces does not stop at high ranking government official positions. Of the 20 largest *chaebol* families in Korea, 9 of their founding fathers came from the Kyongsang provinces (W. W. Lee, 1988, p. 504). Of the top 5 *chaebols,*—if Kim Woo Joong of the Daewoo Group who was born in Taegu is considered to be from Kyongsang province—3 of the founding fathers are from these provinces. Considering that the top 5 *chaebols'* gross revenue equals 61% of the country's gross national product, the concentration of economic power in the Kyongsang provinces is remarkable indeed (Figure 6.4).

The concentration of economic power in the hands of a few *chaebols* resulted largely from the export-promotion policies at the initial stages of Korea's economic development. There are long lists of privileges that were granted to exporters to promote exports through the late 1970s. First, exporters have had literally unlimited access to imported inputs and have paid neither tariffs nor indirect taxes. Wastage allowances of imported intermediate products or raw materials were granted well over the amount required for export production.[9] Even though wastage allowances were later reduced to 10%, they provided exporters with handsome margins by producing goods for the domestic market. In a closed economy where consumer imports are a scarce resource, having access to them virtually guaranteed windfall profits for exporters.

Exporters, at the same time, were allowed preferential access to foreign loans. Between 1965 and 1970, for example, there was a large discrepancy between domestic and foreign interest rates. Korea had high inflation and high interest rates with an overvalued currency. The divergence between the domestic and foreign borrowing rates ranged from 4.4% to 18.0% during this period. For example, during 1966-1970, the foreign interest rate adjusted for foreign inflation averaged about 1.5% whereas the real cost of foreign borrowing faced by Korean borrowers was about –3.1% (Park, 1985,

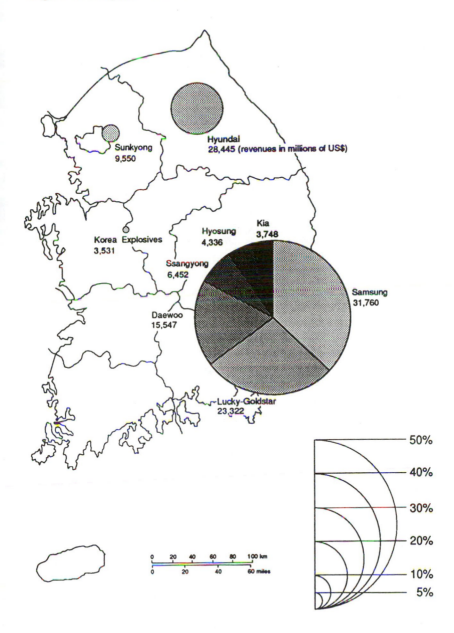

Figure 6.4. Origins of *Chaebols*: Share of Revenues in GNP
SOURCE: Bello and Rosenfeld (1990, p. 64).

pp. 11-12). When the real interest rate faced by borrowers is below market or negative, and an overvalued currency is maintained by government regulation, there is naturally a handsome arbitrage opportunity for those privileged people who have access to foreign loans. The fact that large Korean exporters were consistently able to take advantage of this arbitrage situation clearly indicates that Korea's financial markets were not efficient. Since borrowers expected a stable exchange rate resulting from government regulation, this expectation understated the true cost of borrowing as well, inducing Korean firms to borrow more than they would have done in an efficient financial market. One of the most often cited misallocations of financial resources due to this policy is the large capital investment in heavy and chemical industries that led to a serious economic downturn in the late 1970s.

The privileges mentioned above are only two of the many incentives and profit allocation systems that were given to exporters. With such support from the government, large trading houses grew into *chaebols*. In selecting who should be allowed the benefits among different business groups and exporters, the geographical affiliation, school connections, and kinship network played an important role. Even though it is beyond the scope of this study, the emergence of Lucky Gold Star and Samsung as the top ranking tycoons, and the relative decline of the indigenous capitalists such as Samyangsa Group and Kyongsung Textile Company is a good example of regional affiliations playing an important role.[10]

Intermarriages between the politically powerful families and *chaebols, chaebols* among themselves, and among the politically influential families are quite common. Relationships among the politicians, government officials, military, executives of government-owned corporations, and business elites are close as well (Hattori, 1987, pp. 346-362; Kang et al., 1991, pp. 80-81; W. W. Lee, 1988, pp. 504-505). It is through this network that a political power base was built and the interconnections between politics and business emerged. The fact that about 48% of business heads who previously held nonbusiness occupations came from a background in politics, government, national corporations, or the military is a clear indication that such a network connecting business to politics exists (Itoh, 1984, p. 162). Also, according to Itoh, of business elites who changed occupations, about 53% went into politics, government, national corporations, or the military during the same period.

A large number of military officers placed in high ranking positions in the government and corporations after discharge are from the Kyongsang provinces. The same is true for officials in high ranking positions in the government as well as the business elites mentioned above. The interrelationships among these groups of elites multiplies the impact of concentrated power in the hands of people from the Kyongsang provinces. This in turn induced excessive concentration of investment in industrial facilities and infrastructure in these regions compared to other parts of the country in the past, as was illustrated in Figures 6.2 and 6.3.

Korea did not have natural competitive advantages in heavy industry at the initial stages of its development; thus these industries had to be heavily subsidized in the beginning. The more an industry was supported by the government, the more likely it was that benefits were allocated to regions with political affiliations with the government. Since the allocation of privileged loans and foreign credits were more prominent in the more capital-intensive industries for the reasons explained above, the heavy and chemical industries are more concentrated in the Seoul-Kyonggi and Pusan-Kyongsang areas, while textile industries show relatively dispersed patterns of distribution throughout the country. The best example of this would be locating an electronics complex in Kumi, which used to be a little village not too far from Sunsan, President Park Chung Hee's hometown. The only mitigating factor for the Cholla provinces in heavy industry is that Korea's second largest oil refinery and petrochemical complex are located in Yosu. Recent construction of a large-scale modern steel mill at Kwangyang near Yosu is another exception. This explains the relatively high per capita value-added by the labor force for South Cholla province in 1983 amounting to approximately $US 2,500 in 1990 dollars, when the average per capita value-added from the whole country was $US 1,350 in the same year. It does not necessarily mean that these capital-intensive industries have effective backward linkages with the local economy. This is illustrated by the fact that the total value-added in petroleum and petrochemicals in South Cholla comprised 46.3% of total value-added in the province, when the number of employees in these industries was only 16.7% of total employment. (This does, however, represent a substantial improvement over 1960 when the petroleum and petrochemical sector provided 60.1% of the total value-added and 9.7% of total employment in the province.) There is, however, a limit to the labor absorptive capacity in heavy and chemical industries from the local economy.

The Future of Industrial Development Patterns in Korea

The economic development policies of the Korean government in the 1980s was characterized by a substantial reduction in government control over the economy. Concerted efforts are being made to allow free market mechanisms to take over and correct the distortions introduced by heavy government intervention in the past. Along with these changes in policies, the Korean government is trying to wean *chaebols* from the heavy support to which they are accustomed ("Tough times," Nov. 8). As a part of this policy, the government is attempting to disperse the geographical concentration of industrial development from the Seoul-Kyonggi and Pusan-Kyungsang regions to other parts of the country. This policy has a political motivation of wooing the Cholla provinces from developing increasingly hostile attitudes toward the government. Without having to address the responsibility of Kwangju directly, Roh is trying to appease the Cholla people and to differentiate himself from Chun Doo Hwan of the Fifth Republic by allowing them economic benefits.

There is an economic side to this change in policy that complements the change in the political climate. Korea's real estate prices have skyrocketed in recent years as a result of robust economic growth. When land prices are so high, certain industries that require extensive land, such as the chemical industry, are no longer profitable in Korea. Also due to concentrated development along the Seoul-Pusan arteries, most of the reasonably priced industrial land in these areas is fully utilized and there is little room for expansion.[11] Therefore, the Korean government is planning large-scale ports and infrastructure development along the southwest coast so that it can take advantage of the relatively cheap land prices for industrial development. For example, the land price in Kunsan, recently announced as an industrial complex on the west coast, is approximately $US 52,000 to $US 64,000 per acre at the 1990 exchange rate, while other industrial complexes located in Kyongsang and Kyonggi provinces have unit land price far exceeding $US 130,000 per acre (W. J. Kim, 1988, p. 424).

At the same time, of the $US 20 billion government budget allocated for national and regional development for the period of 1989 through 2001, approximately $US 12 billion will be assigned to the underdeveloped regions including Chungchong and the Cholla provinces (W. J. Kim, 1988, p. 427). Large-scale port construction plans are being drafted for west coast port cities such as Asan, Kunsan, and Namyang. According to the plan, the port capacity of Kunsan, for example, will be increased 40 times. This is quite a contrast to past infrastructure investment patterns where west coast port cities hardly received any investment at all. Express highways connecting port cities along the west coast from Inchon to Kwangyang on the south coast are being planned as well.

As a result of these policies, the spatial distribution of Korean industries is expected to be more evenly distributed in the future. Most of the new industries that will be located along the west coast of Korea will be capital and technology intensive, because the Korean economy already has passed the stage of relying on labor-intensive industries. Since the Chollas' industrial base is dominated by light manufacturing such as food processing, textiles, and clothing, creating a linkage between the existing industrial structure and new technology-intensive industries will largely determine the success of the government's efforts to bring an equal share of income to the Cholla provinces.

Making an effort to equalize the regional concentration of wealth would be one way of appeasing the general population that is becoming increasingly dissatisfied with slowing economic growth and widening income discrepancies. In the face of soaring labor costs, the Korean economy needs major restructuring away from labor-intensive industries to knowledge intensive industries in order to have a relative advantage in world trade. However, the technological level of Korean industry does not allow a smooth transition, for reasons that cannot be discussed in brief in the present chapter. Thus the economic growth perspective in Korea is not too optimistic in the short term. Since Koreans have become accustomed to fast growth in the past three decades, and they face an increasingly uneven wealth distribution as a result of soaring real estate prices and the recent stock market crash, they are starting to demand the rewards of economic growth. There is strong sentiment not to sacrifice for the benefit of economic growth any more. In such an event, the Korean government is faced with a decision whether to continue to aim for high economic growth or concentrate on an even distribution of wealth. Political pressure on the Roh government is the reason behind current development of the southwest of Korea.

Notes

1. Because the statistics published by the Ministry of Construction do not divide the regions along provincial boundaries, it is not possible to compare population and income statistics to provincial data from other sources. However, the Ministry of Construction data provide one of the few reliable regional income statistics able to shed light on the differential levels of regional development in Korea.

2. M. H. Kim (1987) provides various statistics that indicate there is a systematic bias against people from the Cholla provinces.

3. In terms of total agricultural product, the Chollas were prosperous regions comprising 29.4% of the total output of crops produced in the country in 1947 (Ban, Moon, & Perkins, 1982, p. 127). However, because of its high tenancy rate within the region, the poverty index of the Chollas was below the national average before land reform.

4. In 1986 Korea experienced a $US 3 billion overall trade surplus. However, the years between 1984 and 1989 were an anomaly in Korean trade in that Korea recorded trade surpluses for the first time in its history. This was largely due to the three lows—low interest rates, low oil prices, and a favorable exchange rate of the won in relation to the yen—rather than substantial changes in its economic and industrial structure. Before the mid 1980s, Korea was struggling with increasing current account deficits that had to be financed by snowballing foreign debt. The sheer size of debt, amounting to well over $US 40 billion in the mid 1980s, is a good indication of how Korea was still experiencing chronic current account deficits in spite of fast economic growth.

5. Prior to 1990, Korea had three opposition leaders: Kim Young Sam, Kim Dae Jung, and Kim Jong Pil. On January 2, 1990, Kim Young Sam and Kim Jong Pil formed a coalition party, the Democratic Liberal Party, by aligning themselves with Roh Tae Woo. Kim Young Sam has his power base in South Kyongsang around Pusan. Since Kim Jong Pil derives his support from the Chungchong provinces, and Roh Tae Woo draws his main support from North Kyongsang province, the result of this coalition was to alienate Kim Dae Jung whose support comes from the Cholla provinces.

6. According to M. H. Kim's definition, high-level officials are defined as ministers, undersecretaries, and directors at various ministries.

7. The First Republic is the government of Rhee Sueng Man. The Second, Third, and Fourth Republics were headed by Park Chung Hee. Chun Doo Whan was the founder of the Fifth Republic. Roh Tae Woo is the present president of the Sixth Republic.

8. These figures are calculated by dividing the percentage of high-level officers from each province by the percentage of the base population from that province. For example, 43.6% of high-level officers originated from Kyongsang province during the Fifth Republic. In 1985, Kyongsang province had 29.9% of the total population of Korea; 43.6 divided by 29.9 is approximately 1.5.

9. *Wastage allowance* is an accounting term that defines the difference between the volume of imports or production over export, thus allowing a percentage of imports or production to be sold to consumers domestically.

10. As mentioned earlier, Samyangsa Group originated from Gochang in South Cholla province. Kyongsong Textile is one of South Cholla's major industries along with Korea University and *Dong-A Ilbo,* Korea's best known daily newspaper.

11. Note that per unit land price is one variable that determines the rate of return on investment.

References

Ban, Sung Whan, Moon, Pal Yong, & Perkins, Dwight. (1982). *Rural development.* Cambridge, MA: Harvard University Press.

Bello, Walden, & Rosenfeld, Stephanie. (1990). *Dragons in distress: Asia's miracle economies in crisis.* San Francisco: Institute for Food and Development Policy.

Chun, Yool Woo. (1988, July). TK Sadan [TK Division]. *Shindonga,* pp. 254-267.

Hattori, Tamio. (1987, December). Formation of the Korean business elite during the era of rapid economic growth. *Development Economics,* pp. 346-362.

Itoh, Teichi. (1984). Formation of business elites in fast economic growth. *Kaihatsudozokukuno Bisinis Lidashipu* [Business leadership in a developing country]. Asia Kenkyusho [Institute of Developing Economies].

Kang, Chul Gyu, Choi, Joyng Pyo, & Chang, Ji Sang (1991). *Chaebol.* Seoul: Bibong Publications.

Keidel, Albert. (1979). *Korean regional farm product and income: 1910-1974.* Seoul: Korea Development Institute.

Kim, Man Heum. (1988, March). Insa Pyonjoong I Chiyok Kamjong Mandunda [Concentration of high ranking officials from Kyongsang Provinces in the government: Causes of regional confrontation]. *Shindonga,* pp. 486-499.

Kim, Man Heum. (1987). *Hankook Sahoe Chiyok Kamjong Yonku* [Study of regional conflict in Korean society]. Hyundai Sahoe Yonkuso [Hyundai Institute of Social Science Research].

Kim, Wha Joo. (1988, February). Hanbando Eu Saboon Eu Ili Bakuikoita [One fourth of Korean peninsula is changing]. *Wolgan Chosun,* pp. 427-437.

Korea Development Institute. (1989, Spring). *KDI quarterly economic outlook.*

Kuznets, Paul. (1977). *Economic growth and structure in the Republic of Korea.* New Haven, CT: Yale University Press.

Lee, Chan et al. (1988). *Korea: Geographical perspectives.* Seoul: Korea Educational Development Institute.

Lee, Woong Whan. (1988, March). Yongnam Chaebol Eu Inmaek [Human network of Yongnam Chaebols]. *Shindonga,* pp. 500-509.

Mason, Edward, et al. (1980). *The economic and social modernization of the Republic of Korea.* Cambridge, MA: Harvard University Press.

Ministry of Construction (ROK). (1987, December). *Chiyok Kyongjekwonbyol Chonghap Kaebal Keyhoek* [Plans for regional development]. Seoul: Ministry of Construction.

Park, Yungchul. (1985). *Foreign debt, balance of payment, and growth prospects: The case of the Republic of Korea, 1965-1988* (Studies on international monetary issues for the developing countries). [UNDP/UNCTAD Internal Report.]

Research Institute for Human Settlement (ROK). (1985). *Chiyok Charyo Pyonram (Sonamkown)* [Regional statistics (Southwest)].

"Tough times: Korea Goldstar faces a harsh new world under democracy." (1989, Nov. 8). *Wall Street Journal.*

7

Malaysian Industrialization, Ethnic Divisions, and the NIC Model
THE LIMITS TO REPLICATION

PAUL M. LUBECK

The Problem of Replication

Since the first industrial revolution, successful industrialization strategies have invited imitation and replication by economically backward states seeking rapid social and economic transformation. Gershenkron termed this the "demonstration effect," one of the few advantages possessed by late industrializers (Gershenkron, 1982). When applied to the question of states and economic development in the Asian-Pacific region, then the "demonstrated" economic success of the East Asian NICs—Korea, Taiwan, Singapore, and Hong Kong—has, indeed, stimulated much imitation and, inevitably, raises the question whether the policies and institutions responsible for the NIC's success are replicable or transferable, either wholly or partially, to the aspiring NICs of Southeast Asia—Malaysia, Thailand, the Philippines, and Indonesia. Paradoxically, during the 1980s, while Malaysian industrial planners consciously imitated NIC industrial policies, critics charge that they failed to replicate key political institutions or a strong class of indigenous industrialists that, of course, are the trademarks of the NIC model. Given the contradiction between intention and outcome, this chapter pursues the question: Can these aspiring NICs achieve rapid industrialization by replicating NIC industrial policies, even though they have radically different social structures, lack Confucian authority and cultural systems, and are attempting industrialization during a comparatively more sluggish, yet ruthlessly competitive, moment in the history of the international economy?

Appropriately, the Malaysian experience is ideal for evaluating the replicability of the model, for it has launched export-oriented industrialization (EOI), but retains a colonial-origin ethnic division of labor, whereby the Malays control the state apparatus and the Chinese dominate the capital accumulating private sector, a cleavage that undermines close business-state relations so essential to the successful NIC model. Also significant is the fact that all Asian NICs, with the partial exception of Singapore, are ethnically homogeneous societies, a feature that contrasts sharply with the ethnic diversity found in the aspiring NICs. The Malaysian experience forces scholars to consider several interrelated issues: whether the cohesive authority relations that articulate state and society in the NICs implicitly presume ethnic homogeneity; whether a long-standing ethnic division of labor poses an insurmountable obstacle to replicating the model; and, given the latter point, how aspiring NIC industrial strategists might overcome obstacles to industrialization presented by the ethnic division of labor. Let me first examine the achievements and failures of the Malaysian industrialization strategy, and then, in a later section, explore the structural origins of Malaysia's ethnic division of labor as well as the way ethnicity has been treated as an essentialist concept that, purportedly, explains Chinese and Malay investment patterns.

Lessons from the NIC Model

At first glance, Malaysia stands out from other "second tier NICS," not only for registering high rates of economic growth, but also for implementing its "Malaysia Incorporated" and "Look East" industrial policies in obvious imitation of Japan and the Asian NICs. Thus rhetorically, at the very least, Malaysia's industrial strategy is a variant of the East Asian model. What then are the essential features of this model? To be sure, there is variation among the East Asian NICs, arising from historical accidents and different political and social structures. Yet, all are "developmentalist" states, all strategies are administered by comparatively autonomous technocratic elites and all have succeeded by institutionalizing a close relationship between business leaders and state officials in the formation of a dynamic export-oriented regime of capital accumulation (Johnson, 1982). Besides constructing industrial infrastructure (harbors, communications, transportation, and industrial estates) and sponsoring intermediate industries (petroleum refining, steel, and fertilizer), so typical of "deep" import-substituting regimes, the NIC developmentalist state has wedded market rationality to state planning by constructing a "capitalist guided market economy" (White & Wade, 1988, p. 5). "Soft authoritarian" state intervention, to use Johnson's felicitous phase, seeks to augment market rationality, in the long term by reducing risks and uncertainty, as opposed to favoring market distorting interventions that create rent-seeking opportunities for officials and businessmen (Johnson, 1987, p. 141). "Market augmenting" does not, however, mean slavish obedience to free market principles. Not only is state ownership of intermediate and basic industries commonplace, but domestic markets are protected by tariff and nontariff barriers. Amsden convincingly demolishes neoclassical theoretical explanations of Korea's success by demonstrating that "getting relative prices 'wrong' " was, in fact "right." That is, she argues that by insisting on export quotas and other performance standards, Korea's price distortions enhanced growth, private investment, and efficiency over the long term. Firms that met state export quotas were allowed to sell in the domestic market at inflated prices, thus assuring profitability together with EOI (Amsden, 1989, pp. 144-145).

What really happens in practice? Developmentalist state planners constantly assess changing comparative advantages in the world economy in order to upgrade EOI targets that are allocated to domestic producers. While the mix of market-driven competition and market distorting interventions vary situationally according to plan targets, world market demand and productive capacity, that is, from toys to computers, a developmentalist state may provide cheap finance, fiscal incentives, monopoly rents, below-market cost inputs, technological parks, marketing services, or tariff protection in the domestic market. One recognizes, of course, significant variation in the forms of guidance offered by NIC stages in the literature, ranging from the *chaebol*-centered conglomerates nurtured by the corporativist Korean state to the family-centered firms favored by the Taiwanese state (Deyo, 1987; Hamilton & Biggart, 1988). Nonetheless, the essential characteristic of the NIC model rests upon the negotiated relationship between privately accumulating capitalist firms and target-setting state officials; a seminal relationship that links domestic and export-oriented strategies, so as to increase value-added, raise technical expertise, and maintain global competitiveness. Rhetoric aside, whatever slogans like "Look East" intend to communicate, Malaysian industrial policy must be judged by whether state and business elites do, in fact, institutionalize market augmenting policies and whether state subsidies create an innovative, competitive class of manufacturers or a protected, politically dependent class of rentier capitalists. Now let us first examine the case for Malaysia as a fledgling NIC state and then evaluate the critiques of this rosy interpretation.

The Case for "NICdom"

Supporters of the view that Malaysia has successfully entered the pantheon of "NICdom" argue forcefully that the economy has produced very impressive numbers (MIDA, 1990). Indeed, citing conventional statistical indicators, such as recent economic growth (7%-9%/annum), the weight of manufacturing in GDP (26%), the share of export-oriented to total manufactures (50%) and per capita income ($2,182), the financial press has declared Malaysia a NIC (MacFarquhar, 1980, p. 67; *Far Eastern Economic Review* [FEER], September 7, 1989, p. 96). It is the third largest producer of electronic components, after the United States and Japan, and the world's largest exporter of components that are assembled and tested by mostly American firms in export processing zones (EPZs). Recently, Japanese and NIC direct foreign investment (DFI) has mushroomed in other sectors, especially consumer electronics. Interestingly, explanations for the boom in DFI rest not on the exploitation of cheap labor as underdevelopment theorists like Frobel and Kreye argue, for the price of labor is lower in other ASEAN states (Frobel & Kreye, 1980). In fact, Malaysia suffers from a labor shortage, especially acute among skilled electronics workers. The demand for labor attracts an estimated 700,000 to 1 million illegal workers from the neighboring states of Indonesia, the Philippines, and Thailand to work in plantations and domestic service as well as manufacturing. Rather than cheap labor, Malaysia's DFI boom is driven by the interaction of Malaysia's comparative advantages and wide-ranging structural changes in the Pacific Rim economy: that is, by the appreciation of NIC and Japanese currencies, by new inventory and production systems (just-in-time, or JIT) that require local suppliers, by the loss of NIC access to the U.S. market under the tariff-free quotas of the General System of Preferences (GSP) and, relative to ASEAN rivals, by Malaysia's high standard of industrial infrastructure, political stability, civil service discipline, and human capital resources. Further, it can be argued that Malaysia's traditional raw material and commodity exports are efficiently produced and unusually diverse, that is, tin, rubber, palm products, lumber, cocoa, petroleum, and natural gas. Hence, they bolster EOI manufacturing by paying for the foreign exchange costs of importing capital goods and manufacturing inputs as well as by offering forward linkages to resource-based industries using rubber (gloves, tires), palm products (oleo-refining and cosmetics), wood (furniture), and petroleum and natural gas refining (fertilizers, plastics, and petrochemicals). Fortuitously, recent rises in petroleum prices encouraged Bank Negara to revise upward the estimated growth rate to more than 10% for 1990.

Finally, supporters argue that, like Taiwan and Korea, but unlike its ASEAN neighbors, Malaysia has achieved a comparatively equal distribution of income through the implementation of the New Economic Policy (NEP) in 1971 ("The New Economic Policy," 1989). The latter is a program of truly massive state intervention into Malaysia's economy and society, developed in response to ethnonationalist pressure from Malay capital and the shock from the racial riots of 1969 (Shamsul, 1986). To summarize a complex political and legal process, the NEP (1971) was designed:

(1) to eliminate absolute poverty especially among the Malay peasantry;
(2) to abolish the correlation between occupation and ethnicity through an "affirmative action" program requiring quotas for Malays in education, employment and government contracts; and
(3) to restructure the ownership of corporate equity holdings through state funding of Bumiputera (i.e., Malay and other indigenous peoples) "trust agencies" that purchases and holds equities for the Bumiputera community.

To achieve the last goal, the NEP authorized trust agencies to restructure corporate equity ownership among ethnic groups such that, by 1990, the equity share of Bumiputera would be increased from 1.9 to 30%, other Malaysians (Chinese and Indians) would be increased from 23.5% to 40% and foreigners reduced from 60.7% to 30% (Malaysia, 1973). Not unlike other indigenization of industry laws promulgated elsewhere (i.e., Mexico and Nigeria) during the 1970s, NEP represented a bold effort to increase Malaysian control at the expense of foreign equity holdings, to redistribute income to disadvantaged ethnic and class groups, and to abolish a colonial-origin ethnic division of labor, a cleavage that threatened to destroy Malaysia's multiracial democracy and prospects for economic development. Like all "affirmative action" programs, however, the NEP is neither market augmenting nor efficiency inducing in the short to medium term: instead, supporters argue that it has provided the social peace, analogous to social democracy's dampening of class tensions, that has created the institutional basis for economic growth and political stability since 1971. As an official at the Malaysian Industrial Development Authority (MIDA) bluntly stated in an interview: "The Chinese received political stability from the NEP. Racial turmoil attracts neither foreign nor local investment."

The Case for Structural Weakness

However impressive the Malaysian numbers on economic growth may appear when compared to most other second tier NICs, critics assert that the economy is suffering from deep structural weaknesses. From this perspective, massive state intervention into the economy since 1971 neither replicates the positive features of the NIC model, nor the autonomy of state economic planners, nor the articulated relationship between business and the state, nor, in structural terms, a deeper, innovative, and dynamic process of Malaysian, as opposed to foreign, capital accumulation. Instead of "NIC-dom," they see weaknesses, inefficiency, and enclaves. Impressive short-term growth rates, enclave EOI-manufacturing without linkages to the highly protected import-substitution sector, and dependence on raw material export-earnings confirm the existence of deep structural imbalances that require rationalization along market augmenting lines (Edwards, 1990; Jesudason, 1989; Jomo, 1990). Thus the impressive numbers are temporary and illusory, and certainly insufficient evidence for asserting Malaysia's NIC status. Critics stress that, rather than creating a "market augmenting" alliance between business and political elites, one that is committed to strengthening the technical and competitive position of Malaysian manufacturing capital, state industrial policy is riddled with contradictions, irrationalities, and outright corruption. As opposed to strengthening technocratic guidance toward planned goals, the political elite dominates decision making and undermines the comparatively weak technocracy's efforts to rationalize industrial policy. When compared to the high level of policy centralization found in the NIC states, the technocracy's authority is so fragmented among competing agencies (i.e., Malaysian Industrial Development Authority, Economic Planning Unit, State Economic Development Corporations, Ministry of Trade and Industry, HICOM, PETRONAS, etc.) that rational, market augmenting strategies are difficult to implement, even if the political elite consented. Equally important, the necessary consultation between state and business is neglected in favor of interethnic political bargains—money politics—that, though allegedly justified by the NEP, merely line the pockets of an unproductive rentier bourgeoisie who are beholden to a political patronage system that is legitimated by ethnic chauvinism and thus hostile to the discipline of market competition of any kind (Gomez, 1990, 1991).

Regarding income equality, while absolute poverty has probably been reduced to close to NEP targets, relative income inequality within the Malays and other ethnic groups has, in fact, increased significantly since the NEP. Critics, for example, cite the distribution of share ownership in ASN

(Amanah Saham Nasional), the unit trust share agency, which was allegedly created to broaden share ownership for all Malays. Like all the Bumiputera trust agencies, it lacks accountability to share holders. Moreover, less than a third of eligible Malays participate. Worse still from the point of view of inequality, "about three quarters of those participating have five hundred units [i.e., M$500] or less. At the other extreme, half of one percent of participants owns twenty-five thousand units or more" (Hirschman, 1989, p. 80). Furthermore, Hirschman cites Lim and Sieh's (Hirschman, 1989, p. 10) findings that one hundred or so families own almost half the capital in Malaysian corporations. Twenty years later income inequality has increased especially among the Malays, again in contrast to the NIC income profiles.

To be sure, sorting out this debate lies beyond the space limits of this chapter, but several points can be deduced with same certainty. Malaysia has achieved impressive growth figures in manufacturing and successfully emulated certain aspects of export-oriented manufacturing (EOI) in the EPZs. Unfortunately, the structure of production and the relationship between business and the state bear little relationship to either Taiwan or Korea, which are the appropriate comparative cases (MIDA/UNIDO, 1985). It is true that the older domestic manufacturing industries, that is, the ISI sector, are highly protected, dominated by transnational firms and, more significantly, possesses few linkages with the EOI sector: that is, they lack an organic, interactive relationship that would transform the productivity of both sectors as Amsden argues occurred in Korea (Amsden, 1989; see also Edwards, 1990). Despite the boom in direct foreign investment (DFI) in the EOI sector, value added is comparatively low; linkages to domestic suppliers are weak; and efficiency spin-offs that might raise productivity in the domestic ISI sector are absent. The rapidly expanding consumer electronics and appliance industries, to take a glaring example, use electronic chips and components, but there is no strong supplier linkage to Malaysia's components sector. Nor, for reasons discussed below, are Malaysian firms prominent in existing domestic linkages; rather, NIC and Japanese consumer electronics firms are bringing their own supplier firms. If the past record is predictive, any NIC state would certainly have planned to link these sectors and their domestic capitalists would have been assisted, coerced, and subsidized until they created productive linkages.

Curiously, despite the openness of the economy, Malaysia has created a model marked by an extraordinary degree of state intervention into the economy. Yet strong intervention has not performed effectively as a market augmenter, a guided capitalist, planner nor a technocratic prop for domestic

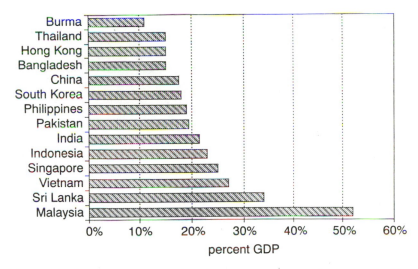

Figure 7.1. Business Indicators: Central Governments' Expenditures as a Percentage of GDP
SOURCE: *Far Eastern Economic Review,* Hong Komng (1990, November 1, p. 75).

manufacturing capital. In practice, enormous sums have been poured into
rural development schemes, heavy industries, Bumiputera loans and NEP
trust agencies. Emulation of Korea's heavy industry program (i.e., HICOM)
produced a nonfunctioning steel mill and a highly protected automobile, the
Proton Saga, which is entirely dependent on Mitsubishi for inputs and management. Observe the astonishing size of Malaysia's central government expenditure relative to GDP presented in Figure 7.1. (Note that the expenditure
of Malaysia's 13 states are not included or it would be even higher!) Undoubtedly, when state expenditure represents more than half of GDP, that is,
almost three times that of centrally planned China, the propensity for patronage and rentier capitalism expands accordingly. At the same time, Figure 7.1
confirms that the financial resources are available to cover subsidies and set
targets, even without foreign aid that was important in the NIC transitions.
If a developmentalist state coalition emerged these resources could subsidize
Malaysian capital with performance standards, improve efficiency and structural articulation between sectors, and/or enhance societal equity. The scale
of these expenditures, together with detailed studies of political party holding companies, noncompetitive public sector contracting, abuses of loan

schemes, and banking scandals, simply contradict the requirement that a NIC-developmentalist state be dirigiste, relatively autonomous and technocratic (FEER, November 1, 1990, p. 75; Gomez, 1990; Haggert & Cheng, 1987). Rhetorical claims of "Looking East" notwithstanding, the structure of Malaysia's manufacturing sector and state industrial policy bear only a distant relationship to the NIC states of Korea and Taiwan.

To respond to one of our original questions, it is now clear that the key relationship between technocratic state elites and Malaysian industrialists is aborted by the separation of economic and political power: The Malays control the state apparatus and the Chinese still, even after 20 years of the NEP, dominate the domestic commercial and manufacturing sector. Rather than aligning with the domestic bourgeoisie, the Malay-dominated state elite have, until now, aligned themselves with foreign capital in exchange for directorships, joint ventures, and other passive, essentially rentier rewards, garnered at the expense of Malaysian-controlled accumulation. Virtually all analysts stress that ethnic competition and cultural differences are the root causes of these structural weaknesses in the Malaysian economy. Jesudason, for example, concludes: "Because of Malay group resentment and envy of Chinese economic success, both aggravated by past Chinese exclusivity in their businesses, the Malay leaders strove to control Chinese business development" (Jesudason, 1989, p. 163). Although this descriptive analysis is true, and indeed suggests how difficult it is to replicate the NIC model in ethnically diverse societies elsewhere in Asia, it would be an error to accept, uncritically, an essentialist explanation that assumes that unchanging, primordial cultural differences are indelibly etched on Chinese and Malay personalities; or one that assumes that the numerically predominant Malays are incapable of altering their rentier mode of accumulation as industrialization deepens. How then does one resolve this conundrum?

First, a sufficient explanation of this cleavage requires a historical-structural explanation for the emergence of the ethnic division of labor from the onset of the colonial period. Second, inconsistencies contained within the dominant explanation—that is, the cultural theory of ethnicity that reproduces ethnic stereotypes recounting the backwardness of the Muslim Malays or the discipline of the Confucian Chinese—must be thoroughly demystified (or "deconstructed" to be more fashionable) in order to suggest routes to alternative futures for both groups. Finally, since no condition is permanent under a regime of rapid industrialization, the evidence suggesting a reconsideration of industrial policy by technocratic Malay elites should be factored into our evaluation.

Structural Origins of the
Ethnic Division of Labor

After reading Jesudason's (1989) description of ethnic competition, it might be easy to forget that our units of analysis, that is, the two ethnic groups now competing intensely with each other—Malay and Chinese—are rather recent social constructions of political solidarity in Malaysia. What were the structural forces that defined their present boundaries? Historically, like the German-speakers of nineteenth-century Central Europe, Malay-speaking groups in the Malay states shared many common cultural elements—language, customary law, and especially Islam—before the British unified the Malay states by gradually introducing "indirect rule." Earlier the Malay peoples in question not only recognized different political authorities, but these authorities were often located in Sumatra, Sulawesi, or Thailand. And, of course, competition, dynastic struggles, and war were common among rival Malay states (Andaya & Andaya, 1982). Hence, the territorial form and ethnonational boundary of Malays in contemporary Malaysia is a product of colonial rule and the political imagination of their community leaders (Anderson, 1983, p. 110).

Similarly the Chinese immigrants to Malaysia, though sharing a common *han* cultural identity, belonged to regionally distinct linguistic groups, which were not mutually intelligible. It is not surprising that the Chinese excluded each other from membership in dialect associations (*Pang*) that were formed by migrants initially attracted to the straits settlements by employment and trade, and later to the interior by the profits from the Chinese-organized tin mining industry. Yen describes the Chinese between 1800 and 1911 as "rigidly divided" by economic competition and because, the leaders "did not foresee a homogenous Chinese society with one dialect, nor did they see the need for such a society" (Yen, 1986, p. 180). The dialect cleavages even "extended to the next world" through different burial grounds that were "intended to separate the spirits of the dead of one *Pang* from an other to whom the dialect would be unintelligible" (Yen, 1986, p. 179). Economic competition between Pangs was so fierce that it ignited a large scale riot in Penang in 1867, involving 35,000 people and lasting 10 days. Hence, history illustrates that the identities of Malaysia's competing ethnic groups are neither natural nor primordial, rather they were invented by leaders who constructed communities in the face of pressures from the world market and later by the constraints imposed by the ethnic division of labor under colonial rule. Is it not possible that new political identities will be constructed as products of rapid industrialization?

In Malaya, as elsewhere, British colonial policy relied on so-called scientific theories of race to organize the social division of labor. Officials assumed each racial and ethnic group possessed inherited predispositions toward performing needed roles in the colonial division of labor, be they martial arts, commerce, wage labor, efficient administration, or subsistence farming. In turn, these beliefs provided the necessary ideological rationalization of colonial Malaya's social order as well as the basis for profitability in the Imperial economic system: The Chinese organized labor and capital to export tin and dominated the intermediary trade between colonial merchant houses and consumers in the interior; the Indians were recruited to work on rubber plantations; and the Malay peasants were encouraged to produce padi rice for local consumption and prevented from planting rubber, a more lucrative crop reserved for plantations and commercial (Chinese) farmers. Alatas (1977) documents the ubiquity of these stereotypes in *The Myth of the Lazy Native,* where he shows how officials constructed a discourse on the docility of the Indians, the indolence and courtesy of the Malay, and the industry and competitiveness of the Chinese. Colonial policy, therefore, not only "consciously sought the ossification of Malay rural society" (Lim, 1984, p. 55), but created an ideology of racial and ethnic stereotypes that "inculcated feelings of superiority and inferiority among, and between, groups" (Abraham, 1983, p. 20). The origins of contemporary ethnic stereotypes lie in the colonial division of labor and in the official discourse on race. Sadly, the subjects still believe the myths and evaluate themselves and others accordingly. Let us examine how the structures of colonial rule inflated ethnic stereotypes and laid the foundation for a weak technocracy and a rentier bourgeoisie.

Structurally, Malaysia's ethnic cleavages emerged from colonial policies that buttressed the Muslim aristocracy on one hand, and crushed economic opportunities for the rural Malays from the commoner strata on the other hand. This is not to argue that the Chinese and Malay were matched equally in the ways of the modern, commercial economy prior to tin mining and British intervention, though a Malay trading class existed in the sixteenth century only to be destroyed by the advance of the Portuguese and Dutch empires. To be sure, originating as self-selected migrants from the highly commercialized regions of southern China, Chinese traders and workers were better positioned than the Malays to garner economic advantages from the colonial economy. Note that these are structural and organizational experiences not dependent solely on cultural values. Worse still for the majority of Malays, British colonial policy not only discouraged Malay rubber producers but introduced a land reservation policy (1913) that deliberately blocked Malay land sales to non-Malays, thus driving down land values by as much as 50% and reducing their creditworthiness (Lim, 1984). Hence, to institutionalize social stability under indirect rule, Malay education was thwarted; immigrants were recruited for clerical and technical positions; and Malay peasants were encouraged to plant low-value food crops without the technical agro-services that the British provided for the plantation sector and, for comparison with the NICs, that the Japanese provided for the peasantry of Taiwan and Korea. All of these policies heightened economic backwardness among the nonaristocratic Malays, thus preventing them from participating in the modern, urban, and commercial sector (Roff, 1967).

Aristocratic Allies
and Rentier Politics

The contrast with Japanese agrarian policy in colonial Taiwan and Korea underscores how indirect rule contributed to the economic backwardness of the Malay and the "rentier" economic orientation of the Malay political elite. However brutally administered in Taiwan and Korea, Japanese agrarian policy was economically progressive in that they expropriated large landlords, transformed the technology of agrarian production and rationalized landlord-tenant relations such that output increased dramatically so that it could be taxed accordingly (Amsden, 1985). Paternalistic indirect rule, informed by Western "orientalism," committed the British to supporting the ruling groups' right to administer customary law and the Islamic religion. Thus the British wedded the power of the colonial state to the decaying cultural authority of a backward feudal ruling class and, because of the organizational and technical superiority of the colonial state, actually strengthened the aristocracy's capacity to exploit their subjects through taxation, licenses, corruption and, above all, indirect control over land title transactions. As salaried officials who dominated recruitment to the civil service, the ruling groups had privileged access to state economic affairs like allocating mining concessions, the purchase of Malay-reserved land, and access to higher education. Talib's study of Trengganu documents the increasing economic insecurity of the peasantry at the same time as the "the new salaried class, by virtue of its political position and social connections, was able to maintain its continued interests in land even after the collapse of its former forms of domination" (Talib, 1984, p. 225).

Structurally, it is readily apparent that today's weak administrative state elite and the rentier bourgeoisie are the immediate progeny of indirect rule. The aristocrats became colonial civil servants; later they formed the leadership of United Malays National Organization (UMNO) as well as providing the first three prime ministers; and now they straddle the public and private spheres as company directors, trust managers, and heads of public corporations. It is for good reason they are labeled the "administocracy" (Jomo, 1986). Hence, the Malay bourgeoisie is weak, relative to the political-administrative class, in large part because "indirect rule" spawned a powerful rentier political class, one yet to be challenged and all too comfortably ensconced within the state. They remain the dominant class. Emerging from colonialism with all the titles and regalia of a nonproductive ruling class, it never felt the competitive pressure nor the financial necessity to pursue commercial and industrial capital accumulation. Initially, the latter role was allocated to the Chinese who formed an alliance with UNMO. Since the NEP, however, aspiring Malay capitalists must rely on the distribution of patronage from the political class whose control over state administration—from Kuala Lumpur to the remotest village—is crucial for obtaining access to wealth or capital (Shamsul, 1986). Even though the NEP expanded the economic power of the political class and opened its ranks to nonaristocrats like Finance Minister Daim bin Zainuddin, the pattern of rentier accumulation established during colonial-rule remains unchanged and, effectively, unchallenged. Interestingly, those among the Malay who became legitimate capitalists have tended to originate from "alien Malay" (Arabs, Indians, and Indonesians) who, though typically Muslim, could not follow the path of the administocracy (Jomo, 1986). This suggests that inherited structures of political domination, not the cultural attributes of the Muslim Malay, are responsible for the weak state technocratic impulse and indirectly for the ethnic division of labor that depended on bargaining among the ethnically based elites. Finally, to return to our comparison with Taiwan and Korea, whereas the American sponsored land reform in those countries abolished the political and cultural power of landlords as a class, essentially finishing what Japanese colonialism began, the contemporary Malaysian situation is just the opposite. The aristocracy retains juridical, political and economic power as a status group with large landholdings, great political influence on state government, and enormous informal influence in the countryside. Since the constitution defines Islam as the official state religion, cultural power is also retained: Each state's Islamic ruler is the enforcer of Islamic law over his Muslim subjects. All of which should be factored in when evaluating obstacles to replicating the NIC model in states like Malaysia.

Ethnic Essentialism or
State Industrial Policy?

If, as argued above, colonial structures were responsible for institutionalizing an ethnic division of labor, nurturing a rentier aristocratic cum administrative class, and blocking avenues of capitalist development for the commoner Malays, how can one explain the persistence of the ethnic division of labor since implementation of the NEP? To be sure, the NEP has thrust the Malay forward as managers, state administrators, professionals, merchants, and to some degree as industrialists. Yet, the problem of industrial linkages remains: Why have neither the Malays nor the Chinese entered manufacturing vigorously so as to develop the network of linkages necessary for the rapidly expanding manufacturing sector? It should be stressed that, while the Malay elite dominates the state apparatus and the coalition government, allied Chinese and Indian elites also share in the distribution of rentier patronage. And given the vast resources expended it is not surprising that the Malay-dominated state has created a Malay bourgeoisie, one largely limited to finance, property and construction, yet weak in manufacturing and generally dependent on state patronage. What, then, explains the weakness of Malay and, to a lesser degree, Chinese industrialists? Jesudason, writing sympathetically to the plight of Chinese business under the NEP, offers two "general reasons" for the failure of Malay businesses:

(1) the failure of Malays to develop the Weberian equivalent of a methodical rational approach to accumulation, and

(2) the very nature of state policies toward Malay business development. (Jesudason, 1989, p. 104)

Let us examine the assumptions and the implications of the first reason. Reference to the search for the "Weberian equivalent" of the Protestant ethic has an almost intoxicating appeal to cultural theorists such as MacFarquhar who hypothesize that a post-Confucian cultural orientation (i.e., family discipline, respect for authority, frugality, etc.) explains why East Asian capitalism has flourished (MacFarquhar, 1980). In his search for the essential culture of capitalism, Peter Berger notes with understandable irony that Weberians in the 1950s argued just the opposite: Confucianism was seen as an obstacle to capitalist development (Berger, 1986; Levy & Shih, 1949). Yet, even though he agrees that Weber was wrong about the potential of Asian capitalism, Berger remains convinced "that, as evidence continues to come in, this hypothesis will be supported" (Berger, 1988, p. 7). If a cultural ethos like Confucianism can be interpreted as an obstacle during one period and later as a "comparative advantage," then it is difficult to reconcile it as a viable independent variable. Instead, this anomaly suggests that any positive effect Confucianism may have on economic development is contingent on a third, probably structural factor, such as an organized-institutional framework or a particular class coalition.

Since all cultural traditions contain valuable moral lessons about honesty, discipline, and authority, often mutually quite contradictory, one supposes that anyone committed to a cultural explanation can, with some diligence, discover a tradition or verse from a sacred text to make the causal connection—from cultural value to observed behaviors—once a state achieves industrialization. Pursuing this line of reasoning, therefore, it is noteworthy that, despite their rich Confucian cultural endowment, Malaysian Chinese businesses have not performed their assigned role as the innovative, manufacturing capitalist as their Confucian counterparts have done elsewhere, or at very least not sufficiently to resolve Malaysia's manufacturing linkage problems. Furthermore, divisions between small-, medium-, and large-scale Chinese capital are significant. Because the major Chinese capitalists are allied with UNMO in a coalition government, they have shared in the same rentier forms of accumulation as the Malay (Gomez, 1991). Jesudason notes that they avoided long term risks by shifting investment away from productive manufacturing to "commercial property and residential housing"; thus "large firms were relatively unhurt by the NEP" (Jesudason, 1989, p. 163). Similarly, Yoshihara argues that the more disciplined Chinese capitalists became "contaminated" by the political networking and rent-seeking practiced by well-connected Malay political actors.

> This in turn affected the business ethics of Chinese capitalists. By working closely with Malay capitalist or Malay politicians, it became possible to make a large sum of money—an accomplishment that would take decades for the most successful Chinese capitalists before the NEP. (Yoshihara, 1988, p. 91)

Hence, Malaysia's structural weaknesses in indigenous manufacturing investment are not easily attributable to the essentialist ethnic attributes of either Malays or Chinese. Rather state industrial policy, or perhaps the lack of one, appears most significant.

Before discussing alternative strategies let us return to Jesudason's (1989) observation that Malays lack the Weberian equivalent of a disciplined, rational approach to accumulation, an obvious essentialist assertion about Malay culture. Writing on this same issue, Morishima argues in the Japanese case that Confucian ethics borrowed from China were reinterpreted in order to support the national goal of industrialization and political independence. Though starting from the same text, "as a result of different study and interpretation [it] produced in Japan a totally different national ethos" (Morishima, 1982, p. 3). A new interpretation combined with a new authority structure capable of institutionalizing new production norms, therefore, explains the success of industrialization in all of the Confucian societies: Japan, Taiwan, and Korea. Success, therefore, requires the combination of two changes: first, a reinterpretation of texts or values, and second, a new organizational structure of authority to institutionalize them. Organized power must exist before the reinterpreted texts may exert their influence.

Leaving aside the issue of organizational structure for a moment, it is readily apparent in the Malay case that any new interpretative framework encouraging methodical, rational accumulation in Weberian terms, that is, as an ethical orientation toward the world, is unlikely to arise solely from rural-origin Malay culture. Why not? Note first that the Malaysian constitution, which describes the special rights of the Malay, defines Malays as practicing Muslims. To reject Islam formally means risking forfeiture of those special rights. Demographically, Malays now constitute the largest urban ethnic group with the highest population growth rate whose rate of urbanization will surpass 50% in the early 1990s. Therefore, just as backward colonial structures created the prototypical rural Malay identity during the period of indirect rule, the rapid rates of urbanization and industrial participation are constructing the material basis for a new urban Malay identity. Not surprisingly, both the social discourse and social boundaries defining the modern urban Malay identity are framed in terms of Islamic texts and values, and not in terms of regionally based Malay equivalents. Hence, it is readily apparent that any reinterpretation of texts underlying a new authority orientation toward accumulation must come from a reinterpretation of the Islamic discourse on development and accumulation. Writing on the modern Islamic resurgence, Muzaffar concludes:

> More than language or any other facet of culture, Islam expresses Bumiputra, or more accurately, *Malay* identity in a manner that has no parallel. Islam touches the life of a Malay at a thousand points. (Muzaffar, 1987, pp. 24-25)

Space does not permit a detailed discussion of the numerous Islamic movements in Malaysia, but it is noteworthy that since independence the most significant opposition to the UNMO alliance has come from the PAS, the Islamic party; that the Islamic student movement's leader was co-opted by UMNO as education minister; and that, in response to the resurgence, the political administrative class has promoted some of the Islamic agenda. Furthermore, since the "reinterpretation" of texts for national development, cited as a prerequisite by Morishima (1982), is already a major intellectual industry among the world's Muslims, it is exceedingly likely that as inequality rises among Malays and the effects of the rentier system of accumulation are challenged, the Islamic discourse on development will be reinterpreted to construct a new authority structure; one designed to rationalize disciplined accumulation. Finally, just like his analysis of Confucianism and capitalism, numerous studies have shown the Weberian analysis of Islam to be false. Paradoxically, Islamization is, in fact, associated elsewhere with the rise of merchant capitalism, for example, Nigeria and in West Africa; and Islamic sects like the Mozabites and Tijaniyyis have reinterpreted Islamic texts so as to associate religiosity with success in the material world, personal frugality and the disciplined accumulation of capital (Abun-Nasr, 1965; Bordieu, 1962; Rodinson, 1978).

Thus it is textually possible for Islam to provide Morishima's reinterpretation of texts for potential Malay manufacturers. But even if this occurred, would it resolve the problems described by Jesudason (19889)? True, redefining *Malay* will not eliminate ethnic cleavages nor ethnic competition. Potentially for the Malays, it could "develop the Weberian equivalent of a methodical, rational approach to accumulation," and thus a sense of much needed confidence. Finally, instead of generating an orientation of clientelism and ethnic rent-seeking, it raises the potential for a cultural orientation toward industrial investment that is universalistic toward community members as well as consistent normatively toward others. And this would surely be a superior ethical orientation toward the material world than that of the present ethnic patronage system.

Regarding ethnic attributes, therefore, the evidence suggests that rentier and nonproductive forms of investment are very common among both the Chinese and the Malays. Ideally, while it is advantageous to possess a highly commercialized, historically deep, ethnic culture, emphasizing discipline, frugality, and reverence for education, culture alone is insufficient without an institutionalized authority relationship between state and business elites. Twenty years after the NEP, there is a new Malaysian dilemma. Armed by the sweeping authority of the NEP, as well as industry licensing laws like the Industrial Coordination Act, the political-administrative class has achieved hegemony over the Malaysian economy. Unlike the situation of 1970, this class now possesses enormous discretionary powers to approve or disapprove projects, to license intermediate industries, and to capitalize aspiring entrepreneurs, a combination that enables it to mediate most economic relations in Malaysia. What has been the result of the increased relative autonomy of the political-administrative class? On one hand, their policies have frightened away Chinese investments in productive manufacturing linkages, while, on the other hand, the hegemonic class has failed to create a disciplined class of industrialists from among their Malay clients in spite of truly staggering expenditures. Hence, without the confidence of the Chinese industrialists or a confident Malay class of industrialists, Malaysia is forced to rely on foreign investment to achieve those rosy numbers in its manufacturing sector, with all the attendant structural weaknesses.

Toward Structural Reform:
The Search for Technocratic Guidance

Given the reality of structural weaknesses in the manufacturing sector, let us conclude by examining the potential for reform represented by the technocracy in the next decade. It is reasonable to assume that ethnic segmentation will remain part of the Malaysian social structure. And because of higher birthrates, the assimilation of Muslims into the Bumiputera, and higher outmigration rates for minorities, the proportion of Bumiputera will rise significantly, probably reaching two thirds of Malaysia's population in the 1990s. It follows that the Malays will continue to exercise control over the state and the economic technocracy. Given the assumption of Malay political dominance, what are the forces that might combine to rationalize state industrial policy in the direction of NIC-like market augmenting strategies, greater domestic investment in linkages, and higher value-added manufacturing?

The inexorable demographic shift toward the Malays coupled with rising income inequality raises the question of whether ethnically based redistribution policies at the core of the NEP can be sustained indefinitely. As the Malay political class becomes increasingly responsible for economic and investment policy and as the Malay rentier bourgeoisie becomes more visible within the economic elite, there will be proportionately less to redistribute to the Malay from others; and, at the level of communal party politics, there will be less plausibility in scapegoating the Chinese for Malaysia's economic problems and structural weaknesses. Recent electoral outcomes reflect these strains already. Ultimately, the lack of competitiveness and low rate of return from both state sponsored and subsidized Malay investments, aggravated by competitive pressures from the international economy, will force factions within the political elite to reform industrial policy. Whatever the outcome of this struggle, the Malay technocracy must play a powerful role in any reformulation.

One of the successes of the NEP has been the creation of a Malay technocratic, professional, and managerial class, one that is increasingly critical of the irrationality and failures imbedded in the present model of accumulation. Mindful of the reconsideration of NEP, which expires in 1991, Malay policymakers both within and outside the state have floated reform packages. Surprisingly, though often described as a think-tank for the Malay establishment, the Malaysian Institute of Economic Research (MIER) recently indicted the NEP for failing to alter the prevailing pattern of Bumiputera underrepresentation in the "commercial and industrial sector," for creating a "rentier entrepreneurial class" and for "the institutionalization of mediocrity" (Salih, 1988, pp. 2-3). Commenting on the future, MIER warned the Malay elite:

> The high degree of dependency created by government-supported programs and politicization of educational goals may also contribute to a closing of the Malay mind, and induce a heightened degree of ethnic polarization that will leave the young[er] generation confused and unprepared for the demands and competition of the twenty-first century. (Salih, 1988, p. 3)

Subsequently, a reformation of the NEP was proposed in a paper coauthored by the director of MIER and a colleague who is now an economic advisor to the Malaysian central bank. Again, they argue for greater competition, reduction in income inequality "regardless of race" and higher rates of "efficiency, innovation, technology and skills." Inattention to the latter, according to their analysis, "shows how much the problems of wastage, inefficient management and shortcomings in skill and manpower, and technological development need to be addressed in . . . the post-1990 economic policy" (Salih & Yusof, 1989, p. 23). Continuing, they dismiss the effort to create a Bumiputera commercial and industrial class by subsidy and patronage as a failure. Hence for these reasons, they argue against the current NEP policy of forced restructuring of corporate equities in Chinese firms (i.e., 30% Bumiputera), acknowledging that forced restructuring of Chinese and others has deterred investment and promoted rentier forms of accumulation (i.e., Ali Baba arrangements). Instead, they argue that fiscal incentives should be used to encourage Bumiputera equity sharing; that Bumiputera ownership of equity should not be a criteria for the establishment or expansion of an enterprise; that take-over actions by Bumiputera trust agencies be limited so that priority can be given to improving the efficiency and productivity of enterprises in which the trust agencies have an ownership stake (Salih & Yusof, 1989, p. 59). Overall, the thrust of their recommendations argue against state intervention on behalf of Malay rentiers and in favor of increasing productivity by forcing the Bumiputera managers, investors, and manufacturers to meet performance standards based upon efficiency. Undoubtedly, just as in other statist economies, there is an intense debate among Malays over the cost and benefit of the rentier model, the question remains whether the technocratic groups will prevail over the political elite that trades on redistribution of rent-seeking opportunities.

Finally, it should be noted that state technocrats charged with monitoring foreign investment and encouraging domestic linkages are also concerned with the irrationalities arising from current state industrial policy. Let us return to the problem of linkages in the booming electronics and electrical sector. Rasiah's work on the electronic components sector shows clearly that linkage and supplier firms have emerged in the Penang region mostly because of competition among international firms, support from the Penang Development Corporation and a ready supply of mostly Chinese small-scale industrialists (Rasiah, 1990). Modest linkage effects were achieved in spite of the relative indifference of the responsible Malaysian (federal) state agencies, largely because most are not Bumiputera owned and managed. Hence, the potential is there but the candidates are Chinese and Indian. If Salih and Yusof's recommendations about equity restructuring were followed, manufacturing linkages would increase immensely. It is important to note that many technocrats who were interviewed about such irrationalities were aware and voiced support of the reforms proposed by Salih and Yusof.

. Finally, structural changes in the Pacific Rim economy have brought changes in foreign investment patterns especially in the booming electronics sector. Instead of originating solely from OECD states, much of the new investment arrives from the NICs, especially Taiwan, Singapore and Hong Kong. Taiwan was the largest foreign investor in 1989 and represented 42% of approved applications in the first nine months of 1990 (*The Star,* 1990). Part of Malaysia's attractiveness arises from Malaysia's Chinese-language schools that enable firms to recruit high quality managers and skilled labor. Since foreign firms that export are exempted from NEP equity restructuring regulations and since state planners must generate employment for the urbanizing Malays, foreign Chinese presence in Malaysia's industrial profile is increasing even in small- to medium-scale industries that supply the NIC firms. Hence, state policymakers have expressed concern during interviews that because NEP equity requirements and other regulations (i.e., ICA) discourage Malaysian Chinese from developing supplier firms but encourage foreign (often Chinese) firms to bring their own suppliers, the state is unintentionally *denationalizing* those very industries that could ameliorate the acknowledged structural weaknesses in the Malaysian manufacturing sector. These are some of the most blatant irrationalities that bedevil industrial policymakers. It is readily apparent that some members of the technocracy are debating policy reforms that would encourage linkage industries regardless of ethnicity. Whether they are capable of overcoming the resistance of political elites remains the pivotal question for industrial policy in the next decade.

References

Abraham, R. (1983). Racial and ethnic manipulation in colonial Malay. *Racial and Ethnic Studies, 6*(1).

Abun-Nasr, J. (1965). *The Tijaniyya.* London: Oxford University Press.

Alatas, S. (1977). *The myth of the lazy native.* London: Frank Cass.

Amsden, A. H. (1985). The state and Taiwan's economic development. In P. Evans, D. Rueschmeyer, & T. Skocpol (Eds.), *Bringing the state back in.* New York: Cambridge University Press.

Amsden, A. H. (1989). *Asia's next giant.* New York: Oxford University Press.

Andaya, B., & Andaya, L. (1982). *A history of Malaysia.* London: Macmillan

Anderson, Benedict. (1983). *Imagined communities: Reflections on the origins and spread of nationalism.* London: Verso.

Berger, P. (1986). *The capitalist revolution.* New York: Basic Books.

Berger, P. (1988). "An East Asian development model?" In P. Berger & Michael H. Hsin-Huang (Eds.), *In search of an East Asian development model.* New Brunswick, NJ: Transaction Books.

Bordieu, P. (1962). *The Algeriens.* Boston: Beacon Press.

Deyo, F. C. (Ed.). (1987). *The political economy of the new Asian industrialism.* Ithaca, NY: Cornell University Press.

Edquist, C., & Jacobsson, S. (1988). *Flexible automation: The global diffusion of new technology in the engineering industry.* New York: Blackwell.

Edwards, C. (1990). *Malaysian industrial policy in the 1990's.* Norwich, UK: University of East Anglia, School of Development Studies.

Far Eastern Economic Review. (various issues)

Frobel, F., & Kreye, O. (1980). *The new international division of labor.* Cambridge: Cambridge University Press.

Gershenkron, A. (1982). *Economic backwardness in historical perspective.* Cambridge, MA: Harvard University Press.

Gomez. T. (1990). *Politics in business: UMNO's corporate investments.* Petaling Jaya: Forum.

Gomez, T. (1991). *Money politics in the Barisan Nasional.* Petaling Jaya: Forum.

Gullick, John, & Gale, Bruce. (1986). *Malaysia: Its political and economic development.* Selangor, Malaysia: Pelanduk Publications.

Haggert, S., & Cheng, Tun-Jen. (1987). State and foreign capital in East Asian NICs. In F. Deyo (Ed.), *The political economy of the new Asian industrialism.* Ithaca, NY: Cornell University Press.

Hamilton, G., & Biggart, N. (1988). Market, culture and authority: A comparative analysis of management and organization in the Far East. *American Journal of Sociology, 94*(Suppl.), pp. 552-594.

Hing Ai Yun. (1984). Capitalist development, class and race. In S. Husein Ali (Ed.), *Ethnicity, class, and development.* Kuala Lumpur: University Malaysia, Persatuan Sains Social Malaysia.

Hirschman, C. (1989). Development and inequality in Malaysia. *Pacific Affairs, 62*(1), pp. 72-81.

Hoffman, Kurt. (1985). Microelectronics, international competition and development strategies. *World Development (special issue), 13*(3).

Horowitz, Donald. (1985). *Ethnic groups in conflict.* Berkeley: University of California Press.

Jesudason, J. (1989). *Ethnicity and the economy: The state, Chinese business, and multinationals in Malaysia.* Singapore: Oxford University Press.

Johnson, C. (1982). *MITI and the Japanese miracle.* Stanford, CA: Stanford University Press.

Johnson, C. (1987). Political institutions and economic performance: The government-business relationship in Japan, South Korea, and Taiwan. In F. Deyo (Ed.), *The political economy of the new Asian industrialism.* Ithaca, NY: Cornell University Press.

Jomo, K. (1986). *A question of class.* Singapore: Oxford University Press.

Jomo, K. (1990). *Growth and structural change in the Malaysian economy.* London: Macmillan.

Lim Teck Ghee. (1984, December). British colonial administration and the "ethnic division of labor" in Malaya. *Kajian Malaysia: Journal of Malaysian Studies, 3*(2).

Levy, M., & Shih, Kuo-Heng. (1949). *The rise of the modern Chinese business class.* New York: Institute of Pacific Relations.

Luedde-Neurath, Richard. (1984, April). State intervention and foreign direct investment in South Korea. *IDS Bulletin, 15*(2).

MacFarquhar, R. (1980, February 9). The post-Confucian challenge. *The Economist,* pp. 67-72.

Malaysia. (1973). *Mid-term review of the Second Malaysia Plan, 1971-1975.* Kuala Lumpur: The Government Printer.

MIDA. (1990). *Statistical information* (various). Kuala Lumpur: MIDA.

MIDA/UNIDO. (1985). Electronics and electrical industry. *Industrial master plan, Malaysia, 1986-1995. Vol. 2, part 8.* Kuala Lumpur: MIDA.

Morishima, M. (1982). *Why has Japan "succeeded"?* Cambridge, UK: Cambridge University Press.

Muzaffar, C. (1987). *Islamic resurgence in Malaysia.* Petaling Jaya: Penerbit Fajar Bakti.

Rasiah, Rajah. (1990). *The electronics industry in Malaysia: Implications for neo-classical and neo-Marxist theories.* Post Graduate Research Seminar Series (unpublished). Cambridge, UK: University of Cambridge, Faculty of Economics and Politics.

Rodinson, M. (1978). *Islam and capitalism.* Austin: University of Texas Press.

Roff, William. (1967). *The origins of Malay nationalism.* New Haven, CT: Yale University Press.

Salih, K. (1988). *The new economic policy after 1990* (Mier Discussion Papers, No. 21). Kuala Lumpur: MIER.

Salih, K., & Yusof, Z. (1989). Overview of the new economic policy and framework for the post-1990 economic policy. *Malaysian Management Review, 24*(2), 13-61.

Shamsul, A. (1986). *From British to Bumiputera rule.* Singapore: Oxford University Press.

The Star. (Kuala Lumpur). (1990, October 7).

Talib, S. (1984). *After its own image.* Singapore: Singapore University Press.

The new economic policy: Where now? (On equity and equitability.) (1989, August 1-15). *Malaysian Business.*

White, G. (Ed.). (1988). *Developmental states in Asia.* New York: St. Martin's.

White, G., & Wade, R. (1988). Developmental states and markets in East Asia. In G. White (Ed.), *Developmental states in East Asia.* New York: St. Martin's.

Yen, Ching-hwang. (1986). *A social history of the Chinese in Singapore and Malaya.* Singapore: Oxford University Press.

Yoshihara, K. (1988). *The rise of ersatz capitalism in South-east Asia.* Singapore: Oxford University Press.

8

The Japanese State and Economic Development
A PROFILE OF A NATIONALIST-PATERNALIST CAPITALIST STATE

HARUHIRO FUKUI

The main purpose of this chapter is to discuss selected aspects of the economic development of modern Japan in order to illustrate and highlight the role of the state as the designer and propagator, and private enterprise as the main beneficiary of an ideology conducive to rapid economic growth at certain developmental stages of a national economy. Like all other ideologies, this ideology is a complex of a number of dogmas, but nationalism and corporatism are the two that are most directly relevant to my explanation of the ideology's impacts on economic developments in modern Japan.

I shall first discuss the origins and evolution of the ideology in post-Tokugawa and pre-World War II Japan, then trace its transformation and impacts on the development of the postwar Japanese economy, and finally touch on recent political-economic changes and their implications for the future of Japanese capitalism in general and its ideological basis in particular. The discussion will demonstrate that capitalism has triumphed in modern Japan, in postwar Japan in particular. This, however, is an unorthodox and deviant species of capitalism that, unlike the orthodox capitalism defined and conceptualized by Marxists, rejects class interests as the legitimate, not to mention the sole, basis of social action and political organization. Its success therefore has more to tell us about the performance of a deviant and heretical variant of late-developer capitalism than about the performance of capitalism as such. My discussion will show that, if effectively inculcated in a literate and skilled work force and supported by an appropriate state and corporate institutions, an anticlass ideology that emphasizes national unity, corporate solidarity, and collective achievement serves the goal of rapid economic development very well.

The Pre-World War II Japanese State and Economic Development

Born in the mid-nineteenth century revolution known as the Meiji Restoration, modern Japan was founded as a state intensely nationalistic in its ideology and paternalistic in its view of domestic society and economy. It evolved during the next 70 years with remarkably little fundamental change either in its ideology or in its behavior. The nationalist/paternalist orientation of the state is owed both to the special circumstances of the revolution and to the special character of the leadership that dominated the post-Tokugawa state.

The special circumstances include both external and internal developments: that is, the growing threat to Japan's territorial integrity and political independence posed by advancing Western colonialism, the apparent inability of the Tokugawa shogunate to cope effectively with that threat, and the increasing disunity and conflict among the Japanese themselves (Saitō, 1981; Tanaka, 1976).[1] Gripped by a deepening sense of national crisis caused by these developments, bands of younger and lower-ranking samurai in outlying domains in southwestern Japan successfully revolted to build a new state in a mold reflecting their preoccupations and commitments. These preoccupations and commitments in turn reflected their underprivileged samurai backgrounds as well as the nature of the national crisis as perceived by them.

The majority of low-ranking samurai in Tokugawa Japan constituted a propertyless salaried class who performed mainly petty clerical duties in the service of either the Tokugawa shogunate or local domain (*han*) governments (Kimura, 1967, pp. 77-195; Omachi, 1970). They thus held a status distinct from and higher than those of farmers, artisans, and merchants. This status distinction was rigidly maintained until the end of the Tokugawa period even as a small but vigorous and thriving bourgeois class emerged in the major cities, notably Edo (later renamed Tokyo) and Osaka (Crawcour, 1965, pp. 17-44; Fujino, 1961, pp. 285-310, 459-492; Fukai, 1980, pp.148-194; Wakita, 1980, pp. 77-92). As the band of revolutionaries from the lower samurai ranks toppled the feudal regime and began to build a new state in the mid-nineteenth century amidst a national crisis, they were determined to ensure Japan's independence and integrity by rapid industrialization to build "a rich nation with a strong army" (*fukoku kyōhei*). Consistent, however, with the traditional distinction between the ruling samurai as managers and the ruled farmers, artisans, and merchants as producers, the new leaders of Meiji Japan attempted to achieve their goals by indirectly nurturing and managing, rather than directly running, new and old industries. During the first post-Tokugawa decade the new Meiji state set up and directly managed, at substantial financial losses in most cases, a number of mining and manufacturing operations, notably coal and silver mines, silk reeling and cotton spinning mills, shipyards, and cement factories (Asai, 1980, pp. 231-232; Smith, 1955). Most of them, however, were sold to a few select businessmen in the 1880s and, until the late 1930s, the state by and large limited its own role to indirectly nurturing private businesses in selected areas by tax breaks, subsidies, tariffs, and so forth.

Thus emerged a distinctively *nationalist/paternalist* state that was to survive the enormous changes in its internal and external environments in the next century, including a series of wars culminating in World War II. This was a state that would, by its very nature, promote domestic harmony, consensus, and unity, and suppress dissensus and conflict. It tried to ensure national unity, on the one hand, by the manipulation of the emperor cult—that is, the myth that the emperor was divine, and imperial rule eternal and inviolable—and, on the other, by ruthless suppression of ideas and ideologies that challenged the orthodoxy. Class theory in general and Marxist class theory in particular was especially offensive to the leaders of this state. Even more offensive and dangerous were actual industrial actions by workers and revolts by farmers inspired by such theory. The appearance of the first Japanese labor union in 1897 was met by the enactment of the Peace and Security Police Law in 1900, while a temporary resurgence of the labor movement in the wake of the Russo-Japanese War (1904-1905) was stalled by the brutal repression that followed the apprehension and prosecution in 1910-1911 of two dozen leaders of its radical wing on the charge of an assassination plot against the emperor (Tsujinaka, 1971). The anticlass and antilabor thrust of the Peace and Security Police Law was substantially sharpened in the Peace and Security Maintenance Law that replaced it in 1924. At the peak of the organized labor movement in pre-World War II Japan in the early 1930s, less than 8% of Japan's total industrial work force was unionized (Sheldon, 1987, p. 256).

Political parties espousing class theory were punished even more harshly. The Meiji state permitted the formation and activities of loyal political parties as early as the mid-1870s, that is, a decade and a half before the Constitution of the Japanese Empire was promulgated (1889), and a bicameral and partially elective parliament, the Imperial Diet, was instituted (1890). In fact, party government by loyal and conservative parties was accepted as the "normal" form of government by the turn of the century and remained so until the early 1930s, when it began to be increasingly overshadowed, but never totally replaced, by military government (Berger, 1988, pp. 97-153; Masumi, 1965-1980; Scalapino, 1967a). Parties espousing class theory, however, were an altogether different story. Japan's first left-wing party of a few hundred members, the Oriental Socialist Party, was banned within two months of its founding in 1882. Several socialist parties were nominally formed during the first two decades of the twentieth century, but each was banned within between two days and one year (Ota, 1971; Yamakawa, 1979). The Japan Communist Party founded in 1922 met a particularly brutal response from the wary and nervous state: It was immediately declared illegal and thereafter subjected to constant police surveillance, harassment, and arrest and imprisonment of its leaders until its ranks, modest from the beginning, were virtually decimated by the mid-1930s (Koyama, 1967; Scalapino, 1967b).

At the same time, however, the Japanese government also followed, to a limited extent, precedents set by European, notably German, governments and attempted to bring about peace and harmony in industrial relations by providing a modicum of legal and economic protection for employees. The Factory Law enacted in 1911, for example, banned employment of children under the age of 12 and night work by women and minors and limited the workday to 12 hours (Mori, 1979, pp. 89-94, 126-134). The government also tolerated labor organizations, such as the Friendship Society (Yūaikai, 1912-1919), that showed willingness to cooperate with management, rather than advocating class ideology (Kobayashi, 1986, pp. 9-10; Suehiro, 1959, pp. 46-47). By the early 1920s, the Factory Law had been revised and several new laws enacted, with the blessing and assistance of the Home Ministry's newly created Bureau of Social Affairs, to provide better protection of employees' health and welfare (Ikeda, 1982, pp. 7-9, 23-30). By this time, corporatism had become a prominent feature of Japanese management's approach to docile and loyal labor, while, with the help of the state, it ruthlessly suppressed left-wing unions.

The leaders of the Meiji state were more circumspect from the beginning in responding to recurrent, and often violent, disputes between rural landlords and tenant farmers than in dealing with militant labor unions. During the Tokugawa period the ownership of land was a privilege reserved to the Tokugawa shogunate, the lords of the 300 or so feudal domains, and a small number of wealthy farmers (Fujino, 1961, pp. 333-400). The Meiji state, however, granted landownership to ordinary farmers in return for the payment of newly instituted land taxes and this led to the emergence of a substantial rural landlord class and its even more substantial but impoverished twin, a class of tenant cultivators. This bifurcation of the rural population in turn led to a series of often violent disputes between landlords and their tenants and, by the early 1920s, to the emergence of a militant national tenant organization. The government attempted, ultimately with considerable success, to defuse the rural conflicts and tension essentially by nurturing owner-cultivators ("middling farmers") with both modest material incentives—subsidies for irrigations works, expanded extension service, construction of agricultural schools, and so forth—and then controlling them through a network of government-sponsored rural organizations (Fujino, 1961; Tabata, 1981, pp. 15-27).

By far the most significant and successful means used by the prewar Japanese state to promote domestic harmony and national unity was, however, systematic indoctrination of the youth in a mixture of the Shintoist emperor cult and the Confucian ideology of loyalty to the state and its existing institutions. Shinto was originally just a variant of simple and primitive shamanistic animism common among rice farmers of monsoon Asia with its characteristic belief in ubiquitous spirits and ancestor worship. In late Tokugawa Japan, however, the animism was transformed, by a small group of nationalist scholars known as the Mito School, into an elaborate theology of a divine nation eternally ruled, or to be ruled, by a succession of emperors who descended directly from the Sun Goddess and who were themselves gods in human guise (Gotō, 1988, pp. 21, 32-40). This theology was further refined and exploited by the early nineteenth century nationalist revolutionaries, first, to bring down the Tokugawa shogunate and "restore" a 16-year-old boy emperor to his heaven-ordained rulership and, then, to unite and mobilize the entire nation in a frantic drive to build a "rich country with a strong army" (*fukoku kyōhei*) under the new government. Within a few years of the revolution, a number of new Shinto shrines were built around the country, all shrines in the nation were then systematically ranked, and Shinto rites regulated by law (Murakami, 1982, pp. 22-26). In short, Shinto became Japan's official state religion. Beginning in 1906, moreover, many of the 190,000 or so shrines scattered around the country were consolidated so that as a rule each and every village had one shrine. This "reform" paved the way for the use of Shinto parishes and parishioners as a tool to combat and quash the radical, and often Marxist-inspired, labor and peasant movements that arose in the wake of the Russo-Japanese War (Murakami, 1982, pp. 50-51).

Shinto in pre-Meiji Japan had evolved in close association with Confucianism, which was imported from China by the fifth century A.D., as well as with Buddhism, which reached Japan about a century later via China and Korea. It was, in fact, Confucianism rather than either Shinto or Buddhism that served as the "state religion" in Tokugawa Japan and the Confucian ideals of social order and harmony maintained by a moral and benevolent ruler and his loyal, disciplined, and industrious subjects that informed both the politics and society of the period (Imanaka, 1972). The Meiji government elevated Shinto above Confucianism—an obvious foreign import—as the new state religion, but it did not cease to exploit the core dogmas of Confucianism for exactly the same purposes as the Tokugawa shogunate had done, that is, to unite and mobilize the nation for tasks set by the state. The 1890 Imperial Rescript on Education thus referred to "loyalty to His Majesty and filial piety to parents" as the eternal "essence" of the Japanese polity (Imanaka, 1972, pp. 42-43; Togawa et al., 1987, pp. 4-5). Thereafter, Confucianism served as a "spiritual pillar" of the nation to help "maintain order in the state, in society, and within the family" and "nurture moral conduct" among the people, as an influential Confucianist organization recently declared (Togawa et al, 1987, pp. 18-19).

The new Shinto-derived state religion, reinforced by the core dogmas of Confucianism, was propagated in Meiji Japan not only by the newly built and embellished shrines and government-sponsored rites but, far more importantly, by a newly established system of public education. In one of their first and most important decisions, the leaders of the Meiji state undertook in 1872 to create a three-tiered system of public education composed of compulsory primary schools and voluntary middle and high schools and universities (Tamura, 1988, pp. 41-52). The enrollment of all children and their exposure to state-sanctioned standard textbooks was the central objective of the system from the beginning, an objective successfully achieved by the turn of the century, although the legally required enrollment period was initially four years and did not reach six years until 1907. By the first decade of the twentieth century, nearly all school-age children were enrolled, although no more than about three-quarters of them regularly attended classes.[2]

Shinto and Confucian dogmas played an important part in primary school textbooks from the beginning but became particularly salient after the 1910s. Children were taught to be loyal, cooperative, and industrious, as well as literate and able, workers in the service of the state. Only a small minority of these children went to one or another kind of secondary school, and an even smaller minority to high schools and universities.[3] The system as a whole emphasized a curious mixture of seemingly contradictory principles: Egalitarianism at the primary school level and elitism at the higher, especially the university, level. Emphasis on performance and achievement served as a sort of hinge between the two opposing principles.

The Meiji government's initial approach to public education was actually quite liberal and emphasized objectivity and universalism in the preparation of curricula. By the early 1880s, however, this initial approach was abandoned in favor of an explicitly and narrowly nationalistic policy with extensive use of Shinto and Confucian dogmas, as reflected in the series of Ministry of Education ordinances issued during the decade, particularly the 1886 decree on teachers colleges (Horimatsu, 1985, pp. 97-99, 114-115, 129-131; Kokumin kyōiku kenkyūjo, 1973, pp. 46-49, 59, 62, 71-73, 80-84; Kubo, 1979, pp. 10-11; Oe, 1974, pp. 42-48). Moral education, that is, inculcation of nationalist ideology was the task assigned mainly to primary and secondary schools and was administered mainly through ethics, Japanese language, Japanese history, and geography courses. After 1903, textbooks used in these four subject areas were screened and selected by the Ministry of Education, a practice extended to texts in mathematics and drawing in 1905 and sciences in 1910 (Horimatsu, 1985, pp. 150-151; Kubo, 1979, pp. 49-51). About half the hours (15 out of 28 hours per week for boys and 15 out of 30 for girls) spent in class by fifth and sixth graders was devoted to these subject areas, while about a third of the time spent in class by secondary school students was consumed by courses in those areas (Kubo, 1979, pp. 146-147, 154). A typical passage in a 1930 ethics text for upper primary school classes taught the pupils that "the easiest way to practice one's patriotism" was to "discipline oneself in daily life, help keep good order in one's family, and fully discharge one's responsibility on the job" (Murakami, 1982, p. 64). By comparison, both curricula and textbooks used at the postsecondary levels emphasized more specialized and technical subjects and were largely free of overtly ideological material (Kokumin kyōiku kenkyūjo, 1973, pp. 94-99).

Outside the formal education system, the increasingly strident and chauvinistic nationalist ideology was disseminated by a number of mass organizations, most sponsored directly or indirectly by the government. Youth associations were set up throughout the country in the 1910s, primarily to combat "alien," particularly, Marxist, ideologies in the wake of the Russo-Japanese War and effectively performed that function especially after they were brought under the centralized direction of a national headquarters in 1924 (Kokumin kyōiku kenkyūjo, 1983, p. 131; Waswo, 1988, pp. 572-576). More than 30 organizations were formed in the 1910s and 1920s for similar purposes, many with a membership running into several hundreds of thousands.

The private sector of the economy, especially its urban industrial part, took full advantage of both the work force thus nurtured and indoctrinated in state-controlled schools and the state-fostered ideological environment of the entire society. The dominant feature of that environment was nicely captured by Governor Murakami Yoshio of Ishikawa Prefecture in his 1904 speech at a prefectural trade school:

> Military warfare has its limits. Meanwhile, industry that lies at the base of national power rises or falls at each passing moment and the world situation compels all (nations) to participate in fierce competition (for industrial supremacy). . . . You must understand that war in peace time goes on constantly. In this kind of war, that is, struggle for survival, those who exploit scientific instruments to expand industry, produce goods at low costs, and thus absorb financial resources will nurture the strength of their own nation, enrich its resources, and thus emerge as winners, while those who fail to do so will gradually lose their financial resources and exhaust the strength of their nation . . . to end up as losers. For this reason, while we win a military war to guard our national security, protect our possessions, and expand our national influence, we must at the same time win the war in peace time so as to gain hegemony in East Asia, enrich our financial resources, and place ourselves in a position to lead [other nations in the region]. (Oe, 1974, pp. 159-160)

Labor unions were formed in the 1910s and thereafter, but they were all either effectively tamed by management and brought under its control or, if they insisted on fighting management, simply destroyed. Japan's first major labor federation that had evolved from the Friendship Society of the 1910s, the Japanese Confederation of Labor (*Nihon rodo sodomei*), embraced militant syndicalism for a short while in the early 1920s. It shifted its position to a moderate cooperationist line, however, following the 1923 Great Kanto Earthquake during which mass hysteria led to mob attacks—often with the acquiescence of or in collusion with local police—that proved fatal to a number of prominent Marxists as well as Koreans (Ikeda, 1982, p. 256). The 1925 Peace Preservation Law then banned all organizations denouncing either the principle of imperial sovereignty or that of private property (Murakami, 1982, pp. 55-56).

Harnessed to a massive amount of industrial machinery and technologies imported from abroad in great haste, the literate, hardworking, largely nonunionized, loyal, and achievement-oriented labor force drove the industrialization of the prewar Japanese economy. Agricultural labor that accounted for about three quarters of the total work force at the end of the Tokugawa period fell to about two-thirds by the turn of the century, less than one half by the early 1930s, and about 40% by the eve of World War II, while manufacturing output rose from 6% of the gross domestic product at the turn of the century to 30% by World War II (Patrick & Rosovsky, 1976, pp. 7-8). Meanwhile, the gross national product grew at an accelerating real annual rate of about 3.5% in the 1920s and more than 5% in the 1930s.

The economy that developed in pre-World War II Japan was clearly a market-based capitalist economy. It was, however, a capitalist economy nurtured in an ideological environment characterized by preoccupation with domestic harmony and unity and strong antipathy toward all divisive ideas and activities, especially Marxist theory of class warfare. It was also a remarkably successful economy that grew at a steadily accelerating rate to become one of the world's major industrial economies within a little more than half a century.

The Postwar Japanese State
and Economic Development

If the success of the state-managed economy in pre-World War II Japan was remarkable, the performance of the postwar Japanese economy has been spectacular. To repeat a somewhat tired cliché, for the 40 years since 1950, it has maintained the highest, and by and large the most stable, average annual growth rate among the major industrial nations. Juxtaposed with its prewar counterpart, the postwar growth curve may give the impression that it has merely extended the prewar curve beyond 1950, with a roughly 10-year interval caused by the war and its immediate aftermath. Such an impression, however, is too simplistic, considering the magnitude of the postwar reforms implemented under the auspices of the Allied occupation authorities. These reforms reached and transformed virtually all important political, economic, and social institutions of the vanquished and occupied nation, from its constitution to business conglomerates (*zaibatsu*), rural landlordism, state Shinto, the status of women, and the educational system, not to mention the entire military establishment and police organizations.[4]

The prime targets of the sweeping reform program were virtually all of the institutions and practices that were responsible for the rapid industrialization and growth of the prewar Japanese economy. The emperor cult was condemned, as were all other forms of ultranationalist ideology, including Shinto and Confucian dogmas. School textbooks were purged of all affirmative references to "undemocratic" ideas and practices. In fact, long before the

Supreme Commander for the Allied Powers (SCAP) issued the first official decree on the subject of school textbooks, the Japanese government acted on its own to remove teaching materials likely to be targeted by SCAP sooner or later. As early as September 20, 1945, the Ministry of Education thus instructed all schools either to black out or treat with extreme care any part of textbooks in use, especially in Japanese language courses, that praised chauvinism or denigrated international peace and amity (Horimatsu, 1985, p. 253; Kubo, 1984, p.200). Most textbooks, especially those in ethics, contained so many potentially offensive passages that they were virtually soaked in the India ink used to black them out and became unusable. SCAP then followed the Japanese government's initiative by ordering suspension of all ethics, Japanese history, and geography textbooks in December and designating additional passages in Japanese language and mathematics textbooks to be blacked out (Horimatsu, 1985, p. 254; Kokumin kyōiku kenkyūjo, 1973, p. 203; Kubo, 1984, pp. 203-204).[5] These old textbooks were first mercilessly gutted and then replaced by brand new textbooks produced under the Ministry of Education's supervision in accordance with a set of strict SCAP guidelines aimed at thoroughly democratizing the entire Japanese educational system overnight.

Meanwhile, an extensive bill of rights guaranteed by the new Occupation-authored constitution to all Japanese citizens explicitly included the "[F]reedom of assembly and association as well as speech, press and all other forms of expression" (Constitution of Japan, Article 21). Left-wing political parties, including the Japan Communist Party, were now fully legal and free to espouse whatever political views they preferred, including Marxist class theory, as were labor unions to bargain collectively with management and any other kind of organizations to engage in any peaceful form of activity to advance the interests of their members. Moreover, most of these reforms, undoubtedly among the most thorough and radical of the kind ever undertaken in modern world history, were not only swiftly and effectively implemented but have since become integral and permanent components of the postwar Japanese polity and society.

The spectacular performance of the postwar Japanese economy has thus occurred despite the sweeping changes in both core institutions and ideology of the modern Japanese state. Any plausible explanation of the Japanese "miracle," then, must contend with the paradox between, on one hand, the real and profound impacts of the postwar reforms and, on the other, the apparent continuity and consistency in the pattern of the growth performance of the Japanese economy before and after those reforms. The following is a preliminary and obviously very incomplete attempt to formulate such an explanation.

As I have argued above, an outstanding feature of the core ideology of the prewar Japanese state was its commitment to building "a rich nation with a strong army" and another, and closely related feature was its preoccupation with national independence, integrity, and unity, and concomitant antipathy toward any ideas or activities that threatened to divide the nation, such as Marxist class theory. The basic ideological means to achieve these goals— for example, the emperor cult, Shinto and Confucian dogmas, and so forth— were designed and developed by the state and exploited by private industrialists and businessmen to train and tame their employees. The state attempted to accomplish its goals by, on one hand, indoctrinating youth with the correct ideology through the public education system and, on the other, indirectly managing and guiding the operations of economic and social groups in the private sector.

This strategy, however, failed to produce a totally loyal and dedicated work force and a great deal of physical coercion and repression had to be used against dissidents and rebels. This was particularly true in the period following the Russo-Japanese War, when class divisions sharpened in a postwar recession, peasant revolts spread, a series of industrial disputes erupted, strikes by copper miners and cotton mill women workers shook the nation, and Japan's first Marxist parties were formed (Ota, 1971, pp. 155-231). The government responded to the crisis with renewed emphasis on Shinto and Confucian teachings, as in a 1908 imperial rescript and in the 1910 revisions of school textbooks (Oe, 1974, p. 104).

The postwar reforms put an end to the state's sponsorship and instigation of the exclusivist and xenophobic nationalist ideology ("ultranationalism") as well as militarism. They also vastly expanded the sphere of private individual and collective activities free from state-imposed restrictions, as well as significantly strengthening egalitarianism in social and economic relations, especially in the education system. They did not, however, attempt to suppress, much less eliminate, either the more moderate form of nationalism—that is, the cultivation of national identity and the defense of national integrity and independence—or the psychological antipathy toward class theory and other divisive ideologies, as opposed to the legal proscription of them.[6] What actually happened, in large measure thanks to, rather than in spite of, the postwar democratic reforms, was in fact deeper penetration of society in general and the corporate world in particular by the anticlass ideology of consensus and cooperation. The promotion of the unionization of labor, land reform, emancipation of women, the democratization of the education system, and so forth, all contributed to the eclipse rather than the popularity of the ideology of class warfare, notably Marxism and its variants.

Like all interpretations of complex social phenomena, the validity of this conclusion cannot be directly proven. A number of well-documented developments in the past four decades, however, provide fairly strong, if not conclusive, circumstantial evidence. To cite only a few examples—the conservative Liberal Democrats, known for their consistent support of moderate nationalism and capitalism, have consistently received no less than about 42% of the valid ballots cast, representing about 30% of all eligible voters, in the House of Representatives general elections since 1955; by comparison, the Communists, known for their opposition to capitalism and suspect in their allegiance to nationalism, have never received more than about 10% of the ballots cast, representing about 7% of all eligible voters, in those elections (Curtis, 1988, appendix). Meanwhile, a series of annual public opinion polls administered by the Office of the Prime Minister since 1958 have shown that more than 70% of adult Japanese by the late 1950s, more than 85% by the mid-1960s, and more than 90% by the early 1970s identified themselves, albeit highly ambiguously and misleadingly, as "middle class" (*churyu*).[7] The argument that this is a case of identification based on "false consciousness" may be correct but does not in any way detract from my point that the ideology of class warfare has been eclipsed by the ideology of national consensus and cooperation.

Another, and far more complex, example is found in the changing role of the education system and the teaching profession. The ideals of the Occupation-sponsored reform and democratization of the system were immortalized in a 1947 law, the Basic Law on Education. The law still remains in effect in its original form and its first article still declares that

> education aims at helping [children] to grow up as members of a peaceful state and society who love truth and justice, uphold the value of the individual, believe in hard work, take responsibility for one's action, display an abundant spirit of independence, and possess both physical and spiritual health. (Kyōiku kihon hō, 1985, article 1)

In a number of subtle ways, however, these lofty democratic ideals have been gradually whittled away over the years by a small but dedicated group of unreformed nationalists among conservative politicians and Ministry of Education bureaucrats with the support and encouragement of big business interests. The revisionist moves include, for example, the passage in 1954 of a pair of laws that made it illegal for school teachers either to make any "political" statement—such as criticizing a government, a political party or a policy—in class or to engage in off-campus political activities; a 1956 law that replaced the popular election of local education board members by their appointment by heads of local governments; and, beginning in 1957, the introduction of a uniform nationwide teacher evaluation system (Nakauchi et al., 1987). The revisionist assault was directed above all at the 600,000-member Japan Teachers Union—one of the largest and most explicitly Marxist of its kind in the world—that threatened to introduce class theory in classroom and thus subvert the core ideology of Japanese education that had already suffered a serious blow at the hands of the postwar Allied occupation.

For purposes of my argument, three aspects of the revisionist movement in the 1950s are particularly important. First, it was a response to a series of formal recommendations presented to the government by employer organizations, notably the Japan Federation of Employers' Associations (*Nihon keieisha dantai rengōkai* or *Nikkeiren*) that, among the major big business groups, concerned itself mainly with management-labor relations. These included, inter alia, a recommendation calling for a wholesale review of the postwar education system (1952) and another urging the promotion of scientific and technical education (1956) (Kokumin kyōiku kenkyūjo, 1973, pp. 256-258; Nakauchi, 1987, pp. 134-135). Second, the revisionist campaign succeeded in significantly limiting the influence of the left-wing Japan Teachers' Union, although not in killing the organization. Third, the campaign succeeded first in sanitizing primary and secondary school curricula against class ideology and then, in the 1960s, in strengthening science and technology curricula at the secondary and tertiary levels (Nakauchi, 1987, pp. 156-164).

The last example that points to the defeat of divisive class theory and the triumph of the ideology of unity and achievement is the spread of enterprise corporatism, a style of management-labor relations long advocated by the leadership of the national federation of private sector unions, the Confederation of Labor (*Dōmei*), and opposed by its public sector rival, the General Council of Japanese Trade Unions (*Sōhyō*). The so-called quality control (QC) circle is a representative product of this form of corporatism and its rapid spread since the 1960s is another indication of the resounding success of the anticlass ideology.

A QC circle is defined as a small group formed at any workplace by all employees who belong to that workplace and who engage, together and on a daily and continuous basis, in voluntary and self-governed activities aimed at improvement of both the quality of their products and management of their work through self-learning and mutual teaching.[8] The idea and methodology of scientific quality control (SQC) developed at a Bell Laboratory in the 1920s were known to a few Japanese statisticians before World War II, but these were introduced to Japanese businessmen and engineers in any significant way only during the postwar occupation by SCAP as a way to improve, primarily for military purposes, Japan's ramshackle and undependable telephone system (NHK shuzaihan, 1987, pp. 67-71, 110-113). The concept was widely popularized in the mid-1950s by the airing of special NHK (Japan Broadcasting Corporation) programs on the subject and QC circles began to appear in the early 1960s and spread "like wild fire" in the 1970s, especially in the automobile, steel, and electrical industries (Kuroda, 1988, p. 313). The national association launched in 1963 with an initial membership of about 200 circles had grown into an organization of nearly a quarter million affiliated circles with nearly 2 million members by 1986, while, according to one estimate, 7 to 10 times as many unaffiliated circles existed with a total membership approaching 10 million, or at least 40% of the total number (about 23 million) of Japanese employees.[9]

The Japanese QC circles as they have evolved over the past three decades are characterized by the wide use of and reliance on statistical data processing and analysis, development of a set of standard and fairly simple statistical measures accessible to employees at all educational levels, and participation by all employees at a given workplace (NHK shuzaihan, 1987, pp. 106-110). They have evolved as part of a wildly effective tool of the corporate strategy to improve the quality and competitiveness of products through employees' own "voluntary" efforts, that is, at minimum costs to management. As a 1969 *Nikkeiren* report pointed out, employers understood the value of "groupism as a distinctive feature of the Japanese national character" and of "the ZD [zero defect] movement and QC group activities . . . as devices effective in encouraging employees' voluntary commitment to work and in raising their morale" (*Nihon keieisha dantai rengōkai*, 1969, pp. 68-71).[10] Through the practice of self-learning and mutual teaching, a QC circle raises the standard of work performance by all employees, including the least able; under the group's collective pressure, all work overtime with nominal compensation, mavericks are brought into line, and recalcitrant dissidents—especially those who believe in class ideology—are forced either to change their ways or quit the job (Kuroda, 1988, pp. 313, 320; Watanabe, 1987, p. 193).[11]

Fervent advocates of enterprise corporatism, QC circles have inevitably competed with and, to an important extent, eroded the ranks of labor unions—themselves formed and operating within individual enterprises rather than entire industries or crafts. The percentage of unionized employees in the secondary and tertiary sectors fell from 28.0% in 1965 to 23.5% in

1985.[12] Moreover, many unions, particularly those at larger corporations, such as Toyota, now accept and cooperate with the ubiquitous QC groups (NHK shuzaihan, 1987, pp. 65-66).

The great success and popularity of enterprise corporatism in general and the QC circle movement in particular has been significantly helped by the so-called lifetime employment and seniority-based promotion and wage (i.e., pay-by-age) systems. These were introduced at management's initiative in prewar Japan primarily as means to recruit, train, and then keep scarce skilled workers, that is, essentially as tools of corporatist policy. In the early postwar period, unions demanded the preservation and expansion of both practices in the name of job security for and equality among all employees, and management went along (Kuroda, 1988, pp. 301-302; Tsuda, 1981, p. 29). Management, however, also used them as weapons to divide and rule labor. For one thing, issues of utmost concern to employees, such as job security, promotions, and wages, now became subjects to be discussed and settled strictly by management and employees of the given enterprise alone, and thus no business of outsiders; for another, within each enterprise some employees were granted lifetime job security and age-based promotion and wage increases, while others were not granted either. Even when the systems were at the peak of their popularity in the mid-1960s, they applied to no more than between 10% and one quarter of the total number of Japan's employees, depending on how broadly or narrowly one defines those terms (Tsuda, 1981, pp. 292-293).

At the beginning of the 1990s, QC circles continue to thrive in Japanese firms, whereas the nation's education system still runs the "reverse course" started in the early 1950s. In a number of important ways, however, Japan's nationalist/paternalist capitalism is undergoing a metamorphosis under the pressure of rapidly and dramatically changing domestic and international environments. In the process, some of its hallmarks mentioned above are being either tossed away outright or drastically modified so that Japan's political economy at the turn of the next century is bound to look quite different from what it has looked like in the past. Let me now turn to some of the major changes underway.

Japanese Capitalism at a Crossroad

First, Japanese capitalism is going through a rapid and traumatic process of internationalization. Capital began to move out of the country by the late 1950s and the outflow picked up considerably in the 1970s and, especially, the 1980s. Until the mid-1970s, Japanese foreign direct investments were concentrated mainly in the production and development of foodstuffs and industrial raw materials. Since then, however, two major considerations have driven Japanese investments abroad: (1) to reduce labor costs by relocating labor-intensive processing or assembling phases of the production of certain manufactures, such as watches, desk calculators, electric fans, and so forth, to nearby Newly Industrializing Countries (NICs) with still relatively cheap and abundant labor; and (2) to get around rising trade protectionism, especially increasingly stringent local content requirements, in the United States and Western Europe, by locally producing many of Japan's staple exports to those markets, such as automobiles, color televisions, semiconductors, and so forth (Toshida, 1989: 19-20, pp. 178-179).

Capital outflow from Japan increased dramatically in the 1980s, not so much because of rising labor costs in Japan as because of rising protectionism abroad and the sharp appreciation of the yen following the September 1985 Plaza Accord that started a successful concerted effort by the governments of the major industrial nations to drive up the value of the yen (and the West German mark) and drive down that of the U.S. dollar. Japanese direct investments abroad grew from about $4.7 billion in 1980 to $12.2 billion in 1985 and to $47.0 billion in 1988 (Keizai Koho Center, 1989, p. 56). The regional distribution of the invested funds significantly changed during this eight-year period: Asia's share, associated mainly with labor cost considerations, declined 25.3% to 11.7%, while North America's and Europe's, both associated mainly with market access considerations, rose, respectively, from 34.9% to 46.8% and from 12.3% to 19.1% (Fukiya, 1988, p. 55; Keizai Koho Center, 1989, p. 56).

That market access considerations were more important than labor cost considerations in Japanese investments in the United States and Europe becomes evident when one compares their wage growth rates. Over the period 1980-1988, real hourly wage rates in manufacturing industries grew considerably faster in the United States and the major West European economies than in Japan.[13] The differences may be explained largely by similar differences in the rates of change in the consumer price index: Japan's increased far more slowly than the other major economic nations'.[14] They were, however, also due to a substantial lag between the growth rate of real wages and that of labor productivity in Japan, that is, a consequence of a poor deal Japanese labor struck, whether willingly or unwillingly, in wage negotiations with management.[15] This lag in turn was due partly to the enormously successful campaign for corporatist control and mobilization of labor in general and activities of the host of QC circles in particular and, partly, to a relatively slack labor market. According to official statistics, Japan's unemployment rate has been consistently and significantly lower than that of the other major industrial nations, but it rose significantly following the 1985 Plaza Accord to reach about 3% by early 1987, a very high level by Japanese standards, while the ratio of job openings to job seekers fell as low as .61 (Keizai Koho Center, 1989, p. 72; Toshida, 1989, p. 74). More recently, however, the Japanese labor market has tightened considerably, with the unemployment rate falling to about 2.5% and the job openings per job seeker ratio rising to more than 1 by the summer of 1988; it continues to tighten as most Japanese industries and firms have seemingly adapted to the impacts of the strong yen.

The capital flight has therefore not resulted in a hollowing out of the Japanese economy in the sense of exporting jobs abroad and creating a serious unemployment problem at home. On the contrary, a shortage of labor, especially young and inexpensive labor, has become such a chronic and acute problem for many Japanese firms, especially for small businesses, despite the above-mentioned temporary slackening of the labor market in the mid-1980s, that a substantial and rapidly increasing number of foreign workers—as many as 200,000 in 1988, according to some estimates—are employed, legally or illegally, for the first time in Japan's history (*Ohara shakaimondai kenkyūjo*, 1989, p. 38). Along with foreign direct investments in Japan itself, which increased from less than $300 million in 1980 to nearly $2.6 billion in 1988 (Keizai Koho Center, 1989, p. 58), the growing presence of foreign workers in Japan brings internationalization home, so to speak.

The internationalization of the Japanese economy that thus proceeds both externally and internally is bound to have significant impacts on many of the ways of Japanese capitalism that I discussed in the preceding sections. It is highly doubtful, for example, that QC circles can be organized and run by foreign workers, whether in Japan or abroad, in the same way that they are organized and run by Japanese employees, even though hundreds of foreigners visit Japanese firms each year to see and learn about the organization and activities of these groups (NHK shuzaihan, 1987, pp. 85-86). Some 300 American firms had set up Japanese-style QC groups by the late 1980s, but only a few, such as Westinghouse of Pittsburgh, are reported to have made any significant impacts on the performance of the firms (NHK shuzaihan, 1987, pp. 91-95, 128-129). As I have argued, the success of Japanese QC circles owes a great deal to nationalist and corporatist ideologies derived largely from Shinto and Confucian dogmas. Absent such ideologies, and especially present an antithetical individualistic ideology, employees and their groups, whatever they are called, will behave differently from their Japanese counterparts.

Second, the lifetime employment and pay-by-age systems, both long regarded as shibboleths of Japanese-style management, are in trouble. As I have already suggested, neither system has ever applied to more than a small minority of Japanese employees in any case. In fact, the two systems could not have been simultaneously applied to the majority, not to mention all, employees in any but an imaginary enterprise with limitless resources; a typical real-world enterprise could not possibly afford to guarantee the majority of its employees "lifetime" job security—that is, employment up to a mandatory retirement age of 55 or 60 or 65—and, at the same time, promise them payment of wages that rise automatically and continuously each passing year as they grow older. The enterprise would be bankrupt in no time. The implementation of these systems therefore required the use of a large number of employees who would work without claim to their benefits, that is, "regular" employees excluded from the systems and "non-regular" employees hired on a part-time or temporary basis (NHK shuzaihan, 1987, pp. 303-304). Women employees accounted for an overwhelming majority of those in the first category and a large majority of the second, and were consequently paid grossly substandard wages. For example, women employed in the secondary and tertiary sectors in 1988 were paid per month on average slightly less than 55% of what men were paid (Rōdōdaijin kambō seisaku chōsabu, 1988b, pp. 132-133).[16] To cut down further on labor costs, many parts needed by larger manufacturers of complex products, such as automobiles and computers, were acquired from a large number of smaller firms serving as subcontractors.

The subcontracting system is critical to the successful operation of the lifetime employment and pay-by-age systems, and it is extremely complex. Just how complex can be seen in the case of the Yamaha Motors Company, a major motorbike manufacturer but not one of the biggest Japanese firms by any means: the company has 83 subcontractors (firms), one of which (the Sakura Industries that makes motorbike mufflers) alone has 70 subcontractors under its own wings, one of which has 40 subcontractors of its own, one of which has an unknown number of subcontractors of its own, and so on, so forth (NHK shuzaihan, 1987, pp. 173, 193-201). For a single motorbike manufacturer alone, then, between 2,000 and 3,000 (no dependable statistics exist) small firms, including a number of tiny family shops at the very bottom of the heap, make up an intricate and quasi-familial network. For Japan as a whole, two thirds of the 868,000 or so firms with no more than 300 employees serve as subcontractors for larger firms. Employees in the smaller contractor firms are paid considerably less than those in the parent firm or larger tractor firms (NHK shuzaihan, 1987, pp. 180, 182).[17]

With all these escape hatches carefully built into them, both the lifetime employment and pay-by-age systems have nonetheless substantially declined in popularity during the last decade, while reliance on nonregular workers and subcontracting has increased. Terms of employment, including both the lengths and types of service and the kinds and amounts of compensation, are determined increasingly on the basis of the type of job and the quality of performance. The mandatory retirement age for most employees has been raised from 55 to 60 by nearly 60% of firms with 30 or more employees and nearly 90% of those with 5,000 or more employees (*Ōhara shakaimondai kenkyūjo*, 1989, pp. 114-115). In the meantime, however, commitment to lifetime job security has significantly declined.[18] Commitment to the pay-by-age system is even rarer these days.[19] One of the two representative hallmarks of Japanese-style management, the pay-by-age system, is thus nearly finished, while the other, the lifetime employment system, appears to be following the same fate.

Third, as far as the majority of Japanese citizens are concerned, Japanese-style capitalism has ceased to deliver as much as they have come to expect. While the Japanese economy was growing at a brisk pace in the 1950s and 1960s, the average real wage in the manufacturing industry steadily and substantially rose each passing year, until the 1973 oil crisis put an end to the period of double-digit growth rates. The average real wage has continued to rise even during the post-oil crisis period—except in 1980 when the mean real wage in the manufacturing sector registered a negative growth rate of −1.6%—but only at much lower rates (0.5%-3.1%) (*Ōhara shakaimondai kenkyūjo*, 1989, p. 71; *Rōdōdaijin kambō seisaku chōsabu*, 1988a, pp. 14-15). The deceleration in the rise of wage rates in the mid-1970s gave rise to serious and widespread disaffection among some segments of the working class for the first time since the early 1950s. For the next decade, however, the disaffection was under control, until a sudden and frenetic surge in urban real estate prices hit the pocket books of urban white-collar and blue-collar workers in the late 1980s.

By the mid-1980s, urban real estate had become a prime object of investment for large and small corporations awash with idle funds accumulated during the years of slow but steady growth of the economy as a whole and booming export trade. In five short years from 1983 to 1988, the average prices of residential and commercial land rose, respectively, by 15% and 23% in the Nagoya metropolitan area, by 34% and 81% in the Osaka area, and 119% and 203% in the Tokyo area (Honma, 1988, pp. 37-40). In the last of these three major metropolitan areas of the country, the price of residential land shot up by nearly 70% in 1988 alone (*Asahi nenkan*, 1989, p. 694). This put even a tiny apartment in the metropolitan areas, especially Tokyo, far beyond the limits of the ordinary wage earner's purchasing power.

The disaffection among growing ranks of urban wage earners was further deepened by the discovery that, despite the impression one would get by simply comparing the CPI in different nations, the prices of most consumer goods, from foodstuffs to electronic gadgets, are actually much higher in Japan than in any other major industrial nation. The introduction of a new 3% across-the-board sales (consumption) tax in 1989, amidst a scandal involving many of the top LDP and government leaders, added fuel to the flame of popular anger and led to unprecedented electoral upsets that have shaken Japan's capitalist regime to its foundations. In the quadrennial Tokyo Metropolitan Assembly elections held in July 1989, the LDP lost 20 of the 63 seats it had won in the 1985 election, while the Japan Socialist Party (JSP) won 24 seats more than the 12 it had won in 1985; in the triennial House of Councillors (upper house) election held almost simultaneously, the LDP lost 33, while the JSP gained 24; and in the House of Representatives general election called in February 1990, the LDP lost 9, while the JSP gained 57 (Baerwald, 1989, 1990; *Asahi shimbun,* July 3 [evening ed.], 5, 25, 1989; *Yomiuri shimbun,* February 20, 1990).

The results of the most recent elections may have reflected the passing moods of a notoriously fickle electorate rather than a long-term trend. On the other hand, they may well have signaled a significant change underway in the political foundation of Japan's postwar political economy, a change that may sooner or later coalesce with the other changes already discussed to transform Japan's 120-year-old nationalist/paternalist capitalist state. Whether the Japanese state and capitalists prove resourceful enough to survive this gravest of the crises they have ever faced since the Meiji Restoration is yet to be seen.

Summary and Conclusions

Like all social phenomena, capitalism comes in different shapes and colors in different cultural and historical environs. I have argued that Japan's is one that is quite different from the classic model where economic rationality is the paramount criterion of worthy conduct and that it is, on the contrary, inspired and guided by an ideology, that is, irrationality. The main thrust of my thesis is undeniably Weberian, except that, in my argument, labor in pre-Meiji or post-Meiji Japan has never been quite a "calling" and an "end in itself" in Weber's or Martin Luther's sense, while a religion-inspired secular ideology (nationalism), rather than a religion itself (Protestantism), has driven the rise and expansion of Japan's late-developer capitalism (Weber, 1930, p. 62).[20] For that matter, my thesis has even closer affinity with Bellah's classic, *Tokugawa Religion* (Bellah, 1957).

I am also ready to admit that an important implication of my thesis is that what happens in political and social arenas, especially educational institutions, rather than what happens in economic arenas per se, is critical to the economic performance of a late-developing capitalist nation, if not that of any capitalist nation. One therefore looks very carefully at a government's political and social policies and society's responses to them, rather than at its economic policies, such as industrial policy or tax policy, in order to understand and explain the long-term pattern of a developing nation's economic performance. For the long-term performance of a developing capitalist economy, how many schools are built, who attends them, and what is taught there is more important than how many factories are built and what types of merchandise are produced.

Weberian as it may be, however, my thesis is not Hegelian; it recognizes the importance of objective material conditions, and class interests and relations based on such conditions. It also recognizes, if only implicitly, the importance of economic policies that affect those conditions. A critical point about modern Japan's economic policies, however, is that, like political and social policies, they have been aimed primarily at ensuring domestic peace and harmony and mobilizing voluntary and enthusiastic cooperation of the populace in the building of a rich nation, with a strong army before World War II and without one after the war.

The successful maintenance of domestic harmony and effective mobilization of popular cooperation have required, among other things, two conditions: the maintenance of a high and stable economic growth rate, and reasonably equal and fair distribution of the results of the economic growth. Statistics show that Japanese-style capitalism has, by and large, successfully met these two conditions. Not only has modern Japan's economy grown at a higher and more stable rate than any other major industrial economy, but the fruits of that growth have been distributed more equitably in postwar Japan, though not in prewar Japan, than in most other nations. A comparison of Gini coefficients based on the latest comparable statistics available show that in the late 1970s and early 1980s Japan had the most egalitarian overall income distribution among the major capitalist industrial economies.[21]

There have been, however, periods in modern Japanese history—for example, the post-Russo-Japanese War, post-World War I, and post-World War

II periods—when the growth rate fell and/or income (or wealth) inequalities rose so significantly that social harmony and cooperative public spirit were seriously undermined. These were periods of crisis for Japanese capitalism, to which it responded just as it was expected to do, that is, with a combination of improvised material and ideological palliatives. It is of great credit to the ingenuity and the shrewdness of leaders of the Japanese state and enterprise that this combination has usually worked in the past.

In the last decade of the twentieth century, however, it is far from certain that Japan's nationalist/paternalist capitalism may once again prove its genius and resiliency and successfully overcome the multiple and complex domestic and international pressures it faces. Even if it may survive the pressures, it will not remain intact. As I have pointed out, it is already being transformed in a number of significant ways. Japanese-style capitalism is thus unlikely to exist in the year 2000 in anything like its present shape and color.

Notes

1. Throughout this chapter, all Japanese personal names are given in the native order, that is, surname first, followed by given name.

2. By 1890, about half the school-age children were enrolled and the percentage figure rose to more than 80% by 1900, more than 95% by 1905, and more than 98% by 1910. See Horimatsu, 1985, pp. 140-141; Kokumin kyōiku kenkyūj, 1973, pp. 84, 88-89; Oe, 1974, pp. 40, 120.

3. The so-called multiple-track system of secondary and postsecondary education in prewar Japan was so complex, especially with regard to eligible ages, that it is difficult to estimate the ratios of students per appropriate groups of population. According to my own calculations, in 1935 secondary school, high school and college, and university students accounted, respectively, for no more than 4%, 1.5%, and 2% of the eligible populations, that is, those at the ages of, respectively, 12-17, 12-19, and 19-21. These estimates are based on data drawn from *Shōwa 16-nen Asahi nenkan*, 1940, pp. 90-91, 452-454; and Horimatsu, 1985, pp. 140-167. Others estimate that in the 1930s no more than about 1% of elementary school graduates could expect to enter any university, and no more than half as many any of the seven imperial universities. See Passin, 1965, p. 104; Pempel, 1978, p. 34.

4. For detailed discussions of the wide-ranging reforms, see *Tokyo daigaku shakaikagaku kenkyūjo* (1974-1975). For an overview, see Fukui, 1988, pp. 155-184.

5. According to a survey conducted by SCAP's Civil Information and Education Section at the time, more than half (773 pp.) of the 1,502 pages of the twelve primary school Japanese language textbooks in use at the time contained language praising militarism, ultranationalism, Shinto dogmas and/or the emperor cult. See Kubo, 1984, p. 200.

6. Needless to say, at no time was encouragement of Marxism or any other anti-capitalist ideology part of the United States' policy for occupied Japan. See Iokibe, 1985, vol. 1, pp. 226-282; vol. 2, pp.227-259.

7. For a critical analysis of the significance and implications of this development, see Imada, 1989, pp. 149-164.

8. Quoted from the *QC Circle Charter* issued in 1970 by the national headquarters of QC circles, in *NHK shuzaihan,* 1987, pp. 26-27.

9. According to one recent survey, as many as 62% of enterprises had at least one QC circle and an additional 20% had similar employee groups, called either Zero Defect (ZD) or JK (for *jishu kanri* or self-management). The Toyota Motors Corporation alone had 6,500 separate circles in 1988, each with six members on average; and one was found in every workplace in the company's technical departments and 80% of its administrative departments. See NHK shuzaihan, 1987, pp. 32, 38, 75-76.

10. President Toyoda Shōichirō of Toyota Motors Corporation believes that improving employees' "motivation" is a far more important function of a QC circle than teaching statistical data processing methods. See NHK shuzaihan, 1987, p. 62.

11. See George Fields's similar comments in NHK shuzaihan, 1987, pp. 14-15.

12. During the same period, the left-wing *Sohyo's* membership fell from 11.7% to 8.3% and the corporatist *Domei's* from 4.5% to 4.0% of the total work force in the two sectors, or by 3.4 and 0.5 percentage points respectively. See Rōdōdaijin kambō seisaku chōsabu, 1988a, pp. 29, 189, 191.

13. The growth rates of wages in the comparable nations were: 40.2%, or 5.0% per year, in the United States; 39.1%, or 4.9% per year, in West Germany; 70.4%, or 8.8% per year, in Great Britain; 44.5% in 1980-1987, or 6.3% per year, in France; and 26.0%, or 3.2% per year, in Japan. See Rōdōdaijin kambō seisaku chōsabu, 1990a, p. 224.

14. Japan's increased by only 16.2% in the eight years, as compared to West Germany's 22.4%, Great Britain's 59.9%, France's 71.8%, and the United States' 43.6%. See Rōdōdaijin kambō seisaku chōsabu, 1990a, p. 228.

15. Labor productivity in the manufacturing sector as a whole rose by as much as 20.1% even in the three years between 1985 and 1988, and by at least twice as much between 1980 and 1988. See Rōdōdaijin kambō seisaku chōsabu, 1990a, p. 164.

16. For a good Marxist analysis of women's status and role in the Japanese economy, see Steven, 1983, chapter 5.

17. The average employee in a small firm with between 10 and 99 employees was paid per month about three-quarters of what the average employee in a large firm with 1,000 or more employees. See Rōdōdaijin kambō seisaku chōsabu, 1988b, pp. 132-133.

18. A recent survey conducted by a committee of labor management experts for the Ministry of Labor found that about 60% of firms with 1,000 or more employees were still committed to lifetime employment for their regular employees, but the remaining 40% practiced a "half-lifetime" system. See *Ohara shakaimondai kenkyūjo,* 1989, p. 109; Rōdōdaijin kambō seisaku chōsabu, 1990b, p. 56.

19. According to a 1988 Ministry of Labor survey, only about 17% of firms with 30 or more employees still offered their regular employees automatic annual wage raises on the basis of seniority, while the remaining 83% paid their employees on the basis of either job and performance alone or a combination of seniority and performance. See Kuroda (1988, pp. 198-199), *Ohara shakaimondai kenkyūjo* (1989, p. 117).

20. If one could replace religion by nationalist ideology, however, I could have easily borrowed and used Weber's lines, such as: "It [labor] cannot be evoked by low wages or high ones alone, but can only be the product of a long and arduous process of education" or "The ability of mental concentration, as well as the absolutely essential feeling of obligation to one's job, are here (in certain workers) most often combined with strict economy . . . which enormously increase performance." Weber (1930, pp. 62-63).

21. According to my calculations based on World Bank data, the comparable Gini values are: Japan (1979) = 0.2700; U.S. (1980) = 0.3292; U.K. (1979) = 0.3148; West Germany (1978) = 0.2952; France (1975) = 0.3424; Sweden (1981) = 0.3060; and the Netherlands (1981) = 0.2596. The Netherlands alone among the 24 Organization for Economic Cooperation and Development (OECD) member states had a more egalitarian pattern of income distribution than Japan. Data from World Bank (1989, p. 222, table 30).

References

Asahi nenkan 1989-nen ban [Asahi yearbook, 1989 edition]. (1989). Tokyo: Asahi shimbunsha.

Asai, Yoshio. (1980). Sangyō kakumei [An industrial revolution]. In K. Takahashi, et al. (Eds.), *Nihon kindaishi yōsetsu* [A summary discussion of modern Japanese history]. Tokyo: Tokyo daigaku shuppankai.

Baerwald, Hans H. (1989, September). Japan's House of Councillors election: A mini-revolution? *Asian Survey,* pp. 833-841.

Baerwald, Hans H. (1990, June). Japan's 39th House of Representatives election: A case of mixed signals. *Asian Survey,* pp. 544-559.

Bellah, Robert N. (1957). *Tokugawa religion: The values of pre-industrial Japan.* New York: Free Press.

Berger, Gordon M. (1988). Politics and mobilization in Japan, 1931-1945. In Peter Duus (Ed.), *The Cambridge history of Japan. Vol 6: The twentieth century* (pp. 97-153). Cambridge, UK: Cambridge University Press.

Crawcour, E. Sydney. (1965).The Tokugawa heritage. In William W. Lockwood (Ed.), *The state and enterprise in Japan.* Princeton, NJ: Princeton University Press.

Curtis, Gerald L. (1988). *The Japanese way of politics.* New York: Columbia University Press.

Duus, Peter. (Ed.). (1988). The twentieth century (The Cambridge history of Japan, vol. 6). Cambridge: Cambridge University Press.

Fujino, Tamotsu. (1961). *Bakuhan taiseishi no kenkyū* [A study of the history of the shogunal-domainal regime]. Tokyo: Yoshikawa kōbunkan.

Fukai, Jinzō. (1980). Kinsei toshi no hattatsu [The development of cities in early modern Japan]. In Shirō Matsumoto & Tadao Yamada (Eds.), *Genroku-kyōho-ki no seiji to shakai* [Politics and society in the genroku-kyoho (1688-1735) period] (Kōza: Nihon kinseishi [Series on early modern Japanese history], vol. 4). Tokyo: Yūhikaku.

Fukiya, Kenji. (1988). 1979-nendai ikō no kokusai shūshi to taigai tōshi [The balance of international payments and foreign investments since the 1970s]. In Sengo nihon keizai kenkyūkai [Association for the study of the postwar Japanese economy] (Ed.), *Nihon keizai no bunsuirei [Watersheds in Japanese economic development].* Tokyo: Bunshindō.

Fukui, Haruhiro. (1988). Postwar politics, 1945-1973. In Peter Duus (Ed.), *The Cambridge history of Japan. Vol 6: The twentieth century.* Cambridge, UK: Cambridge University Press.

Gotō, Sōichirō. (1988). *Tennōsei kokka no keisei to minshū* [The formation of the emperor-system state and the people]. Tokyo: Kōbunsha.

Honma, Yoshihito. (1988). *Tochi mondai sōtenken* [A comprehensive survey of the land problem]. Tokyo: Yūhikaku.

Horimatsu, Buichi. (Ed.). (1985). *Nihon kyōikushi* [A history of Japanese education]. Tokyo: Kokudosha.

Ikeda, Makoto. (1982). *Nihonteki kōporatizumu no seiritsu* [The formation of Japanese-style corporatism]. Kyoto: Keibunsha.

Imada, Takatoshi. (1989). Shakai kaisō to seiji [Social strata and politics]. In Inoguchi Takashi (Ed.), *Gendai seijigaku sōsho* [Contemporary political science series, vol. 7]. Tokyo: University of Tokyo Press.

Imanaka, Kanji. (1972). *Kinsei nihon seiji shisō no seiritsu* [The formation of political ideologies in early modern Japan]. Tokyo: Sōbunsha.

Iokibe, Makoto. (1985). *Beikoku no nihon senryō seisaku: Sengo nihon no sekkeizu* [The United States' occupation policy: The blue-print for postwar Japan]. 2 Vols. Tokyo: Chūokoronsha.

Keizai Koho Center. (1989). *Japan: An international comparison 1990*. Tokyo: Keizai Koho Center.

Kimura, Motoi. (1967). *Kakyūbushi ron* [On the lower-ranked samurai]. Tokyo: Hanawa shobō.

Kobayashi, Tango. (1986). *Nihon rōdōkumiai undōshi* [A history of the Japanese labor union movement]. Tokyo: Aoki shoten.

Kokumin kyōiku kenkyūjo. (Ed.). (1973). *Kindai nihon kyōiku shōshi* [A short history of education in modern Japan]. Tokyo: Sōdo bunka.

Koyama, Hirotake. (1967). *Nihon marukusushugishi gaisetsu* [An overview of the history of Japanese Marxism]. Tokyo: Haga shoten.

Kubo, Yoshizō. (1979). *Tennōsei kokka no kyōiku seisaku: Sono keisei katei to sumitsuin* [The educational policy of an emperor-system state: The formative process and the Privy Council]. Tokyo: Keisō shobō.

Kubo, Yoshizō. (1984). *Tainichi senryō seisaku to sengo kyō iku kaikaku* [The occupation policy for Japan and the postwar education reform]. Tokyo: Sanseidō.

Kuroda, Ken'ichi. (1988). Kyōsōteki shokuba chitsujo to rōmu kanri [Competitive workplace order and labor management]. In Sengo nihon keizai kenkyūkai [Association for the study of the postwar Japanese economy] (Ed.), *Nihon keizai no bunsuirei* [Watersheds in Japanese economic development]. Tokyo: Bunshindō.

Kyōiku kihon hō [Basic Law of Education]. (1985). In *Iwanami roppō zensho: Shōwa 61-nenban* [Iwanami compendium of the six codes: 1986 edition]. Tokyo: Iwanami shoten: 487.

Masumi, Junnosuke. (1965-1980). *Nihon seitō shiron* [A historical study of Japanese political parties], 7 vols. Tokyo: Tokyo University Press.

Mori, Kiichi. (1979). *Nihon no kindaika to rōdōsha kaikyū* [The modernization of Japan and the working class]. Tokyo: Nihon hyōronsha.

Murakami, Shigeyoshi. (Ed.). (1982) *Kokka shintō to minshū shūkyō* [State Shinto and popular religions]. Tokyo: Yoshikawa kōbunkan.

Nakauchi, Toshio, et al. (1987). *Nihon kyōiku no sengoshi* [The history of postwar Japanese education]. Tokyo: Sanseidō.

NHK shuzaihan [The Japan Broadcasting Corporation reporters' team). (1987). *Nihon kaibō 2: keizai taikoku no gensen: QC undō wa naze nihon de seikō shita ka* [An anatomy of Japan, vol. 2: Sources of an economic superpower: Why the QC movement has succeeded in Japan]. Tokyo: Nihon hōsō shuppan kyōkai.

Nihon keieisha dantai rengōkai [Japan federation of employers' associations]. (1969). *Nōryokushugi kanri: Sono riron to jissai* [Performance- and ability-based management: Theory and practice]. Tokyo: Nihon keieisha dantai rengōkai.

Ōe, Shinobu. (1974). *Kokumin kyōiku to guntai: Nihon gunkokushugi kyōiku seisaku no seiritsu to tenkai* [Public education and the army: The creation and development of militarist education in Japan]. Tokyo: Shin nihon shuppansha.

Ōhara shakaimondai kenkyūjo [Ohara Institute of Social Research]. (Ed.). (1989). *Nihon rōdō nenkan* [Japan labor yearbook], vol. 59. Tokyo: Rōdō jumposha.

Ōmachi, Masami. (1970). *Sōmō no keifu: Meiji ishin no teiryū* [The lineage of grassroots samurai: An undercurrent of the Meiji restoration]. Tokyo: San'ichi shobō.

Ōta, Masao. (1971). *Meiji shakaishugi seitōshi* [A history of socialist parties in the Meiji period]. Tokyo: Minerva shobō.

Passin, Herbert. (1965). *Society and education in Japan.* New York: Columbia University Teachers College.

Patrick, Hugh, & Rosovsky, Henry. (1976). Japan's economic performance: An overview. In Hugh Patrick & Henry Rosovsky (Eds.), *Asia's new giant: How the Japanese economy works.* Washington, DC: Brookings Institution.

Pempel, T. J. (1978). *Patterns of Japanese policymaking: Experiences from higher education.* Boulder, CO: Westview.

Rōdōdaijin kambō seisaku chōsabu [Ministry of Labor Secretariat, Policy Planning and Research Department]. (Ed.). (1988a). *Rōdō tōkei yōran 1988-nenban* [Handbook of labor statistics, 1988 edition]. Tokyo Okurashō insatsukyoku.

Rōdōdaijin kambō seisaku chōsabu [Ministry of Labor Secretariat, Policy Planning and Research Department]. (Ed.). (1988b). *Dai-41-kai rōdō tokei nempō* [The 41st Year Book of Labor Statistics]. Tokyo: Rōdō hōrei kyōkai.

Rōdōdaijin kambō seisaku chōsabu [Ministry of Labor Secretariat, Policy Planning and Research Department]. (Ed.). (1990a). *Rōdō tōkei yōran 1990-nenban* [Handbook of labor statistics, 1990 edition]. Tokyo: Okurashō insatsukyoku.

Rōdōdaijin kambō seisaku chōsabu [Ministry of Labor Secretariat, Policy Planning and Research Department]. (Ed.). (1990b). *Rōdō tōkei nempō* [Yearbook of labor statistics]. Tokyo: Rōdō hōrei kyōkai.

Saitō, Nobuaki. (1981). *Meiji ishin kakumei* [The Meiji restoration revolution]. Tokyo: Sairyūsha.

Scalapino, Robert A. (1967a). *Democracy and the party movement in prewar Japan: The failure of the first attempt.* Berkeley and Los Angeles: University of California Press.

Scalapino, Robert A. (1967b). *The Japanese communist movement, 1920-1966.* Berkeley and Los Angeles: University of California Press.

Sheldon, Garon. (1987). *The state and labor in modern Japan.* Berkeley: University of California Press.

Shōwa 16-nen Asahi nenkan [1941 Asahi yearbook]. (1940). Tokyo: Asahi shimbunsha.

Smith, Thomas C. (1955). *Political change and industrial development in Japan: Government enterprise, 1868-1889.* Stanford, CA: Stanford University Press.

Steven, Rob. (1983). *Classes in contemporary Japan.* Cambridge, UK: Cambridge University Press.

Suehiro, Gentarō. (1959). *Nihon rōdōkumiai undōshi* [A history of the Japanese labor union movement]. Tokyo: Kyōdō tsūshinsha.

Tabata, Terumi. (1981). *Nihon no nōson fukushi* [Rural welfare in Japan]. Tokyo: Keisō shobō.

Tamura, Eiichirō. (1988). *Nihon no kyōiku to nashonarizumu* [Japanese education and nationalism]. Tokyo: Akashi shoten.

Tanaka, Akira. (1976). *Meiji ishin* [The Meiji restoration] (Nihon no rekishi [Japanese history], vol. 24). Tokyo: Shigakukan.

Togawa, Yoshio, et al. (1987). *Jukyōshi* [A history of Confucianism] (Sekai shūkyōshi sōsho [World religions series], vol. 10). Tokyo: Yamakawa shuppansha.

Tokyo daigaku shakaikagaku kenkyūjo. (Ed.). (1974-1975). *Sengo kaikaku* [The postwar reforms], 8 vols. Tokyo: Tokyo daigaku shuppankai.

Toshida, Seiichi. (Ed.). (1989). *Nihon keizai no nagare wo yomu* [Reading currents in the Japanese economy]. Tokyo: Tōyō keizai shimpōsha.

Tsuda, Shinchō. (1981, July). Nihonteki keieiron no kiso shikaku [The basic perspective for a Japanese theory of management]. *Keizai hyōron*, (July).

Tsujinaka, Isao. (1971). *Meiji no rōdō undō* [Labor movements in the Meiji period]. Tokyo: Kinokuniya.

Wakita, Osamu. (1980). Kinsei toshi no seiritsu [The formation of early modern cities]. In Kōtarō Takahashi, et al. (Eds.), *Nihon kindaishi yōsetsu* [A summary discussion of modern Japanese history]. Tokyo: Tokyo daigaku shuppankai.

Waswo, Ann. (1988). The transformation of rural society, 1900-1950. In Peter Duus (Ed.), *The Cambridge history of Japan. Vol 6: The twentieth century* (pp. 97-153). Cambridge, UK: Cambridge University Press.

Watanabe, Osamu. (1987). Gendai nihon shakai no ken'iteki kōzō to kokka [The authority structure of contemporary Japanese society and the state]. In Isamu Fujita (Ed.), *Ken'iteki chitsujo to kokka* [Authority structure and the state]. Tokyo: Tokyo daigaku shuppankai.

Weber, Max. (1930). *The protestant ethic and the spirit of capitalism* (Talcott Parsons, trans.). New York: Scribner.

World Bank. (1989). *World development report 1989*. New York: Oxford University Press.

Yamakawa, Hitoshi. (1979). *Shakaishugi undō shōshi* [A short history of the socialist movement]. Tokyo: Shakaishugi kyōkai shuppankyoku.

PART III

SOCIAL POLICY

In this concluding section of the book, we examine in greater detail the central importance of state interventions in the production and reproduction of labor. The three chapters examine the ways in which the East Asian states actively promoted the exploitation of cheap female labor to foster economic development, along with other social and labor policies intended to keep labor inexpensive and relatively quiescent during the early years of industrialization, when development depended on the exportation of cheap commodities.

In Chapter 9, Lucie Cheng and Ping-Chun Hsiung document the central role played by female labor in the recent growth of the Taiwanese economy (this theme is taken up in a comparative context in the following chapter by Salaff). They argue that patriarchy and capitalism have reinforced one another to promote economic development. In Taiwan (as elsewhere in the world), women are shown to bear the "double burden" of providing labor in the larger economy as well as at home: Taiwan's economic success results in large part from "the specific use of women's labor as chief wage workers, unwaged family workers, and unpaid service providers." Yet while women provided the cheap labor that underpinned Taiwan's EOI, they have not reaped the fruits of their efforts.

Women now comprise more than one third of the work force in Taiwan, with labor force participation rates approaching 50%. The most rapid growth in female labor occurred during the explosion of EOI during the late 1960s and early 1970s. Yet despite the presence of substantial numbers of women in the work force, female labor force participation is highly volatile, reflecting ebbs and flows in the world economy, the local business cycle, and family situation. In Taiwan women enter the work force at an early age, withdraw when they get married and have children, and then reenter in their late thirties, as child-rearing responsibilities diminish. They also tend to retire from the work force earlier than men—around age 55—often to care for elderly males in their homes. When they do work, women are paid less than men, a fact that is trumpeted by the Taiwanese government to court foreign investment (the presumed docility of female workers is another frequently cited selling point). In industries such as agriculture, mining, manufacturing, construction, and commerce, there has been a progressive erosion of female earnings relative to male earnings since the early 1970s.

As Cheng and Hsiung demonstrate, the exploitation of women has been particularly severe in the sex industry, a major source of foreign exchange. Prostitution and open sex are used to lure millions of tourists—from the United States, Japan, and elsewhere—to the brothels, massage parlors, bath houses, and even barber shops of Taiwan. Government-distributed tourist booklets frequently contain advertisements touting the sexual attractiveness of Taiwanese women. It is estimated that as many as a third of a million women are involved in the sex industry at the present time.

Women provide an important source of unpaid domestic labor, a pattern that is actively pursued through state policy and reinforced by the traditional Chinese emphasis on women's roles in maintaining harmony and educating children. The amount of work that even middle-class Taiwanese women do at home is substantial. Homemaking duties frequently combine with unpaid or poorly paid labor intended to supplement factory output for the export sector. While homework is not uncommon in industrial nations, Taiwan is one of the few countries actively to pursue such cheap labor through state policies. Cheng and Hsiung discuss at length two examples of this "capitalist patriarchal state of Taiwan": the "living-room factories" and the "Mother's Workshops," both originating in the 1968 community development program. Under the former program, the Taiwanese government provides special incentives for families to purchase sewing machines and learn sewing skills for homework. This simultaneously increases the supply of cheap female labor while reducing its cost, since expenditures do not have to be made on facilities, energy, dormitories, or management. Nor are women who work at home provided with health insurance, minimum wage guarantees, or similar protections. The living-room factories are supported by the Mother's Workshops, which attempt to "educate" women into being good mothers and productive workers at home. Women are trained in community beautification, safety, vocational skills, sanitation, health, nutrition, culture, leisure, and even interior decoration. Government-sponsored workshops also train mothers in family virtues: etiquette, womanly comportment, the promotion of harmony in the family, the proper use of make-up, and—importantly—the skills necessary to be effective workers in living-room factories.

Women work long and hard in Taiwan; in Cheng and Hsiung's view, they are the untold story of that country's phenomenal economic growth. They provide a flexible work force that is secure, unprotected, and cheap. Without this form of patriarchal domination, Cheng and Hsiung conclude, Taiwanese capitalism would not have proven so successful.

In Chapter 10, Janet Salaff further examines the critical role played by women in the economic development of Hong Kong, Singapore, and Taiwan. She first examines the threefold nature of the Chinese family. It is patrilineal and patrilocal, a form that privileges the bond between the family and the son, while requiring the daughter to establish ties with her husband's family at the expense of her own. The family also functions as an economic unit, pooling the labor of the married daughters. Finally, Chinese mothers have close bonds with their children, creating a "uterine family" that assures an economic contribution by daughters despite their exclusion from the patriliny.

During the postwar period large families (reflected in growing dependency ratios) forced unmarried sons and daughters into the work force. Girls in particular, having already experienced the household division of labor, were readily absorbed into the larger economy; as adolescents they first serve as unpaid household laborers in "putting-out" systems (as Cheng and Hsiung document), moving into outside factory work as they grow older. During the early days of industrialization, unmarried daughters were expected to work, often delaying marriage so that the sons could continue their educations. The girls' wages contributed to household income, viewed as a form of compensation for the costs of their upbringing. In return, the daughters received a modest increase in disposable income, along with the satisfaction that derived from contributing to the family in a culture where such contribution is highly valued. Salaff finds that daughters contribute as much as three quarters of family income, rendering their labor a significant source of the household's living standard.

A large proportion of newly married couples initially live with the husband's parents, at least until the birth of their children removes the mother from the work force, creating an economic burden on the parents' household. The ability of a newly married woman to work depends on her level of education, the wage she can earn outside the household, and her ability to shift her homemaking responsibilities to unmarried sisters. Since women's wages are typically extremely low, most married women drop out of the work force while they are raising children. In recent years, however—as wages and women's educational attainment have increased—there is some evidence that women are remaining more active in the work force. Once women become mothers-in-law and grandmothers, they often reenter the work force, this time realizing a fair degree of economic independence.

Salaff concludes that family cycle, demographics, and the external economy interact to produce the labor patterns associated with EOI in the East Asian NICs. While the role of female labor was key to early development, in today's maturing economies an increasing number of women are demanding (and receiving) education and higher wages. As a result, growing numbers of women—including those who are married—are choosing to work outside the home. This will undoubtedly have a profound effect on family structure and economic development in the coming years.

In the final chapter, Frederic Deyo undertakes a broad comparative review of the various forms of social policy that have been used by the East Asian states to secure legitimacy. He argues that under EOI, economic policies typically drive social policies. Four different forms of social policy are examined: economic development itself, which, Deyo argues, has significant welfare implications as employment and wages rise; direct social welfare expenditures on health, housing, education, transportation, food, and various forms of public assistance; incomes policies, which influence wages and benefits; and income security programs, through pension programs, unemployment compensation, disability and health insurance, and other forms of social security. All four forms of social policy have been effectively utilized to promote economic development goals.

Economic development, as others in this volume have shown, was explicitly intended to secure legitimacy by reducing unemployment and boosting incomes—a strategy pursued with varying degrees of success in all four countries. By promoting development through the export of labor-intensive manufactured goods, labor surpluses typically turned into shortages within two decades; this, in turn, has resulted in a shift toward higher value-added manufacturing.

Unlike development strategies, direct expenditures on social welfare differ considerably across the four NICs. The provision of housing, health care, and subsidized foodstuffs helped to ease the upward pressure on wages, particularly in Hong Kong and Singapore, which provided vast public housing estates for workers. Public housing, Deyo argues, has been provided not in response to workers' demands, but rather as an instrument of development itself, sharply reducing the cost of labor and hence cheapening the cost of exports. In general, Deyo finds the percentage of government expenditures on the social wage to be highest in the two higher-urbanized city-states, with Hong Kong currently outspending Singapore even after the latter's more sizeable defense expenditures are subtracted from the base. Taiwan also spends more than Korea on social welfare, both per capita and relative to GDP. During the 1980s, all four countries increased social spending relative to other government outlays, a result that doubtless reflects some "maturing" of their developmental economies. Presently, if one looks only at social expenditures, South Korea and Singapore spend the highest percentage (roughly 63%) on education of the four NICs, with Hong Kong spending the lowest (34%); Taiwan spends the highest percentage on social security and welfare (41%); Singapore and Hong Kong spend the highest percentage on health (18%); while Hong Kong spends the highest percentage on housing and community service (36%, Singapore having completed its vast public housing programs by the early 1980s).

Incomes policies have changed considerably in recent years in the four countries. During the early phases of EOI, when cheap labor was the key to growth, strict controls over labor were the norm; the need to keep wages down—to assure international competitiveness—often led to a high degree of repression. In recent years, the turn away from cheap export manufacturing—necessitated by growing labor shortages, themselves the result of developmental success—has led to growing expenditures on the human capital formation, particularly education and health. As wage restraint becomes less compatible with economic growth, controls have been eased. There are, however, significant historical differences between the four NICs. South Korea, which emphasized heavy industry requiring large labor concentrations, until recently exerted the most repressive controls over its work force; South Korea's history of pitched battles and bloody repression is well known. While Taiwan also depended on cheap labor for its early developmental success, its form of economic organization (small, interlinked, family-based firms rather than large factories) did not so readily admit of labor repression, a pattern reinforced by historically paternalistic employer-employee relations. In Singapore, early (1960s) leftist leanings of the since-dominant People's Action Party assured the widespread provision of the national pension scheme (Central Provident Fund), public housing, and national health care. Since that time, labor has been fully incorporated and controlled, permitting repressive wage policies during the 1970s and human capital formation subsequently. Hong Kong combines the family-firm structure of Taiwan with larger factory employment; the steady influx of immigrants from mainland China, however, has helped to assure a relatively abundant (and docile) work force fearful of deportation.

Policies aimed at providing income security have varied across the NICs. In South Korea, social insurance guarantees have been primarily directed toward public sector workers, the military, and school teachers. In general, protections have tended to be privately financed and contributory in nature. Taiwan has a similar profile, although with somewhat broader state guarantees than South Korea. Singapore's Central Provident Fund—which was established prior to industrialization—provides a strong social insurance program, while Hong Kong guarantees such protections only to civil service workers.

In recent years, economic restructuring in all four NICs has led to a shift toward higher value-added production, entailing new investments in human capital formation. The highly interventionist governments of South Korea and Singapore have, not surprisingly, devoted more resources to education and training than have those of Taiwan and Hong Kong. More paternalistic labor relations have also helped to assure stability in Taiwan and Singapore. In South Korea, which has continued to emphasize heavy industry, a highly proletarianized work force has become increasingly militant, demanding (and, in the past few years, receiving) significant wage increases, a national pension plan, and national health insurance.

Taiwan has similarly experienced a liberalization of labor policies, although the economy continues to be characterized by small, paternalistic firms and weak labor. The government of Singapore—like that of South Korea—has played a key role in economic restructuring, primarily in the direction of greater corporatism in the form of house unions and the privatization of some social, educational, and welfare programs. Restructuring—even including the encouragement of higher-wage, higher value-added production—remains in the service of economic development. Finally, Hong Kong has experienced no major shifts in social policy, with continuing flows of immigrants assuring a pool of low-wage, largely female workers for export industries.

Deyo concludes that East Asian development has emphasized the "effective utilization of human resources." While the strength of the developmental state varies across the four countries (with Singapore and South Korea at one pole, Hong Kong at the other, and Taiwan occupying an intermediate position), in all four cases social policy has been subordinate to (and in support of) state developmental objectives. Social policies, in general, have increased labor productivity, provided education and training, and—in various ways—helped to control and/or subsidize wages. The state has thus in various ways played a key role in assuring rapid economic growth.

9

Women, Export-Oriented Growth, and the State
THE CASE OF TAIWAN

LUCIE CHENG

PING-CHUN HSIUNG

During the last decade, three areas of scholarship have developed independently of each other: development studies, feminist studies, and studies of the role of the state. Not until recently has there been some cross fertilization among the three areas (Charlton, Everett, & Staudt, 1989). This chapter, drawing on the insights of these fields, is an effort to contribute to the ongoing discussion of the relationship between economic development and the system of male domination. We argue that as patriarchy and capitalism have penetrated the family, enterprises, and the state they have promoted the exploitation of women as low-waged and nonwaged income-generating workers, and as nonwaged domestic workers responsible for the reproduction of labor and for care of the elderly. The twin ideologies that dominate state and society actively promote "the double burden" as an acceptable and even aspired-to woman's role in the service of national development. This role, in turn, is a necessary, although not a sufficient contributor to the nation's economic advancement in a competitive world system. We will ground our discussion on the period of rapid economic growth in Taiwan from the mid-1960s to the late-1970s and will include more recent data when relevant.

Among the many factors that have been identified as responsible for Taiwan's economic "miracle," perhaps the least controversial is the availability of an elastic and cheap labor supply. Several scholars have pointed out that women are an especially important component of this labor (Bian,

1985; Chou, 1989; Diamond, 1979; Gallin, 1984a, 1984b; Koo, 1987; Kung, 1983; P. K.-C. Liu, 1984; Y.-L. Liu, 1985; Tsay, 1985). Despite their contributions to the economic growth of Taiwan, women as a group have not benefitted equally in comparison to men. Women are still underrepresented in the upper echelons of occupations (Y.-L. Liu 1985, p. 40), and their average wage continues to be a fraction of their male counterparts' (Bian, 1985, pp. 270-271; P.K.-C. Liu, 1984, p. 96). How is this gender difference maintained and reproduced? Research has focused on gender-specific socialization patterns, the influence of cultural traditions, and discriminatory practices of employers. We attempt to integrate these discussions by examining the role of the state vis-à-vis women and development. We will show how, under the "economy in command" orientation and with the support of a male-dominated civil society, the state manages to ensure the availability of an elastic and cheap female labor force by perpetuating and institutionalizing a patriarchal, capitalist ideology. The advancement of Taiwan's position in the world system is dependent on the specific use of women's labor as cheap wage workers, unwaged family workers, and unpaid service-providers.

Women's Labor and Economic Development in Taiwan

Discussions of women's labor and economic development have largely concentrated on female labor force participation and employment. Taiwan is justifiably proud of its record on the quantity and quality of its female work force. In 1951, shortly after the Guomindang (GMD, the Nationalist Party) government relocated to the Islands, the male labor force participation rate was 90.0% and the rate for females was 42.1%. Both rates decreased until 1966 when male participation dropped to 81.4% and female to a low of 32.6%. The reasons for these decreases are not entirely clear. Based on age-specific data by sex, P. K.-C. Liu and Hwang (1987) attribute them to rising levels of education, a low economic growth rate, compulsory military service, high fertility rate, and statistical artifacts due to a change in reporting definition. In any case, the early trend of decline for female labor force participation is generally seen as benign or even to some extent "positive," a result related more to improvement of the quality of labor and intensified childbearing and not so much to traditional gender discrimination. This conclusion masks the fact that negative effects of demographic factors on women's labor force participation are not natural, but are socially produced. There is no doubt that the expansion of educational opportunities for women has had many beneficial results. Among these has been an improvement in the quality of female labor force. Unfortunately, more education for women may not mean more gender equality. As Greenhalgh (1985) observes, up to a point the relationship between women's education and the decrease in their labor force participation reflects increased gender inequality. Young women were given the opportunity to finish junior high and high schools before entering the labor force to help their brothers gain more education. The increase in education for women in Taiwan has not increased women's status vis-à-vis men. Instead, it has resulted in higher returns to their families from their exploitation. Parents tended to increase investment in their daughters' education just enough to enable the child to gain a well-paid job.

The negative relationship between fertility and labor force participation observed by P. K.-C. Liu and Hwang (1987) is more a social construct than a physical inevitability. For example, the requirement that women leave the labor force for an extended period to assume responsibility for child care is a "social" rather than a "biological" one. By tying rewards exclusively to individual productivity while ignoring societal needs, what appear to be gender-neutral capitalist employment practices actually punish women.

Elasticity in Women's Labor Force Participation

Most discussions of gender and labor force participation in Taiwan begin with 1966 when the impact of economic restructuring was first reflected in the labor market. From that year on, women's labor force participation rate, despite its zigzag pattern, has shown an upward trend. By 1987, 3.1 million or 38.1% of the total labor force, were women (Directorate-General of Budget, 1989, p. 5). In comparison to 1966, when 32.6% of all females 15 years and older were in the labor force, the percentage for 1987 is 46.5. Three characteristics of women's labor force participation support the argument that women are especially important to Taiwan's economic growth: the timing of the increase, its long-term growth pattern, and women's low wage level.

The sharpest rise in women's labor force participation occurred between 1966 and 1973, the period marked by labor-intensive, export-oriented industrialization. During that period, as Table 9.1 shows, the female labor force participation rate rose from 32.6% to 41.5%, while male rates remained relatively stable with some decline. This trend reflects a change in the economic policy of Taiwan which in turn is conditioned by the transformation of the international division of labor.

Massive restructuring of capitalism in the mid-1960s created an opportunity for peripheral and semiperipheral countries to seek advancement in the world system. Taiwan was able to mobilize its resources to take advantage of this opportunity. Adequate foreign investment and domestic accumulation, enough state autonomy from both the constraints of world economy and powerful domestic interest groups, political stability, and access to markets provided the conditions for Taiwan to develop a viable economic policy based on export (Crane, 1982; Evans & Pang, 1989; Winckler and Greenhalgh, 1988. The pursuit of labor-intensive, export-oriented development required a particular kind of labor force, one relatively large in number, flexible in flow, and inexpensive in price. Female labor, for reasons that we will discuss later, fits these requirements especially well. The ready supply of female labor has reduced labor costs and increased Taiwan's competitiveness in the world market (Bian, 1985; Gallin, 1990). In addition, the use of female labor helps to ease the impact of inflation in core countries such as the United States (Mies, 1986). The elasticity of female labor relative to male labor is indicated by the greater fluctuation in women's participation rates over time. In contrast with male rates, female rates are more sensitive to changes in the world economy (Chiang & Ku, 1985, pp. 8-9). The rise and decline of female rates corresponds to business cycles in Taiwan (Chou, 1989, pp. 437-438).

Table 9.1 shows the difference in annual growth rates of male and female labor force participation. While male rates hover between 1.3 in 1980 and 4.9 in 1974, female rates not only have a much wider range, but also show a much wider zigzag pattern. The growth of women in the labor force peaked in 1973, when the rate reached 16%. This increase is due to labor-intensive industrialization. The growth rate, however, dropped to 0.3% in 1974 and reached a negative of −0.8% in 1975 when Taiwan's economy was severely affected by the oil crisis. Afterward, it took almost a decade for women's participation rate to reach the same average level of growth as before the economic recession. A comparison of the unemployment rates between women and men shows similarly greater elasticity for women (Table 9.1). There are more frequent fluctuations in women's rates and the difference between each change is generally larger.

Table 9.1 Labor Force Participation and Unemployment by Gender, Taiwan, 1965-1987

	LFP Rate[a]		Growth Rate[b]		Unemployment Rate	
	Male	*Female*	*Male*	*Female*	*Male*	*Female*
1965	82.6	33.1	2.1	0.8	2.3	5.9
1966	81.4	32.6	2.1	2.0	2.3	4.9
1967	80.9	33.7	3.0	7.5	1.8	3.5
1968	80.2	34.4	2.8	5.9	1.6	2.0
1969	79.2	35.4	2.9	7.0	1.6	2.6
1970	78.9	35.5	3.9	4.2	1.5	2.2
1971	78.4	35.4	3.5	3.7	1.5	2.1
1972	77.0	37.1	2.2	8.9	1.2	2.1
1973	77.1	41.5	3.4	16.0	1.1	1.7
1974	78.2	40.2	4.9	0.3	1.3	2.0
1975	77.6	38.6	2.7	–0.8	2.1	3.1
1976	77.1	37.6	2.7	0.8	1.6	2.1
1977	77.8	39.3	4.2	8.1	1.7	2.0
1978	78.0	39.2	4.5	3.2	1.6	1.9
1979	77.9	39.2	2.5	3.4	1.2	1.5
1980	77.1	39.3	1.3	3.0	1.1	1.5
1981	76.8	38.8	2.2	1.7	1.2	1.6
1982	76.5	39.3	2.3	4.1	2.3	2.3
1983	76.4	42.1	1.8	9.6	2.7	2.7
1984	76.1	43.3	2.0	5.2	2.4	2.5
1985	75.5	43.5	1.7	2.8	2.9	2.9
1986	75.2	45.5	2.0	7.1	2.8	2.5
1987	75.2	46.5	2.2	4.4	2.0	2.0

SOURCE: Directorate-General (1988), pp. 52-53.
NOTES: a. Percentage of LFP
b. Increases in number of workers in labor market

Table 9.2 Labor Force Participation Rate by Age and Gender, Selected Years

	1966		1974		1983	
	Male	Female	Male	Female	Male	Female
15-19	54.6	54.7	49.9	52.4	76.4	39.2
20-24	84.0	46.6	78.7	54.3	36.2	60.9
25-29	97.3	28.9	96.6	36.7	75.9	46.5
30-34	98.1	28.7	98.8	37.8	95.3	46.9
35-39	98.3	33.2	98.8	53.5	98.1	48.9
40-44	96.9	30.6	98.5	47.9	98.1	48.0
45-49	95.1	27.4	96.1	41.4	96.1	52.9
50-54	89.1	20.0	89.0	32.6	89.8	35.0
55-59	71.4	11.7	82.8	19.4	79.7	26.8
60-64	46.2	6.0	52.7	7.0	60.2	15.6
65+	17.2	1.5	11.8	1.0	15.4	2.7

SOURCE: Tsay (1985), p. 303.

Women's employment is not only more susceptible to the business cycle, it is also more affected by individual and family life-cycle events. Age, marital status, and number of children play a more significant role in determining women's than men's labor force participation. Women tend to withdraw from the marketplace between age 25 to 34; that is, after the worker's marriage and the birth of her first child. They reenter the labor market after 35 as their family responsibilities lighten. A great majority leave the labor market entirely after 55 years of age, perhaps to care for the elderly members of the family. Males, on the other hand, stay in the job market until they reach retirement age (Table 9.2).

The differential impact of marital status is more obvious when we compare female and male rates in Table 9.3. While gender makes a difference in labor force participation, the difference is the smallest for single persons. For

Table 9.3 Percentage of LFP for Male and Female by Marital Status and Age, Taiwan, 1984

Age	Male			Female		
	Single	*Married*	*Divorced/ Widowed*	*Single*	*Married*	*Divorced/ Widowed*
15-19	30.2	90.8	—	33.4	30.7	100.0
20-24	70.5	97.3	100.0	76.8	34.1	91.3
25-34	91.2	98.9	94.7	86.1	41.8	71.5
35-44	89.0	98.4	96.2	76.0	50.0	63.2
45-54	83.3	94.6	90.3	61.5	39.5	43.3
55-64	50.3	75.4	56.7	42.6	21.8	20.5
65+	10.4	18.0	8.5	32.4	4.3	1.7

SOURCE: Liu (1985), p. 25.

those who are married, male rates are more than double those of female's for all age groups. The presence of children under six years of age greatly reduces the likelihood of married women's labor force participation (Y.-L. Liu, 1985, pp. 76-77). When employment and promotion rules are developed with male workers in mind, women are disadvantaged because of interruptions caused by domestic responsibilities. Women's more frequent and early exits from the labor market for reproductive and caring purposes perpetuate their exploitation as cheap labor.

Women's Labor as Cheap Labor

Just how cheap has women's labor been in Taiwan? We will examine both the difference between male and female wages, and women's wages alone. The Taiwan government has publicized the cheap wages and docility of its labor force to attract foreign investment. A number of scholars have emphasized low wage and lack of benefits as characteristic of female labor (Cumings, 1987; Deyo, 1989; Kung, 1983). In fact, many would argue that these features are the raison d'être of female employment in capitalism. As

Table 9.4 Gender Distribution by Industry, Taiwan, Selected Years

	1966		1970		1980		1988	
	M	F	M	F	M	F	M	F
Agriculture, etc.	42.6	46.0	35.1	40.6	20.2	18.1	15.2	10.6
Mining	2.0	0.4	2.7	0.8	0.9	0.3	0.5	0.2
Manufacturing	17.2	17.5	19.7	21.9	29.3	39.9	31.7	39.0
Utilities	1.0	0.2	1.0	0.3	0.6	0.1	0.6	0.1
Construction	4.8	0.6	7.0	0.7	11.7	2.0	10.6	1.9
Commerce	11.4	13.7	14.0	16.1	15.0	17.9	17.7	22.5
Transportation, etc.	5.9	1.7	7.0	1.9	7.7	2.3	7.3	2.1
Finance	15.2	19.9	13.6	17.8	2.0	2.5	2.9	3.8
Services	—	—	—	—	12.8	16.8	13.7	19.9
N	2,702	945	3,121	1,425	4,357	2,191	4,946	2,986

SOURCE: 1966, 1970, 1980: P. K.-C. Liu & Hwang (1987), p. 100. 1988: Directorate-General (1988), pp. 8-9.
NOTE: Numbers (N) are in thousands, for age 15 and older.

Tables 9.4 and 9.5 show, after two decades of development, women workers are still concentrated in the most labor-intensive industries where wages are typically low (see Table 9.4), as well as at the lower end of the occupational ladder of all industries (see Table 9.5).

As in other countries, women's wages in Taiwan are only a fraction of their male counterparts. In fact, the gap between male and female earnings not only has persisted but, in some occupations and industries, has widened over the past two decades (P. K.-C. Liu, 1984, pp. 95-98; P. K.-C. Liu & Hwang, 1987; Y.-L. Liu, 1985, pp. 56-66). Table 9.6 shows that in five out of nine industries there has been a deterioration of women's wages relative to men's during the past decade. The gains in wage equality observed in the 1970s had mostly eroded by the 1980s. Using 1980 data, P. K.-C. Liu (1984) found that the wage differentials cannot be explained by human capital variables.

Table 9.5 Occupational Distribution by Gender, Taiwan, Selected Years

		1970		1980		1984		1988[e]	
		M	F	M	F	M	F	M	F
Professional &	(a)	0.3	—	0.3	—	0.3	—		
Technical Workers	(b)	2.6	0.6	2.4	0.6	2.8	0.8		
	(c)	9.4	12.0	11.0	14.5	10.9	14.3		
	(d)	22.8	23.8	26.9	33.1	26.2	32.6	6.2	7.8
Administative &	(a)	0.1	—	—	—	—	—		
Managerial Workers	(b)	9.3	1.0	2.6	0.1	2.5	0.2		
	(c)	5.3	1.6	1.1	0.2	1.1	0.2		
	(d)	6.8	2.0	1.8	0.3	1.6	0.2	1.3	0.2
Clerical Workers	(a)	0.5	0.3	0.6	0.5	0.5	0.8		
	(b)	6.3	8.3	14.6	13.6	14.4	14.5		
	(c)	13.0	12.8	15.6	26.9	15.3	26.4		
	(d)	19.7	14.7	21.4	21.4	20.1	22.4	11.5	20.3
Traders	(a)	0.1	—	—	—	—	—		
	(b)	4.7	4.5	3.1	0.9	3.0	0.8		
	(c)	32.8	38.5	30.7	30.2	31.7	30.3		
	(d)	0.9	1.2	0.7	1.1	1.0	1.1	14.4	15.1
Service Workers	(a)	—	—	0.1	0.3	—	0.2		
	(b)	1.6	1.6	2.4	1.1	2.1	1.1		
	(c)	11.8	21.8	14.6	20.3	15.3	22.3		
	(d)	22.3	39.7	22.6	27.6	23.4	30.5	7.3	11.8
Agricultural &	(a)	98.0	99.5	98.4	99.0	98.4	98.7		
Related Workers	(b)	1.0	0.6	—	—	—	—		
	(c)	0.6	—	0.1	—	0.1	—		
	(d)	0.7	—	0.2	—	0.3	—	15.1	10.6
Production,	(a)	1.1	0.2	0.6	0.3	0.6	0.2		
Transportation, &	(b)	74.5	83.3	74.9	93.6	75.2	82.6		
Related Workers	(c)	27.2	13.2	26.9	7.8	25.6	6.4		
	(d)	26.8	18.6	26.4	16.5	27.4	13.2	44.1	34.2

SOURCE: P. K.-C. Liu & Hwang (1987), pp. 140-141; Directorate-General (1988).
NOTES: a. Agriculture
b. Manufacturing
c. Service
d. Commerce
e. All Industries

Table 9.6 Proportion of Average Monthly Female Wage to Male Wage
             by Industry, Taiwan

	1973	1978	1984	1988
Agriculture	—	56.8	51.9	55.0
Mining	37.2	65.8	53.6	55.2
Manufacture	54.4[a]	61.0	61.1	57.6
Utilities	68.5[a]	75.1	74.0	81.6
Construction	65.4	75.8	68.0	71.9
Commerce	—	72.6	68.0	68.4
Transport	71.7	71.2	75.0	76.7
Financial Services	—	59.2	68.0	65.1
Social and Personal	71.3	72.7	75.7	72.8

SOURCE: 1973: Directorate-General (1974), p. 682; 1978 and 1984: Y.-L. Liu (1985), pp. 61-62; 1988: Directorate-General (1988), pp. 90-91.
NOTE: a. For manufacturing and utilities, the percentages are calculated from data for 1972.

Gender discrimination is widely recognized in Taiwan, although not widely condemned. A study of employment advertisements in newspapers reveal that males are preferred for higher-paying jobs, while for lower-paying jobs ads often stipulate that "only females may apply" (*Funu Xinzhi*, 59, 1987, p. 8). The state, on the one hand proclaims that men and women are equal, but on the other condones gender discrimination in its own employment practice (Zheng & Bo, 1987). Women are excluded from participating in civil service examinations for certain prestigious government jobs, such as high level jobs in the customs department, the diplomatic services, international journalism, and the labor department. For some civil service jobs, the number of women can not exceed a certain quota. For example, in 1985, the civil service examination for consular personnel was slated to admit 50 persons, but the public was informed that no more than 7 would be women (Zheng & Bo, 1987, p. 8). When confronted with these and other discriminatory practices, government officials often respond by saying that it is better for women and for society if women concentrate on what they do best.

Table 9.7 Percentage Distribution of Women and Men as Unpaid Family Workers, Selected Industries, 1966-1986

		Agriculture		Manufacturing		Commerce		Services	
		M	F	M	F	M	F	M	F
1966	(a)	28.7	74.9	4.4	12.1	8.3	41.6	2.0	7.2
	(b)	48.8	51.2	48.6	51.4	31.9	68.1	34.9	65.1
1971	(a)	23.0	78.9	2.8	9.7	8.2	43.2	2.0	5.7
	(b)	38.4	61.6	32.3	67.7	27.0	73.0	36.5	63.5
1976	(a)	20.9	71.4	2.5	4.7	6.6	36.3	1.3	4.6
	(b)	38.0	62.0	44.6	55.4	26.5	73.5	34.2	65.8
1981	(a)	16.1	65.8	2.4	4.6	6.2	36.3	1.4	5.2
	(b)	37.1	62.9	43.1	56.9	22.0	78.0	28.6	71.4
1986	(a)	16.5	67.3	1.9	5.3	6.6	36.3	1.4	5.8
	(b)	34.7	65.3	30.7	69.3	19.9	80.1	22.5	77.5

SOURCE: Chou (1989), pp. 450-457.
NOTES: a. Proportion of total male/female employed who are unpaid
b. Proportion of total unpaid workers who are male/female

For example, the Minister of Interior proclaimed publicly that women should take pride in freeing their husband from family worries and not be so concerned about whether or not they themselves can become department heads (*Funu Xinzhi,* 5, 1982, pp. 13-14). The labor force participation and employment rates overestimate the progress women have made in remunerative work since both include a large number of unpaid family workers, most of whom are female. As Table 9.7 indicates, although unpaid work done by males and females has declined, there has been an increase in the proportion of unpaid work done by females since 1966. In every industry, the proportion of unpaid female workers exceeds that of their male counterpart. Among unpaid family workers, women exceed men by a large margin. What labor can be cheaper than unpaid labor?

The expansion of women's paid and unpaid income-generating labor is directly tied to the state's export-oriented growth strategy. Fiscal and tax policies favoring firms willing to export (Directory, 1963, pp. 164-174; Yu, 1981) provided incentives for families to send their women to work or to respond to the state-sponsored "living-room factories" program to take advantage of family and neighborhood female labor. By linking domestic and paid work in the same space, women's labor was intensified and their work days lengthened. The increase in women's labor force participation and employment does not necessarily indicate an improvement in women's lives, nor does it indicate a rise in women's status. On the contrary, it may simply reflect an intensification of women's exploitation resulting from the addition of nondomestic employment with meager reward to the burden of domestic work. Women's increased employment is a requirement for the survival of capitalism; it is not to be confused with a victory in gender equality.

Women, the Sex Industry, and the State

An often ignored area of women's labor that has contributed significantly to capital accumulation in Taiwan is their sexual labor. Discussions on this topic are quite numerous, but most have focused on its morality and the physical exploitation of women, not on its economic role. Since the 1950s, Taiwan has been considered a haven for male tourists. In addition to registered brothels, commercial sexual services under various guises are widely available. These include barber shops, bath houses, massage parlors, bars, coffee houses, and restaurants, some of which are conveniently labelled by the government as *teding* or *tezhong yingye* or specialized businesses. Table 9.8 shows that while the number of brothels declined after peaking in 1967, the number of *Jiujia* or "restaurants with waitresses" more than doubled during the same period. Unfortunately, data on these specialized businesses are no longer published, although it is widely known where one can buy sexual services (*Funu Xinzhi*, 66, 1987, p. 10). Most recently, a new type of sex business has come into being that is graphically referred to as the "beef market."

Two conditions greatly facilitated the growth of the sex industry in Taiwan and other developing countries: American military presence and the United States' initiative to tie tourism to Third World development. One of the well-known but relatively unexplored consequences of the Korean War and the Vietnam War is the increase of the sex trade in Asia. Used as favorite R&R sites for American soldiers, cities in Taiwan, South Korea, Thailand, and other Southeast Asian countries became lucrative markets for the exploitation of women's sexual labor (Kim, 1987; Truong, 1990). The infrastructures developed for the sex industry continued to serve a burgeoning tourist trade after the wars ended.

Table 9.8 Number of Sexually Oriented Businesses in Taiwan, 1946-1973

	Hotel	Tea & Coffee Room	Restaurant w/Waitress	Cabaret	Brothel
1946	866	—	—	11	216
1947	969	—	—	—	—
1948	932	—	—	—	—
1949	902	—	—	—	—
1950	801	—	31	—	—
1951	842	346	56	—	—
1952	892	546	88	—	—
1953	961	786	86	—	—
1954	1,093	930	54	—	—
1955	1,137	930	52	—	—
1956	1,251	1,001	—	—	—
1957	1,326	984	—	—	249
1958	1,479	1,043	—	—	349
1959	1,576	1,030	—	3	424
1960	1,671	963	—	8	463
1961	1,782	1,002	—	11	476
1962	1,897	793	—	15	453
1963	2,014	825	—	17	412
1964	2,143	801	—	27	529
1965	2,272	859	—	32	509
1966	2,403	756	—	31	489
1967	2,949	765	76	46	636
1968	2,662	629	163	33	452
1969	2,802	596	449	25	384
1970	2,864	568	429	25	355
1971	2,916	511	372	25	337
1972	2,974	485	342	25	319
1973	2,997	451	407	25	311

SOURCE: Directorate-General (1974), pp. 188-189.

The development of Third World tourism is closely related to the global political economy (Truong, 1990). Truong argues that in order to save the heavy investment banks had made in aircraft industries in the 1950s, the U.S. government began to promote tourism as a development strategy for the

Third World, especially for Asian countries (Truong, 1990). Tourism was hailed as a peace-maintaining, harmony-producing industry. But the political and cultural functions of tourism were not enough to induce developing countries to spend millions of dollars to buy passenger airplanes, construct luxurious hotels and build other tourism infrastructure. After a concerted effort of the United States, tourist projects became eligible for financial and technical assistance from the international development programs of the World Bank, the United Nations, and other international agencies. It was the attraction of tourism as a way to gain foreign currency that prompted many Asian countries to use tourism as a development strategy.

The Taiwan government began to promote tourism in the mid-1950s, immediately following the conclusion of the Korean War. Since then, heated debates over its efficacy have periodically taken place in the Provincial Assembly and among the populace. Supporters of tourism combine economic, political, and cultural arguments. They point to its potential in earning foreign exchange, attracting foreign investment, and expanding foreign trade (Deng, 1975, p. 402). Politically, tourists are described as valuable messengers who can tell the world about the progress in Taiwan and therefore raise its international status. In addition, tourism can promote Chinese traditional culture (Zhou, 1966). Opponents, however, argue that the net economic advantage of tourism has not been demonstrated, and the negative social effects overshadow all the other advantages (Y. Li, 1987; Qu, 1984). Women's organizations and human rights activists have accused the government of colluding with sex traders by not enforcing existing laws or passing new legislation that would legalize prostitution rather than making invidious and useless distinctions between "public" or registered sexual laborers and "private" or underground ones (*Funu Xinzhi,* 1986-1987). Even supporters admit that due to the profit-seeking motives of some businesses, tourism has led to the burgeoning of the sex trade and has "affected the moral fiber of Taiwan" (Zhan, 1966, pp. 5-9). In fact, the government keeps the price of sexual labor low by prohibiting women in the "specialized businesses" to form unions on the grounds that their occupation "violate the good mores of society" (*Funu Xinzhi,* 69, 1988, p. 14).

Tourism is an "experience commodity" that necessitates the commoditization of personal services (Truong, 1990). Tourists are to be made feel welcome and "at home." Promotional campaigns endorsed by government agencies and tourist industries attempted to build a market by focussing on aspects of hospitality, such as female submissiveness, caring, and nurturing, as well as sexual temptation (Directory, 1963, pp. 178-180). Tourist booklets distributed at government handicraft stores and offices contain advertisements that magnify the sexual appeals of Taiwan women. Operators of sex package tours give detailed descriptions in words and pictures of the kinds of sexual services available and their costs to show that foreign visitors can enjoy uninhibited sex. A government publication, praising the achievement of Taiwan since its recovery from Japanese occupation, highlighted the "inexhaustible sources of pleasure" available (Deng, 1975, pp. 403-404).

To combat sexually transmitted diseases, which would threaten the tourist business as well as embarrass the government, a number of laws were promulgated to control prostitution and other sex trade. These laws take two general approaches: to make sexual contacts safe by requiring prostitutes to obtain and display health certificates, and to limit the number of specialized businesses by increasing the licensing fees and tax. Although neither approach has been successful, these laws did provide an official guide to relatively safe sex, and increased the revenue of the state. The link between women's sexual labor and foreign trade is a popular theme among well-known local writers (Huang, 1981). While we have no way to determine the specific dollar contribution of the sex industry to the economy, it is certain that it forms an important part of the tourist revenue. Tourism is included in economic discussions as an export, its revenue ranks fourth to sixth of all exports during the last two decades (Deng, 1975, p. 402). Table 9.9 shows the increase in tourist revenues from 1956 to 1973, the period of export-led growth.

As Table 9.9 also shows, the number of tourists has jumped from 15 thousand to more than 824 thousand during the same period. The increase is largely due to the influx of Japanese tourists. In 1957, Americans outnumbered all tourists with 70%; by 1973, American tourists comprised less than 20% while Japanese made up 72% of all tourists (Directorate-General, 1974, pp. 516-517). Japanese males are notorious as consumers of sexual tours, and their behavior has been the target of continuing demonstration by Japanese women as well as women in other Asian countries (*Funu Xinzhi,* 1987; Kim, 1987; Truong, 1990). When the International Lions Club met in Taipei, newspapers splashed pages of materials on where visitors can go to "buy spring." Taiwan women demonstrated with banners in Chinese, English, and Japanese languages: "Welcome to Taiwan for Friendship, but not for sex tours" (*Funu Xinzhi,* 62, 1987, p. 6).

Traditional ideology of self-sacrifice and submissiveness plays an important role in the sex trade, as girls "volunteer" or are forced by their real or adoptive parents to trade sexual labor for family survival or for the education of their male siblings (*Funu Xinzhi,* 47, 1986, pp. 2-3; X. Lu, 1986). While no official figures are available, women workers in the sex industry are

Table 9.9 Tourist Industry In Taiwan

	Total Number of Tourists	Growth Rate (%)	Total Revenue from Tourism (U.S.$)	Growth Rate (%)
1956	14,974	—	935,876	—
1957	18,159	21.3	1,134,938	21.3
1958	16,709	8.0	1,044,313	−8.0
1959	19,328	15.7	1,208,000	15.7
1960	23,636	22.3	1,477,251	22.3
1961	42,205	78.7	2,637,914	78.7
1962	52,304	23.9	3,269,000	23.9
1963	72,024	37.7	7,202,000	120.3
1964	95,481	32.6	10,345,000	43.6
1965	133,666	40.0	18,245,000	76.4
1966	182,948	36.9	30,353,000	66.4
1967	253,248	38.4	42,016,000	38.4
1968	301,770	19.2	53,271,000	26.8
1969	371,473	23.1	56,055,000	5.2
1970	472,452	26.9	81,720,000	45.8
1971	539,755	12.2	110,000,000	34.6
1972	580,033	7.5	128,707,000	17.0
1973	824,393	42.1	245,882,000	91.0
1974	819,821	−0.6	278,402,000	13.2
1975	853,140	4.1	359,358,000	29.1
1976	1,008,126	18.2	466,077,000	29.7
1977	1,110,182	10.1	527,492,000	13.2
1978	1,270,977	14.5	608,000,000	15.3
1979	1,340,382	5.5	919,000,000	51.2
1980	1,393,254	3.9	988,000,000	7.5
1981	1,409,465	1.2	1,080,000,000	9.3
1982	1,419,178	0.7	953,000,000	−11.7
1983	1,457,404	2.7	990,000,000	3.9
1984	1,516,138	4.0	1,066,000,000	7.7
1985	1,451,659	−4.3	963,000,000	−9.7
1986	1,610,385	10.9	1,333,000,000	38.4

SOURCE: Directorate-General (1987), p. 397.
Revenue income for 1956-1961 from Taiwan Shengzhengfu Xinwenchu (1965), pp. 18-32.

popularly estimated at more than 300,000 in 1989, including those brought from Southeast Asia and girls as young as 11 from local ethnic groups. Their customers include a large number of overseas Chinese and foreign visitors looking to satisfy their sexual appetite at an affordable price, and more importantly, with state protection. Women's sexual labor, like women's labor in other areas, is consciously exploited in Taiwan's strategy for national development. It functions as an exotic commodity for "tourist attraction and helps to fill airplane seats and hotel rooms. National accounts benefit from taxes on accommodation, food, drinks and services. Unlike their flesh, the contribution of prostitutes' labor to the process of accumulation remains invisible." (Truong, 1990, p. 128). The state condemns the women who are engaged in this trade and periodically arrests those who lack official certification, yet the state also encourages the continuation of exploitation by treating sexual labor as a tourist attraction.

Women's Unwaged Domestic Labor

National statistics do not reveal the necessary but monotonous, fragmented, and time-consuming domestic work that most women do without wage. Studies continue to show that men do not participate in household labor to any appreciable degree in most societies, including Taiwan (Y.-H. Lu, 1984; Miller & Garrison, 1982). Those who share this work with women do so selectively and reluctantly. Taiwan women, socialized to believe that domestic work is part and parcel of womanhood, may complain, but do not generally expect help from their menfolks.

What is the relationship between women's unwaged domestic labor and economic development? At the most basic level, women, as housewives and mothers, reproduce the labor force that creates growth. But women's unwaged domestic work is more than the physical reproduction of labor. Surveys indicate that housewives are the principal agents of domestic consumption. In Taipei, household expenditures in 59.4% of all families are managed by the wife, and another 14.7% by other women in the family (*Funu Xinzhi,* vol. 16, 1983, pp. 6-7). The model of the middle-class housewife in Taiwan involves a highly developed consumption style, which provides a market for ever-increasing commodities and services. It is no wonder that consumer education is almost exclusively directed toward females, and women are beginning to realize their potential in influencing the behavior of large corporations.

Through the maintenance of the family, women provide stability and emotional support to its members. Chinese tradition views women's role in maintaining harmony at home and in the neighborhood as critical to national development (Diamond, 1973; P. K.-C. Liu & Hwang, 1987). Both Taiwan and the People's Republic of China continue to promote this image through mass campaigns, education, and media indoctrination.

The heated debates in the 1970s in Europe and in the United States among scholars and politicians regarding "wages for housework" point to the economic value of this unpaid work (Kaluzynska, 1980). Unpaid domestic work became a public issue in Taiwan when *Funu Xinzhi,* the leading feminist magazine, reported in 1983 that the economic value of a housewife in middle-income families was about NT$35,500 a month, more than the salary of an associate professor in a university (*Funu Xinzhi,* vol. 16, 1983, p. 17). This estimate only includes cooking, laundering, cleaning, caring for the elderly, and tutoring children twice a week. Excluded are the economic value of household management and consumption-related labor typical of housewives such as shopping for food, clothing, and daily necessities. More recently, the magazine *Money (Qian)* calculates that depending on the number and ages of children, a middle-class wife has to earn a minimum of NT$18,620 to $36,620 per month to make her employment outside worthwhile (*Qian,* p. 162). The cost to the family of having the housewife employed outside for wages is staggering when we consider that the median monthly income of college-educated women is NT$17,146.

Various types of caring, such as child care, care for the elderly, and care for the infirm performed by women without pay reduce the cost of social welfare for the state. These savings have been especially significant for Taiwan since it has allocated a large percentage of its resources to security and defense. Women's unpaid domestic labor frees capital to be directed toward more productive investment as defined by the state.

It has been argued that the benefits of economic development will trickle down to women. However, the experience of advanced countries gives us little confidence in this prediction. Economic development has not reduced the burden of women's household labor as expected. A male-dominated state apparatus does not treat women's interest as a high priority. Machines and services considered by women to be most useful to alleviate their work load are not easily accessible in developing countries. When household mechanization occurs, it changes the way some housework is done, but does not greatly reduce the time spent in doing housework. The time that is reduced in an area of work often is taken up by other housework, or by a rise in housework standards.

Mechanization and commercialization of housework create opportunities for waged work for all women but produce different consequences for women of different classes. Working-class women will make the machines and provide the household services to allow middle-class women to seek better employment. Both classes of women are increasingly required to earn a wage to prevent the family from slipping from its standard of living. While middle-class women will gain some alleviation from their domestic responsibilities, working-class women who cannot afford to buy the machines or hire others to perform the services will continue to be burdened. Data from Taiwan indicate that among married female professional and managerial workers, more than 15% rely on servants for child care (Y.-H. Lu, 1984, p. 367).

Economic growth has created more leisure, but this leisure has not led men to share domestic work with women. In fact, it is women's unpaid domestic labor that creates leisure time for men. Studies have shown that employed men have more leisure time than both employed women and full-time housewives (Waring, 1988, p. 163). Men prefer to spend their leisure with other men. In the United States they drink, play cards, attend sports events, go camping or fishing, or watch TV. In Taiwan, men may engage in other activities, but it is doubtful that they will do housework.

The flexible nature of domestic labor is especially conducive to exploitation. Much housework does not have to be done in a specific amount of time because the standards are variable: high or low standards of cleanliness, ironed or unironed clothes, and so forth. Therefore, it does not prohibit women from taking on either unpaid family income-producing work, or waged labor. In other words, it allows women to be doubly burdened without appearing so. The blind acceptance of a patriarchal concept of labor defined by men and based on the characteristics of male labor prevents the recognition of a large portion of women's labor as labor.

Waged Work and Unwaged Work: The Continuity of Women's Work

Mies (1986) argues that we are accustomed to viewing women's work with concepts developed on the basis of men's work under capitalism. Most men work for a certain number of hours a day, away from home, and uninterrupted by household concerns. Men are paid regularly and their jobs are to a varying extent protected by the state. Women's work does not have the same characteristics. Women are primarily household workers, although an increasing number are engaged in income-generating activities. Many work in the informal economy, insecure and unprotected. Their work is continuous and with frequent interruptions, but the interruptions are an integral part of women's work. It is misleading to think of women's work with categories developed for the accounting of men's work. Thus feminist scholars have argued the need for a new concept of labor built upon the concrete labor of women (Beneria, 1982; Mies, 1986; Waring, 1988). Some case studies of the working lives of women in Taiwan's export economy may be helpful in this construction.

Women's daily work schedules are arranged around their familial responsibilities as wife, mother, and daughter-in-law.

1. May-cheng comes to paint glasses at the small factory around 8 in the morning after her husband leaves for work. Around 11, she goes back to her apartment, which is five doors down the alley, to prepare lunch for him. After her husband leaves for work around 1 o'clock, she comes back to work until 5:30 or 6 when she goes home to prepare for dinner. She continues to paint the glasses at home after dinner while she waits for water to do the family's laundry or other chores. She doesn't go to sleep until after midnight.

2. A-hsia and her sister-in-law share the responsibility of caring for their father-in-law. They each take care of him for 15 days per month. During the half month of A-hsia's turn, she gets up around 6 and prepares both breakfast and lunch for him before she comes to work because he insists on eating his noon meal at 11:45. A-hsia goes home at 12 o'clock to eat the leftovers. She comes back to the factory at 12:50 and goes home to cook around 5:10. After dinner, she comes back to work in the factory until 9.

3. This week is A-chou's turn to stay at home and look after her father-in-law who has been confined to bed for the last 10 years. She can only work in the factory from 1 to 3 when he takes his nap. She rushes into the factory, squats on the floor, and removes as many rubber bands from the drawers as she possibly can. During the whole time, the only word she utters is "good-bye" when she leaves.

Women often have to compromise their waged labor outside the family with their unwaged labor in the family business. When a man is thinking of getting married, he calculates how much he has to spend for the engagement party, bride price, and wedding, and how much of his investment will be recovered when his wife joins the labor force.

When I congratulated Lin, an owner of a factory who just got engaged, he talked about his bride-to-be: "I don't intend to get a decorating vase. I also don't need sex; if I want sex, I can get cheap sex on the street. I heard that she is very good at bookkeeping. People say that she is really thrifty and hardworking too. The other day, I ran into her in the market, she was riding a 125 cc motorcycle. You know, she is really physically very strong." When I asked him how much he had to spend in total, he said it will be about NT$400,000. "It is worth it. People think I have a pretty good deal, you know," Lin said.

It is quite understandable why many women quit their jobs in the factory after their marriage; the totality of their labor, for income and for reproduction, is required by the family as unwaged labor.

> Lu finished elementary school and didn't want to continue because she didn't think she could pass the unified entrance examination for junior high. She went to work in a garment factory in the Tan-zi Export Processing Zone for more than 10 years. Her marriage was arranged by her parents. She had to quit her job because the factory run by her husband's family needed her labor. She didn't get paid working in the family's factory. It was only last year when the family business slowed down that Lu start looking for jobs outside. Even after Lu found a job in the neighborhood, she still had to compensate for her missed unwaged labor in the family factory by coming up with a special work arrangement:
>
> Lu's schedule starts around 7 in the morning. She has to get ready for work by 7:15. Before leaving home for waged work, she first works in the family factory for 30 minutes. She and her two sisters-in-law take weekly turns to cook for workers in the family factory. Lu works for wages in Xin-liang, a hardware store, from 8 to 12 during the weeks when it is not her turn to cook lunch, and returns at 1 p.m. In other weeks she leaves Xin-liang at 11 and gets back at 12:30 instead of at 1 p.m. when other workers come back from their lunch. After she finishes work at the hardware store, she resumes work in the family factory again from 4:30 to 5:30. Lu is paid hourly by the hardware store because she does not work 40 hours every week.

The complex and overlapping work schedule reflects the integration of women's productive and reproductive roles and their waged and unwaged labor.

How is the continuing exploitation of women's labor in all its complexity maintained, and the resulting gender inequality perpetuated? What role does the state play?

The Capitalist Patriarchal State of Taiwan

Several scholars have argued that the GMD state of Taiwan has been and continues to be a patriarchal state (Diamond, 1975; Gallin, 1984a, 1984b). This is best seen through the activities of its Women's Department and a semiofficial organization, the Chinese Women's Anti-Aggression League. Both of these institutions advocate patriarchal values and sponsor programs and projects that are mere extensions of women's familial roles. Women are encouraged to participate in

> voluntary sewing of clothing for military personnel, collection and donation of cash, clothes, and foodstuffs for needy military dependents, the operation of 35 milk-bars for needy children, the maintenance of schools and orphanages for war orphans and the children of civil servants and military personnel, assistance to retired servicemen, collections of clothing for Vietnamese refugees, and aid for KMT (GMD) soldiers returned from Burma and Vietnam, and relief services to needy women and overseas Chinese girl students in Taiwan. (Diamond, 1975, p. 15)

Women's subordination in Taiwan is not simply a continuity of traditional values and culture. It is a product of patriarchal capitalism in which the interests of the capitalist, the state, and the international market are served (Gallin, 1984b; Gates, 1979). As Gates (1979) puts it, "the KMT has fostered patterns that are more than conservative, for it has not simply maintained or returned to tradition. Instead, it has encouraged certain tendencies through new political means and a changing economy to a higher level than they could possibly have reached in the past."

Through the mass media and educational system, the state plays an active role in encouraging "an ideological environment that relegates women to menial labor and household tasks." The result is a patriarchal capitalist system whereby women's unpaid domestic and underpaid public labor are appropriated "without altering cultural definitions of male and female roles or transforming the structure of male status and authority within the family." (Gallin, 1984a, p. 398). A study of elementary and middle school textbooks used in Taiwan shows that scientists, positive political leaders, and scholars are invariably males; and those caring for households are all females. Furthermore, the personal qualities associated with male characters are ambition, courage, persistence, wisdom, adventurousness, and so forth, whereas those associated with female characters are filial obedience, courtesy, and warm-heartedness (*Funu Xinzhi,* 1988).

Fostering Women's Double Burden:
The Community Development Program

As pointed out earlier, the adoption of an export-oriented development strategy necessitates the availability of a flexible and cheap labor supply, and women have met that need extremely well. But women's employment is also feared as potentially threatening to men and to family stability. These two concerns are reflected in the state's Community Development Program that promotes the perpetuation of women's double burden. In 1968, the government designed a 10-year community development program that was later extended several times. The goal of this program is to "improve the people's material as well as spiritual lives" (Taiwan Shengzhengfu Shehuichu, 1987, p. 19). The program not only deals with problems in food, clothing, living, transportation, and leisure, but also proposes to enhance Chinese traditional moral values and social norms in the local community. Women are important in the Community Development Program both as a target group for special training and as essential implementers of the Program. Their participation has been crucial to the success of the Program.

Organizational Structure

There are Community Development Committees at the provincial, district/county, and town/village levels. The Governor, Mayor, Chief, and other officials serve as the chair of the Committee at each respective level to monitor and evaluate the Program. In addition, each community has a Community Council with 9 to 17 members, one of whom is designated as the Director. Members are theoretically elected by the heads of households in the community, and the Director is either elected by council members or handpicked by the district/county official. Until 1983, more than one fourth (26%) of the council members and another one-fourth (24.4%) of the Directors were designated by the state (Taiwan Shengzhengfu Yanjiu Kaohe Weiyuanhui, 1983, pp. 67-68).

The incorporation of the newly established Community Development Program into the preexisting bureaucratic system means that women have been excluded from the decision-making process at the governmental level. Furthermore, since council members are elected by the heads of households rather than by individual residents in the community, women have almost no chance of becoming members of the Council in their own community. The exclusion of women in decision making at the local level is all the more serious when the state increasingly penetrates into the life of the community.

The result of this organizational pattern is seen in a survey conducted in 1983 to evaluate the achievement of the Community Development Program. Of the total 1,810 Council members from 127 communities, less than seven percent (6.7%) were women (Taiwan Shengzhengfu Yanjiu Kaohe Weiyuanhui, 1983, p. 54). When residents who hold decision-making positions in community affairs were asked who they thought best suited to be the director of the Council Committee, less than one percent (0.9%) mentioned women in the neighborhood (Taiwan Shengzhengfu Yanjiu Kaohe Weiyuanhui, 1983, p. 131).

Program Contents

There are three substantive areas of the Community Development Program: basic engineering/construction projects, production and social welfare, and ethics and morale. Within each of these three major areas, programs or activities are designed and carried out in local communities. The *Keting gongchang* or "Living-Room Factory," and the *Mama jiaoshi* or "Mother's Workshop" programs are directly related to women. These two programs illustrate that the state ideology on women's role remains patriarchal in essence though its emphasis shifts as Taiwan's economy develops.

Living-Room Factories

The "living-room factory" program is also referred to as the family subsidiary employment program. It is designed to solve the labor shortage problem by mobilizing surplus labor in the community/family to engage in production. State officials reasoned that by introducing homework and similar forms of production into the local area, people's living standard will be improved while national productivity is increased, thus "community development and economic development will enhance each other." (Economic Construction Commission [EEC], 1978, p. 1).

After surveys conducted under state sponsorship found that there were many "idle women" in local communities, a proposal to establish "living-room factories" was developed (EEC, 1978, p. 2). The government provided special loans for families intending to purchase machines to do homework. Workshops were conducted to train housewives to apply themselves to productive work. Many "living-rooms" were converted into "factories," housewives became workers, and work became "housewifized."

One of the consequences, of course, has been that those families whose female members do homework in their living-rooms experienced an improvement in their living standards. However, a greater benefit can be claimed by others. Capitalists were relieved of a labor shortage because a new segment of the population was incorporated into the production line. This helped to ease the pressure for potential wage increase. Since many living-rooms were converted into "factories" and the workers worked at home, capitalists were able to avoid expenditures on factory facilities, energy, dormitories, and management. The incorporation of women into living-room factory work is capitalist patriarchal because those homeworkers were treated more as homemakers who were willing to work, rather than workers who worked at home. They were not provided with health insurance to which most factory workers were entitled. Nor were they protected by the minimum wage regulations, since they were paid on a piece-rate basis. The society as a whole was able to benefit from productivity increases, consumer price stabilization, and economic growth. The state boasts that the informal/subsidiary employment arrangement typical of living-room factories reduces potential conflict between capitalists and workers (EEC, 1978, p. 3).

The consequences of homework in industrial Europe and America are well-known (Daniels, 1989). What distinguishes the Taiwan case is the active promotion of homework by the state, and the institution of national programs such as the Mother's Workshops to ensure that women will not lose sight of their responsibilities as "good wives and fine mothers."

Mother's Workshops

Mama jiaoshi, or the Mother's Workshop Program, a companion of the "living-room factories," is a subarea within the project of ethics and morality enhancement. Many state officials have underlined the importance of the program in itself and for the success of the Community Development Program as a whole. In 1984 Zhao Shoubo, Director of the Department of Social Affairs of the Province, stated:

> Mama Jiaoshi is a sound idea and a wonderful institution. To educate a woman into a good mother is equal to educate the whole family well. If every family lives in comfort and happiness, the society will be peaceful and prosperous, united and harmonious. Ultimately, the whole country will be strong and well-off. Therefore, the Mother's Workshop Program has a great responsibility. (Zhao, 1984, p.27)

An editorial in the official journal *Shequ Fazhan* (Community Development) points out that, among the 77 programs and activities proposed by the government to achieve the goals of the Community Development Program, at least 39 cannot be accomplished without the Mother's Workshop Program.

> Programs on community beautification. environmental improvement, community safety, vocational and skills training, sanitation and health instruction, nutrition improvement, cultural and leisure activities, interior decoration,

neighborhood harmony, adult education and public service, and so forth, are within the scope of the Mama Jiaoshi. . . . Unless these are taught, learned, discussed, and absorbed by women through the Workshops, these programs forever remain only as slogans. (*Shequ Fazhan Jikan*, 28, 1984, p. 4).

The Mother's Workshop Program, according to its initiator, Governor Xie Dongmin who later became the Vice-President of the Republic of China (1989), is also designed to "alleviate societal uneasiness and disorder created by economic development . . . such as increases in divorce rate and adolescent crimes, negligence of the elderly, and widespread hedonism and prodigality." As a government document (Taiwan Shengzhengfu Gonggao, 8027, 1973) states,

Chinese society is built upon the family and sustained by traditional virtue. And, the mother is the center of a family. Only competent and virtuous mothers can raise stable families. The prosperity of the society and the strength and growth of the country all depend upon people's morality, which is contingent upon stable families. Therefore, we conclude that promoting virtuous and responsible motherhood is the most crucial issue today.

The state claims that the most important aim of the Mother's Workshop Program is to "propagate government orders, promote developmental and educational programs in the local community, and celebrate national festivals. Taking care of mother's interest and need is only secondary" (Zhao, 1984, p. 24). In other words, various courses held in the local community in the name of Mother's Workshop are simply means through which the main objectives set by the state can be accomplished.

Numerous Mother's Workshops were conducted in local communities. Beginning in 1977, the state has sponsored regular training courses for supervisors and instructors of local Mother's Workshops. The state has also published a 10-volume set called *Mother's Readers* to guide these workshops. Written in simple Chinese language and heavily illustrated, these volumes are no more than 30 pages each. Their subjects include family planning, child care, prenatal care, infant care, food and nutrition, housecleaning, family finance management, family life management, and clothing selection, construction, and care (Taiwan Shengzhengfu Shehuichu, 1977a). Additional materials, such as "Supplementary Readings for the Mother's Workshop," were published periodically (Sili, 1985). By 1989, a total of 8,130 supervisors had been trained by the government and more than 160,000 copies of the Readers have been distributed.

Table 9.10 Number of Mother's Workshops Sponsored by County/City, 1987

Number of Workshop Classes per Community per Year	Number of County/City
1+	1
3	1
6	4
8	1
12+	2
24	1
Non-specified	11
Total Communities	21

SOURCE: Taiwansheng (1987), pp. 20-40.

The influence of the Program can also be shown by the number of Workshops held. By 1984, a total of 4,063 communities had implemented the Community Development Program in Taiwan. About 90% of them held Mother's Workshops in their communities in 1984 alone. One third of the counties/cities in the province (7 out of a total of 21) have a community sponsor rate of 90%. Among them, three counties/cities have Mother's Workshop in every local community (Zhao, 1984, p. 26).

In 1987, local officials and representatives from 21 counties/cities responsible for the Mother's Workshop Program gathered at a conference called by the Department of Social Affairs. Every county/city gave a summary report on what has been accomplished. Ten reported statistics on how many classes of Mother's Workshop were organized in the local community of their counties/cities. The number of classes sponsored by each local community varied widely, and ranged from once a year to twice per month (see Table 9.10).

In urban areas most participants are middle-class housewives (Zhao, 1986), although women from various class backgrounds have attended the Program as well (Taiwansheng 74-75, 1987). Especially in rural areas, the Mother's Workshop Program has played important educational roles, such as distributing information on family planning, infant care, and nutrition.

Workshops are usually held at community centers over the weekend, and are centered around four areas, ethics and morality, sanitation and public health, homework and productive skills, and leisure activity and social services. The ultimate goals of ethics and morality education are to get women in the community to "practice proper etiquettes, respect womanhood virtues, pay attention to motherhood, and increase harmony in the family" (Zhao, 1984, p. 25). Women are taught, for example, how to prepare nutritious food for the family, what the proper make-up is when attending social gatherings with their husbands, and how to take care of the elderly with chronic diseases. Training on productive skills is connected with the "Living-Room Factory" program. Courses on leisure activity planning and social services encourage women to organize themselves "to visit the aged, orphans, the handicapped, the mentally retarded, and military and poor families [in the local community]" (Zhao, 1984, p. 26). A person in charge of the training courses for supervisors of the Mother's Workshops Program once said, "in a modern society, women have to play at least four different roles: they have to be pretty women, lovely wives, responsible mothers, and successful professionals" (M.-X. Xie, 1985). An example of the content and attendance of these workshops is provided in Table 9.11 for Tainan County between 1985 and 1986.

As Table 9.11 shows, more than one thousand classes were conducted with more than ten thousand participants in Tainan County in 1985 and 1986. The figures do not distinguish frequent participants from one-time attendants. However, the table does show that the most frequently sponsored courses are recreationally oriented. Women have also actively participated in courses on make-up, family relationships, homemaking, and public health.

State officials have lamented that some Mother's Workshop Programs have focused too much on recreation. Vice-President Xie claimed that "mothers in the community become indulged in such activities [folk dancing]. They neglect their husband and overlook their children. As a result, more problems have been created in the family" (J. Li, 1985, p. 59). Another government official points out that:

> The purposes of the Mother's Workshop is to bring forth sweet and happy family, thereby a stable and harmonious society eventually. Courses on parenting and occupation skills are means to achieve these goals. The Mother's Workshop is not limited to skill training, such as cooking, flower arranging, or folk dancing. Some local communities have focussed on such trivial activities and lost sight of the main objectives of the program. (Zhao, 1984, pp. 24-27)

Several points can be made regarding the "Living-room Factory" and the Mother's Workshop programs. First, the ways women were incorporated in the programs reinforced their submissive and dependent status in the family and society. Women's waged work was based on its subsidiary and supple-

Table 9.11 Activities and Attendancy of Mother's Workshops, Tainan County, 1985-1986

Courses & Activities	Total Classes		Attendance		Average Attendance per Class	
	1985	1986	1985	1986	1985	1986
Family relations (Mother & Son, Spouses, Mother-in-law & Daughter-in-law)	100	35	1,342	976	13.4	27.6
Public health (Sanitation, Family Planning, Emergency Care)	90	57	1,402	1,004	15.6	17.6
Homemaking (Cooking, Flower Arrangement, Interior Decoration)	308	170	2,735	1,725	8.9	10.1
New Knowledge (Crime Prevention, Make-up, Social Skills)	84	79	1,628	1,234	19.4	15.6
Productive Skills (Bamboo Handcrafts, Embroidery, Knitting, and Toys, Ornaments, and Pin Making)	66	61	851	612	12.9	10.0
Recreational Activities (Camping, B-B-Q, Folkdancing)	707	659	3,522	4,126	5.0	6.3
Social Services (Visit Elderly, Poor, and Community Services)	68	79	536	350	7.9	4.4
Total	1,423	1,150	12,016	10,018		

SOURCE: Taiwansheng (1987), pp. 32-33.

mentary character, even though their income was essential to the family. Women were not treated as workers but as housewives in need of some pocket money. Female workers at a living-room factory were told by local officials to lie about their wages to visitors to hide the fact that they were paid below the minimum (Personal communication). They were also subjected to all the hazards of chemical pollution, unstable income, and other problems faced by workers in the informal economy. Second, women's roles as mother and caretaker were reinforced by programs emphasizing their "moral obligation" to the family, and to other people in need. Women were asked to take up the "double burden" for the good of the whole society. Third, the Community Development Program was a top-down program. It is based on the male-dominated bureaucratic structure and ignores preexisting social networks in the community, which are often centered around women. The failure to take into account these local personal networks has excluded women's participation in the decision-making process, and by that exclusion has created many unnecessary difficulties for the success of the state-sponsored programs.

Conclusion

The demand for flexible labor in the contemporary world system means that women are especially courted. They are often said to prefer flexible work because of their own desire to care for their families. Stable families, harmonious neighborhoods, and orderly society can be achieved through the fulfillment of motherhood. Working for wages is encouraged by the state as long as it does not interfere with women's role as wives, mothers, and daughters-in-law. And the best way for society to induce women to do both is to provide opportunities for flexible work. It is not flexible work that we object to, but its evaluation. Flexible work is cheap, insecure, unprotected, and taken for granted. Here a socially produced condition is taken as natural, and perpetuated by the state, the society, and the family. The success of the export-oriented growth strategy of Taiwan is related to a system of male domination that provides incentives for firms and families that exploit women's labor. Beyond economic strategies, the state controls and disciplines female workers by perpetuating the "double burden" ideology through educational institutions and state-sponsored community programs such as the "Living-Room Factory."

References

Beneria, Lourdes. (Ed.). (1985). *Women and development: The sexual division of labor in rural societies*. Westport, CT: Praeger.

Bian, Yu-yuan. (1985). Funu laodong dui jingji fazhang zhi gongxian [The contribution of female labor to economic development—A case study of Taiwan]. In Population Studies Center (Ed.), *Funu zai Guojia Fazhan guochengzhong de Jiaose Yantaohui Lunwenji* [Proceedings of conference on the role of women in the national development process in Taiwan] (pp. 261-274). Taipei: National Taiwan University, Population Studies Center.

Charlton, Sue Ellen, Everett, Jana, & Staudt, Kathleen. (1989). *Women, the state and development*. Albany: SUNY.

Chiang, Lan-hung Nora, & Ku, Yenlin. (1985). *Past and current status of women in Taiwan*. Taipei: National Taiwan University, Population Studies Center.

Chou, Bi-ar. (1989). Industrialization and change in women's status: A reevaluation of some data from Taiwan. In Hsin-huang Michael Hsiao, Wei-yuan Cheng, & Hou-sheng Chan (Eds.), *Taiwan: A newly industrialized state* (pp. 423-461). Taipei: National Taiwan University, Department of Sociology.

Crane, George T. (1982). The Taiwanese ascent: System, state and movement in the world economy. In Edward Friedman (Ed.), *Ascent and decline in the world-system* (pp. 93-113). Beverly Hills: Sage.

Cumings, Bruce. (1987). The origins and development of the northeast Asian political economy: Industrial sectors, product cycles, and political consequences. In Frederic Deyo (Ed.), *The political economy of the new Asian industrialization* (pp. 44-83). Ithaca, NY: Cornell University Press.

Daniels, Cynthia R. (1989). Between home and factory: Homeworkers and the state. In Eileen Boris & Cynthia R. Daniels (Eds.), *Homework*. Urbana and Chicago: University of Illinois Press.

Deng, Wenyi. (1975). Sanshinianlai de Taiwan Guanguang Luyu Shiye [Tourist industries in the last thirty years in Taiwan]. In Taiwan Shengzhengfu Xinwenchu (Ed.), *Taiwan Guangfu Sanshinian* [Thirty years after Taiwan's recovery from Japanese occupation] (pp. 337-409). Taizhong: Author.

Deyo, Frederic C. (Ed.). (1987). *The political economy of the new Asian industrialization*. Ithaca, NY: Cornell University Press.

Deyo, Frederic C. (1989). *Beneath the miracle: Labor subordination in the new Asian industrialism*. Berkeley: University of California Press.

Diamond, Norma. (1973, September). The middle class family model in Taiwan: Woman's place is in the home. *Asian Survey, 13*, pp. 853-872.

Diamond, Norma. (1975). Women under Kuomintang rule: Variations of the feminine mystique. *Modern China, 1*(1), pp. 3-45.

Diamond, Norma. (1979). Women and industry in Taiwan. *Modern China, 5*(3), pp. 317-340.

Directorate-General of Budget, Accounting and Statistics, Republic of China. [Various years]. *Zhonghuaminguo Tongji Nianjian* [Statistical yearbook of the Republic of China]. Taipei: Author.

Directorate-General of Budget, Accounting and Statistics, Republic of China. (1974). *Zhonghuaminguo Tongji Tiyao* [Statistical abstract of the Republic of China]. Taipei: Author.

Directorate-General of Budget, Accounting and Statistics, Republic of China, and Council for Economic Planning and Development, Republic of China. (1989). *Taiwan Diqu Renli Yunyung Diaocha Baogao* [Report on the manpower utilization survey in Taiwan area]. Taipei: Author.

Directory of Taiwan. (1963). Taipei: The China News.

Economic Construction Commission. (1978). *Ruhe yi Shequ Fazhan Fangshi Tuixing Jiating Fuye zhi Yanjiu* [How to promote family subsidiary work through community development]. Taipei: Author.

Evans, Peter, & Pang, Chien-kuo. (1989). State structure and state policy: Implications of the Taiwanese case for newly industrializing countries. In Hsin-huang Michael Hsiao, Wei-yuan Cheng, & Hou-sheng Chan (Eds.), *Taiwan: A newly industrialized state* (pp. 3-30). Taipei: National Taiwan University, Department of Sociology.

Funu Xinzhi [Awakening]. (1982-1989). [Various Issues.] Taipei.

Funu Xinzhi. (Ed.). (1988). *Liangxing Pingdeng Jiaoyu Shouce* [Handbook on gender equal education]. Taipei.

Gallin, Rita S. (1984a). The entry of Chinese women into the rural labor force: A case study from Taiwan. *Signs, 9*(3), pp. 383-398.

Gallin, Rita S. (1984b). Women, family and the political economy of Taiwan. *Journal of Peasant Studies, 12*(1), pp. 76-92.

Gallin, Rita S. (1990). Women and the export industry in Taiwan: The muting of class consciousness. In Kathryn Ward (Ed.), *Women workers and global restructuring* (pp. 179-192). Ithaca, NY: Cornell University Press.

Gates, Hill. (1979). Dependency and the part-time proletariat in Taiwan. *Modern China, 5*(3), pp. 381-407.

Greenhalgh, Susan. (1985, June). Sexual stratification: The other side of "Growth with Equity" in East Asia. *Population and Development Review, 11,* pp. 265-314.

Hsiao, Hsin-huang Michael, Cheng, Wei-yuan, & Chan, Hou-sheng. (Eds.). (1989). *Taiwan: A newly industrialized state.* Taipei: National Taiwan University, Department of Sociology.

Huang, Chunming. (1981). *Shayunala Zaijian* [Sayonara goodbye]. Taipei: Yuanjing.

Jones, Gavin. (Ed.) (1984). *Women in the urban and industrial workforce, Southeast and East Asia.* Canberra: Australian National University.

Kaluzynska, Eva. (1980). Wiping the floor with theory: A survey of writings on housework. *Feminist Review, 6,* 27-54.

Kim, Elaine. (1987). Sex tourism in Asia: A reflection of political and economic inequality. In Eui-young Yu & Earl H. Phillips (Eds.), *Korean women in transition* (pp. 127-144). Los Angeles: California State University, Center for Korean-American and Korean Studies.

Koo, Hagen. (1987). The interplay of state, social class, and world system in East Asian development: The cases of South Korea and Taiwan. In Frederic Deyo (Ed.), *The political economy of the new Asian industrialization* (pp. 165-181). Ithaca, NY: Cornell University Press.

Kung, Lydia. (1983). *Factory women in Taiwan.* Ann Arbor: University of Michigan Press.

Li, Jianxing. (1985, December). Shequ Mamajiaoshi yu Shequ Jiaoyu [Community Mother's Workshops and community education]. *Shequ Fazhan Jikan, 29,* pp. 58-59.

Li, Yuanzhen. (1987, February). Chuji Wenti, Bubu Jiannan [Difficulties in facing the problems of young prostitutes]. *Funu Xinzhi, 57,* 1.

Liu, Paul K.-C. (1984). Trends in female labour force participation in Taiwan: The transition toward higher technology activities. In Gavin Jones (Ed.), *Women in the urban and industrial workforce, Southeast and East Asia* (pp. 75-99). Canberra: Australian National University.

Liu, Paul Ke-chih, & Hwang, Kuo-shu. (1987). *Relationships between changes in population, employment and economic structure in Taiwan.* Taipei: Academia Sinica.

Liu, Yu-lan. (1985). *Taiwan diqu funu renli yunyung huigu yu zhanwang* [Utilization of women's labor in Taiwan: Past and future]. Taipei: Meizhi Tushu Gongsi.

Lu, Xiulian. (1986). *Qing* [Affection]. Taipei: Dunli.

Lu, Yu-hsia. (1984). Women, work and the family in a developing society: Taiwan. In Gavin Jones (Ed.), *Women in the urban and industrial workforce, Southeast and East Asia* (pp. 339-367). Canberra: Australian National University.

Mies, Maria. (1986). *Patriarchy, accumulation on a world scale.* London: Zed Books.

Miller, Joanne, & Garrison, Howard H. (1982). Sex roles: The division of labor at home and in the workplace. *Annual Review of Sociology, 8,* pp. 237-262.

Population Studies Center. (1965). *Funu zai Guojia Fazhan guochengzhong de Jiaose Yantaohui Lunwenji* [Proceedings of conference on the role of women in the national development process in Taiwan]. Taipei: National Taiwan University, Population Studies Center.

Qian [Money]. (1990). 5, pp. 156-186. Taipei.

Qu, Haiyuan. (1984). Seqing yu Changji Wanti [Sex and the prostitution problem]. In Guoshu Yang & Qizheng Ye (Eds.), *Taiwan Shehui Wenti* [Social problems in Taiwan] (pp. 543-571). Taipei: Juliu.

Shequ Fazhan Jikan [Community Development Quarterly]. [Various issues.] Taipei: Zhonghuaminguo Shequ Fazhan Yanjiu Sunlian Zhongxin.

Sili Shijian Jiazheng Jingji Zhuanke Xuexiao. (1985). *Mama Jiaoshi Buchong Jiaocai* [Supplementary instructional materials for Mother's Workshops]. Taizhong: Taiwan Shengzhengfu.

Taiwan Shengzhengfu. (1973). *Gonggao* [Public document] No. 8027. Taizhong.

Taiwan Shengzhengfu Shehuichu. (1977a). *Mama Duben* [Mother's readers]. 10 vols. Taizhong: Author.

Taiwan Shengzhengfu Shehuichu. (1987). *Taiwansheng Shequ Fazhan Houxu Dierqi Wunian Jihua Gongzuo Shouce* [Handbook of the second five-year community development program of the provincial government]. Taipei: Author.

Taiwan Shengzhengfu Xinwenchu. (1965). *Taiwan Guangfu Ershinian* [Twenty years after Taiwan's recovery]. Taipei: Author.

Taiwan Shengzhenqfu Yanjiu Kaohe Weiywanhue. (1983). *Taiwansheng Shinianlai Shequ Fazhan Chengxiao zhi Pingjian ji Weilai Fazhan zhi Yanjiu* [Evaluation of the Ten-year Community Development Program in Taiwan and Its Future Direction]. Taipai: Taiwan Shengzhengfu Yanjiu Fazhan Kaohe Weiyuanhui.

Taiwansheng 74-75 Niandu Shequ Mamajiaoshi Fudao Renyuan Zuotanhui Zonghe Jishi [Proceedings of the 1985-86 community Mother's Workshop supervisors seminar]. (1987). Taipei: Author.

Truong, Thanh-Dam. (1990). *Sex, money and morality: Prostitution and tourism in southeast Asia.* London: Zed Books.

Tsay, Ching-lung. (1985). Xingbie chayi [Sex differentials in educational attainment and labor force development in Taiwan]. In Population Studies Center (Ed.), *Funu zai Guojia Fazhan guochengzhong de Jiaose Yantaohui Lunwenji* [Proceedings of Conference on the Role of Women in the National Development Process in Taiwan] (pp. 277-308). Taipei: National Taiwan University, Population Studies Center.

Waring, Marilyn. (1988). *If women counted: A new feminist economics.* San Francisco: Harper & Row.

Winckler, Edwin A., & Greenhalgh, Susan. (Eds.). (1988). *Contending approaches to the political economy of Taiwan.* Armonk, NY: M. E. Sharpe.

Xie, Meng-xiong. (1985, December). Shequ Mamjiaoshi yu Jiazheng jiaoyu [The community Mother's Workshop and homemaking education]. *Shequ Fazhan Jikan, 29,* pp. 60-61.

Yu, Zongxian. (1981). Duiwai Maoyi [Foreign trade]. In Chia-lin Cheng (Ed.), *Woguo Jingji de Fazhan* [Economic development of our country] (pp. 301-384). Taipei: Shijie Shuju.

Zhan, Chunjian. (1966). Dangqian Fazhan Guanguang Shiye de Tujing [Directions of tourism development]. In Huiyan Zhou (Ed.), *Guanguang Shiye Lunji* [Essays on tourism], vol. 1. pp. 4-16. Taipei: Zhongguo Wenhua Xueyuan.

Zhao, Shoubo. (1984, December). The current status and future prospective of Mother's Workshops in Taiwan. *Shequ Fazhan Jikan, 28,* pp. 24-27.

Zhao, Shoubo. (1986). Qianghua Mamajiaoshi de Gongneng [Strenthening the function of Mother's Workshops]. In *Taiwansheng Mamajiaoshi Fudao Renyuan Yanxihui Shouce* [Handbook for supervisors of the Mother's Workshops, 1986] (pp. 1-2). Taipei: Author.

Zheng Zhihui & Bo Qingrong. (1987, March). Zhengshi Zhiye Funu soshou de Jiuye Qishi [Looking seriously at the discrimination faced by working women]. *Funu Xinzhi 58,* pp. 1-9.

Zhou, Huiyan (Ed.). (1966). *Guanguang Shiye Lunji* [Essays on tourism] vol. 1. Taipei: Zhongguo Wenhua Xueyuan.

10

Women, the Family, and the State
in Hong Kong, Taiwan, and Singapore

JANET W. SALAFF

Hong Kong, Singapore, and Taiwan have since the early 1970s entered the ranks of the newly industrialized countries (NICs) based on manufacturing for export, in which women play key roles. Their great transformations occurred when few scholars expected them to prosper, and many other Third World nations, in contrast, had suffered from a decline in their living standards (Bello & Rosenfeld, 1990; *World Bank Report*, various years). Instead of declining, the "three dragons" bargain sharply for investors and markets. How they accumulate and invest capital and supply labor fascinates many scholars. A number of studies compare the state infrastructures that encourage investment in export-oriented industries in these places (Deyo, 1987; Henderson, 1989; Huang, 1989). Fewer have looked at how the state powers its labor supply, my concern here (Ong, 1987; Ward, 1990; D. Wolf, 1989). The present chapter describes how the Pacific Rim NICs proletarianized its populace by requiring families to earn money in industries and fitting the labor force into these industries. I discuss how the state buttresses the household authority over its members, and why anybody's daughter will do.

This chapter analyzes the strong Chinese family, conduit for state policies that deal with the economy and the sexual domain. Particular social-historical forces compel families to use the new economic institutions to chart their course. To start with, these include demographic pressures and the newly created commodity economy. Within the framework of the new economic options, the family turns to a familiar means, control over its labor power, to accomplish its goals of survival and progress. In fact, the Chinese family has more than one goal. We will see how the family presses women to work at three stages of their life cycles to meet a number of family goals. For instance, these family demands on the individual reach their fruition in myriad small family industries (Hamilton & Biggart, 1988). I introduce the concept of *substitutability,* to help us understand how women's earnings can replace those of men in each of these three life cycle stages. Although Singapore contains more than one ethnic group, here I focus solely on the Chinese to describe more precisely how family members enter the labor force.[1] The data are drawn from the early 1970s through the early 1980s. This period takes us from the early labor-intensive industry through to changes in the industrial mix for a more skilled labor force. This decade-long time span shows the ways the proletariat was reproduced at a crucial time in the evolution of the new industrial countries on the Pacific Rim.

Family Strategies
Encouraging Women to Work

As the states set new economic directions, forcing people into the money economy and providing opportunities to work, families in the three countries respond to the need to earn cash and the means to do so. Unable to live off the land, or grow or make goods themselves, people must earn money to survive. They must buy food, clothing, furnishings, education, and housing. Few any longer live in squatter or rural *kampung* villages, pick durian, ramutan, or star fruit, raise chickens, or sprout beans. They must work and now they have the opportunity to work. Young family members are not just attracted by wage work opportunities, but are forced by necessity to work. In this way government actions have created a stock of labor power.

But more than exterior conditions draw women to work. Families exploit the environment to get cash, in accord with the ecology and within the bounds of social structure. The location and timing of the new work opportunities differed from early work opportunities. Industrial work is located within daily traveling distance from the home, but outside it, and demands continuous work for a long period every day of the week, in all seasons. An industrial worker can no longer work around the home at piecework, peddling, domestic labor, or child care. And so to send members out of the home for wage work in industry means they must be expendable to the household or they must find others to do the work they formerly did at home.

In the places under study, the majority of these workers were women. But different cohorts of women were drawn into factory work at different stages of the industrializing process. This has to do with both the demand for workers and their supply. How this is so will be seen in the following cases of workers from Hong Kong, Taiwan, and Singapore. I first look at unmarried Hong Kong and Taiwan factory women at the height of the export-oriented industrial strategies in the mid-1970s. I compare them to young Singapore Chinese married women from working- and middle-class backgrounds around 1980. I then discuss older Taiwanese working women working in the mid-1980s.[2]

Types of Family

In supplying labor to the industrial work force, the Chinese family chooses those it can free from home tasks. Who these members are varies by family life cycle. This is because the Chinese family is not a single unitary type. It is a set of constructs that press upon its members with different meanings. These meanings and the members' responsibilities and obligations under each of the three family regimes vary by their life-cycle stage and gender. And so the workers that the family supplies also vary by the life-cycle stage of the family. We distinguish three conceptual units. The stage of the family's life cycle determines which of these three family units is stressed.

The first of these units, the *patriliny,* is the family core, composed of men linked by descent and with equal rights to inherited property (A. Wolf & Huang, 1972). It is this family that comes into mind when we envision the large extended family of Chinese literature, with three or four generations under one roof, under the authority of the older patriarch. This family type is dominant in the three areas discussed here, even though few households actually contain several generations. It is not necessary for several generations to live under one roof for the patrilineal concept to hold weight. Few families in the two city-states inherited land, and Taiwanese landholdings are small. Immigrant families in Hong Kong, and to some extent Singapore, grew up without a full set of paternal kin. In Taiwan, refugees from China and urban migrants from the village might also leave their kin behind. High wartime mortality also meant a low probability of survival of grandparents and parents in the region. But even though an ideal form of patrilocal household cannot come into existence, the patriliny still remains a guideline for behavior. This demands that families bear sons for economic and religious reasons. In such a patrilineal family, ties of women to their kin cause potential loyalty conflicts, which the patriliny attempts to dilute. Daughters are expected to sever their ties with their parents on marriage, and more fully turn their loyalty and energy to their husband's line.

The second conceptual family unit, the domestic or economic family (*jia*), focuses on present-day economic survival, rather than line of inheritance. All members of the economic family contribute to the common budget and draw their expenses from this common purse. Since all workers support the family, this permits substitutability: The earnings of any worker can help the household. The family's drawing upon the labor of the children and women stems from the economic family concept. Even after marriage, ties to women's kin are tolerated and even may be encouraged if they contribute to the economic well-being of the household. For instance, a woman's mother can help watch her children so that she can work, although according to the patrilineal concept, married women should not turn to their natal family for help (Judd, 1989).

The third family unit is formed by the bonds of sentiment between women and their children. Since the mother lacks the same rights as her husband in the line, she compensates by building bonds of support with her children. Emotional exchanges underlie these bonds of support. Where the father is emotionally distant from his offspring, as is common in Chinese families, the mother can more easily build up these alliances. Margery Wolf calls the female-centered family the "uterine family." The willingness of daughters to contribute to the economic family, despite their exclusion from the patriliny, family inheritance, and family future, is ensured by the sentimental bonds of support built in this family unit (M. Wolf, 1972).

Demographic Pressures and the Family Life Cycle

The choice of which member the family would send into the labor force was also shaped by the demographic processes. Most crucial of these were the demographic outcomes of the previous years of high birthrates, universal marriages, and low death rates. The high post-World War II birthrates in the three areas, and good chances for survival, created sizable families. Hong Kong women aged 40 to 44 in 1971 averaged 4.3 live births.[3] Youths who were born from 1948 to 1960, and were in their teens through twenties in the

Table 10.1 Ratio of Wage Earners to Family Dependents, 1960 to 1974

Respondents	1960	1965	1970	1973	1974
Working Class					
A-li	1:8	3:7	3:7	4:6	4:6
I-ling	1:4	2:4	3:3	3:3	3:3
Mae-fun	1:7	3:5	4:3	4:3	3:3
Wai-gun	2:7	3:6	3:6	4:5	5:4
Upper Working Class					
Ming	1:6	1:7	3:5	3:5	3:5
Middle Class					
Ju-chen	1:9	2:7	3:7	4:6	3:6

mid-1970s, had many brothers and sisters. Comparable large families are found among Singapore and Taiwanese mothers of the same age cohort. These large families gave rise to problems in societies without social assistance. Demographic pressures combined with the impossibility of surviving outside the wage economy created a situation that was not experienced in the same form during earlier historical periods, when higher mortality limited surviving births.

Let us look at the dependency ratio—the burden on wage earners as measured by the ratio of wage earners to dependents. In the families of my Hong Kong study, there was usually only the father as the single earner. The earnings of one working-class man were not enough for s sizable family. Worse, often the father's contribution diminished—he became ill, died, took a second wive, or deserted the family. This problem, a result of World War II wartime turmoil, was found in all three societies. For example, two fifths of the fathers in the 100 Singapore couples I studied had passed away before their children had grown up. Their early demise left the household of many children without a breadwinner. But even households with an adult male wage earner faced hard times because of high dependency ratios and low working-class wages. In the families I studied in Hong Kong, the dependency ratios ranged from 1:4 to 1:9 when respondents were youngsters, ca. 1960 (Table 10.1). These demographic pressures led in additional workers, to add to or substitute for the earnings of the father/household head. The first to enter the wage force were unmarried daughters.

Working Daughters. The high dependency ratio made the need to earn money overwhelming. But the mothers in the families could not earn much. Hong Kong and Singapore mothers were burdened with many small children, labor-intensive household chores, and insufficient help at home, and they lacked education or industrial labor force experience. In Taiwan they had farm tasks to perform. So mothers rarely worked for a wage outside the home. The demographic situation that intensified the problem also suggested the means to resolve it—sending children out to work. As youngsters, girls and boys already helped run the household. This was partly because of sheer household size. Sheer size in an organization entails rules of interaction, structuring authority, obedience, and emotional intimacy (W. J. Goode, 1982). The more functions filled, the more call there is for a strict definition of roles by age, sex, generation, and lineage (Winch, 1963). The family at the stage we are studying here is sizable enough to require a number of rules, which are generally accepted.

In addition to sheer family size, the labor-intensive household economy draws young daughters into the household division of labor, and sets the stage for their later employment. First was early training of children to participate in family tasks. By age 5 most girls learned many necessary tasks, and by age 12 all hauled water, cooked, washed clothes. As they neared adolescence, the older girls did putting-out work (piecing together plastic flowers, transistors, pressing metal eyelets, beading). They did this as part of a family-wide project, carried out in the home, and they received no individual wage or recognition. This was most common in Hong Kong, the earliest entrant to the new world economic order. In Taiwan, young girls often had housekeeping tasks that were associated with agriculture. They fed pigs, nipped the ends off bean sprouts. Singapore girls similarly performed subsistence work, helped in a family hawker enterprise, or did domestic work in other households.

Sex roles marked different expectations. When the young women born in the post-World War II years were growing up, there was rarely enough money to send both sons and daughters to school. Based on the patrilineal construct, looking toward the future they would share with their sons, parents saw daughters as "goods upon which one loses." Daughters would leave the domestic family upon marriage, while boys were the future of the family. Thus, in the 1950s and 1960s, girls received less schooling than boys. Certain that they would work for only a few years until their marriage, with enough education to give them literacy but not enough for them to enter skilled jobs with a future, young women were a prime labor force for low-waged, export-oriented industries. Their brothers, however, were to be contributors to the domestic economy throughout their lives, albeit unevenly due to their own domestic economic burdens. If there was a sum of money available for only one or two of the children to study, the boys were chosen. It was hoped that they could repay the family at a higher rate of return. Thus young daughters became the natural substitutes for their brothers in the labor force.

With this bridge of hard work—performing household tasks and working in family putting-out projects—working-class Hong Kong daughters who matured in the early to late 1960s entered the paid labor force between ages 12 and 14. They were child labor in the accepted definition of the International Labour Organization. Apart from working at home on the farm, some Taiwan daughters who matured at this time worked as bar girls until a few years later when factory work became available. Singapore girls started to work later still when factories began to reach out for them. Middle-class families in all countries were more likely to delay the entry of their daughters to the work force until they completed some or all of high school. They went to work at around age 16.

The young woman who went to work after primary school entered the new low-waged manufacturing work just then opening up in the 1960s. She gave most or all of her income to the household. Thereupon, family living standards markedly improved, as seen through the family dependency ratio. Take as an example Wai-gun's family of nine—seven children and two working parents. The proportion of dependents in the household dropped from 78% to 67% with just one daughter's entry into the labor force alone (Table 10.1). A turning point came in the fortunes of this family when the older working daughter reached aged 23, and the next younger sibling joined her at work: two parents and two daughters supported the household that included five school-age children (for a dependency ratio of 4:5). Eventually, the dependency ratio even reversed, with more workers than nonworkers in the household. And this was a common occurrence.

Parents long looked forward to the transition from a consuming to an earning household. They tried to stretch out the period, within limits. The lengthening of the daughters' years of contribution to the domestic economy was accomplished not only by their early entry to the labor force. Parents might also postpone their daughters' exit through marriage. Hong Kong parents sought a full decade of daughters' income contribution, the number of years largely determined by the desire to ensure younger siblings' schooling at a higher level. If the daughter was herself a younger sibling, the length of time she needed to contribute her wages to the household economy was reduced. Even so, Hong Kong daughters, younger and older, sought to repay their parents for the costs of their upbringing. Kung's study of Taiwanese factory women similarly notes the daughters' desire to repay their parents for the their upbringing (Kung, 1983). Thus for the daughters, early work substitutes for early marriage.

Social class differences came into play. Middle-class daughters with the longest period of education entered the labor force at an older age. They then were expected to contribute to the family budget for a number of years, and as a result delayed marriage longer than working-class women. It was not only parents who sought to delay their offspring's marriages, of course. Filial daughters themselves postponed marriage until their family dependency ratio improved, and the household could do without their input. The 1980 census of Taiwan shows that marriage age is directly associated with educational level in Taiwan (*Extract Report,* 1982, p. 62). Among the reasons for this delay is undoubtedly the period of posteducational employment, much of which aids their natal families.

We introduced the concept of substitutability. The young woman worker abandons her household roles, in her parents' or husband's household, and she also gives up her education for paid wage labor. She works at slightly different factory jobs than her brothers or father, but it is wage work nonetheless. She is in fact substituting for the work of men.

Families reward daughters very little for their employment and their input to the household. But the young women do get something out of their input, which keeps them in the exchange. Part of what they get is material. They earn money they can use themselves when their household income takes a turn for the better. Sometimes they also obtain a greater decision-making role in the family. Part of what they get is moral. Knowing that their families truly need their material input, they feel satisfied they are meeting their filial obligations as daughters. Thus we can look at the exchange through the three types of family forms. The patriline requires women to support the family of the male line (first their parents, later their husbands after marriage). The economic family demands material input to the household economy. And the uterine family ties give emotional satisfaction to women that help out at home. Thus the exchange is neither entirely material nor moral. Nor is it of short-term duration.

Although their wages were low, the Hong Kong and Taiwanese working daughters interviewed lived at home, and they at first earned so little that they only paid for bus fare and basic expenses of their own. As they gained work experience, they contributed more to the family coffers. In low-income households, purchases varied by the dependency ratio, a product of the life cycle. When, as young unmarried daughters, women first entered the labor

Table 10.2 Occupational Profiles, Family Members and Income

Occupation of Several Respondent's Family Members	Household Income per Month[a]		Percentage Contribution of All Daughters to Household Income, 1973
	1963	1973	
Mae-fun			
Father ————	$85	$120	
Mother —			
Sister ———	25	80	
Mae-fun ———	25	80	42%
Brother ————		100	
(seven members in family)	$135	$380	
Wai-gun			
Father ———	$50	$80[b]	
Mother ——	30	60	
Wai-gun ———	20	80	52%
Sister ———		70	
(nine members in family)	$100	$290	
Suyin			
Father ———	$15[b]	$20[b]	
Mother ——	30	60	
Suyin ———	30	120	73%
Sister ———	30	100	
(eight membrs in family)	$105	$300	
Chin-yiu			
Father ———	$—[b]	$200	
Mother —			
Chin-yiu ————	30	160	66%
Sister ————	30	170	
Sister ———		70	
(seven members in family)	$60	$600	
I-ling			
Father ———	$—[b]	$200	
Mother ——	30	60	
I-ling ———	30	100	28%
(six members in family)	$60	$360	

NOTES: a. All dollars are given in U.S. dollars at the rate of $5 HK = $1 U.S.
b. Father contributing little due to unemployment, layoffs, illness, or residence elsewhere.

Never worked = —
Unskilled = ——
Semiskilled = ———
Skilled = ———
Low-paid clerk = —————
Well-paid clerk = —————

force within the context of a high dependency ratio, their wages helped their families buy necessities—rent, and food for the entire family. Medical care was an optional, but costly item, and families improved their care when extra money became available. Working women's income enabled extended education for younger siblings past the years provided by their governments. Gradually, their input moved the household living standard from a bare survival level to even modest prosperity (Table 10.2). As the dependency ratio improves, daughters in working-class families help raise the family living standard through the better education of their younger brothers. But since everyone in the society chases more education, there is a spiraling of credentials, and youngsters must remain in school longer just to keep in the same place. Nevertheless, the ability to help with younger brothers' education is most feasible when daughters have been working for a decade. By this time, too, telephones, televisions, small semiautomatic washing machines, and other consumer goods add to the household comfort of the working class, made possible through the combined earnings of the employed children.

Middle-class working daughters also add their earnings to their natal families. Many help their parents launch a small business, such as hawking, or a small subcontracting firm. The high savings propensity of the Chinese in Hong Kong, Singapore, and Taiwan, and their willingness to risk investment in the local economy has been documented (Topley, 1969). Earnings of the children that add to the family budget boost the export-oriented manufacture economy. The extent to which children aid their parents in building a small fund of capital for investment is worthy of future study.

The material consequences of women's work were crucial, much more so than a widening of their proper sphere. Although working daughters obtained a meaningful outcome from their employment, their employment cannot entirely be seen as a transaction between their families and themselves as equal parties, in which they have power to work or not to work. Unmarried Hong Kong, Taiwan, and Singapore women have less power in their households than their parents. Nevertheless, working daughters widened their sphere of decision making as it affected their own lives. So long as they could put in a good-sized portion of their wages to their family budget, Hong Kong and Taiwanese daughters kept some for their own spending money. They could thereby join peer activities, dress better, and use their free time in ways they themselves decided. By entering the spreading consumer economy, they became enmeshed in the new capitalist system. But working daughters could not greatly expand their input into decision-making processes in their families in either setting, and their wages did not confer upon them power to realign their dependence on the family itself.

Opting out (becoming a "swinging single") was limited by the expectation that women remain at home until marriage, despite earning money. This expectation was based on the slim wages they received as "dependents." It was reinforced by slurs cast on women who leave home ("loose women"). In addition, the Hong Kong and Singapore states dominate the housing market, and allot public housing only to families in need. It is thus hard for most women earners to live alone or with other women. They cannot leave home. In Taiwan, working daughters from rural areas lived in the main in tightly supervised factory dormitories, and those who moved into private flats found it was too expensive to meet their obligations to their families. Those who could live at home and commute to work did so, to save money. Although work did not confer a period of accepted physical independence from the family, women who lived apart from their families had the greatest chance to choose recreational activities and friends of their own. Hong Kong and Taiwan daughters enjoyed this period of making friends, participating in the newly expanding consumer culture, and going on group dates. These opportunities were more accessible when the working daughters lived in factory dormitories, and less accessible when they lived at home (Kung, 1983).

Daughters' wage labor for the family meets expected behavior associated with that family life stage. Their subordination to the family construct is often harmonious. Remaining at home and aiding the household in fact occurs only for a certain limited period. Sometimes, however, these different concepts come into conflict. While people will attempt to minimize the conflict of expected behaviors, at times conflict cannot be avoided, and the result may be particularly painful. Conflict is often structural as well, as when the three sets of family concepts clash (W. H. Goode, 1960).

An example is the case of a young Hong Kong working daughter, Wai-gun, depicted in Tables 10.1 and 10.2 above. She had worked since she was 11, and had contributed her wage to the family budget since she was 12 years old, first as an electronics assembler, then as a higher-paid garment seamstress. In 1971, when I first met her, she was employed at Fairchild Semiconductor factory. She was one of three contributors, including her parents and herself, in a family of nine members. As eldest daughter, she was the only child that worked for wages. By 1974, however, two younger siblings entered the labor force; there were five wage-earners and four dependents. Wai-gun's place in the domestic economy was now less essential. She was allowed to use more of her money for recreation and hobbies. She was also preparing to marry. Her intended was an eldest son, whose father was a businessman in the Philippines, and who lived with his mother in Hong Kong. The couple planned to marry in the near future, and saved money for the event. Then, unfortunately, Wai-gun's father became critically ill and passed away, while her mother, whose health was never strong, also began to deteriorate. Soon she was unable to earn money, and in 1976 the family dependency ratio unexpectedly took a turn for the worse. The eldest son left school to go to work, while the second daughter left work to nurse her mother. Three children (Wai-gun, her third younger sister, and first younger brother) supported four younger children and their ill mother (dependency ratio of 3:5). Now Wai-gun could not withdraw her earnings from the household, and thus could not marry. At this time, her fiancé was under pressure by his father to further the family line. He was expected to marry and bear a son in the patrilineal tradition. Thus the two potential partners were enmeshed in different family constructs—Wai-gun in the domestic economy, her fiancé in the patrilineal construct. Their relationship broke up under conflicting family demands. He returned to Fujian province in China and found a village bride in an arranged marriage. She turned her energies again to the household needs of her family. In this case, the progress of the family cycle was sent off course by the unexpected turn of events. The energies of the daughters, ready to be freed, were again reined in and turned to their natal household.

In sum, the young girl who matures into adolescence and then early adulthood in the early industrialization era finds her work life determined by demographic pressures. The three types of family units form the bounds within which demography is defined. The long-term stress on males, the domestic economy that supports the household, and the bonds of affection between mother and daughter propel her to add to the household economy.

Working Mothers. Household structure and composition also shape postmarriage patterns of work for women. The patrilineal construct prevails. Patrilocal residence is common for young couples. Most Hong Kong youth studied planned to move in with one set of parents after marriage, preferably the husband's. In Singapore, patrilocal residence was also common. Three fifths of the young couples I studied in 1975 had once lived with kin, most with the husband's family. By the time one or two children were born, just under half of the Singapore families studied still lived with kin, and two fifths still lived with the husband's parents. In Taiwan, too, recent retrospective survey data find a sizable proportion had lived with their parents after marriage, again most with the husband's parents.

The eldest son marries first by custom, and brings his wife into the household of his parents. If she is still in the labor force, this creates an extremely favorable dependency ratio. But it cannot last. The couple usually has children soon after marriage. From a low dependency ratio in the parental household, once again there is an unfavorable dependency ratio. When the next son plans to marry, it is hard to put all couples under one roof in a high-rise flat. The first son and his wife and children typically move out, and the newlyweds take their place, improving the dependency ratio once again.

Some married women work and some do not, but there is a relation between the two. Married women with young children are not automatically able to continue working. They must negotiate their work status with the wider kin group. They have to find substitutes for their household and mothering roles in other women. Their negotiation reflects the bargaining power of women in the labor force. Those with the better women's jobs are usually best able to bargain to stay.

In the patrilocal household of newly married Singapore women in my study, there are several working-age women, the bride, the bride's mother-in-law, and her sisters-in-law. Which ones go out to work depends on their earning power. Given the low wages of most at the time, it was hardest for the working-class bride with only a modest education to remain in the labor force, since she could not earn much in the kinds of women's jobs that were available. Expected to turn her energies to her new household, she will be requested to quit her job and do the housework. She might, thereby, free her unmarried sisters-in-law for work. But married women with above-average education who work in the slightly better paying women's jobs, like electronics assembly, might continue to work so long as other women are willing to undertake the housework in their stead. Actually, few Singapore women in my study at the turn of the 1980s earned a wage that justified their leaving their homemaking burdens to others. After all, women are designated to take over men's homemaking burdens. They work for a wage lower than would be charged if men paid full market value for the services needed to support them (M. E. Barrett & McIntosh, 1982). Thus women's wages are set by the presumption that they depend on their families for support, and do not themselves support others. Women's wages are further depressed by the large number of women who compete for a narrow range of "women's" jobs.

My study, which tracked through 1981 women recruited to work before 1975, found that as soon as they have children, women find it difficult to work in the prevailing low-paid women's jobs. They simply do not earn enough to justify giving their homemaking burdens and obligations to others. This leads to the typical *n*-shaped female labor force pattern of the region of the time, with high rates of labor force participation, peaking in their twenties, but dropping after that. Only 18% of Singapore women with two children were still in the labor force in 1973; similarly 23% of currently married Taiwan women were economically active in 1980 (*Extract Report,* 1982, p. 120).

This, however, has been changing: as the educational levels for women rise, they lengthen their work experience; the wage rates for electronics assemblists are also rising, and so is the families' need for cash (Lin, 1989, p. 118). In Hong Kong, in 1986, the proportion of economically active women peaked at age 20 to 24 at 84%, and dropped to 34% at ages 35 to 39, rose slightly, then gradually declined to one quarter by age 55 to 59. In Singapore, in 1987, the female activity rate peaked at ages 20-24, when 80% of females are economically active, and the proportion dropped to 56% at ages 30-34, and down to 17% at age 55 to 59 (*Yearbook of Labour Statistics,* 1988, pp. 32, 37).

Under these conditions, especially those of the time of my study, when work was not common for women with children, a newly married woman's right to work is decided upon as part of a household-wide strategy. Here, too, the division of labor can depend on household size, where many people may be accommodated and many functions performed. The older generation sets the division of labor. Where there are several adults in the household, the elders can choose the women with the strongest wage-earning power to work. In order to go out to work, women must find others to do the household chores, child care, and other internal ministering of the household for them. In a large household there is considerable work to do. A large household with a strong dependency ratio, however, also has the potential for a division of labor in which young women can find backup services of others in their homes.

My Singapore research of the mid-1970s showed that the nature of factory demands for women was crucial in determining who would go to work and who would remain as backup workers in the home. Women with above-average education, some technical skills, and longer industrial work experience were the most eligible for better paying factory jobs, such as in multinational electronics firms. Thus although most women had worked prior to marriage, many had done traditional types of work on farms, in workshops, or small factories packing peanuts, making gold paper used to burn for the dead, or in soy sauce factories. Their labor force experience could not command a good wage earning job after marriage. Those married women who worked were among the better educated, the women with superior class backgrounds in my sample.

Women whose families were in great need, whose husbands were quite poor, might also work for a wage, but typically they could only get low-paid

Table 10.3 Comparison of the Residences of Full-Time Wage-Earning Wives and Homemakers, Singapore ca. 1975

| Form of Residence | Wives' Employment Status | | | | | |
| | Wage-Earners | | Homemakers | | Total | |
	%	(Number)	%	(Number)	%	(Number)
Stem or Extended	65		31		49	
Neolocal	35		69		51	
	100	(52)	100	(48)	100	(100)

Table 10.4 Interaction Patterns of Working Wives and Housewives, Phase 1, Singapore ca. 1975

| | Wives' Employment Status | | | |
| | Wage-Earners | | Homemakers | |
	%	(Number)	%	(Number)
Isolates	10		35	
Interactors	90		65	
	100	(52)	100	(48)

work. They were then subsidized by other women in the household, who responded to their great need. Alternatively, some of them might do nonindustrial work in the neighborhood, take in washing, wash floors part-time for neighborhood women. This underground economy work was not registered in labor force statistics.

That household support is key in aiding married women to work is seen in a comparison of full-time wage-earning women and homemakers in our study (Table 10.3). Women who lived in the same home with other kin (stem or extended households) were more likely to work than women who lived neolocally. In addition, however, a number of women carved out support systems that crossed household walls and drew upon several kin in a community area. These women are "interactors" (see Table 10.4).[4] Thus wage-earners invariably had kin-based support systems to help them out.

The example of a Singapore woman, Tan Giok Bee, a domestic servant in the mid-1970s, shows the high level of overall cooperation between family members that goes into married women's work. She received only four years of primary school, quit to care for her five younger siblings, until at age 17 she entered domestic service like her mother and her older sister. She worked six days a week for only S$180 a month for foreign families living in Singapore.[5] She left temporarily to care for each of her three newborn daughters. After the first birth she tried another line of work and spent a year making incense sticks, but found that she could not fit the fixed factory hours to her demanding regime of household tasks. One of her daughters was subject to epileptic seizures, and caring for this child imposed an added burden on her. "I prefer to work as an *amah* [domestic servant] because I don't have to keep strict hours on this job. Sometimes I can go home early or choose my own day off, when I have to take my daughter to the hospital on a working day. Her husband, Poh Wah, a tinsmith, also earned a poverty-line wage of S$250. The couple lived with their three daughters in a rented two-room HDB flat with elder Mother Tan. Tan Giok Bee's mother-in-law helped care for the children, but because the elderly woman was not well, Tan Giok Bee still had to do much of the housework, the errands, and services entailed in mothering. Tan Giok Bee gave mother-in-law a small sum of cash in exchange for the child-care help. A typical day's chronology of household care arrangements for Tan Giok Bee is given in Table 10.5. (Poh Wah was, we note, not part of these arrangements.)

Many working women who lived in small households found it necessary to engineer child care arrangements of this type. With the wider help, however limited, Tan Giok Bee was thus able to put in a full working day, but she could not manage to work at the higher paying factory jobs just then opening up. Her earnings were not enough to live on, and she "borrowed right and left" from her mother, who lived with two working sons and one daughter. Without the help of kin, Tan Giok Bee could not afford to work for the low wage she earned. In turn, she could support her mother-in-law at a modest level. Interviewed six years later, Tan Giok Bee told us that her mother-in-law had passed away. Tan Giok Bee's household burden even increased somewhat. Although her eldest children could care for themselves, the girls did not do the housework. Tan Giok Bee was pressed into a heavier double day than before, and she had to reduce her working hours to do so. Other women also enter and create complex interpersonal relationships, and may, if their husband's mother cannot help them, draw from relatives on both sides, which helps them to remain in the labor force after marriage. In turn, their work often gives employment and needed support to their kin.

Married Singapore women directed their wages toward their economic family. Poverty stricken married Singapore women who worked could help

Table 10.5 Chronology of Help for Domestic Servant Tan Giok Bee

In 1975

6:30	Tan Giok Bee rises to prepare breakfast for her three daughters (ages 8, 10, and 11).
7:00	Tan Giok Bee takes middle daughter to primary school, then continues to the neighborhood market to shop for the day's vegetables.
8:00	Tan Giok Bee does the day's laundry by hand.
9:00	Tan Giok Bee leaves home for her job.
9:00–12:30	Mother Tan cares for the two children at home, cooks and serves them lunch.
13:00	The younger and elder girls walk to primary school for the afternoon session.
14:30	Tan Giok Bee returns from work, takes a nap, and on alternative days prepares dinner for the family.
19:00	Tan Giok Bee's husband returns from work to eat dinner.
20:00	Poh Wah goes out for an evening of drinking with his co-workers.

Chronology of Help for Tan Giok Bee in 1981

6:30	Tan Giok Bee rises.
7:00	Tan Giok Bee markets for the day's vegetables.
7:30	Tan Giok Bee cooks breakfast and lunch for her three daughters (ages 14, 16, and 17)
7:30	The younger two girls leave for secondary school, and the eldest goes to work as a dental receptionist.
9:00	Tan Giok Bee leaves home for her job as a household servant.
2:00	Tan Giok Bee returns home and does the day's laundry by hand.
15:30	Tan Giok Bee takes a nap and then prepares dinner for the family.
19:00	Poh Wah returns from work to eat dinner.
20:00	Poh Wah sits in front of the color television for a quiet evening at home.

pay for tutors for their own children, to improve their performance on competitive state examinations. Even middle-class women saw their work as possible only if they could successfully field their family obligations to others. Women enjoyed an enlarged sphere of action due to having money of their own, but with their funds they bought clothes for their children, rounded out the family budget, and/or provided small sums to their mothers or other kin, which could not legitimately be drawn from their husband's or the wider household budget. They could join peer outings with workmates on special occasions, and purchase presents with their earnings. However, in virtually all cases studied, married women placed the major part of their earnings at the disposal of their family, usually their nuclear family. They obtained a widened sphere for their small nuclear unit within the patrilineal construct (Cohen, 1976).

Working Grandmothers. Women have a greater chance to come into their own when they become mothers-in-law and grandmothers. It is at this point that the dependency ratio improves once again, and from the older woman's perspective, she is the one to benefit. As they age, women may have a chance to take direct control over their expenditures. A 1984 survey of married couples in Taiwan, most of whom did not live with their parents, found that if both worked they spent on average $113US on their parents a month (this sum was 8% of their income). Twenty-six percent of the parents depended entirely and 36% depended partly on their adult children to live.[6] Although they can count on such a sum of money, many older women try to augment this sum with their own earnings.

The study I conducted on firms that include older women as blue-collar employees found these middle-aged Taiwan working women are typically married with grown and even married children. They fell into two groups. One group was protected and nurtured by their grown offspring. They have the freedom to spend money on themselves. As also shown in a Taiwan labor force survey that looked into the expenditure patterns of employees by age, the spending patterns of women in their late fifties differed greatly from their younger counterparts. They are finally able to use their earnings as "pocket money." This factory or service sector wage is often the first real sum of money they have ever fully controlled. They spend their earnings variously on renting video tapes, gambling, group outings and excursions, dinners, and *kala-okay* hi-fi sets for singing parties, and drinking. In one factory, one section is known plant wide for the leisure activities organized by a 55-year-old illiterate worker who has become an informal leader. Apart from investing in household furnishings for a new apartment, in the main she felt free to spend her earnings on her enjoyment, depending on her retired husband and employed son to maintain the household economy. Her daughter-in-law ran the household. Her co-workers stressed to me that this dowager was able to enjoy herself because she did not have a "double day." In my view, the strength of the filial tie was also crucial, which meant that her son and daughter-in-law were willing to support their mother, and permit her this modicum of freedom with her earnings.

Apart from those with a solid family, some are on their own because they have broken families, and must support themselves. These are divorcees, or women with nonearning husbands or sons. They suffer from their low wages, and their lack of a wider economic household and uterine family to provide them with old age security they had looked forward to. They cannot spend their money on leisure and instead barely make ends meet. It is quite possible that the current period is an unusual one, in which the youths are still willing to meet their obligations in line with the three types of family forms. Later cohorts, brought up in school systems and society that do not extol the elderly so much, and with fewer siblings with whom to share this care, may find the burden of the aged too heavy. Then the need for the state to come forth with a universal social insurance system will be unprecedented.[7]

State Strategies in Promoting
Export-Led Industrialization:
The Overall Picture

The Hong Kong, Taiwan, and Singapore states have developed export-oriented economies. They propelled the populace into the money economy, which required families to earn cash. The three states do not direct industry in the same ways. Huang (1989), who compared the states of Taiwan and Singapore, stressed how their similarities in relation to the society enabled them to chart the development policy.

> In both Taiwan and Singapore, the state leaders have been able to make decisions quite independent of the major social forces and groups in their own societies. This relative autonomy of the state to its civil society makes possible the relatively smooth shift to development policy from import substitution to export promotion without much resistance from groups of vested interests. (Huang, 1989, p. 98)

We have also seen the lack of responsiveness of the Hong Kong colonial state to the society.

Taiwan and Hong Kong, where the state plays the smallest economic role, depend more closely on the Chinese family firm as its industrial arm than does Singapore. Nevertheless, in establishing their industrial frameworks, all three make use of the Chinese family and its controls over the individual. In all three countries, the family helps put into place an economy that draws on female wage labor. The labor they use depends on the women's family cycle position. In the early stages of industrialization, they mostly drew upon the inexpensive labor of unmarried women, to a lesser extent married women, and still fewer middle-aged and older women. As the labor force became experienced and wages rose, and full employment of unmarried women was reached, married women were kept on the job and recruited for new positions. Finally, middle-aged women may be hired, especially in firms that pay too little to attract younger better educated women, but where the older women are able to earn "women's wages" because they either are not needed in the home, or they urgently need their income to support themselves. In these ways there is an articulation of the family structure and its economy with the development program.

Notes

1. There are many differences in the family regimes of Malays and Indians, as reflected in surveys on their family economies and studies on why may work and how their money is used (Ong, 1987; D. Wolf, 1989). I cannot cover all these materials in the present chapter, but a truly comparative family study would be welcome.

2. These cases come from the following sources: my in-depth study of 28 unmarried working-and middle-class women in Hong Kong, research by Linda Gail Arrigo (1984) and Lydia Kung (1984) on Taiwan factory women of the same ages, my case histories of 100 Singapore women, and data on 220 employed Taiwan women. My Hong Kong, Singapore, and Taiwan studies employed purposive sampling to meet quotas. The ages of the Hong Kong women studied were 20 to 24 in 1973, after which I studied them over a several-year time period. The Singapore women were married, with at least one child, and aged 20 to 30 when interviewed in the mid-1970s; they were also studied over time, the mid-1970s and early 1980s; the Taiwan data covers women of all ages from 20 firms with different types of work experience.

Kung did a two-pronged study (1983-1984), an ethnography of a market town and neighboring agrarian communities, and participant observation in an electronics factory west of Taipei (the capital city). Most of her respondents were unmarried. Arrigo (1984) also studied an American electronics firm in depth, through participant observation, survey, and case study methods. Although Kung and Arrigo did not explicitly select their sample of women workers within a particular age bracket, the labor force participation pattern of Taiwan women at the time limited most workers to the same age group of those I studied in Hong Kong, that is, their late teens and early twenties. For further discussion of sampling and other findings, see the following studies (Arrigo, 1984; Kung, 1984; Salaff, 1981, 1988).

3. These data come from the Census; the mothers were the ages of the mothers of the young employed women I studied.

4. "Interactors" are couples whose wives or husbands visited the same kin two or more times a week. Typically, kin cared for their children during the week, which helped wives work. Some women or their husbands worked with kin. Many of the exchanges that occurred aimed to reduce the homemaking burdens of these young mothers. Thus women could often draw upon this support system and go out to work.

5. In Singapore dollars, at the approximate rate of S$2.25 = US $1.

6. A Survey by China Youth Corps, reported in *Free China Journal,* June 17, 1984. Sixty percent of the adult couples surveyed did not live with their parents, 30% did, and in 17% of the cases the parents lived with each of their sons in turn, a common Taiwan solution for spreading the burden of support among offspring.

7. The "Conference on Economic Development and Social Welfare in Taiwan," sponsored by the Academia Sinica, Economics Research Centre, held in January, 1987, in Taipei, stressed this issue.

References

Arrigo, Linda Gail. (1984). Taiwan electronics workers. In Mary Sheridan & Janet W. Salaff (Eds.), *Lives: Chinese working women* (pp. 123-145). Bloomington: Indiana University Press.

Barrett, Michele E., & McIntosh, Mary. (1982). *The anti-social family.* London: Verso.

Bello, Walden, & Rosenfeld, Stephanie. (1990). *Dragons in distress.* San Francisco: Institute for Food and Development Policy.

Cohen, Myron. (1976). *House united, house divided.* New York: Columbia University Press.

Deyo, Frederic C. (Ed.). (1987). *The political economy of the new Asian industrialism.* Ithaca, NY: Cornell University Press.

An extract report on the 1980 census of population and housing, Taiwan-Fukien area, Republic of China. (1982). Taipei: Census Office of the Executive Yuan, R.O.C., Director General of Budget, Accounting, and Statistics.

Goode, William H. (1960, August). A theory of role strain. *American Sociological Review, 25,* pp. 483-496.

Goode, William J. (1982). *The family.* Englewood Cliffs, NJ: Prentice-Hall.

Hamilton, Gary G., & Biggart, Nicole Woolsey. (1988). Market, culture, and authority: A comparative analysis of management and organization in the Far East. *American Journal of Sociology, 94* [Supplement], pp. S52-S94.

Henderson, Jeffrey. (1989). The political economy of technological transformation in Hong Kong. *Comparative Urban and Community Research, 2,* pp. 102-155.

Huang, Chi. (1989, April). The state and foreign investment: The cases of Taiwan and Singapore. *Comparative Political Studies, 22*(1), pp. 93-121.

Kung, Lydia. (1983). *Factory women in Taiwan.* Ann Arbor: University of Michigan Research Press.

Kung, Lydia. (1984). Taiwan garment workers. In Mary Sheridan & Janet W. Salaff (Eds.), *Lives: Chinese working women* (pp. 109-122). Bloomington: Indiana University Press.

Judd, Ellen R. (1989). Niangjia: Chinese women and their natal families. *Journal of Asian Studies, 48*(4), pp. 525-544.

Lin, Vivian. (1987). Women electronics workers in southeast Asia: The emergence of a working class. In Jeffrey Henderson & Manual Castells (Eds.), *Global restructuring and territorial development* (pp. 112-135). Newbury Park, CA: Sage.

Ong, Aihwa. (1987). *Spirits of resistance and capitalist discipline: Factory women in Malaysia.* Albany: SUNY.

Salaff, Janet W. (1981). *Working daughters of Hong Kong.* Cambridge, UK: Cambridge University Press.

Salaff, Janet W. (1988). *State and family in Singapore: Restructuring an industrial society.* Ithaca, NY: Cornell University Press.

Topley, Marjorie. (1969). The role of savings and wealth among Hong Kong Chinese. In I.C. Jarvie & Joseph Agassi (Eds.), *Hong Kong society: A society in transition* (pp. 167-227). London: Routledge and Kegan Paul.

Ward, Kathryn. (Ed.). (1990). *Women workers and global restructuring.* Ithaca, NY: ILR Press.

Winch, Robert F. (1963). *The modern family.* New York: Holt, Reinhart & Winston.

Wolf, Arthur, & Huang, Chieh-shan. (1972). *Marriage and adoption in China, 1845-1945.* Stanford, CA: Stanford University Press.

Wolf, Diane. (1989). *Gender, households, and rural industrialization: Factory daughters and their families in Java.* Unpublished manuscript.

Wolf, Margery. (1972). *Women and the family in rural Taiwan.* Stanford, CA: Stanford University Press.

World Bank Report. [Various years.] Washington, DC: World Bank.

Year book of labour statistics. [Various years.] Taipei: Executive Yuan, R.O.C.

11

The Political Economy of Social Policy Formation
EAST ASIA'S NEWLY INDUSTRIALIZED COUNTRIES

FREDERIC C. DEYO

Sustained rapid industrial development in South Korea, Hong Kong, Singapore, and Taiwan, East Asia's Newly Industrializing countries (NICs), has spawned a sizeable literature seeking to explain this remarkable economic expansion. Especially prominent in this literature is an ongoing debate over the role of the state in economic change. While this debate has centered mainly on the relevance of state policy for economic growth and export expansion, relatively little attention has been accorded the related issue of the state's role in provision for social welfare. Given the close linkage between economic development policy and the welfare role of the state, one's perspective on the developmental role of the state is reflected in one's understanding of social policy.

This chapter examines social policy differences among the East Asian NICs. It assesses the relationship between social policy and economic development policy in these countries, showing that under a development strategy of human-resource-intensive export oriented industrialization (EOI), social and economic development goals are often compatible and closely linked. Indeed, it is argued that with a few such exceptions as Singapore's early postindependence experience and recent political change in South Korea, East Asian social policy has been driven primarily by the requirements and

AUTHOR'S NOTE: I am indebted to Manuel Castells, Paul Evans, Jeffrey Henderson, Su-Hoon Lee, Minjoo Oh, Janet Salaff, Michael Shafer, and Richard Stubbs for critical comments on an earlier draft of this chapter.

outcomes of economic development policy, unlike the situation in Latin America, where extrabureaucratic political pressures have played a more prominent role in shaping social policy.

It is shown that temporal change in social policy among the East Asian NICs is in part explained by evolutionary changes in economic strategy, while cross-national variation in social policy is closely related to corresponding differences in the developmental roles of states as well as in the nature of the employment systems through which the East Asian NICs have wedded domestic labor to the requirements of export-oriented industrialization.

Major Components of Social Policy

At the most general level, social policy refers here to state policies, practices, and institutions that directly influence the economic welfare and security of popular sector groups (farmers, workers, middle classes, etc.). Such policy may be understood by reference to four major components. First, social policy is embedded in economic development policy insofar as economic policy has intended welfare consequences or reflects implicit or explicit socioeconomic priorities. Indeed, politically unacceptable levels of unemployment in the late 1950s and early 1960s were an important stimulus to policy reforms that ushered in labor-intensive export manufacturing and the attendant achievement of near-full employment and rising wages by the 1970s.

Social policy relates secondly to direct government provision for social welfare, in part through public services and subsidies that benefit major social sectors. Subsidized health, public housing, education, child care, subsidized foodstuffs, public transportation, and welfare payments and public assistance programs fall into this category typically referred to as the "social wage."

Third, social policy includes incomes policy, that assemblage of measures that influence wages and benefits in both public and private sectors.

Finally, the state may influence income security through pension schemes, disability and health insurance, unemployment insurance, and other measures typically included in social security systems. These schemes may apply to government workers or they may be mandated for private sector firms. In the latter case, there may be substantial variation in the extent of state financing.

This chapter compares social development policy among the East Asian NICs, looking in turn at social policy embedded in development strategy, the social wage, incomes policy, and social security. Discussion concludes with an explanation for policy differences among these countries, focusing especially on the relationship between social policy on the one hand, and economic political imperatives on the other.

Social Priorities Embedded
in East Asian Development Policy

At the very outset of East Asian policy reforms that ushered in the export-led industrialization strategy of the 1960s, it was recognized that political stability and legitimacy depended in large measure on reduction of high levels of unemployment and enhancement of wages and standard of living. Acceptance of the need to adopt a strategy to achieve these ends, coupled with an absence of significant nonlabor agricultural, mineral, or other economic resources, encouraged an emphasis on light, labor-intensive manufacturing that might generate quick gains in employment. The success of this policy is seen in rapid declines in unemployment in these countries, bringing about, in fact, growing labor shortages by the 1970s. Indeed, many observers have argued that given the massive provision of jobs and wage gains under a successful strategy of labor-intensive industrialization, social policy would have been extraneous and irrelevant to welfare gains, or worse, that "premature" welfare programs might have reduced the competitiveness of East Asia's export-oriented manufacturing, thus undercutting both economic growth and associated employment gains.

By the mid-1970s, a policy shift toward promotion of higher value-added manufacturing prompted greater investment in "human capital" along with new strategies to enhance labor force stability and productivity. This strategic shift was associated with increased emphasis on education and training and on enhanced workplace benefits. Additionally, increased production for domestic consumer and producer markets paralleled by growing wage pressures in a tightened labor market encouraged substantial and continuing wage gains. Thus, economic policy changes in the 1970s eventuated in important gains in worker welfare.

Social Wage

If the East Asian NICs have generally shared a common development strategy since the 1960s, they have diverged in their social security and

Table 11.1 Social Expenditures in the East Asian NICs

	Per Capita ($US)	As % of GDP		As % of Total Government Expenditures	
South Korea	1987: 148	1980: 4.6	1987: 5.0	1980: 26.6	1987: 29.1
Taiwan	1988: 301	1981: 5.9	1988: 6.0	1981: 27.7	1988: 30.5
Singapore	1987: 862	1980: 5.1	1987: 10.6	1980: 30.6	1987: 29.5
Hong Kong	1987: 652	1980: 8.1	1987: 7.8	1980: 50.2	1987: 53.1

SOURCE: United Nations (1988); Republic of China (1990).

welfare policies. Some indication of these differences may be gleaned from available data on public social welfare expenditures (for education, social welfare, health, housing, and community services). Table 11.1 compares social expenditure outlays among these countries.

In large measure, the marked differences in per capita social expenditure between South Korea and Taiwan on the one hand, and Singapore and Hong Kong on the other, reflect differences in degree of urbanization and in corresponding differences in the need for government provision of social services. In order to take this fundamental structural difference into account, subsequent discussion emphasizes separate comparisons between South Korea and Taiwan, and between Singapore and Hong Kong.

Unlike per capita data, which reflect absolute levels of social expenditures, social expenditure as a percentage of Gross Domestic Product (GDP) measures the extent of the social wage relative to the size of the national economy. Here we again note moderately lower expenditures in South Korea than in Taiwan throughout the 1980s. More interesting is the reversal between Singapore and Hong Kong. Whereas Hong Kong's social expenditures were higher than those in Singapore at the beginning of the decade, only a few years later, social outlays in Singapore exceeded those in Hong Kong.

A useful measure of government policy priorities is provided by social expenditures as a percentage of total governmental outlays. This percentage rose moderately in three of the four countries, thus indicating greater attention to social development. It is apparent here that social expenditures have comprised a far smaller proportion of total expenditures in Singapore than in Hong Kong. The difference between the two city-states is only in part ex-

Table 11.2 Categories of Social Expenditure as a Percentage of Total Social Expenditures

		Education	Social Security and Welfare	Health	Housing and Community Service
South Korea	1980	64.4	23.9	4.6	7.1
	1987	62.5	22.5	9.0	6.1
Taiwan	1981	42.2	46.5	5.8	5.5
	1988	47.2	40.9	5.3	6.6
Singapore	1980	47.8	4.4	22.7	25.1
	1987	49.0	4.4	12.2	34.5
Hong Kong	1980	30.6	8.8	15.0	45.6
	1987	34.4	11.5	18.2	35.9

SOURCE: United Nations (1988); Republic of China (1990).

plained by the greater defense outlays in Singapore. As a percentage of non-defense expenditures, social expenditures comprise 34.5% of the total in Singapore, versus 54.8% in Hong Kong.

A further examination of the relative emphasis given the various components of social expenditures permits a fuller understanding of these cross-national differences. Table 11.2 shows recent social expenditures broken down by functional category.

These data provide a starting point for developing a social policy "profile" for the East Asian NICs. Taiwan stands out here in its relatively lower outlays for education and health services, and its greater emphasis on social security and welfare than South Korea. Similarly, Singapore's lesser emphasis on social security and welfare, and greater stress on education, contrasts with Hong Kong's stronger commitment to welfare. It should be noted in this regard that Singapore's housing expenditure increased dramatically during 1986 and 1987, in the context of a major reconstruction project. Similarly, Singapore's low social welfare expenditures in part reflect comprehensive welfare programs for workers provided by trade unions closely allied with the ruling People's Action Party.

Incomes Policy

Abandonment of import-substitution strategies in favor of export-led de-velopment in the 1960s had a further important consequence for social wel-fare. The global competitiveness of East Asia's manufactured exports was based in part on cheap, productive labor. This consideration, along with a further determination to prevent early wage gains from restraining employ-ment growth, implied a low-wage policy extending well into the 1970s. In Singapore and South Korea, wage restraint invoked direct wage controls and restrictive policies toward trade unions. Beginning in 1974, Singapore's Na-tional Wages Council (NWC) issued annual guidelines to be applied in wage negotiations. Until 1979, these guidelines held wage gains to levels below productivity increases. Beginning in 1968, the Singapore government sin-gled out "Pioneer Industries" (labor-intensive export industries promoted by the government) as free from any obligation to negotiate pay levels above the minima recommended by the NWC. Similarly, South Korea's Economic Planning Board issued yearly wage recommendations that held wage gains to a fixed percentage of inflation and productivity gains. And in Taiwan, trade unions were generally prohibited from pressing for large wage increases.

On the other hand, growing labor shortages soon created strong upward pressure on wages. These wage gains, it should be noted, flowed less from political pressures, as in Latin America, than from labor market outcomes of successful development strategies themselves. Indeed, subsequent policy change was in part driven by rising wages as East Asian planners sought to encourage productivity gains through capital and technology deepening and skill development during the 1970s and 1980s, in order to maintain globally competitive labor costs. In the case of Singapore, this policy shift was re-flected in a marked realignment in wage policy, as the ruling party sought to preempt this otherwise slow readjustment by actively promoting wage in-creases in the late 1970s in order to discourage further investment in low-skill, labor-intensive manufacturing.

Income Security

The relatively minimal early social expenditure of South Korea (see Table 11.1) and its emphasis on human capital formation through education rather than community welfare (see Table 11.2) reflect a single-minded com-mitment to rapid, state-induced industrialization at whatever social cost necessary. A major exception to this "production first" approach relates to provision, under the 1963 Social Security Act, of pension, medical, and other benefits for civil service, military, and private school teachers (Chang, 1985) (public school teachers receive coverage as members of the civil service). Indeed, a substantial portion of total government social insurance and welfare expenditures target this politically important category of workers. Beyond this protected segment of the workforce, social insurance provision has been uneven and minimal (Park, 1975).

In response to political pressure, a national pension insurance plan was enacted in 1973, but this was only implemented in 1988, in the context of powerful new political forces associated with the democratic reforms of the late 1980s. Financing is almost entirely contributory in nature, and coverage during the first phase of implementation extends to only 4.4 million workers. Similarly limited is coverage under the 1983 Industrial Injury Compensation Insurance Act, which provides medical coverage for work-related injuries. This and other worker welfare programs are contributory in nature, thus avoiding large government expenditures (Chang, 1985). In fact, over half of all social welfare expenditures are privately financed. In addition, given inadequate public enforcement and widespread employer violation of newly mandated social insurance requirements, nominal work force coverage greatly exaggerates actual coverage. South Korea, it should also be noted, has yet to ratify most ILO conventions relating to worker rights and welfare.

In Taiwan, as in South Korea, government workers enjoy broad, if shallow, social security benefits. Private sector social insurance policy centers on state-mandated employer provision against death, disability, severance, and retirement for workers (International Commercial Bank of China, 1983). Coverage under the Labor Insurance Act of 1958 (as subsequently amended) is almost entirely contributory in nature although the government does help finance social insurance for self-employed persons under a voluntary insurance program (Chan, 1985). Under the 1984 Labor Standards Law, pension and severance benefits are obligatory for employers. While employer refusal to implement provisions of the 1984 law somewhat reduces effective coverage (Lee, 1989), it is clear that state-mandated social insurance is more fully developed here than in South Korea. But it must also be recognized that such insurance is almost entirely enterprise based.

The Labor Insurance Act of 1979 established, for the first time, limited unemployment insurance, but this program was indefinitely suspended "because of low levels of unemployment," and, significantly, because it was felt it would lead to "welfare dependency" (Chan, 1985). Assistance to unemployed is largely confined to public assistance for the very poor.

Singapore is unique among the East Asian NICs in having developed a comprehensive national pension plan (the Central Provident Fund, or CPF) prior to the period of rapid EOI development. While there is no national unemployment insurance program, severance pay and worker compensation programs are required of employers. Indeed, many social insurance programs (e.g. medical insurance) have been shifted to companies themselves during recent years.

The colonial government of Hong Kong has established a comprehensive social insurance scheme, covering severance, illness, and retirement for civil service workers (Hong Kong Social Welfare Department, 1989). But unlike Singapore, Hong Kong lacks a public social insurance program despite growing pressure for establishment of a colony-wide provident fund (Chow, 1985). Under recent legislation enacted during the mid-1980s, employers are now required to provide severance benefits for workers who have been employed at least 10 years. As of 1985, only about 14% of all workers were covered by pension and severance schemes. Many employers have been known to fire workers just before their tenth year of employment in order to avoid this legal obligation. While Hong Kong has ratified many (49) ILO labor standards conventions (International Social Security Association, 1989), enforcement in this area is similarly deficient.

Social and Economic Development Policy:
The Question of Compatibility

Beginning in the 1930s and 1940s, social development policy in Argentina, Brazil, Mexico, and elsewhere in Latin America has been powerfully driven by extra-bureaucratic political forces. In some instances, such policy was preemptive and anticipatory, as under Cardenas in Mexico. In other cases, it was in reaction to existing political opposition and pressure, as in Brazil in the early 1960s and Chile in the early 1970s. Often, where such opposition severely threatened economic growth and the interests of economic elites, it was met by repression (e.g. Argentina, 1976; Brazil, 1964; Chile, 1973) rather than by accommodative social policy reforms. In most cases, pursuit of a capital intensive, exclusionary, and inequality-generating development strategy (Evans, 1979) heightened the incompatibility between economic and social policy, thus generating powerful currents of political and class conflict.

East Asian industrialization, on the other hand, has been relatively more compatible with positive social policy, especially during the period of economic restructuring and in the areas of social wage and incomes policy. To the extent this is true, it would tend to explain the continuing expansion of social development expenditures (Table 11.1) and policies during recent years, despite a general absence of effective political pressure from popular sector groups.

East Asian export-oriented industrialization has from the very outset centered on the effective utilization of human resources. In particular, in the absence of significant mineral or agricultural resources, low-cost labor has defined the competitive edge of these small, crowded countries. Labor cost containment in turn has entailed some combination of the following elements: low wage and compensation levels, high productivity, and low levels of labor conflict. During most of the period of rapid industrialization, labor conflict has been minimal (Deyo, 1989). But the relative importance of compensation levels on the one hand, and productivity and skill on the other, was reversed during the 1970s.

During the early period of light-industry-based development, plentiful, low-wage labor provided the key to export expansion and economic growth. At this time, a clear incompatibility existed between some elements of social policy and economic policy. In particular, a repressive incomes policy and a reluctance to impose income security expenses on employers often required strict political controls over labor. On the other hand, expansionary social policy in other areas often supported, rather than undermined, industrial expansion (Salaff, 1988, p. 27). In particular, provision of housing, health, subsidized foodstuffs, and other elements of social wage acted as a wage subsidy by reducing the cost of living and thus reducing upward pressure on wages. It will be suggested below that the massive housing programs in Singapore and Hong Kong may be understood in this way.

The later shift to higher-value-added industry greatly enhanced the degree of compatibility between social and economic development policy. Such increased compatibility related especially to the need for higher levels of skill and productivity in the context of declining unemployment and concomitant upward wage pressures. Most obvious is the productivity benefit derived from "human capital investment" in education (especially vocational training) and health. Similarly, as industrial restructuring proceeded, incomes policy could be relaxed. And as work force stabilization and enterprise loyalty were increasingly sought by employers as a precondition for increased investment in worker training, mandated enterprise-level social security benefits became ever more supportive of continued industrial transformation.

The extent of compatibility varied as well by the nature of the employment systems through which domestic labor was wedded to international capital, technology, and markets. Where proletarian labor controls relied extensively on the power of labor markets to discipline workers, especially during early industrialization, an enhanced social wage and income security measures that might have sheltered workers from the discipline of labor markets were incompatible with economic expansion. On the other hand, where labor controls relied to a greater extent on employer paternalism, social wage and income security measures were more compatible with economic policy.

It is clear, too, that the nature and extent of state guidance and intervention in the development process conditions the extent to which simple compatibility between social and economic policy is reflected in actual enactment of social development measures. Developmental states, whose governments have attempted systematically to restructure their economies by directly influencing investment decisions in targeted industries, are prone systematically to implement development-enhancing social measures. Less interventionist states, where economic growth is encouraged through more indirect means, tend to exhibit a looser correspondence between economic and social policy. Thus may be understood the greater social policy priority accorded education than social welfare (Table 11.2) in the more developmental states of South Korea and Singapore than in Taiwan and Hong Kong during recent years of industrial restructuring. It should be noted, however, that large public housing expenditures in Hong Kong, and publicly financed and privately mandated social security and welfare in Taiwan, have also played important, if less direct, roles in economic development. I return to this point below.

Having argued that East Asian development has posed a less sharp polarity between social and economic development policy than elsewhere, it should be reiterated that such polarity has presented itself most clearly at various developmental junctures and for particular aspects of social policy. In addition, even where social and economic development priorities have not clashed, governments have often been reluctant to pursue proactive social policy measures in the absence of strong political pressures. In both these instances, social policy has been determined more by political forces than by developmental considerations. Thus, in order to understand social policy differences and trends in East Asia, it is necessary as well to take into account the power of popular sector groups and organizations to influence governmental policy. The remaining discussion provides a brief overview of the way in which these developmental, economic structural, and political factors have influenced East Asian social policy during the early period of light-industry-based export-oriented industrialization in the 1960s, as well as during the more recent period of economic restructuring. Because during the earlier period, social and economic development policy were relatively less compatible, political factors acquire special importance. Conversely, given the greater compatibility of social and economic priorities under restructuring, economic requirements become more salient during the 1970s. Finally, political developments in the 1980s, flowing in part from rapid economic and class transformation, have resulted in a renewed importance of political forces, especially in South Korea.

Early Light-Industry-Based Development

In South Korea, as elsewhere, labor-intensive export-oriented industrialization was adopted in part to generate rapid gains in employment and thus to garner working-class support for ruling groups. But during the early phase of EOI, the implementation of such a strategy entailed more specific elements of social policy that bore down heavily on working classes. Most important in this regard were a low-wage policy alongside minimal provision for social services or income security. At the outset of export-led development in the 1960s, high unemployment levels sufficed to maintain low wages. Subsequent upward wage pressures were contained by progressively tougher political controls over the late 1960s and 1970s.

The need for deep, repressive labor controls in South Korea followed in part from a development strategy that encouraged large-scale industry and proletarian employment systems. Lacking either Singapore's corporatist union structure or Taiwan's enterprise paternalism, proletarianized Korean workers were better positioned to form locally independent organizations and unions, despite higher level political controls at the federation level. As union pressure mounted during the 1970s, the government's only available response was one of repression. The vicious cycle of repression and protest that issued from this early pattern was eventually to contribute to the democratic opening of the mid-1980s. In the shorter term, however, repression sufficed to scuttle demands for greater provision for social welfare and social insurance, to hold wages down, and to confine social policy primarily to education and training. Such exclusionary policies buttressed the economic power of employers, who in most cases were able freely to evade even those few wage and benefit requirements the government did enact, and encouraged continued reliance on proletarian labor strategies.

If early EOI development in Taiwan relied as strongly on low wages as in South Korea, a low-wage policy relied to a far lesser degree on state repression. The key to understanding this difference is to be found in characteristics of industrial structure and employment systems.

Industrial development in Taiwan centered more than elsewhere on elaborate subcontracting networks among small and medium-sized family-based firms. These firms, embedded as they were in the rich associational life of local communities, provided workers with a modicum of security against economic deprivation albeit at very low wage levels. Enterprise paternalism, given further encouragement under national legislation mandating a number of employment benefits, greatly enhanced the power of employers. The resulting weakness of trade unions, further ensured by preemptive political controls imposed under martial law at the outset of KMT rule in Taiwan, resulted in extremely weak social pressure for a proactive social policy. The major exception to this pattern was substantial social provision for government employees, a potentially important political support group for the ruling party.

At the outset of self government in Singapore in 1959, the ruling PAP drew substantial political support from leftist trade unions. This early circumstance, unique among the East Asian NICs, partly explains the relatively early provision of a national pension scheme, public housing, and a national health care system as well as a continued professed public commitment to welfare socialism. It should also be noted, however, that the developmental advantages of some of these programs were clear at the outset. The CPF, for example, has comprised a major source of finance for many government projects.

The chosen mode of developmental intervention has also influenced Singapore's social policy. Far more than its counterparts elsewhere, the PAP has employed labor policy as a central element in its broader economic strategy. Of particular importance has been the utilization of a tightly controlled NTUC to encourage and monitor compliance with various government policies. It is likely that without the impetus for PAP corporatist inclusion of the unions provided by a powerful labor movement in the early 1960s, a far less proactive social policy would have emerged in Singapore. On the other hand, it is also clear that the substantial leverage provided the PAP by Singapore's preemptively controlled labor movement was an essential element in maintaining a highly effective policy of wage compression over a 10-year period up to the late 1970s. This wage depressing policy, along with a number of welfare programs self-financed by trade unions, largely compensated for substantial employer costs incurred by required CPF contributions.

While patriarchal and paternalistic employment systems among Hong Kong's many family firms provided a close structural and political parallel to Taiwan, the concomitant growth of large-scale factory employment defined an important departure from the Taiwanese pattern. Continuing inflows of mainland immigrants provided cheap, politically vulnerable labor for local and foreign employers who operated outside traditional social relationships of mutual obligation. In these factories, transitory employment of low-skilled persons, especially young women at very low wages, adequately fulfilled the requirements of cheap, manageable labor for export production. Workers in this factory sector, like their counterparts in Hong Kong's smaller family firms, presented little challenge to employers or to the colonial government to adopt social insurance or welfare protection for workers (Deyo, 1989; Henderson, 1989). This weakness of organized labor, along with a determination on the part of the government to intervene only minimally in the colonial economy, has encouraged a continuing reluctance to introduce private-sector social insurance legislation. A major exception to this more general pattern of political insulation from popular sector pressure is to be found in the widespread riots of 1966-1967 that prompted expanded government welfare and social security programs in the 1970s (Chow, 1985).

On the other hand, lack of substantial expenditure in such other areas as economic services and defense in this nondevelopmentalist colonial dependency means that social expenditures comprise a relatively large portion of total government expenditure (Table 11.1). Most important has been a sizeable outlay for public housing. While Hong Kong's vast housing program may in part be explained by continuing waves of immigrants from the mainland and a corresponding need to accommodate their housing needs, the political weakness of this group, alongside a more general political insulation of the colonial regime from popular sector groups, would seem to require a more persuasive account of so massive a public undertaking. One possibility is that public housing in fact comprises an exception to the more general pattern of developmental nonintervention. Castells (1984) and Salaff (1988) argue that public housing has provided an important indirect stimulus to industrialization. Such housing resulted first in the elimination of informal sector nonwage work in traditional local communities that were displaced by such housing, while at the same time forcing newly housed families, and especially women, to enter the work force for the first time to earn wages for rent and other necessities. Beyond this impetus to work force expansion, public housing also attracts and accommodates light industry complexes that draw their work force largely from the local population of housing residents. Such complexes provide employment for many women whose household duties would otherwise preclude travel to more distant work. Finally, subsidized public housing, along with price-depressing government controls over food imports from China, acts as a wage subsidy for employers by holding down the cost of living (Henderson, 1989; Schiffer, 1991). In these ways, proactive social policy has encouraged industrial development.

Economic Restructuring and
Divergent Social Policy

Growing labor shortages and increased wage pressure in the 1970s, along-side growing protectionism in core economies, posed well known threats to continued export expansion among the East Asian NICs. But if an earlier crisis of import substitution eventuated in a convergence on light-industry-based export manufacturing, the new crisis precipitated more divergent responses in economic policy, in the employment systems that were associated with those responses, and in the empowerment of popular sector groups. These divergencies, in turn, had varied consequences for social policy.

Shared by all four countries was a need to restructure into higher-value-added economic activities, whether in manufacturing or other sectors, in order to accommodate increased wage costs. Economic growth somewhat reduced this cost-based pressure through an enhanced domestic market for both consumer and producer goods. On the other hand, export markets remained critical for continued growth while import liberalization, in part the result of external political demands, added further pressure for increased productivity and efficiency.

Economic restructuring in manufacturing required substantial new investments not only in physical capital, but also in expanded and upgraded education and training programs. As noted earlier, the more interventionist governments in South Korea and Singapore have devoted a far larger portion of social expenditure to education than their less developmental counterparts in Taiwan and Hong Kong. Although not shown in Table 11.2, Singapore's expenditure priorities shifted dramatically from housing and community services to education during the 1980s. There, as in South Korea, substantial attention has been directed to the expansion of vocational and technical training, at secondary and tertiary levels and in separate training institutes, as an essential instrument of state efforts to promote industrial restructuring.

As important, restructuring encouraged the development, particularly in Taiwan and Singapore, of more paternalistic labor relations that might encourage greater work force stability, better morale, and heightened enterprise loyalty in order to enhance productivity and returns to investments in worker training.

South Korea's ruling party, under greater political threat than its counterparts elsewhere, continued its reliance on political repression to contain labor costs and heightened inflationary pressures during the late 1970s and early 1980s. It should be noted that this repressive response was more effective during earlier years when U.S. backing for anticommunist regimes was most assured, and became less effective during the late-1970s with the diminution of this external regime support. An alternative turn to enterprise paternalism would probably have been impossible to achieve in the context of extreme hostility and volatility in labor relations during this period.

In addition, restructuring policies emphasized, to a greater extent than elsewhere, automobile, shipbuilding, and other heavy industry. While in the short term, repression sufficed to keep production and labor costs down and to resist growing pressure for positive social policy, continued prolatarianization along with rapid growth in heavy industry encouraged increasing labor militancy culminating in the protracted strike wave of 1987-1988. Such heightened political pressure resulted in substantial wage increases, the launching of a national pension scheme, and extension of coverage under the medical insurance program to the entire national population.

Taiwan's enterprise paternalism was in fact well adapted to the requirements of restructuring, insofar as workers were already closely bound to the fate of their companies through a range of economic and noneconomic sanctions and obligations. A continuing liberalization in state development policy over the 1970s and 1980s (Li, 1989), and a corresponding dependence on the continued vitality of small firm entrepreneurship for growth, built on this strength in traditional employment systems. Indeed, earlier social insurance requirements mandated for local employers were further expanded during the 1970s, especially under the provisions of the 1984 Labor Standards Law, thus encouraging a further deepening of enterprise paternalism (Liu, 1988). As a consequence, direct government social programs retained their self-consciously "residual" character. The power of organized labor has remained negligible. Indeed, despite appeals for labor representation during deliberations on the introduction of the new Labor Standards Law, union officials failed to participate. By default, therefore, labor's interests were largely represented by the Ministry of Labor.

As in South Korea, the Singapore government has played a dynamic role in engineering economic restructuring. This greater role is reflected, as well, in social policy reforms. In Singapore, a number of new measures encouraged paternalism in employment relations. Large industry-wide unions were decentralized, and house unions were encouraged. Many social insurance programs were partially decentralized to firms. A portion of CPF contributions reverted to enterprise-level social funds, while educational and welfare programs, and, later, medical coverage, devolved to firms. In these ways, the PAP emulated Taiwanese efforts to enhance work force stability and enterprise loyalty. It should be noted that throughout this recent period of transition, expanded government commitment to social welfare has been driven primarily by the needs of evolving development policy, rather than by the pressures of political dissent. Even Singapore's dramatic break with an earlier low-wage policy in 1979 was based almost entirely on a perceived need to phase out low-skill, light industries in favor of higher value-added production.

While social insurance and welfare outlays increased somewhat in Hong Kong, there, too, social policy underwent no decisive shift over the 1970s and 1980s. High rates of immigration until well into the 1970s encouraged a continued reliance on low-wage, export manufacturing (e.g., textiles) in lieu of a shift toward higher value-added manufacturing. This, along with the impending reality of the colony's reversion to Chinese control and a continued commitment to economic liberalism, ensured an absence of government reconstructive intervention in the economy. With the exceptions of housing, land, and food policies, with their supportive links to industrial expansion, social outlays were minimal and largely custodial, rather than developmental. Hong Kong continues to lag far behind Singapore in educational expenditures. To the extent economic restructuring has been systematically encouraged, it has centered on renewed growth in financial and service activities associated with Hong Kong's traditional entrepôt role.

Conclusion

With the exceptions of Singapore in the early 1960s and South Korea in the late 1980s, East Asian social policy has been more strongly shaped by the developmental priorities of politically insulated states than by extra-bureaucratic political forces as in Latin America. Political autonomy, whether or not associated with developmental states, has in turn been variably rooted in social organizational and economic structural factors that have muted labor opposition, or, alternately, in political regimes that have either co-opted or repressed popular opposition movements.

But political autonomy has not resulted in an absence of proactive social policy. Indeed, in some instances East Asian social policy has been far more progressive than that in other developing countries. That state autonomy has not eventuated in dismal social policy records, particularly during recent years, is in part explained by the nature of development strategy. East Asian export-oriented industrialization has centered on the effective utilization of human resources. Under such circumstances, economic development has been energized by social policies that have enhanced labor productivity, encouraged enterprise training, and subsidized wages. To this extent, economic development and proactive social policy have been mutually supportive.

The systematic use of social policy to pursue economic development goals has been most pronounced where states have intervened most directly in the development process. While developmentally supportive social policy is clearly in evidence in Taiwan and Hong Kong, it has been largely indirect and sometimes ambiguous in its intended purpose. By contrast, the government role in education, wage determination, and other elements of social policy has been more explicitly and directly linked to economic growth in South Korea and Singapore.

References

Castells, Manuel. (1984). *Small business in a world economy: The Hong Kong model, myth and reality*. Paper delivered at the Seminar on The Urban Informal Sector in Center and Periphery. Baltimore, MD: Johns Hopkins University.

Chan, Gordon Hou-Sheng. (1985). Taiwan. In John Dixon & Hyung Shik Kim (Eds.), *Social welfare in Asia*. London: Croom Helm.

Chang, In-Hyub. (1985). Korea, South. In John Dixon & Hyung Shik Kim (Eds.), *Social welfare in Asia*. London: Croom Helm.

Chow, Nelson. (1985). Hong Kong. In John Dixon & Hyung Shik Kim (Eds.), *Social welfare in Asia*. London: Croom Helm.

Deyo, Frederic C. (1989). *Beneath the miracle: Labor subordination in the new Asian industrialism*. Berkeley: University of California Press.

Evans, Peter. (1979). *Dependent development: The alliance of multinational, state, and local capital in Brazil*. Princeton: Princeton University Press.

Henderson, Jeffrey. (1989). Labour and state policy in the technological development of the Hong Kong electronics industry. *Labor and Society*, 14. pp. 20-21.

Hong Kong Social Welfare Department. (1989, June). Changes in social security provisions in Hong Kong. *Asian News Sheet*, 19(2).

The International Commercial Bank of China, Republic of China. (1983, November-December). The social welfare system and social welfare expenditures of the Republic of China. *Economic Review*, pp. 6-14.

International Social Security Association. (1989, June). ILO in Asia and the Pacific: A review of events and activities in the field of social security. *Asian News Sheet, 19*(2).

Lee, Joseph S. (1989, April 25). Labor relations and the stages of economic development. *Industry of Free China, 71*(4).

Li, K. T. (1989). *The evolution of policy behind Taiwan's development success*. New Haven, CT: Yale University Press.

Liu, Paul K.-C. (1988, October-November). Employment, earnings, and export-led industrialization in Taiwan. *Industry of Free China, 70*(4-5).

Park, Chong Kee. (1975). *Social security in Korea: An approach to socio-economic develop-ment.* Seoul: Korea Development Institute.

Republic of China, Executive Yuan. (1989). *Statistical yearbook.*

Salaff, Janet. (1988). *State and family in Singapore: Restructuring an industrial society.* Ithaca, NY: Cornell University Press.

Schiffer, Jonathan. (1991). State policy and economic growth: A note on the Hong Kong model. *International Journal of Urban and Regional Research, 15.*

United Nations, Economic and Social Commission for Asia and the Pacific. (1988). *Statistical yearbook for Asia and the Pacific.* Bangkok, Thailand: Author.

Name Index

310   STATES AND DEVELOPMENT IN THE ASIAN PACIFIC RIM

Subject Index

About the Contributors

Richard P. Appelbaum is Professor and Chair of the Sociology Department at the University of California at Santa Barbara, where he also directs the UCSB Center for Global Studies. He received his B.A. from Columbia University in 1964, and M.P.A. from the Woodrow Wilson School of Public and International Affairs at Princeton University in 1966. After serving as a technical consultant to the National Planning Office of Peru he returned to graduate school, receiving his Ph.D. in sociology from the University of Chicago in 1971. Dr. Appelbaum has conducted research and published extensively in the areas of social theory, urban sociology, the sociology of housing and homelessness, and—most recently—the geography of economic development. His most recent books include *Rethinking Rental Housing* (with John I. Gilderbloom; Temple University Press, 1988), and *Karl Marx* (Sage, 1988). He is a principal author of H.R. 1122 (101st Congress), "A Comprehensive National Housing Program for America," and has testified before Congress on the problems of homelessness. Dr. Appelbaum's work has received a chapter award from the American Planning Association, and the Douglas McGregor Award for excellence in behavioral science research. Most recently, he has received grants from the Haynes Foundation and the University of California Pacific Rim Program to undertake a comparative study of several industries that span Los Angeles, northern Mexico, Hong Kong, Taiwan, and South Korea.

Manuel Castells is Professor of Planning and of Sociology at the University of California at Berkeley. He has been a Visiting Professor at the University of Hong Kong, and a Senior Visiting Fellow at the National University of Singapore. He has also lectured at Taiwan National University and at Seoul National University.

He has published 15 books, including *The Economic Crisis and American Society* (1980), and *The Shek Kip Mei Syndrome, Economic Development and Public Housing in Hong Kong and Singapore* (1990).

Lucie Cheng is Professor of Sociology and Founding Director of the Center for Pacific Rim Studies at the University of California, Los Angeles. She writes on international migration, ethnic relations, and gender issues. Her publications include *Labor Immigration Under Capitalism* (with Edna Bonacich), and "Women and Class Analysis in the Chinese Land Revolution," among others.

Soohyun Chon is presently the Academic Coordinator at the Center for Korean Studies at the Institute of East Asian Studies and a lecturer in geography, both at the University of California, Berkeley. She obtained her Ph.D. in economic geography from the University of Michigan (1984) and an MBA in finance from the University of Chicago (1985). She is currently working on a book dealing with the Industrial Structure Comparison between Korea and Taiwan: Implications for Future Industrial Growth.

Frederic C. Deyo is Associate Professor of Sociology at State University of New York at Brockport. He has written extensively on East Asian industrialization and labor, and is author of *Beneath the Miracle: Labor Subordination in the New Asian Industrialism.*

Haruhiro Fukui is Professor of Political Science at the University of California, Santa Barbara, and specializes in Japanese domestic politics and foreign policy. He has recently been a Visiting Fellow at All Souls College, Oxford University, and a Visiting Professor at the International University of Japan. He recently co-edited *Japan and the World* (Macmillan, 1988) and *The Politics of Economic Change in Postwar Japan and West Germany* (Macmillan, in press).

Gary Gereffi is Associate Professor in the Sociology Department at Duke University. He is the author of *The Pharmaceutical Industry and Dependency in the Third World* (1983) and co-editor (with Donald Wyman) of *Manufacturing Miracles: Paths of Industrialization in Latin America and East Asia* (1990). His current research is on international subcontracting and export networks in the garment, footwear, automobile, and computer industries in East Asia, Latin America, and the Caribbean, and the United States.

Nigel Harris, an economist, is Professor of Development Planning in the University of London, and former director of the Development Planning Unit at University College, London. He is the author of numerous works on economic development, class structures, trade, and urbanization in developing countries. He is currently working on the fourth volume of a work seeking to analyze the national implications of an integrating world economy. The volumes are: *Of Bread and Guns: Crisis in the World Economy* (1983); *The End of the Third World* (1986); *National Liberation* (1991). The final volume will concern the world labor market.

Jeffrey Henderson was born and raised in northern England and studied sociology and politics at the Universities of Birmingham, of California at Santa Barbara, of Leeds, and of Warwick. Currently Senior Fellow in Sociology and Comparative Management at the Manchester Business School, University of Manchester, he was until recently Reader in Sociology and Urban Studies at the University of Hong Kong. He has taught previously at the University of Birmingham and has held Visiting Professorships at the Universities of New England and of California at Santa Cruz. Additionally, he has held Visiting Fellowships at the Universities of Lodz, of California at Berkeley, of Melbourne, of Glasgow, and of Warwick. He has researched and published in the areas of race relations, labor processes, urban theory, and public housing (for which he was a recipient of the Donald Robertson Memorial Prize in 1983). More recently he has been concerned with the dynamics of global restructuring and high technology industrialization. His current research is concerned with transnational corporations, local linkages, and state policy in East Asia and Central Europe. He is a Corresponding Editor of the *International Journal of Urban and Regional Research* and his most recent book was *The Globalization of High Technology Production* (Routledge, 1989).

Ping-Chun Hsiung was a doctoral student in the Department of Sociology at the University of California at Los Angeles. She completed her dissertation on class, gender, and the satellite factory system in Taiwan. She is Assistant Professor in the Department of Sociology at the University of Toronto, Scarborough College.

Eun Mee Kim is an Assistant Professor of Sociology at the University of Southern California. Kim has been conducting research on various aspects of economic and political development of South Korea. Kim's articles on foreign capital, investment patterns of U.S.- and Japan-based multinational corporations, *chaebol* (Korean large business conglomerates), and democratization have been published in *Studies in Comparative International Development, Asian Affairs,* and *Pacific Focus.* Kim is currently working on a book about the political economy of state and capital in Korean development.

Hagen Koo is Associate Professor of Sociology at the University of Hawaii. His research interest is in the political economy of East Asian development and class formation in South Korea. He is completing a book, tentatively titled *Work and Class in South Korean Industrialization.*

Paul M. Lubeck is Professor of Sociology and History at the University of California, Santa Cruz, where he teaches sociology, political economy, and development studies. He has published extensively on NICs, Islamic social movements, and capitalist development in Africa. His book, *Islam and Urban Labor in Northern Nigeria,* received the Herskovits Prize in 1987. Taking Malaysia as a case study, his current research explores the tension between industrial policy formation and globalization processes in multiethnic states.

Janet W. Salaff did her studies in Sociology at the University of California, Berkeley, with a specialty in Chinese studies. She came to the Department of Sociology, University of Toronto in 1970, and has been teaching in Toronto since. Professor Salaff has researched the changes of family life as industrialization has permeated Asia. Among her main books are: *Working Daughters of Hong Kong: Female Filial Piety or Power in the Family?; Lives: Chinese Working Women; State and Family in Singapore: Restructuring an Industrial Society.* She is currently completing a manuscript comparing Chinese farmers and Chinese cowboys and cowgirls in Inner Mongolia. Professor Salaff has lived in Hong Kong, Taiwan, Singapore, and China for periods of time.